SLADE GORTON

A HALF CENTURY IN POLITICS

John C. Hughes

THE WASHINGTON STATE
HERITAGE CENTER

GORTON CENTER
SLADE GORTON INTERNATIONAL POLICY CENTER

NBR THE NATIONAL BUREAU
of ASIAN RESEARCH GLG

Book design by Suzanne Harris / Integrated Composition Systems
Cover design by Laura Mott

Printed in the United States of America
By Thomson-Shore

This is one in a series of biographies and oral histories published by the Washington State Legacy Project. Other history-makers profiled by the project include former governor Booth Gardner; Northwest Indian fisheries leader Billy Frank; Congresswoman Jennifer Dunn; former first lady Nancy Evans; astronaut Bonnie J. Dunbar; Bremerton civil rights activist Lillian Walker; former chief justice Robert F. Utter; former justice Charles Z. Smith; trailblazing political reporter Adele Ferguson; Federal Judge Carolyn Dimmick, and Nirvana co-founder Krist Novoselic. For more information on The Legacy Project go to http://www.sos.wa.gov/legacyproject/

Cover photo: Gorton listens to testimony from National Security Adviser Condoleezza Rice at a 9/11 Commission hearing on April 8, 2004, in Washington, D.C. *AP Photo/Charles Dharapak*

For Sally and Patsy

Contents

Slippery Slade?

K ELLIE CARLSON WAS COLD from her nose to her toes. Just out of college, she was an entry-level legislative assistant on Capitol Hill at $14,000 per year. Washington, D.C., was a far cry from Pullman, Washington, not to mention the wide spot in the road where her dad lost his shirt in the forest products business when logging was slashed to save the spotted owl. Working for U.S. Senator Slade Gorton was her dream job. After rent, groceries and a car payment, however, she was always flirting with dead broke by mid-month.

One evening in the winter of 1995 several staffers were accompanying Slade to a reception on Capitol Hill. "Kellie, where's your coat?" he scolded fatherly halfway down the block. "Go back to the office and get your coat."

"I don't have a coat," she said so softly it was almost a whisper. "Please, Slade, don't embarrass me."

"You don't have a coat?"

"Well, not a winter coat, but I'm going to get one when I get paid."

"Tomorrow," he said when the event was over, "Sally and I are going to Delaware for a walk on Rehoboth Beach. You're coming with us. There's an outlet mall there, and you're going to get yourself a coat."

Mortified, she wanted to say "Tomorrow isn't pay day." But she just nodded and worried herself home.

Next morning they drove to the outlet mall—Slade, Sally, Kellie and Brig, a big old slobbery dog, stuffed into an un-senatorial Geo Prizm.

At $70, the cheapest winter coats were still more than she could afford.

"I just wanted to throw up. It was so embarrassing."

Then Slade handed her some coupons he'd been saving. "This is your contribution," he said. "Sally and I will take care of the rest."

"They took me to lunch and we came home. It was a wonderful day. Whenever I hear someone from Seattle say what an arrogant, aloof man he is I want to shout 'You don't know the real Slade Gorton!'"

It's a green wool coat—a good Republican cloth coat—that she treasures to this day.

Which brings us to the paramount duty of every biographer: Answering "What's he really like?"

He's complicated. There's the man behind the coat, the boss who inspired such loyalty, and he who does not suffer fools gladly; the nimble hardball-player who elevated running against Greater Seattle to an art form.

If they got this far, his old enemies are still gagging over the coat story.

IT WAS ED DONOHOE, the acerbic Teamsters union columnist, who hung "slippery" on Slade Gorton 50 years ago. Donohoe had a nickname for everyone. Governor Dan Evans, the Eagle Scout who led Gorton into politics, was "Straight Arrow." A. Ludlow Kramer, the secretary of state, was "Lud the Dud." Watching Gorton at work as Evans' legislative tactician in the 1960s, helping engineer a coup that overthrew the speaker of the House, Donohoe said the Democrats were left to grouse about how hard it was to win an argument with someone "so goddamn smart." Gorton's redistricting battles with Bob Greive, the Senate majority leader, were a high-stakes political chess match the likes of which the State Legislature has seldom seen.

As Washington's attorney general, Gorton was one of the first major Republican officials to call for Nixon's resignation. He was also a far-sighted consumer protection activist. As a U.S. senator, his insistence on deficit reduction infuriated Ronald Reagan. His support for the National Endowment for the Arts left Jesse Helms sputtering. He outraged Native Americans. Environmentalists intent on curtailing logging and breaching dams elevated him to their "Dirty Dozen" even while he was preserving vast tracts of scenic land and pressuring Detroit to adopt higher mileage standards. He was 6–2 in statewide races, defeating a legend to get to the U.S. Senate. The two he lost were remarkably close.

One of Gorton's heroes, Teddy Roosevelt, always said the spotlight comes with the territory when you're "the man in the arena," living the strenuous life, doing things. Gorton has been in the arena without interruption since 1956 and shows no signs of slowing down.

THE ALARM IS SET for 6:45. It rarely goes off. At 83, he's clear-eyed at dawn, checking the Weather Channel to see if he should wear tights under his running shorts. Then he's out the door, rain or shine, for a two-mile jog with Trip, his faithful Yellow Lab. When they return some 30 minutes later, he shaves and showers before breakfast. When it's chilly, he wants oatmeal. Usually, though, it's the same concoction he learned to love at Boy Scout camp—shredded wheat, corn flakes, Rice Krispies and fruit, garnished with Grape Nuts. Sally surveys the hall to see how well he and Trip wiped their feet. "I used to tell my friends I've done more than most people have done by the time I get him out the door," she sighs. They've been married for 53 eventful years.

He usually heads to one of his offices or the airport. As a lawyer, lobbyist, foundation member and political strategist, he still spends a lot of time in D.C. Fun is a good book. They're piled high everywhere. Spring is his favorite season because baseball begins. Without him, Seattle wouldn't have the Mariners.

Capable of breathtaking political somersaults, he *is* slippery. But definitely not in the sense that Bill Clinton was "Slick Willie," his silver tongue and roving eye compromising his brilliant promise. Clinton's intellectual equal, Gorton is virtually viceless, except for his impatience, which can morph into arrogance if things get tedious. He bristles when his integrity is challenged.

After his crushing first defeat in 1986, his friends staged an intervention that rinsed out some of the hubris. He learned to resist the temptation to finish your sentences; stopped telling reporters they had just asked singularly stupid questions; grew more thoughtful. His first grandchild, a chubby-cheeked charmer, was a revelation. She's now an officer in the U.S. Navy. The fourth, a handsome boy who turned out to be autistic, taught him even more. The coupon-clipping closet softie made more appearances. Confronted by a dullard, however, his eyes still reveal that he's weighing whether to respond with a large butterfly net or a blow dart.

"You may have noticed that I'm not the world's warmest person," he quipped to his biographer.

Do tell.

"He's not a schmoozer," says Sally, chuckling at the understatement. "When he plays Pickleball, he always aims for your toes. He hates to lose."

Besides books, baseball and dogs, he likes York Mints and meat loaf. The man often accused of being humorless actually laughs a lot, especially at himself. He can be spontaneously mischievous. Shortly after Al and Tipper Gore's famous passionate kiss at the Democratic National Convention, Slade grabbed Sally at a Republican gathering and gave her a smooch that brought down the house. She wanted to kill him.

WITH HIS LEAN FRAME, tall forehead, angular chin, toothy smile and big, bespectacled eyes, Thomas Slade Gorton III is a cartoonist's dream. For a roast, admirers commissioned a Bobblehead from David Horsey, the *Seattle Post-Intelligencer's* Pulitzer Prize winner.

Gorton at his office in the Gorton Center. On the wall behind him are some of the quills from his U.S. Supreme Court appearances. *Dan Schlatter/Puget Sound Business Journal*

Many have observed that Gorton and Hillary Clinton seem to rub a lot of people the wrong way for some of the same reasons. They're remarkably bright, self-assured and polarizing. Gorton, as pollsters put it, has high negatives.

When President Reagan visited Seattle in 1986 to help raise funds for Gorton's Senate re-election campaign, the *P-I's* Joel Connelly wryly observed that the menu de jour—cold salmon and chilled vichyssoise—"served inadvertently to sum up the senator's personality." The Gorton womenfolk were not amused. Connelly, a fellow Episcopalian, found himself in the same pew with them one Easter Sunday morning and remembers the ritual exchange of "Peace" as palpably grudging.

Even Gorton's best friends couldn't resist the temptation to caricature. Joel Pritchard, Washington's former lieutenant governor, who could have made a decent living doing standup, used to quip that if Slade and the famously gregarious Governor Booth Gardner had been in med school together, Slade would have received an A in Surgery and an F in Bedside Manner, while Booth would have flunked Surgery and aced Bedside Manner. Hearing this, the Boothies would laugh, then protest that their guy deserved at least a C in Surgery. Gorton's friends would just laugh. Pritchard, who admired both men, had hit the bull's-eye.

John Keister, the host of KING-TV's *Almost Live!*, ought to have given Gorton one of his Emmys. When Slade threw out the first pitch before a Mariners' game, Keister reported, "His throw was accurate, but his face scared some of the younger children." And when Gorton was captured blinking incessantly under the Klieg lights at a news conference while Phil Gramm droned on about the Republican budget, Keister said they finally determined he was trying to send a coded message: "Help me! This man has eaten a lot of beans."

It would be a snap to fill an appendix with all the things they've called Gorton since 1958 when he was elected to the first of five terms in the state Legislature. Besides "Slippery Slade," there's: Slade the Blade. Skeletor. Cyanide Slade. The new General Custer. The Darth Vader of Northwest Politics. Living proof that not all cold fish comes in a can. Just about the coldest, craftiest guy you would ever want to send 3,000 miles away to represent you in Congress. An evil genius giving off unmistakable signals of his inner corruptibleness. As independent as a hog on ice. A kind of David Bowie of American politics, an agile chameleon who goes out of fashion only long enough to re-emerge with a new face. Brilliant but enigmatic. Fiercely partisan. The prickly, patrician scion to the Gorton's of Gloucester fish fortune. Pluperfect WASP.

Those are all quotes. Gorton's good friend from their days in the U.S. Senate, the effervescent Rudy Boschwitz of Minnesota, doesn't recognize that man. To him, Gorton is a "mensch," kind, decent, admirable; one of the highest honors Yiddish can bestow. Jamie Gorelick, a Clinton Democrat who served with Gorton on the 9/11 Commission, found in him both a gallant big brother and "a wise bipartisan consensus-builder." Former staffers like Kellie Carlson are intensely loyal, proud of having worked for him. From the summer intern to the chief of staff, he was courteous and thoughtful. Never "Senator," always "Slade."

The son of a feisty, college-educated mother, Gorton began opening doors for female lawyers during his three terms as Washington's attorney general. Women who worked on his U.S. Senate staff have formed the Gorton Legacy Group to advance the careers of women in law and politics. It would be inaccurate, however, to call him a feminist. He's gender and color blind. What matters is whether you're smart and willing to work hard.

Still, if you play Slade Gorton word association, "racist" pops up. For instance: "This half of the 20th century leaves history with relatively few prominent U.S. politicians whose careers, spanning decades, were based on overt, vile racism. Future museums will show their awe-stricken, repulsed visitors portraits of George Wallace in the schoolhouse door; Jesse Helms, in the early days, as a '50s Raleigh TV commentator railing against the Negro menace; and Slade Gorton's relentless, despicable attacks on Native America." So wrote Geov Parrish, a Seattle Web-journal columnist lathered into a paroxysm of revulsion over Gorton's challenges to tribal sovereignty. Gorton's battles with the Indians unquestionably are the most contentious episode of his life story. As state attorney general, he challenged all the way to the U.S. Supreme Court the landmark 1974 Boldt Decision granting treaty tribes the right to catch up to 50 percent of the fish in their "usual and accustomed" places. As a U.S. senator, he threatened to slash nearly half of the tribes' federal funding unless they agreed to waive sovereign immunity from civil lawsuits. No one should have special rights, he insists.

The tribes' anger, poured into a war chest bolstered by casino revenues, helped send him into retirement. However, neither Al Ziontz, one of the most respected attorneys in Indian country, nor Ron Allen, a former president of the National Congress of American Indians, believes Gorton is a bigot. "He was our toughest opponent," says Allen. "He made us better, smarter and more savvy. I don't think Slade hates Indians. He just has strong opinions based on his review of what he considers the facts. He has always been a great lawyer—an insatiable reader with an incredible intellect. He can debate anything—constitutional law or scripture, for that matter. He cared about the salmon and the environment and said the tribes should play a role. But when it came to sovereignty issues we collided time and again. . . ."

Gorton finds all forms of bigotry "appallingly un-American." In 1963, he outraged the potent right wing of the State Republican Party by testifying as a character witness for a liberal Democrat, a legislative colleague smeared as a communist. John Goldmark, moreover, was a Jew, they whispered loudly. Anti-Semitism reminds Gorton of Mark Twain's observation that it is "the swollen envy of pygmy minds." When he was running for attorney general in 1968, a year fraught with violence and upheaval, Gorton shocked many by refusing to mince words: "I have always been for law and order," he said, "but too many people today use the phrase when they really mean 'Keep the niggers in their place.'" He worked tirelessly to protect Chinese students in the wake of Tiananmen Square.

When the spotted owl debate erupted, Gorton became a chainsaw populist, championing timber communities and welcoming the wrath of King County's "chattering classes" with all their "self-assured liberalness." The greens called him a cruel demagogue. He retorted that they were "anti-human" hypocrites, masters of the sophistry they claimed he employed.

"Slade recognized there was more to Washington State than Puget Sound," says Dan Evans. The former three-term governor and U.S. Senator has been Gorton's friend for a half century.

THE LATTER-DAY CHARGE that Gorton is a conservative ideologue—or, for that matter, any variety of ideologue—is demonstrably silly. A charter member of the progressive "mainstream" Evans wing of the Washington State GOP, he went on to vote conservative about 60 percent of the time during his 18 years in the U.S. Senate. VoteMatch called him a "Moderate Libertarian Conservative." As a member of Majority Leader Trent Lott's inner circle, Gorton gravitated right in his last term, 1995–2001, yet still ranked as only the 33rd most conservative senator on *National Journal*'s annual analysis of roll-call votes. A progressive as a state legislator and attorney general, Gorton as a U.S. senator was always closer to the middle on social issues and more conservative on foreign policy. He developed genuine friendships with a number of Democrats, notably his seatmate, Henry M. Jackson.

Gorton got a gold star for attendance, missing only one percent of all roll-call votes. As a sponsor of bills, he was somewhere between a leader and a follower—a consensus-builder who co-sponsored five times as many as he introduced. He actually read practically everything set before him, sniffing out ambiguities and opportunities. To his opponents' distress—and grudging admiration—he was an absolute master of the congressional "rider," attaching pet projects to unrelated legislation with crafty dexterity. One such was the timber "salvage" rider that thwarted environmentalists bent on curtailing logging. Another was the famous "midnight rider" he cooked up to secure permits for a cyanide-leach gold mine in Eastern Washington. Gorton often caught them napping because he and his staff were one of the hardest-working teams on Capitol Hill. The senator accused of being aloof prided himself on constituent relations.

Losing his Senate seat in 2000 turned out to be a blessing in disguise, personally and arguably for his country as well. To bipartisan praise, Gorton went on to serve with distinction on blue-ribbon panels studying the Bush-Gore vote-counting snafu in Florida and the explosion that killed 15 and injured 180 at BP's Texas refinery in 2005. That commission warned of attitudes that, largely unaddressed, contributed to the disaster in the Gulf of Mexico five years later.

His service on the 9/11 Commission ranks as the singular achievement of a half century in public life. Cross-examining witnesses with remarkable acuity; working behind the scenes to bridge divisions; boring into bureaucratic fiefdoms to unearth the facts, politics be damned, Gorton was a star.

He's so alive that it's hard to imagine him ever being dead. When he's gone, however, they'll be debating what he was really like for a long, long time.

He won't much care:

"I've had an absolutely marvelous life!"

Members of the "Gorton School of Public Affairs"—as opposed to "Clinton's School of Affairs That Have Become Public"—pose with Slade in 1998. Kellie Carlson is first at left in row two. Creigh Agnew and Mariana Parks are third and sixth from left in the first row. Veda Jellen is looking over Slade's left shoulder in the third row. Heidi Biggs is second from left in the third row, while JoAnn Poysky, Gorton's longtime administrative assistant, is fourth from left. *Law & Politics magazine*

1 | The Gortons and Slades

I T WAS THE WINTER OF 1637. Rubber-legged and shivering, Samuell and Mary Gorton and their young son, Samuell Jr., disembarked in America 140 years before the Declaration of Independence. Samuell had long since declared his own. Within months he was pushing the feudal Massachusetts establishment to grant independence to the Rhode Island colony. They called him cantankerous, even "crazed." Some said there was the glint of a messiah in his blue-gray eyes. In defending freedom of conscience, Gorton was unquestionably obstreperous; a genuine legend in his own time, whipped and banished but undaunted. Samuell's progeny were prolific, patriotic and bright, but he set the bar, especially as a fisher of men. "He was a real rebel," his great-great-great-great-great-great-great-grandson says with an approving smile.[1]

Slade Gorton's American roots run 10 generations deep, starting with Samuell, who was born into a pious, prosperous family in the village of Gorton in the parish of Manchester in Lancashire County, England, in 1593. Of Saxon stock, the Gortons were first recorded there "well before the Norman Conquest of 1066 A.D." Tutored in Greek and Hebrew, Samuell likely memorized the Bible. The name of his fourth child, Mahershalalhashbaz, is from the Book of Isaiah.

Samuell grew tall and lean, a dominant attribute in the Gorton gene pool. Apparently apprenticed to a cloth merchant as a teenager, he established himself as a clothier in London and in 1628 married

Samuell Gorton, an iconoclastic reformer, arrived in America in 1637. *Gorton family album*

Mary Maplett, the daughter of a well-to-do haberdasher. Sixteen years his junior, she too was well educated, unusual for a girl in that era. Mary was a sturdy, adventuresome woman of great character and faith. She bore nine children who survived childhood.[2]

Samuell's true calling was spreading the Gospel. He was an egalitarian radical, holding that women could and should be preachers, which scandalized many. *"There is no distinction between male and female in point of ruling or not ruling, speaking or not speaking,"* Gorton declared. He was equally passionate about the separation of church and state. Civil war was brewing in England over the controversial reign of Charles I, whose marriage to a French Catholic and overtures to high-church clericalism confirmed the Puritans' worst suspicions. Samuell and Mary resolved to start a new life in America, only to discover that its advance billing as an exemplar of religious freedom had been greatly exaggerated by the colonial chamber of commerce. In Boston, at least, the welcome mat wasn't out for noncomformists with an "exasperating spirit of independence."[3]

The growing Gorton family soon moved to Plymouth, where they attended the compulsory Sabbath services. Samuell was also conducting his own meetings twice daily. "He preached like no one in New England," William Gerald McLoughlin testifies in *Rhode Island, a Bicentennial History.* Gorton denied that heaven and hell were "states of the soul following death," asserting that "God rewards or punishes us daily by his spiritual presence or absence from our hearts." He rejected literal interpretations of Old Testament stories, asserting that every true believer could become a priest by studying Christ's words. Most controversial of all, Gorton held that since all men and women were equal under Christ, the courts of men had no business questioning anyone's religious beliefs. "Any erection of authority of the State within the Church, or the Church within the State, is superfluous and as a branch to be cut off."[4]

Many early accounts claim Gorton's religious opinions were "obnoxious" to the people of Plymouth, but a new examination by an English historian, Grahame Gadman, concludes that "Gorton's form of worship was in fact closer to what the original Pilgrim Fathers brought with them in 1620," while the Plymouth Colony was migrating toward the religious beliefs of its "less tolerant and economically dominant Massachusetts neighbors."[5]

THE LAND-GRABBING MASSACHUSETTS ESTABLISHMENT viewed Gorton as a dangerous firebrand. When the Gortons' maid was hauled into a kangaroo court for smiling in church, Samuell was a character witness, reading aloud from Scripture with animated zeal and urging the citizens to "stand for your liberty." The maid's fate is unreported, but Samuell was accused of sedition and banished from Plymouth. "The Gortons were turned out of their home at the height of the worst blizzard so far experienced by the New England settlers."[6] Mary was nursing an infant.

Eventually, they made their way to Aquidneck Island (Newport), only to discover another haughty governor, William Coddington, intent upon establishing his own fiefdom. Gorton and his allies succeeded in having him temporarily deposed, broadened the electorate and basically instituted one-man, one-vote government. It has been called "America's first experiment in civil democracy," Gadman notes. When the governor regained power, Gorton and several of his followers—Gortonists or Gortonites, as they were called—were arrested on trumped-up charges. After yet another judicial charade, Samuell was publicly flogged and banished once again. "Still half naked and bleeding from the lash, he dragged his chains behind him to pursue Governor Coddington as he rode away, promising to repay him in kind."[7]

Gorton and two followers returned to London around 1645. They found a champion in the Earl of Warwick and were instrumental in obtaining a patent for Rhode Island to become an independent colony. Appearing three times before a commission on foreign plantations, Samuell eloquently defended his settlement's political independence from the threat of dominance by Massachusetts.

In 1651, he became president of the Rhode Island colony and in 1657 penned the earliest known American protest against slavery. The Gorton Act abolished "life servitude" in the colony some 200 years before Lincoln's Emancipation Proclamation. Samuell also "stood for the rights of Indians, paying them for his lands when many other colonists merely appropriated their real estate." Gadman concludes that "more than any other figure in New England Gorton's enlightened approach resembles what we recognize today as modern Christianity."[8]

WHEN SAMUEL GORTON IV married Ruth Slade in 1742, another illustrious English name entered the family—this one with roots in Cornwall on the southwest tip of Great Britain. The first Slade Gorton, born in the 1750s, was the seventh of 11 children. He served under General Washington in 1775 and 1776 as the New England militia men who surrounded Boston to bottle up British troops were molded into the Continental Army. Senator Gorton has his ancestor's bayonet in his library.[9]*

---

* The legacy of Samuell Gorton, the patriarch, includes another noted Washington State politician—the late congresswoman Jennifer Dunn. Senator Gorton and the vivacious Republican from Bellevue were tenth cousins, once removed, but could have passed for brother and sister.[10]

Taken in 1891 outside the Slade Gorton Company at Gloucester, Mass., this photo was framed with wood from the wharf on which the men are standing. From left: Thomas "Tommy" Slade Gorton Sr. (the senator's grandfather); Slade Gorton (the senator's great-grandfather); an unidentified Gorton son-in-law; Isaac Gould, a skipper and fisherman; Tom Carroll, the general manager, and Nathaniel L. Gorton, the senator's grand-uncle. Gould was lost at sea aboard the fishing schooner *Columbia* in a 1927 gale. *Gorton family album*

The seventh-generation Slade Gorton whose great-grandson was destined to carry his name to Congress founded the legendary Gorton fish company in 1883 after the Massachusetts cotton mill he managed burned down, according to most accounts. Gorton, 51, and 240 others found themselves jobless. The story goes that he was prodded by his enterprising second wife, Margaret Ann, to take up fishing and soon began to pack and sell salt cod and pickled mackerel in kegs stamped "Slade Gorton Company." In the 1880 Census, however, his occupation is already listed as "fish dealer." In the 1870 enumeration, it says he "works in cotton mill." An account by Mathias P. Harpin, a prolific New England author, says Gorton went to work as a weaver as youth, but bristled at the low pay and long hours. "While in the company store one day his attention was drawn to the salt cod hanging from hooks in the ceiling. . . . This gave him an idea. He decided to become a fishmonger. He went to Newport, met fishermen at Long Wharf, bought cod by the barrel and sold it by the pound. . . . Going from village to village, he sounded his horn as he approached and housewives came running."

As his sales increased, Gorton began to buy fish by the ton at Gloucester when trawlers arrived from the Grand Banks. Soon he branched out, selling to wholesalers and supplying taverns, hotels and restaurants. "He was warm, affable, young; full of drive and ambition. Honesty was his watchword. His fish were always fresh and preserved in ice." This account has all that happening in the 1860s before the death of Gorton's first wife, Maria. Clearly he was selling fish earlier than 1883 and likely operated the fish business on the side for years or was in and out of the cotton mill business. That squares with accounts that have the company starting in 1868 or 1874. Perhaps it was the mill fire that forced Slade Gorton to become a full-time fish dealer. That he was good at it is indisputable. His sons proved to be masters of marketing.[11]

THOMAS SLADE GORTON SR., the senator's grandfather, joined his older brother Nathaniel in the company as a young man. By 1889, the company's codfish were being shipped nationally. Gorton's was becoming a household name. Tommy and Nat inherited the business in 1892 when their father died of a heart attack at 60. Just before the turn of the century, the company patented the Original Gorton Fish Cake, and in 1905 The Gorton's Fisherman ("The Man at the Wheel") made its debut as the company's symbol. Today it anchors the Logo Hall of Fame. The company merged with John Pew & Sons and two other old-line Gloucester firms in 1906 and boasted a fleet of speedy fishing schooners and 2,000 employees on sea and shore, where it occupied 15 wharves.[12]

Thomas Slade Gorton Jr., the senator's father, had a classic apprenticeship. He loved to tell the story about the day he was swept off a Gloucester schooner in the storm-tossed Atlantic. Luckily, the first mate saw the lad being slurped up by the swirling sea and managed to retrieve him.

Something of a hellion as a youth, the senator's father was stubborn, tough and intensely competitive. At 12, he took a leap on a dare. Jumping out of a church gallery, his intention was to grab a dangling light and swing Tarzan-style to the other side of the sanctuary. Unfortunately, he and the fixture came crashing down in a heap of chagrin and shattered glass. (When he was 45, he finally paid his penance, donating a magnificent chandelier to the First Baptist Church in Gloucester.) At 15, Junior got himself kicked out of Holderness, an Episcopal prep school in New Hampshire. Sent fishing by his unamused father, he defiantly joined the Marine Corps during World War I. The war was over before he made it overseas but he made his mark as a tough little prize fighter. By the time Gorton was discharged, he had acquired some self-discipline to match all that energy.

THE GORTONS OF GLOUCESTER found themselves in dire straits in 1923 when Benito Mussolini's Fascist Blackshirts gained control of Italy. For the greater good of the new Roman Empire, *Il Duce's* government confiscated a huge shipment of salt cod and refused to pay the bill. Gorton-Pew Fisheries had a major cash-flow problem. State Street Bank & Trust Co. of Boston snapped up the company. William Lowell Putnam, a well-known Boston lawyer, became its president.[13]

"My grandfather kept his job for life," Senator Gorton says, "but my father, who thought he was going to inherit the business because he was the only male child, was sorely disappointed." He became a mouthy junior manager under the new ownership. (When he was finally able to move back to Boston, successful in his own right, the senator's father refused to do business with any bank or business related to the Putnam family, the old-line Massachusetts investment bankers and lawyers he blamed for his fate—although, truth be told, they'd done him a backhanded favor.)

Gorton's father—"Tom" to his friends and "Slade" in the trade—knocked around the fish business for Gorton-Pew for several years. He managed

the New York office and took night-school classes in business and economics. He also met the senator's feisty Louisiana-born mother, Ruth Israel. His relationship with Gorton-Pew, however, was heading for the rocks. Management grew weary of a whipper-snapper telling them they were making an expensive mistake by not applying for duty drawbacks, the refund of Customs duties. They shipped him off to Chicago.

Tom and Ruth's first child, Thomas Slade Gorton III—a slender boy with inquisitive blue-gray eyes—was born there on Jan. 8, 1928. He was always called Slade,

Slade as a toddler, 1929. *Gorton family album*

not Tom or Tommy. He had a small hole in his palate, the source of the distinctive little cough that punctuates his speech to this day. By first grade, when his nose was buried in books, they also discovered he was blind as a bat. He acquired his first pair of thick glasses, a Gorton trademark in the years to come.

When Slade was a year old, his father founded his own wholesale fish business with $1,200 in working capital. He set up shop at 735 West Lake Street, in the cold gray shadow of Chicago's elevated railway—the "El"— six weeks before the Stock Market crash of 1929. Gorton's net profit for that first year was $148. Grandfather Gorton was mad as hell that he'd left the company, predicting he'd lose his shirt. Eventually the two stubborn Yankee fishermen made up. Gorton-Pew Fisheries was less forgiving. It tried to put Tom Gorton out of business by dumping seafood in Chicago. He outsmarted them. Friendly with the fish broker, he promptly cooked up a dummy firm, XYZ Company, and bought frozen and salt fish right back at below-market prices. The broker didn't care. Gorton also made friends with the bankers, who were delighted to have someone making deposits rather than withdrawals. He prided himself on having friends of all ethnicities. Jewish merchants particularly admired his work ethic and his fish.

SENATOR GORTON'S MATERNAL GRANDFATHER, Edward Everett Israel, was a hard-shell prohibitionist Presbyterian of Welsh extraction. He is also the only other documented elective office-seeker in the history of Slade's family. Grandpa Israel ran for senator and governor several times in Louisiana as a candidate of the Prohibition Party. "He got maybe 3,000 votes in a statewide election," Slade says, but was undeterred.

Grandpa was a huge baseball fan. He had a tryout as a major-league catcher in the 1890s. His major weakness in the secular world, in fact, was the St. Louis Cardinals. But he couldn't go to a baseball game—even listen to one—on Sunday. The Sabbath was a holy day. Slade's kid brother, Mike, says grandpa used to fudge. He'd turn down the volume and put his ear right next to the radio so grandma wouldn't know what he was up to.

The Israels also believed fervently in the power of education. Slade's mother and Aunt Dorothy were graduates of Louisiana State University in an era when few women finished college. Slade's mother had a strong independent streak. "First, she left Louisiana, went to New York City and became a medical technician. Second, she left the Presbyterian Church and became an Episcopalian. And third, we would occasionally have wine with dinner when we were growing up," Slade remembers. When his grandfather—they called him "Pa"—came to visit, he would regale them with stories of his boyhood adventures rafting on the Mississippi and exploring caves. "He had us on the edge of the bed, telling us how he'd got lost in a cave and followed the flickering light of a candle, shades of Tom Sawyer and Huckleberry Finn," Mike Gorton says.

WORKING 15–HOUR DAYS through the depths of the Depression and World War II, the senator's father made a success out of Slade Gorton Company. He was a sharp businessman—Chicago was one tough town—but unwaveringly scrupulous. During World War II, the Office of Price Administration regulated seafood prices. Gorton knew the regulations so well that the Chicago OPA Administrator would frequently phone him to ask him questions. Gorton refused to overcharge or sell on the black market to boost his profits.

Much has been written over the years about Gorton's "patrician" background. He guffaws at the characterization of himself as an Ivy Leaguer with a tennis racket and a roadster. He grew up in the mostly middle-class Chicago suburb of Evanston, the oldest of four children—Slade, Mary Jane, Mike and Nat. "Probably by the late 1930s my father was doing pretty well, but it all went back into the business, except what was necessary for the family to live decently. He still loved the East and did most of his buying in New England, so we would go back in the summer to Gloucester for sometimes as long as six or eight weeks." On those meandering, thousand-mile drives, Slade was fascinated by the diverse landscape of America. He liked Massachusetts, devoured history and loved hearing about his ancestors, yet the family business held no allure.

"I was the first son, the one who would inherit the business," Slade says. When he was around 12, he started going to work with his father every Saturday morning. "Pop loved to talk about the business. It was his life. It was the way he had grown up. He had suffered that devastating loss and he just tested himself against the family history."

Slade pitched in to help unload trucks, work in the freezer and slice fish. To the tourists at Seattle's Pike Place Market, fish-tossing looks like great fun, but the real world of the warehouse "was a grimy, slimy, smelly place, and I knew very early that I wasn't going to work 15 hours a day, six days a week at the fish business. So for that I was a great disappointment to my father. Two strong personalities collided. It is my great good fortune that my brother Michael, who followed me to Dartmouth, got his MBA and went to work with my father."

Mike Gorton, a savvy businessman with a warm smile and manners to match, became the chairman of Slade Gorton & Company, based once again in Boston, while Slade's niece, Kim Gorton, in due course ascended to CEO and president. By the 21st century, Slade's stock in the company had largely devolved to his children. Other than serving on its board for a while, he was never active in the company's management. His youngest brother, Nat, became a respected federal judge in Boston. Their sister, Mary Jane, a voluble sprite, went to Wellesley College and became an art historian, college professor and passionate advocate for abandoned and otherwise abused animals.

Gorton's of Gloucester, now a subsidiary of a Japanese seafood conglomerate is unrelated—save for its history—to the Boston firm owned and operated by the Gorton heirs.

"POP AND SLADE didn't get along that well from his teenage years into early adulthood," Mike Gorton attests. "Since Slade was exceptionally bright and doing so well in school, Pop wanted to groom him for the fish business, but Slade made it clear he had no desire to do so." Loud arguments often ensued. In fact, they were still ensuing decades later. The clan was getting ready to go out to dinner one night when Slade and Pop

"Pop" (Thomas Slade Gorton Jr.) and Mom, Ruth Israel Gorton, with Mary Jane, Mike and Slade around 1935. Brother Nat arrived three years later. *Gorton family album*

"got into a rip-roaring argument about something we can't remember,"
Mike says, laughing at the memory. "To diffuse tension we all more or
less got up to leave. As Slade opened the front door, Pop picked up a baseball and fired it at his head. His aim wasn't that good so it harmlessly flew
over Slade's head, out the door and into the yard. That ended the argument and released the tension!" Mike Gorton says the strong-willed old
fisherman and his equally independent and opinionated namesake had
"a deep-down fondness and respect for one another."

Three years older than Mary Jane, nearly six years older than Mike and
10 years older than Nat, Slade was a good big brother, particularly to the
boys. Mary Jane says he would punch her in the arm from time to time to
make her tougher. She admired her big brother but was resigned to being
the odd girl out among three competitive, sports-nut boys. Since Pop
worked long hours in the seafood business, including many weekends,
Slade was Mike and Nat's male role model. They'd go to the movies, watch
him and his pals play pickup baseball, football or pond hockey. As they
grew older, he'd make sure they were included in the games. There were
no Little Leagues. You just got your friends together and played baseball
or touch football on the nearest vacant lot. Sometimes they'd see the
Cubs at Wrigley Field or the Blackhawks at Chicago Stadium. In the sum-
mertime, Pop would actually take a break. He and Slade taught the
younger boys how to sail, fish and dig clams, also encouraging their interest in tennis. In the winter, they'd go sledding and skating. Pop ended
up with a back brace one year after an exuberant game of ice hockey. "My
father's great pleasure in the fall was getting together a number of our
friends and going up to Wilmette Beach on Sunday afternoon to play
touch football," Slade says. "However, none of us were ever any good. I
went to a big high school. There was no chance I was ever going to be on
a varsity team."

Slade's favorite places growing up were the Public Library, Wrigley
and, surprisingly, church. By 12, he had plowed through Plutarch's Lives,
the classic study of notable Greeks and Romans. Around the dinner table,
Slade and Pop also talked politics. At 14, Slade discovered what he wanted
to be when he grew up. It was the spring of his freshman year at Evanston
High School. America was at war when Dr. Walter Judd addressed an all-
school assembly. A physician and devout Christian, Judd had been a medical missionary in China, ultimately driven out by the Japanese. He came
home in 1938 to urge America to reject isolationism. In 1942, Judd was
preparing to run for Congress in Minnesota. He told the teenagers that
public service was the highest calling—that they had the power to make

the world a better place. Slade walked out of the assembly and said to himself, "I want to be a Walter Judd." He came home and told his mother that someday he was going to be a U.S. senator.

GORTON LOOKS BACK on high school as the worst time of his life. "I was too young. I started grammar school early so I went to high school a year younger. There were 3,200 kids there and I was lost and unhappy." The most formative aspect of his childhood was something most would never guess. It wasn't school or sports. It was being a soprano in the all-boy choir of St. Mark's Episcopal Church in Evanston, Illinois. "My parents dumped me in it at the age of 9 or 10 under the tutelage of a taskmaster whose name was Stanley Martin. If a boy attended every rehearsal and every service for an entire month and was not disciplined—and you were very often disciplined—he got a dollar in silver, handed out coin after coin by Mr. Martin. That was the best discipline I ever had in my entire life. He was a talented musician and he wanted his boys to be good sing-ers, but that was not the most important part of the experience, as far as he was concerned. Most important was whether you *cared*; whether this meant something to you and whether you would subject yourself to his discipline."

At rehearsals, Mr. Martin presided imperiously from a grand piano. The boys were arrayed in two rows on either side, the older ones in the back rows. The mischievous big boys periodically would boot the little boys in the butt. "If the little boys jumped, they were the ones who got chewed out. And Stanley Martin could chew you out without ever saying a vulgar or off-color word better than anyone I've ever known. Bang! His hands would come down on the keys. He'd stand up, waving his arms: 'That was it! You missed your cue!' There was almost no praise. Every now and then on Tuesday he would say, 'Last Sunday morning wasn't bad.' You absolutely lived for that. Then on Friday nights when the tenors and basses came for a joint rehearsal, he'd say, 'Now, when Willie Good-enough was a soprano this was a decent choir!' Willie Goodenough and the others would almost break up. You didn't really get it until you learned years later that he'd say, 'When Slade Gorton was a soprano we had a de-cent choir in this place!' I learned very early in life what it was like to be excommunicated by the Roman Catholic Church in the 14th Century be-cause every now and then there was a kid who couldn't take the discipline and was kicked out. They might as well have been dead as far as everyone else who was there was concerned. They were no longer part of the hu-man race."

On Pentecost every year, the anniversary of the choir's founding, Mr. Martin presented the worthiest with gold medals. The easiest to earn was for perfect attendance. "And perfect attendance meant every rehearsal and every service for the entire year," Gorton says. "One of my two best friends, who lived across the street from me, got scarlet fever the month before the awards. In those days that meant you had your house quarantined. He had to be strapped into his bed because he was going to miss a perfect attendance medal!"

Every year, Mr. Martin awarded a General Excellence medal. One boy—at most two—received the coveted award. Slade has his framed. "You got to wear them on your vestments on Christmas, Easter and Pentecost. During those years in the choir, I learned to read music, to tell the subtle differences between one chorus and the next and how to tell a good anthem from a yawner." Gorton attends a performance of Handel's *Messiah* every year, following the score intently with sheet music. The timbre of his tenor yields hints that his boyhood soprano was lovely.

Gorton was a member of the choir for more than 12 years, sitting in whenever he was home from college, even during law school. "My voice changed and I soon became a baritone, but that experience and that man teaching you that if you are going to do something you damn well better do it right was simply overwhelming. There were all kinds of little things I learned from being a member of that choir. Not only does the attitude of discipline and excellence last, but the music appreciation lasts."

Growing up, he also developed a lasting appreciation for the Republican Party. The first time he heard his mother swear or saw her cry was after the 1936 election. James Farley, FDR's campaign manager, had predicted that Alf Landon, the GOP candidate, would carry only Maine and Vermont. "That damn Farley was the only one who got it right!" mother declared. Slade was 8. That's his first political memory.

Four years later, when Roosevelt was seeking an unprecedented third term, Gorton's father stuffed Wendell Willkie literature in every shipment of fish. The dining room window of the Gorton home featured a Willkie-for-president sign. When the window was shattered by a brick, the sign went back up with the new window. In short order, there was another brick, another window and the same sign. Gortons are stubborn.

Slade was too young to vote in 1948, but he favored Arthur H. Vandenberg, a progressive senator from Michigan, over Thomas Dewey for the GOP presidential nomination. Vandenberg was one of the founders of NATO and also backed the Marshall Plan to rebuild Europe after World War II. "That was always my segment of the Republican Party," Slade says. "Then in 1952 when I was just about ready to leave home, my father and I had a passionate disagreement. He was for MacArthur. I was for Eisenhower."

A SOLID STUDENT, Slade was conflicted about college but ended up at one of the best. "I wasn't going to go to Louisiana State where my mother went. My father had not gone to college at all, but we kids were damn well going to go. I went to Dartmouth because my older cousin was sent there for his Navy training. He became an officer and said it was a great place. I was admitted to a couple of smaller schools, but Dartmouth was certainly the only Ivy League School that I applied to and an easy choice when I was accepted."

Slade at Dartmouth College, 1950.

He started college right after high school graduation in 1945 and finished his freshman year in January. Even though the war was over, the draft was still active and college deferments had ended. Slade was drafted in April of 1946. After basic training, Private Gorton was sent to the Army's Weather Observer School learning to tell cumulonimbus from nimbostratus. Then the demobilizing military decided to discharge draftees early. Gorton served 11 months and five days, which was fortuitous in two respects: The G.I. Bill paid most of the rest of his last three years at Dartmouth "and when Korea came along if you hadn't served a year it didn't count."

"I liked college," Slade says, "and I did well—Phi Beta Kappa—but I didn't have any idea what I was going to do next. In fact, I made one of the dumbest decisions I've ever made."

2 | Dumb and Dumped

S OME IMAGINE SLADE GORTON EMERGED from the womb wearing wingtips and horn-rimmed glasses, with a set of 3–by-5 index cards outlining his goals for kindergarten. The truth is he wasn't always so self-assured. At 22, he was indecisive, smitten and silly. During his senior year at New Hampshire's branch of the Ivy League, he was about to acquire a degree in International Relations yet clueless about what to do next. Everyone said he should go to law school, so he applied to several and was accepted by two of the very best, Yale and Stanford.

"Yale had a bunch of what seemed to me to be outrageous requirements, so I turned them down. Stanford offered me a full ride, but it never crossed my mind that I would actually go west, so I turned down Stanford too." By summer he realized he'd made a huge mistake. The fallback position was moving back home to Evanston and starting law school at Northwestern. Years later, when Sandra Day O'Connor was in Seattle for a seminar after her retirement from the U.S. Supreme Court, Gorton told her his story. "You turned down a full ride to Stanford!" O'Connor said, shaking her head. Gorton could have been at Stanford with her and William Rehnquist, a future chief justice.

"It was a hell of a mistake for me to go to Northwestern and live at home at the age of 22. I didn't get along with my parents and I had a girlfriend at Smith College whom they detested." The girlfriend transferred to Juilliard in New York City, so Slade promptly transferred to Columbia. His father was furious. "That's it!" he said. "You're on your own. Do what you want, but you're not getting any support from us."

The girl dumped him practically before he was unpacked and Columbia wouldn't give him a scholarship because the Gortons had money— much less than perceived but at least the aura of money. Now he was really on his own. It turned out for the best. He landed a construction job for the summer and learned some important lessons in the workaday world. When school started, he worked a 12–hour weekend shift at the magnificently gothic Riverside Church, running the elevators and mind-ing the switchboard. He was also a waiter at the Men's Faculty Club, which meant he could eat for free. Before Christmas vacation, he found yet another job as a temp at the New York Post Office.

Columbia generously granted him 27 hours of credits for his first year at Northwestern but Gorton was disappointed to learn he had to take *Civil Procedure One* all over again with the first-year students. At Columbia, however, it was largely a course in logic taught by a brilliant sage, Jerome Michael, Columbia Law School Class of 1912. On the first day of class in 1951, Gorton immediately deduced that Professor Michael had subjected his pupils to the same catechism for decades. The professor bowed his head and scanned the list of some 200 students until, aha, he found the one with the most unusual name.

"Mr. Hamburger!"

Hamburger dutifully arose.

"Mr. Hamburger, have you read the cases assigned for this, your first day of class?"

"Yes sir."

"Very good. And would you give me the name of the first case you were assigned to read?"

"Jones vs. the Acme Loan Company, sir."

"Very good, Mr. Hamburger. And would you tell me who the plaintiff was in that case?"

"Jones, sir."

"Very good, Mr. Hamburger. And would you tell me how you know Jones was the plaintiff?"

The silence was deafening. For 20 years or more, Slade learned later, the professor invariably had been told, "Because Jones' name was listed first." That's the wrong answer. The appellant, in fact, is the party who files the appeal—the loser of the original trial.

Hamburger paused for a moment to study his notes, then looked up with a beatific smile: "Because, sir, in the second paragraph in the opinion it says 'the plaintiff's mother,' and everyone knows that loan companies don't have mothers."

Professor Michael could do little but nod. Hamburger was the man of the hour. "It was a *wonderful* first day in law school at Columbia!" Slade says, laughing at the still vibrant 60–year-old memory.

BY THE NEXT SUMMER, Gorton had acquired a foxy, ambitious new girl-friend, Virginia Craft—"Crafty Ginny" to Slade and his pals—and an internship at Ropes & Gray, Boston's oldest and most prestigious law firm.

One of its stars in the 1870s was Oliver Wendell Holmes Jr., whose career on the U.S. Supreme Court is the stuff of legends. Gorton was assigned to work for Elliot Richardson, who reportedly had posted the fourth-highest grades in the history of Harvard Law School. It was a humbling experience to work for someone so brilliant and charismatic. Twenty years later, when he was Washington's attorney general and Richardson headed the Department of Justice, Gorton followed the Watergate scandal with extra fascination as Richardson resigned in the "Saturday Night Massacre" after President Nixon fired Watergate special prosecutor Archibald Cox. Several Northwest journalists observed that Gorton seemed a clone of the slender, cerebral Richardson.

A Harlan Fiske Stone Scholar, Gorton was offered a full-time job at Ropes & Gray when he graduated. He turned it down, with no regrets. "It was a wonderful experience, but I didn't want to spend the rest of my life keeping my nose above water in this magnificent law firm." There was another reason: Gorton was glued to the TV at a friend's house during the 1952 Republican National Convention—televised nationally for the first time. One of the stars of the five-day drama was Don Eastvold, a 32–year-old lawyer from Tacoma. Tall and handsome, Eastvold had been a moot court champion at the University of Washington Law School. He won a seat in the State Senate from Pierce County's 29th District in 1950. Now he was running for attorney general.

An Eisenhower delegate, Eastvold's deft management of a floor fight at the Washington State GOP Convention carried the day for the party's young liberals, who solidly backed Ike for president over Robert Taft, the rock-ribbed conservative from Ohio. The stakes were much higher when the party convened in Chicago in July. Eisenhower and Taft were virtually deadlocked for the nomination. A decisive battle erupted over the credentials of the pro-Taft Georgia delegation. With Eastvold in the trenches, Ike's troops finally prevailed. Eastvold's performance was hailed by *Time* magazine as "bold and brilliant." *Life* described him as the general's "youthful captain."[1]

"Beware a young man with a book," Eastvold declared in prime time, reprising an old adage among lawyers as he brandished a copy of a law book featuring a Supreme Court decision he said buttressed Ike's position. Gorton and some 70 million other Americans watched Eastvold give a dynamic nominating speech for the next president of the United States. Eastvold became the youthful face of Republican politics in Washington State. "My gosh," Slade said to himself, "that looks like a wonderful place." Moreover, "one didn't have to have an awful lot of smarts to know what political future an impecunious Yankee Republican Protestant had in Boston. So I said no to Ropes & Gray and decided to go to Seattle, knowing that the day I told Crafty Ginny this news would be the last date I would ever have with her, for she had decided that the man she married would be governor of New York. As it was, it was a nice goodbye." Ginny ended up as the wealthy widow of a Kentucky horse-breeder.

LAW DEGREE IN SUITCASE, Gorton bought a one-way bus ticket to Seattle. "I can read a map, Slade," his mother said. "I know you're going as far from Boston as you can get."

He stepped off the bus at the Greyhound Station in downtown Seattle—it's still there at 811 Stewart St.—on a Monday morning in the summer of 1953 with $300 in his jeans and a single suitcase. For a nickel, he invested in a copy of the *Post-Intelligencer* and found an ad in the classifieds for a boarding house in the University District.

In those days, Seattle's law firms, like the city itself, were relatively small. The biggest had about 30 lawyers, which struck Gorton as ideal. Better yet, Seattle society—unlike Boston—was open to newcomers. "It didn't matter whether your family had been here for several generations or whether you were brand new."

His timing was right in another respect. The bar exam cram course was beginning that very night. As the first Saturday session was winding down, the instructor said, "If there is a Slade Gorton here would he come up and see me?" Slade presented himself. The instructor extended his hand. "Ken MacDonald, Dartmouth '39. Would you like to spend the weekend at my house?" MacDonald, a former Bostonian who had survived serious wounds as an infantry sergeant during World War II, was already a much-admired civil rights attorney in Seattle. "They were wonderful to me," Slade recalls, "and I saw a lot of the very liberal MacDonald family. It was just Dartmouth; that was the only connection."

He was in Seattle for only five months before he dodged the draft.

Although his parents had moved to Boston, Slade was still under the jurisdiction of the Evanston Draft Board. The easiest person in the world to draft was someone who no longer voted or lived there, so he showed up on their radar the minute his deferment ended with his graduation from law school. As luck would have it, Alan Farnsworth, a doppelganger friend from Columbia—professors couldn't tell them apart—had received an Air Force commission and was helping process appointments to the Judge Advocate General corps. Lieutenant Farnsworth put his pal's application on top of the stack.

Gorton passed the bar and received a reserve commission in the Air Force around mid-October of 1953, with orders to report to the JAG School in Alabama during the first week of January. But his draft notice ordered him back to active duty with the Army in late December. The choice between cloud counting as a private or lawyering as a lieutenant was instantaneous. He pleaded his case with the Air Force, which back-dated his induction to Dec. 15.

At Polk Air Force Base near Fort Bragg, North Carolina, in 1954, Gorton became the staff judge advocate as a first lieutenant, assisted by Second Lieutenant Leonard A. Sheft, a Jewish kid from Brooklyn who went to Yale. Sloppy, brash and brilliant, Lenny had a French wife who could work wonders with leftovers. Slade and three other single officers were living together off base. Monique, who had barely eluded the Nazis, became their worldly ex-officio big sister.

Gorton's most memorable case during those three years on active duty was defending a homesick teenage airman. Stationed in Oklahoma, the kid went home on leave to the mountains of North Carolina to see his girl and failed to report back as prescribed. The Air Police cuffed him without resistance and deposited him at Polk, the closest Air Force base, where he was charged with desertion. AWOL, a lesser charge, is absence without official leave. Desertion is absence without leave without the intent to return. "It's subjective," Gorton explains. "To prove desertion, you've got to prove beyond a reasonable doubt that the guy did not intend to go back. With AWOL they tap you on the wrist, maybe give you 30 days and put you back on duty. For desertion, in those days, you got two or three years in the federal pen."

Gorton's client swore he was working at a gas station and saving for a bus ticket. "I was going to go back." Not much of a story, but a story nevertheless. Lieutenant Gorton put the kid on the stand and he told his story. The prosecutor obviously didn't believe a word of it but shrugged off cross examination. The lieutenant colonel who was president of the court panel leaned over the bench and asked, "Airman, how much does a bus ticket from Rockingham, North Carolina, to Oklahoma City cost?" Gorton's life flashed in front of his eyes in about a tenth of a second. "You dumb schmuck," he said to himself, "you never thought to ask him that question." But the airman, without hesitation, chirped, "27 dollars and 38 cents, sir." Lieutenant Gorton smiled thinly. The court panel recessed, but quickly returned with its verdict: "Guilty of AWOL. Not guilty of desertion." When he returned to his office, Slade called the bus station. A ticket from Rockingham to Oklahoma City cost only 15 bucks. He laughed out loud and said to himself, "That kid did really well!"

Gorton was released from active duty in the summer of 1956, arriving back in Seattle just before the primary election. He met the Pritchard brothers, Dan Evans and a whole crew of other bushy-tailed young Republicans, and plunged head-first into Washington politics.

They told him Don Eastvold was a bum.

3 | The Change Agents

"**H**E WAS A BRAND-NEW GUY in our town," Joel Pritchard recalled 40 years later, and two things were immediately clear: "Slade Gorton was super smart and he loved politics." He couldn't have fallen in with better companions. The Pritchard brothers seemed to know everyone who was anyone.[1]

Organizational wizards, Joel and Frank had matching jaunty grins. They'd been Seattle's leading young Republicans for several years when Gorton put on his civvies, joined a small law firm and went doorbelling or debating most every night. When Slade and Joel discovered they'd both been inspired as teenagers by hearing Walter Judd talk about public service they figured their friendship was foreordained.[2]

The Pritchard brothers grew up in an intellectually feisty family. Father was a GOP precinct committeeman but pro-Roosevelt in 1940 as the U.S. edged ever closer to joining the war. Mother voted for Willkie, a former Democrat. In any case, by 1952 they all liked Ike—and Governor Arthur Langlie. A paragon of rectitude, Langlie was on Eisenhower's short list of possible running mates.[3]

The 1956 primary election campaign was in full swing when Slade joined the party. The Republicans had their work cut out. Langlie was challenging U.S. Senator Warren Magnuson. Don Eastvold was running for governor. After a controversial term as attorney general, Eastvold now found himself in a surprisingly tight primary battle with Emmett Anderson, the lieutenant governor. A decent fellow, Anderson unfortunately had all the charisma of an Elks Club exalted ruler, which he was. Eastvold, however, was a heavy drinker and womanizer, which offended Langlie, the Pritchards and their new friend, Gorton.

Denounced by Langlie, Eastvold lost in the primary to Anderson, who went down to defeat in November at the hands of State Senator Al Rosellini, the first Italian Catholic governor west of the Mississippi. Magnuson, meantime, crushed Langlie in a no-holds-barred contest one writer characterized as a brawl between a Fifth Avenue minister and a First Avenue longshoreman.[4]

Any way you cut it, 1956 was a disastrous year for the GOP in Washington State. Gorton and the Pritchards, together with Jim Ellis, the attorney for Seattle's influential Municipal League, took some comfort in the election of Dan Evans, an upstanding young engineer, to the House of Representatives from King County's 43rd District.

Gorton joined the Young Republicans of King County and the Evergreen Republican Club. He was flattered to be invited to meet once a month at Bob Dunn's used car dealership with the Pritchard brothers and five or six of their progressive friends. At one strategy session, he wondered if they could muster any support from the old guard:

"What do they think?"

"There is no *they*," Joel shot back. "It's what *we* want to do. We're the change agents."

They all smiled and nodded. "I'll never forget the way Joel said it," Gorton says. "I knew I'd made the right choice in coming to Seattle."

SETTLING IN AS THE ROOKIE ASSOCIATE at Grosscup, Ambler, Stephan & Miller—six attorneys in all—Gorton was also mentored by one of the partners, Pendleton Miller. The scion of a pioneer Washington family, Miller's father went to Yale, came back home, practiced law for a few weeks, decided he really didn't like working and turned instead to tending his investments and a life of leisure. "Pen Miller reacted by feeling there was an absolute obligation to work and contribute to society," Gorton says. "He was a wonderful person, still working in his mid-80s the week before he died."

Early on, Gorton also joined Jim Ellis' campaign to create a "Metro" superagency in King County to clean up Lake Washington, which was absorbing 20 million gallons of raw and only partially treated sewage daily. Regional problems required regional solutions, Ellis said. Traffic and sprawl would only get worse if myopic fiefdoms were allowed to persist. Ellis advocated land-use planning, new parks, greenbelts and rapid transit. It would take years to achieve, in fits and starts, but he was a resilient visionary. Opponents on the far right called his plan "communism in disguise." The suburbs were especially suspicious of the dogged young bond lawyer and his button-down followers.

"One of the charms of democracy—and one of its exasperations—is that each town council, each committee, each city government, is an ego unto itself," Emmett Watson, Seattle's favorite columnist, observed as Ellis "and those he rallied with him went out on the revival circuit, so to speak, to try and open a lot of closed-door minds."[5]

Pritchard and Gorton were part of the Municipal League's speakers' bureau, the Town Criers. "Slade was so good at it," Pritchard marveled. In truth, he was winging it. "That's where I think I learned public speaking," Gorton says. "I got two C's in my entire college career and one of them was in public speaking. So I learned an awful lot about public speaking during those Metro campaigns." He volunteered to work the circuit outside Seattle. "Seattle was going to vote for it; everyone knew that, but there was a lot of opposition in the rural areas. I got to go to places where the vote was going to be five- or six-to-one against it." Metro lost in the rural areas the first time around, so Ellis shrewdly pulled back the boundaries here and there to jettison the losing precincts. The second time around, they were victorious. In the years to come, Gorton would play a key role in shepherding Ellis' programs through the Legislature and Congress. In the late 1960s, a rapid transit bond issue was the major casualty. The voters' short-sightedness would haunt them down the road.

THAT FIRST CHRISTMAS out of the service, Gorton flew east to see his folks, stopping in New York to have dinner with his friends from Polk Air Force Base, Lenny and Monique Sheft. The visit led to a close call with a scandal that could have derailed his political career.

It was the height of the TV quiz show craze. Americans were mesmerized in 1956 by the drama of a brainy cabbie from Baltimore competing for staggering sums on CBS' *The $64,000 Question*. NBC upped the ante with *Twenty One*, where a college student named Elfrida Von Nardroff took home $226,500.

Monique leaned over her salad and wagged her fork.

"Slade, you have more useless knowledge in your head than anyone else I know. You ought to be on *Twenty One*."

"Sure Monique," he said with a skeptical grin. "Why don't you set it up?"

"Nothing easier! Lenny knows the producer. Lenny, call the producer!"

Lenny called the producer, told him his brilliant Air Force buddy—magna cum laude from Dartmouth—was in town and would be great on the show. "Send him to the studio tomorrow," the producer said.

Gorton aced a test for prospective contestants. "Be back here next Wednesday night and you'll be the contestant waiting in the wings," they said. "If somebody loses you get on."

Nobody loses. Night after night, Charles Van Doren, a charming English professor, was locked in prime-time combat with Herb Stempel, a quirky young guy attending college on the GI Bill. Wearing headphones in their glass-enclosed "Isolation Booths," they dueled round after round at $2,500 a point, with 50 million Americans slack-jawed over their TV dinners. "You guys sure know your onions," host Jack Berry marveled. Van Doren won $129,000 and ended up on the cover of *Time*.

Gorton went home, with instructions to call the studio next time he was in town. In April, he was back. Van Doren's run had finally ended but there was a new champ who refused to lose. They invited Gorton to appear on their new daytime show, *Tic-Tac-Dough*.

"A little black lady school teacher from North Carolina had won 900 bucks and got to be 'X' in the game," Gorton recalls. She also learned that the next contestant was a Phi Beta Kappa lawyer. "I quit!" she said. "I'll take my money and go." Gorton right off had the advantage of being X and won $900. He was making $800 a month as a junior associate at the law firm. Gorton called his boss and asked if he could stay a few more days. That Monday he won two more games and headed home with $3,800—some $30,000 in 2010 dollars; enough to buy a nice house and a new car in 1957.

A year later, a letter arrived from the game-show producer. Gorton quotes it virtually verbatim from memory: "Dear Slade, *Tic-Tac-Dough* has been so successful in the daytime that it is now going on primetime once a week at 10 times the value per square. We're starting the nighttime show with winners from the daytime show. The next time you're in New York would you drop by the studio to see whether you qualify?"

"Qualify? What the hell did that mean? Of course I qualify. I'm a daytime winner. But I'm not going back to New York anytime soon." He tossed the letter in the back of a desk drawer. Six months later, a huge scandal erupted. Fuming about his loss to the more telegenic Van Doren, Stempel blew the whistle. The show was fixed. Van Doren repeatedly denied it but came clean when he was hauled before a congressional committee. "That's what they meant by 'qualify,'" Gorton says. They wanted to know if you'd play along with the script to boost ratings and sell more Geritol. The daytime version wasn't fixed, because the turnover in contestants actually helped, "but they found out with the night-time show that they could build up the drama by having the same person stay on night after night," Gorton says, "so they fed that person the answers."

THOUGH HIS TV CAREER was short-lived, Gorton's political career was on the upswing. In the 1957 legislative session, R.R. "Bob" Greive of Seattle, the Senate Democrats' new majority leader, presided over the first redistricting of the state since 1933. Greive had deftly politicized a League of

Women Voters initiative intended to reform the process. One of the few crumbs that filtered down to the Republicans was a new North Seattle district with no incumbents. Gorton asked Dan Evans for advice. "Go for it!" he said. Also enthusiastic were the Pritchards. Joel's hat was already in the ring for a seat in the House from the 36th District.

Slade found a place to live in the 46th, then sought the blessings of his bosses. "Running for the Legislature was not seen as a fitting thing for a young lawyer to do. Pen Miller ran interference for me. I don't know exactly what he said, but probably it was, 'Look, he can't win the race. Why make him disaffected? Let him go ahead and do it and get it out of his system.' So it was Pen Miller who enabled me to begin my political career." It was in his system to stay.

So was Sally Clark, a reporter for *The Seattle Times*. She was very smart and very attractive, with a pert pageboy and a confident air. They met on Feb. 7, 1957, when three girls from Duluth who skied every weekend with guys who lived at the College Club hosted a mix-and-meet at a little red house they'd rented at Leschi. Slade called her the next day and came courting in a nerdy seafoam green postwar Studebaker. "For weeks thereafter every Friday night we went to a movie and every Sunday we went skiing," Sally says. "I couldn't figure out who he was dating on Saturdays. Then I found out he was going to bed early so he'd be rested up for skiing. I foolishly followed him down slopes that were way too steep for me." When her new beau was on *Tic-Tac-Dough*, her editors invited her to join them in the publisher's office, which featured the only TV in the building.

For Sally, it wasn't love at first sight, "but he was certainly the most interesting young man I'd met in some time. He could talk about something other than cars and football, which is about all other fellows liked to talk about. He was so intelligent and knew about so many things. He grew on me, and little by little those other guys fell by the wayside." They were married on June 28, 1958. After a four-day stay in San Francisco, they drove a "huge boat of an old Ford" back to Seattle and went doorbelling the evening they got home. The honeymoon was over. The new Mrs. Gorton understood politics. Dad was a Democrat; mother a Republican, "especially around Election Day. Then they would go to the polls and cancel each other out." Sally had been a reporter since her junior year in high school, practically running the weekly in her hometown of Selah after the owner got himself elected county commissioner. First at the *Yakima Herald-Republic* and then at the *Times*, she had interviewed the wives of many well known politicians.

"Sally knew perfectly well what she was getting into," Slade says, smil-

Slade and Sally on their wedding day, June 28, 1958, with their parents,
Clarissa Clark and Thomas Slade Gorton Jr. and Ruth Gorton. Sally's father,
Harry Baker Clark, was deceased. *Gorton Family Album*

ing at the memory of all the ups and downs they experienced over their
next 42 years in politics. "I thought he'd outgrow it," she quips.

TO DAN EVANS, GORTON was precisely the sort of live wire the Republicans
needed in the Legislature. Using a Polk Reverse Directory and a map of the
43rd Legislative District, Evans won election to the House in 1956 by applying his engineer's mind to campaigning. "I had tediously traced each
street and marked down the name of anybody I knew who lived there. I had
several hundred potential workers and donors in my district as a result.
Slade and I did the same thing for the 46th district. Being a newcomer,
he knew only a handful but I knew quite a few, having lived close by."

A lot more than quite a few, Slade says. "Dan knew about 700 people in
that district and I knew seven! He was the model, the absolute model, of
what a Republican should be at a time when we were trying to recover"
from the setbacks in 1956. "Slade ran a first-rate campaign and worked
much harder than any of his opponents," Evans says. "I began to appreciate

his brilliant mind and his determination to focus intently on his goals."

Joel Pritchard won, too. The 1958
crop of greater Seattle Republican
freshmen also included James Andersen, an ex-infantryman who was
gutsy and smart. Chuck Moriarty,
an ambitious lawyer elected to the
House with Evans two years earlier,
was appointed to the Senate during
the 1959 session so the Seattleites
had a foothold in both chambers. A

Slade holds a postcard from his first
run for the Legislature in 1958. *Dan
Schlatter/Puget Sound Business Journal*

nucleus of dynamic young moderates—"Dan Evans Republicans" or "new
breed" Republicans they'd soon be called—was now in place. As they
gained power, Gorton's elbows were the sharpest. "He stomped on a lot of
people," said Don Eldridge, who was elected to the House in 1952 from
Skagit County, "but he had his eye on the target. . . . Slade sort of has to
grow on you. He was not bashful about anything and very talented."[6] The
first impression he left with many was that of an ambitious, smarty pants
Ivy Leaguer—an interloper. Tom Copeland, a second-term Republican
from Eastern Washington vying with Evans for leadership of the caucus,
was impressed by Gorton's intellect but said he was lucky he landed in
Seattle. If he had arrived in Walla Walla "and put up a sign that said 'I just
came here from Boston and I know exactly what to do for this district in
the Legislature and I will go there and be your salvation' . . . he'd have
been dumped on his ass so fast that it would make his head swim."[7]

Eldridge always said it was clear early on that Evans and Gorton were
destined for bigger things but they were fortunate to have had Pritchard
as a mentor. "Everybody liked Joel. He could kind of joke his way into almost any circumstance."[8] He also possessed uncanny political intuition
as chief strategist for the insurgents.

Evans decided to run for assistant minority leader. It was an exciting
time, Gorton recalls, "and of course all of the young Seattle guys are going to vote for him." The 33 members of the House GOP Caucus met in
Spokane the same weekend as the Husky-Cougar Apple Cup football
game. As Gorton walked into the room, a tall, bespectacled young man
with an eager face rushed up, hand outstretched, and declared, "I'm Dick
Morphis. How old are you?" "Thirty," said Gorton. "Goody," said Morphis.
"I'm still the youngest!" Morphis, a character, ran a rest home in Spokane.
His nickname was "Rigor."

Elmer Johnston, the quintessential old guy in the caucus, also introduced himself to Gorton. "It's wonderful to have you young people here," he said, "and you'll do very, very well in this body as long as you do exactly what I tell you," which wasn't what the young people had in mind.

Johnston invited Gorton and Pritchard to his imposing Spokane home for more mentoring. "Now boys, if you've got to have something for your district, I can work with (Speaker) John O'Brien," he counseled. "We get along and we can work things out." Pritchard smiled. "Elmer, Slade and I didn't come down here to work things out and to get along with John O'Brien. We came down to make some changes." If there was anything in their districts that they needed "we'll work it," Pritchard assured him. "That's the way we're going to play the game." Johnston smiled, shook his head and said, "Well, OK, boys . . ."

Evans was soundly whipped in his bid for leadership. Youth must be served, just not that year. The upstarts didn't waste time licking their wounds. They regrouped and emerged even more determined.

For the 1959 session, Moriarty and Pritchard rented a house just up the street from the Capitol. There was room for four. Evans, not yet married, made it a threesome. Who else could they get? "How about Gorton?" Pritchard piped up.

Sally Gorton, great with their first child, Thomas Slade Gorton IV, became the den mother. "I was treated like the queen bee," she recalls. "I never had to lift a finger. They had wisely arranged for a cleaning lady. Slade and I had the master bedroom and the other guys were upstairs. We went out to dinner practically every night and they talked politics. They were so young; so full of energy to change things. I'll never forget something I heard Joel say: 'You can get a lot done if you don't worry who's getting the credit.' It was a wonderful time."

State Reps. Joel Pritchard, Dan Evans, Chuck Moriarty, Jim Andersen and Slade Gorton in 1959. The future held the governor's office, the U.S. House and Senate and the State Supreme Court. Moriarty was the only political dropout. *Washington State Archives*

4 | The Freshman

FROM DAY ONE, REPRESENTATIVE GORTON, R-Seattle, actually read the fine print of all the bills set to be debated the next day. "Every damn one. I would work my way to an answer logically, step-by-step." Well, most of the time. Some defied translation, whether by sheer bureaucratic turgidity or design. This irritated Gorton to no end. He noted, too, that a swarm of lobbyists was always lurking in "Ulcer Gulch," the legislative passageway, to woo the lazy and complaisant.

In 1959, Washington legislators were paid $1,200 per year. There was a shoe shine stand, manned by a stereotypically affable Negro, outside the House chambers. Inside, practically everyone but Gorton and Evans was smoking incessantly. Chet King of Pacific County still had his spittoon. "We had no offices; no secretaries; no nothing," Gorton recalls. "You sat there at your seat in the House chamber," boning up on bills and handling correspondence as best you could. The lobbyists could be on the floor until 15 minutes before a session started and an hour afterwards. "We mostly escaped to the private dining room downstairs," Evans recalls.

Gorton and Pritchard, being freshmen, were way back by the water fountain, watching how the lobbyists operated down in front. "You learned pretty quickly that the people who got lobbied the most were the ones who were likely to vote the way the last guy who talked to them wanted them to," Gorton says. "Joel turned to me one day and observed, 'He who can be pressured will be pressured.' No one ever put it better."[1]

Although outnumbered two-to-one, the Republicans were a vocal minority. "As much fun as it was," Gorton says, "there were only two things that happened during that first session that would not have happened had I not been there." The first was a securities reform act. With Gorton as the Republican sponsor, it won approval "over the almost-dead body of Elmer Johnston," the penny mining stock lawyer from Spokane who had tried to convince the young fellows it was best to go along to get along. The second thing taught him you can't always judge a bill by its cover.

THE SESSION WAS WINDING DOWN when Gorton encountered an incomprehensible bill on trade regulation. "For the life of me, I couldn't figure out what it was designed to do. All I knew was that I wasn't wild about the sponsors—two D's and one R." He found the R and asked what it was all about. "Oh," said the Republican, "it's to end gasoline price wars." Gorton wrinkled his brow. "How can this be good?" He was a young lawyer, living on a young lawyer's salary, with a wife and young son. He *liked* gas wars. The upshot was that the bill would not allow gas stations to post their prices anywhere but on the pump.

In one of his first speeches, Gorton argued forcefully for free enterprise and the American consumer. "But the bill passes 82 to 17 or something like that and shoots over to the Senate." Jealously guarding its prerogatives, the Senate ignored the House bill and passed a virtually identical one of its own, which arrived on the House floor on the last day Senate bills could be considered. Now it required a two-thirds vote to go from the second reading to the third on the same day. "I really went to work," Slade remembers, leaning forward as he relishes the memory. "I got all my Evans-type 'R' friends and went over to the liberal Democrats, including John Goldmark and Wes Uhlman, and we recruited them to oppose the bill. Lo and behold we got 36 votes against it and the bill died."

Since his law firm's stable of clients included Texaco, Gorton had purposely avoided consulting any of his bosses. He was back at his desk in the House chamber the next morning when a lobbyist strolled up.

"Great job on that bill, Slade! Where do I send your case (of booze)?"

"Who the hell are you?"

"I'm the lobbyist for Standard Oil and all the other oil companies. We think it's great that you killed this bill!"

In an instant, Gorton grasped that it was the guys who owned the gas stations who were backing the bill—not the oil companies.

"Get out of my sight before I deck you!" he sputtered.

"I was just so furious. Here was a guy who presumably had a lot of information on the issue and yet did nothing to inform the person who was fighting it. Doubtless, he then sent a huge bill to his clients."

After the session adjourned, Gorton wrote a letter to Texaco. They'd wasted their money if they paid that lobbyist so much as a red cent, he said. "I reached a conclusion back then that 90 percent of all the money ever spent on lobbyists was wasted. But the problem with the community that hired lobbyists was that you never knew which 10 percent *did* work. As for the 10 percent side, I think we have probably benefited from the

course of this evil." He cites the example of a farsighted lobbyist who created a multi-billion dollar green industry in Washington State.

THE NATIONAL PROHIBITION ACT died in 1933 after 14 controversial years.
Its thirst quenched by brazen rumrunners and moonlighting cops, Washington had been one of the least compliant states in the nation. With the
repeal of the 18th Amendment, states were then given considerable leeway
in regulating the manufacture and sale of alcoholic beverages. "It's influence that they have over nothing else that goes into interstate commerce,"
Gorton notes.

Regulation of wine sales was fiercely debated during his 10 years in the
Legislature. An array of trade restrictions against California wines, buttressed by court decisions and huge markups, protected the tiny "domestic"
producers, which remained mired in muscatel mediocrity. Most wine
drinkers dismissed Washington wines as ghastly stuff that only a wino
could swallow. Every session, the California wine growers would lobby
for repeal of the exclusionary legislation, to no avail until they hired Tom
Owens, aka "Tommy Raincoat," a lawyer Gorton, Evans and a host of other
legislators admired for his honesty. "Tom lobbied for them on the up-and-
up," Gorton says, and finally convinced the Legislature in 1969 that competition wouldn't destroy the Washington wine industry, it would transform
it. "I know of no presentation in any legislative body in which I ever served
that has more totally and completely kept its promise than that one."[2]

In his second term, Gorton was the principal sponsor of legislation
placing stiff restrictions on billboards along major highways. He had
strong support from Evans and a number of Democrats, including Wes
Uhlman. At 26, Uhlman was one of the youngest legislators in America
and a future Seattle mayor. Gorton agreed with Ladybird Johnson, the
First Lady, that billboards are a blight on the American landscape. Unimpressed was Alfred Hamilton, a Lewis County farmer who belonged to
the John Birch Society. He erected a billboard along Interstate 5 that featured Uncle Sam exposing an ever-changing litany of liberal plots to undermine American values.

GORTON'S REPUTATION for parsing every bill became legendary in the
Legislative Building. Dick White, the state's longtime code reviser, said
the funniest backhanded compliment his staff was ever paid came courtesy of Slade, who "came in with blood in his eye one day and just raised
the roof off of my office because there had been a comma misplaced" in a
public power bill. [H]e accused us of deliberately doing it. And of course I

resisted it, but (Slade) said, 'I know you did it. Your people don't make that kind of mistake.'"[3]

Reflecting on his 10 years as a member of the Washington Legislature and 18 more in the U.S. Senate, Gorton concludes that "the average IQ of the State House of Representatives with whom I served two generations ago compared reasonably favorably with the United States Senate. Now, bluntly, I don't think that's true today because of one of the great reforms in our legislative history, which had unintended consequences. When I began my career in the House, the Legislature met only once every two years and for not much more than 60 days, even including a special session. They were genuine amateurs at that $100 a month. I had no staff at all until my last term when I became the majority leader, at which point I got a secretary and an intern." Today, he notes, many maintain that the Legislature is staff-dominated.

Gorton recognized early on that assembling the Legislature only every other year was becoming an anachronism. "The problem is that you don't end up having the same people or the same quality of people. When a legislative body meets as long as ours does today, it is almost impossible to have much of another career. And when the pay is at a relatively low five figures, young people who have not had another career really can't live on it and support a family. Probably two-thirds to three-quarters of the kinds of people we could persuade to run for the Legislature in the late 1950s and '60s could not conceive of doing so today and that is reflected in Olympia."

Another huge difference between 1958 and 2011 is the nature and expense of campaigns. To win a seat in the House in 1958, Gorton raised and spent $1,100 in the primary and general elections combined. "We had our battles, but it was less partisan."

Well, usually. As he campaigned for re-election in 1962 and worked with the League of Women Voters on a redistricting initiative, Gorton also monitored, with mounting disgust, an Eastern Washington battle that had turned vicious. A Democrat whose integrity he admired was in the crosshairs. The fallout would have major repercussions for Slade's bid for a fourth term two years later. It also cemented a growing bond of mutual admiration between two ostensibly strange bedfellows, Slade Gorton and Bill Dwyer. Only 33, Dwyer was already one of the sharpest trial lawyers in America. Actually, it was three ostensibly strange bedfellows, because it began with John Goldmark.

A HARVARD LAW SCHOOL GRADUATE, Goldmark was 45 in 1962. Suntanned and handsome, with a graying crew-cut and muscular arms, he

looked more like a rancher than a lawyer because that's what he was.
Goldmark, his vivacious wife Sally and their two young sons had abandoned the East for a ranch with no electricity in the wilds of Okanogan
County after John saw combat in the South Pacific as a U.S. Navy officer
during World War II.[4]

Goldmark had served three terms in the Washington Legislature and
was chairman of the powerful House Ways & Means Committee. "John
Goldmark philosophically was everything I
wasn't," Gorton says. "He was not only a
Democrat, he was quite a liberal Democrat.
I loved to debate him in the House because
he was an eloquent speaker. He was the best
spokesman the Democrats had."

Gorton and Goldmark were of similar
temperament, Dwyer said. "Impatient of
the foolish and venal, Goldmark lacked the
statehouse politician's air of genial mediocrity." Emmett Watson, Seattle's favorite columnist, always recalled that when he first
met Goldmark "he seemed prickly and impatient; too questing, too demanding; no
time for small talk." When Watson introduced Goldmark to his college-age daughter, he asked her all sorts of probing questions about her goals, hopes and dreams.
"Well, what did you think of him?" Watson

State Rep. John Goldmark,
a Democrat from Okanogan,
in 1961. *Washington State
Archives*

asked that night. "I think he's the kindest man I've ever met." "How so?"
"Because he was taking a genuine interest in *me*."[5] If she had met Gorton,
she might have said the same thing. Smart young people bring out the
best in him.

In the 1962 Democratic primary, Goldmark was challenged from the
right in his own party. Donations from the private-power lobby, the John
Birch Society and other arch-conservatives boosted his opponent. Front-
page stories and editorials in the local weekly branded him a pinko. Albert F. Canwell, the celebrated 1940s communist hunter from Spokane,
appeared at a forum sponsored by the American Legion to warn the locals
that the godless Marxist-Leninist menace was burrowing into their midst.
Canwell revealed a skeleton in Sally Goldmark's closet. Years before
meeting John, when she was an idealistic young New Deal worker during
the Depression, she had joined the Communist Party. One night when

they were dating, John derided communism as an oppressive ideology. She told him her secret and suggested he wouldn't want to marry such a person. John said he didn't care. He loved her. Instead of pressuring her to quit the party, he felt certain she would grow out of it. She quickly did, feeling foolish at her naiveté.[6]

Now, besides sleeping with the enemy, the right-wingers said John Goldmark's membership in the ACLU was prima facie evidence he was "the tool of a monstrous conspiracy to remake America into a totalitarian state." Both Goldmarks "are in fact under Communist Party discipline," they would later charge.[7]

"It was a brutal, nasty campaign and Goldmark was slaughtered," Gorton recalls, voice tinged with revulsion. While Goldmark lost his seat in the Legislature, his indignation was intact. If he went away quietly it might usher in a whole new era of red-baiting in Washington politics, he told Dwyer. He wanted to sue for libel. Dwyer and his co-counsel, a facile Okanogan attorney, took the case for no fee and with little hope of winning a sizable judgment. That it would be "the first libel case of its kind before a rural jury" was tantalizing to Dwyer.[8] He was a renaissance man who loved Shakespeare, mountain-climbing and causes that seemed lost. Soon after arriving in Seattle, Gorton had defended an antitrust case against Dwyer and learned "just how damn good he was. I decided that if I were ever in really big trouble and completely in the right I would want Bill Dwyer to be my lawyer. And if I were ever in really, really big trouble and completely in the wrong I would want John Ehrlichman to be my lawyer." A gifted attorney, Ehrlichman would lose his moral compass somewhere in the West Wing. Growing success never altered Dwyer's mantra. It was *This above all: to thine own self be true."*

GOLDMARK SUED Canwell, Ashley Holden, the publisher of the weekly *Tonasket Tribune,* and two others for libel. The trial began on Nov. 4, 1963. Okanogan's old three-story courthouse, with its spartan courtroom, seemed plucked from *To Kill a Mockingbird.* Dwyer knew Gorton admired Goldmark. He asked him to be the last in a diverse array of 12 reputation witnesses.

"When Bill called, I knew that if I said yes it would cost me. And I knew that if I said no I'd be a coward," Gorton says. "Looking back, that may have been the pivotal moment of my career in politics. There had been no incident in those first three terms that had really tested my character. I said yes." That moment of decision reminds him of the hymn from James Russell Lowell's poem, "To Every Man." From memory, Gorton recites:

> Once to every man and nation,
> comes the moment to decide,
> In the strife of truth with falsehood,
> for the good or evil side;
> Some great cause, some great decision,
> offering each the bloom or blight,
> And the choice goes by forever,
> 'twixt that darkness and that light.

In making that choice for the good side as opposed to doing the political calculus, "the unintended consequence was that it took me out of being just another young state representative. I became someone *The Seattle Times* and other media would pay attention to." In his riveting book about the Goldmark case, Dwyer wrote, "An outstanding young lawyer thought to have a brilliant political future, Gorton was willing to tell the truth as he saw it about John regardless of what it might cost him with the right wing of his party."[9]

"In 1963, I had never set foot in Okanogan County in my life," Gorton recalls. "How well I recall the dull, cloudy November day when I drove over." He testified to Goldmark's honesty and straightforwardness. "His reputation (in the Legislature) was excellent," Gorton told the court. "It was not questioned." The defense cross-examined aggressively, trying to get him to characterize Goldmark as an extreme leftist. "[H]e was a leading member of the liberal group of the Democratic Party," Gorton replied evenly, and that "included the great bulk of the Democratic Party in the Legislature."[10]

When President Kennedy was assassinated in Dallas by an avowed Marxist three weeks into the trial, the plaintiffs feared their case was also mortally wounded. But Dwyer was masterful. The jury, which deliberated in the courthouse attic for five days, decided that a man's good name had been tarnished by innuendo. It awarded Goldmark $40,000 in damages, the second-largest libel verdict in state history. He never received a cent, however. The U.S. Supreme Court, in the famous *New York Times Co. v. Sullivan* case, ruled a few months later that "actual malice" had to be proven by a public figure in a libel or defamation case. The Goldmark verdict was reversed. "At least Goldmark was vindicated by winning in front of a jury of his peers," Gorton says.

Canwell was incensed by Gorton's testimony. "Of course, Slade Gorton, Joel Pritchard, Evans, all of these people who wormed their way into the Republican Party were no more Republicans than I am a Zulu. They were opportunists who moved into a vacuum," Canwell grumped years later.[11]

IN 1964, GORTON FOUND HIMSELF in a bare-knuckle primary of his own. The John Birch Society already viewed the emerging Evans wing of the party as a coven of leftists. When Gorton "defended a commie" that was proof positive. The Association of Washington Business was also suspicious. The right-wingers funded a candidate against Gorton in the 46th District primary. Only 23, Jim Toevs was clean-cut, articulate and a true believer. He had headed the Washington State Draft Goldwater Committee. Slade was worried. "But the race ended up making my political career because it was a primary in which people were widely interested in that very tough year."

Toevs (pronounced "Taves") borrowed a gimmick that helped an unknown Republican from Mercer Island upset an incumbent two years earlier. The night before the election, the candidate mobilized hundreds of volunteers to fan out all over the district. Voters awoke to find their front yards dotted with Popsicle sticks that featured a flag and a five-by-seven card with a portrait of the candidate and the highlights of his platform.

"They pulled the same stunt on me" the night before the primary election, Gorton says. As luck would have it, however, they started out in a neighborhood that was home to two of his most energetic supporters, Fred and Ritajean Butterworth. Ritajean spotted the enemy troops snollygostering from lawn to lawn and called Dick Williams, Slade's campaign chairman. "The boys were out roaming around—God knows where—looking for trouble," Ritajean recalls, but they roared back. Soon Williams, the Butterworths, Ken McCaffree and several other campaign workers were playing pick-up sticks almost as fast as the little signs went in. They arrived at Gorton's house with a trunk load and burned them in his fireplace. Slade was particularly angry that Toevs' cards featured assertions he wouldn't have time to refute.

"Finally, about 3 o'clock in the morning the Toevs people have gone ballistic," Gorton recalls with glee. "Of course what they're doing is every bit as illegal as what we're doing. Our guys got to the point where it was much easier to yank the stick out of the ground, leave it there and just collect the card. There were neighborhoods that looked like a kindling truck had crashed."

Toevs and several supporters screeched to the curb at the Gortons and piled out. "I told him to get the hell off my property or I'd punch him," Gorton says. Toevs' recollection is that he intercepted Gorton's car and chased Slade back to his house. They agree that they went nose to nose.

Gorton had campaigned relentlessly. He defeated Toevs two-to-one and went on to easily win re-election in November.

Fifteen years later, when Goldmark was stoically fighting lymphoma, Gorton spoke at a recognition dinner in Seattle for John and Sally Goldmark. "In 1959 when I first became a member of the state Legislature, I took it as an article of faith that I would not like John Goldmark and that we would vote on opposite sides of almost every significant issue. The last half of that prediction turned out to be all too correct," Gorton told the crowd. "The first part did not, because it was from John Goldmark that I learned the most important political lesson of my entire life. . . . That the character and the courage of the individual within our system counted for far more than anything else."[12]

5 | A Power Struggle

THE MOST CONTENTIOUS STANDOFF in the history of the Washington Legislature was all about power, literally and figuratively. For Gorton, it was "marvelous OJT" in coalition-building and in due course a game changer.

House Bill 197 was introduced by Olympia Republican Harry Lewis and other supporters of private power early in the 1961 session. It mandated a vote of the people before a public utility district could acquire the operating assets of an investor-owned utility. Gorton was the legal adviser for the proponents of "Right-to-vote," including the Evans crew and a collection of conservative Democrats from private power districts. Notable among the Democrats were William S. "Big Daddy" Day, a 6–3, 300–pound chiropractor, and Margaret Hurley, who had "legs any chorus girl would envy." She could be as tough as she was pretty when you got her Irish up.[1] Day and Hurley were from Spokane, home of Washington Water Power.

Representative Bob Perry, another of the Democrats backing HB 197, was a business agent for the Electrical Workers Union in Seattle. Gorton and Pritchard quickly sized him up as a schemer. But he was hard not to like. It would be revealed later that Perry was also on Washington Water Power's payroll. The PUD Association had a war chest of its own.

HB 197 "precipitated the last great battle in the public-private power controversy that had been a major element in the politics of the state for over 40 years." Dan Evans said the bill "actually was nothing more sinister" than requiring a public vote before any county could shift from private power to a PUD. But to Ken Billington, the veteran public power lobbyist, it was "a very cleverly worded piece of legislation, having all the flag-waving appeal of the right to vote." Billington said the fine print revealed a "heads I win, tails you lose" proposal that private power dearly loved.[2]

Gorton, truth be told, had no abiding conviction that he was on the right team on this one. In later years, in fact, he would be a staunch supporter of public power. But it was *his* team, by God, "and Harry Lewis, a freshman, was getting beat up on by the likes of John Goldmark, whom I immensely enjoyed debating at every opportunity just for the hell of it."

Wily John L. O'Brien, having narrowly won a record fourth term as speaker, wielded the gavel with impunity during the filibuster that staved off HB 197 and paralyzed the House. The son of Irish immigrants, O'Brien was a deceptively affable self-made man. His father, a Seattle cop, died in a shootout when Johnny was 9. O'Brien kept a wary eye on the hive of ambitious young Republicans in his midst.

The Evans team had recruited and elected more progressives, allowing Dan to score a 21–18 victory in the race for minority leader. Evans' growing statewide reputation was burnished by his decisiveness during the fight over the power bill. In the course of four tedious days, the members were locked in their chamber "under call," hour after hour, as the opponents resorted to every form of parliamentary jujitsu in the book and some holds no one had ever attempted. There were hundreds of amendments and 45 roll call votes. Sixty-one of the 99 members engaged in the debate, with Gorton, Evans, Hurley, Goldmark and Norm Ackley, a sharp young Democratic attorney, getting in some of the most withering licks. Goldmark said the bill was "essentially a fraud" because its proponents were hailing it as the right to vote. "Democracy," the Okanogan rancher asserted, "is representative government. It is based on having people selected because their friends and neighbors decide somebody should be entrusted with responsibility and they send them to a place to inform themselves and make decisions. It is not a question of referring every single thing back to the people."[3]

Eight exhausting hours into Day 1, Speaker O'Brien fielded a motion to advance the bill to a third reading. He ignored calls for a roll call vote, declared it defeated and banged his gavel so hard that the head broke off and went flying, almost hitting one of the Republicans in the front row. With that, O'Brien declared "Adjourned!" and disappeared through the curtains behind the rostrum as the proponents erupted in indignation. No one had ever seen Evans so angry.[4]

When the battle resumed, Ackley pointed out that if private power won the first vote required by the proposed law, any future attempt by a PUD to seek a second vote or reverse the first vote would be automatically blocked. Gorton conceded the point and won some grudging new admirers across the aisle. He and Ackley drafted a clarifying amendment that passed.

"I think the people for this bill are just as patient as those against it," Gorton predicted confidently. By Day 4, however, the opponents had pieced together a tenuous 51–47 majority by turning up the heat on Democrats from public utility district counties. They moved to send the bill back to the Rules Committee. Poised to move immediately for reconsideration, Evans voted in favor, but O'Brien's gavel once again was too fast for him.[5]

The regular session was followed by an equally volatile special session in both chambers. Republicans and fiscally conservative Democrats in the Senate passed a floor resolution censuring Governor Rosellini when he threatened to veto their conservative budget. It was one of the least productive sessions in state history, with Gorton's billboard control law as its most notable enactment. The session's real legacy was the festering resentment that led to a game-changing insurrection in 1963. Evans believes the seeds of his victory in the 1964 governor's race were sown during the debate over HB 197. So, too, Gorton's rise to majority leader and beyond.[6] O'Brien's days as speaker were numbered. His biographer would describe him as "a martyr" to the cause of public power.[7]

After years of research, legislative historian Don Brazier concludes that the 1961 power struggle is "the single most significant event" in the history of the Washington Legislature. "Dan's right. If it hadn't been for that hassle he might never have had a chance to become governor."

THE POLITICAL FALLOUT was still radioactive when the Democrats held their state convention in Bellingham in June of 1962. The private power delegates from Spokane backed State Senator Al Henry of White Salmon over O'Brien for permanent convention chairman. O'Brien prevailed but paid a price. The platform that emerged featured a strong public power plank as well as another slap in the face to conservatives—an amendment calling for weakening the anti-communist McCarran Act. The federal law enacted in 1950 at the height of the Red scare required communists to register with the U.S. Attorney General and reveal their sources of income and expenditures. Congress overwhelmingly overrode President Truman's veto to pass it. (Truman called the bill "the greatest danger to freedom of speech, press and assembly since the Alien and Sedition Laws of 1798.") The platform also called for the elimination of state loyalty oaths, another remnant of the Canwell-McCarthy era.

Spokane delegates, including State Representatives Bill McCormick, "Big Daddy" Day, Margaret Hurley and her husband, Joe, a former legislator, bolted the convention, together with Bob Perry. "This platform is the Communist Manifesto," Joe Hurley snorted.[8] O'Brien buttonholed Maggie Hurley and accused her of disloyalty. She suggested that his memory needed refreshing. In 1955, after injuring her ankle in an auto accident, she made a dramatic wheelchair entrance to cast the vote that elected O'Brien speaker for the first time. There'd been a lot of water over the dam since then. In 1959, she had to get right in his face when he tried to shove her aside "and put some buddy-buddies on the Rules Committee." She hated his "quizzical way of looking at you as though he was superior in knowledge, ability, power and authority, and you were nothing but a worm."[9]

The Republicans in the House came tantalizingly close to winning a majority in the 1962 elections. Statewide, they captured nearly 53 percent of the vote, gained eight seats and were within 228 votes of winning the two more they needed. It was now 51–48.

The 1963 Legislature was under federal court order to achieve "rational" redistricting, as opposed to the "invidiously discriminatory" lines drawn by the Democrats six years earlier to thwart the League of Women Voters. Evans, Gorton and Pritchard believed that if they couldn't gain control, or at least more leverage, Bob Greive, the majority leader in the Senate, would relegate the GOP to minority status for another decade.

PERRY CONTACTED GORTON and floated the capital idea of forming a coalition to gain control of the House. "Bob was one of first people I met in my first term," Gorton recalls. A labor Democrat from the 45th District in North Seattle, Perry had once worked the rough-and-tumble docks of San Francisco. "He was a man with no formal education, but a voracious reader and magnificently self-educated. We sat across the aisle from each other in my second term and became friends." The day after the 1962 election, Perry told Gorton, "Let's do it!" O'Brien's days as speaker were numbered.

Gorton huddled with Evans and Pritchard. Not much to lose, they concluded, though caution was crucial. They floated the idea with the House Republican caucus. "Look, the dissident Democrats, have come to us," Gorton said calculatingly. "We don't know if there is anything to it, but how about putting together a subcommittee that is authorized to deal with them to see what they have to offer? We won't make any commitments and we'll come back to the caucus when we get something tangible."

Many of the old guard members were fidgety, but the plotters got the go-ahead. Gorton, Evans, Pritchard and Elmer Johnston, the Republican from Spokane who'd been so wary of the freshmen four years earlier, were assigned to follow up on Perry's overture.

The 1963 session would be the stuff of legends.

6 | The Coalition

I T WAS SUNDAY, JAN. 13, 1963, the day before the 38th session of the Washington State Legislature. The Republican members of the House and their spouses were enjoying a get-together at the Governor Hotel in downtown Olympia. As the party wound down, Dan Evans sidled up to Gorton, Don Eldridge and Tom Copeland, three members of his leadership team. He told them to meet him in the parking lot of the Elks Club in a few minutes and they'd go for a ride.

A chilly drizzle slickened the road as Evans headed through west Olympia and turned north onto Cooper Point Road, which winds through a narrow peninsula that pokes into Puget Sound. "We were looking over our shoulders to see if anyone was following us," Gorton says.

They turned onto a long dirt road flanked by towering old-growth evergreens. It led to a clearing and a small house. Light from a fireplace flickered through the windows. Otherwise, the place was as dark as the moonless night. To Evans, it felt like a B movie.

Evans knocked on the door. Bill Day, a moose of a man, welcomed them with a conspiratorial grin. The chiropractor from Spokane had rented the place for the session. Sitting around the fire were Bob Perry, Maggie Hurley, Dick Kink, Chet King and Bill McCormick. In a lifetime of politics, they were "six of the toughest Democrats" Evans ever bargained with. Si Holcomb, chief clerk of the House every session but one since 1935, was there too, together with his assistant, Sid Snyder, who got along with everyone. Holcomb's eyesight was poor, so Snyder suspected nothing unusual when asked to drive him to a meeting with Day. "Everyone had heard all the talk about a coalition," Snyder says, "but I thought we were just going to talk about the opening day agenda. I'm not sure they actually wanted me there, but there I was."

There was no love lost between Snyder's boss and the speaker of the House. "Si had chafed under John O'Brien's rather abrupt and abrasive style," Evans says. "It was one of those cases where human relationships played a very big role." Holcomb was also sore at the speaker because

O'Brien found out he was making hay on the side by selling services and told him to knock it off. "He had a list of lobbyists who wanted copies of bills, the daily calendar and other papers delivered to their rooms and he charged them for it," Snyder says. "O'Brien didn't like it."

It was the first time the Republicans had met with all six of the dissident Democrats. Gorton as usual cut to the chase, advancing Evans as the coalition candidate for speaker. "Well, they didn't want any part of that," Evans recalls with a chuckle. It had to be Day. Truth be told, Evans wasn't particularly excited to become speaker under contentious circumstances, and in return for Day as speaker the Republicans would win major chairmanships and achieve majorities on the important committees, including Rules & Elections and Apportionment.

Gorton and Bob Perry, as different as cheese and chalk, had some sort of weird intellectual chemistry going. Perry assured the other dissident Democrats that Gorton would not allow the gerrymandering of their districts.

It was not for nothing that Snyder called Holcomb "Sly Si." The chief clerk presides over the opening session until a speaker is elected. He was part of the plot because the coalitionists knew they could count on him to wield a mean gavel of his own. His job was riding on the outcome. "If this whole thing failed," Copeland said, "I don't think John O'Brien would have kept him around for one minute."

The deal done, they shook on it and headed back into the night. Gov. Rosellini would brand it an "unholy alliance." It seemed like heaven to the conspirators.[1]

The press expected fireworks, not an ICBM. Everyone knew Evans and the dissident Democrats were trying to craft an alliance to oust O'Brien. Few believed they could actually pull it off. When the Democrats caucused in December, O'Brien had 38 votes for speaker, Day nine and Kink three. Perry was crowing on every corner that O'Brien would never get the 50 he needed. Evans, Gorton and Pritchard weren't showing any of their cards. Fearing leaks, they kept their own caucus in the dark for weeks.

Adele Ferguson, the only woman in the Capitol press corps, delighted in scooping the guys. In a story that led *The Bremerton Sun's* front page a week before the Legislature convened, she said the game was afoot. The O'Brien regulars assured her all the holdouts except Perry were back under the tent, having been promised plum committee assignments. Baloney, Perry told her. "O'Brien is as dead as last year's garbage." Day was diplomatic. "There are going to be a lot of problems facing the Legislature this time," he said. "Redistricting; a deficit situation beyond belief. Tremendous problems. We need to use the best brains we have in a bipartisan effort to represent the people."

"Would Day give the Republicans committee chairmanships?" Adele asked, notepad in hand.

"Absolutely!" said Big Daddy.[2]

THE 48 REPUBLICAN MEMBERS of the House, including Mary Ellen McCaffree, a freshman from Seattle, took their seats in a caucus room at the Legislative Building at 10 a.m. on Jan. 14. McCaffree was nervous. After two eventful terms as president of the Seattle League of Women Voters, she shouldn't have been. Realizing her knowledge of redistricting would prove invaluable, Evans, Gorton and Pritchard recruited her to run for the Legislature. The Democrats had wooed her as well.[3]

Evans locked the door, related the events of the night before and said the Cooper Point coup was a go. But it had to unfold just so. Jaws dropped when Evans announced that the speaker was going to be Day. Gorton, Pritchard and Eldridge, the caucus chairman, nodded reassuringly. Some saw it as a pact with the devil but Evans said, "What the hell do we have to lose?" If they pulled it off they could drive the agenda, oversee redistricting and gain momentum for an outright majority. If they failed, they'd still have their 48 votes and the promise of support on key legislation from the dissident Democrats. They were ideological soul mates on issues that resonated with the Republican agenda: modernizing the committee structure and finding more money for schools without resorting to new taxes, not to mention private power.

"This is pretty heady wine," said Damon Canfield, the assistant floor leader.[4] The Yakima Valley farmer was a man of few words so when he said something people listened. Still, "we had a lot of people who were very, very concerned," Copeland recalled. Some members of the old guard were in a state of shock. They were saying, "Oh my, we would have to be responsible; we would be in the majority. Can we depend upon the members of a coalition?"[5] Leadership patiently fielded every question, then asked for a show of hands. The usually mild-mannered Dwight Hawley, who had represented King County since 1950, was the only one "who just couldn't stomach the thought" of voting for Day.[6]

In another corner of the Capitol, traffic was heavy in and out of O'Brien's office all morning, with Day and Perry conspicuous by their absence. At 11:15, one of the speaker's aides strolled smiling out to the floor and told the scribes, "It's in the bag for O'Brien."

The Republicans broke huddle at 11:55. Evans emphasized once more that they couldn't tip their hand too early when the voting for speaker got under way. O'Brien was already anxious. Don't give him a chance to call a time-out and regroup. They'd spring the trap on the third ballot.

POKER-FACED, THE REPUBLICANS filed into the House chamber at high noon. "Day or O'Brien?" the gantlet of reporters asked. "No comment." "How long ago did you decide who you'd go for?" "No comment." As they were taking their seats, Dick Morphis discovered he'd been relegated to the back despite having more seniority than Pritchard and Gorton, the newly appointed assistant floor leader. "So in the midst of this huge stress," Slade was stunned when "Rigor" bounced down the aisle in a snit and complained to Evans that he deserved a better seat. Normally a model of affability, Pritchard snapped, "Shut up, Dick, and get back to your seat or I'll deck you!" Morphis turned pale and scurried back to his seat. Gorton stifled a chortle.

O'Brien sat in the back row. His thin smile betrayed his anxiety. Day and Perry were uncharacteristically dour. Copeland, the Republican whip, demanded the doors be locked. O'Brien, Day and Evans were duly nominated for speaker in speeches testifying to their wisdom, integrity, infectious congeniality and love of state and country. On the first ballot, the Republicans cast all 48 of their votes for Evans. O'Brien received 45, Day six. On the second ballot, the Republicans held ranks. O'Brien lost a vote when Bill O'Connell, a Democrat from Tacoma, defected to Day. Just before the third ballot, a worried O'Brien approached Hurley, who had nominated Big Daddy for speaker.

"How can you do this to me, Maggie?" O'Brien said, palms uplifted.

"I didn't do it to you, John," she said. "I did it for my voters."[7]

Out of the corner of his eye, O'Brien saw Day's smirk and realized there was no use talking to him either. "By this time, word of the impending confrontation in the House had swept through the Capitol like wild fire." The Senate had recessed to take in the drama across the marbled hall. The galleries and wings were packed.[8]

Evans swiveled in his seat to nod to Alfred O. Adams, sitting one row back. "Doc, it's time," Evans said. Silver-haired, portly and dignified, Adams was a retired orthopedic surgeon. His name was first on the roll call. It galled the hell out of him to be voting for a chiropractor—a *Democrat* chiropractor, no less—for speaker of the House, but he was a trouper.

The clerk will call the roll:

"Adams?"

"Day!" Doc boomed out. Heads whirled and the galleries gasped. The

Republicans were switching their votes to Big Daddy. O'Brien had swapped seats with Mark Litchman, the majority leader-designate, and was now prowling down in front. He couldn't believe this was really happening to him. Bud Huntley of Whitman County was seated next to Adams. He looked on bemused as O'Brien put a hand on Adams' shoulder and implored, "Doc, let's talk this over a little bit." "We've been talking this over for the last four years," said Adams, stony-faced.[9]

O'Brien tried to stall. "Let's sit down and talk about it," he pleaded to three rows of Republicans. "There's nothing to talk about," said one.

Litchman leaned over Evans, asking for a chance to make a deal. Evans wouldn't even look up. Halfway through the roll call, O'Brien stood next to Evans' desk. "We'd like a recess," he begged. "Give us some time, Dan. Do us this courtesy. Can't we work something out?" Evans shook his head and said, "School's out, John." O'Brien glared down at him. "It was the most dramatic thing I've ever seen," Gorton says.

"O'Brien's face collapsed like a jiggled soufflé" as the roll call continued, Adele observed from her front row seat at the press table. Three members of his team raced to the speaker's platform, with Perry in hot pursuit. Holcomb refused to recognize O'Brien, who was now livid.[10]

In a strategic maneuver, Bob Schaefer, the Democrats' floor leader, cast his vote for Day. Si Holcomb banged the gavel. "O'Brien 41, Day 57, Evans one. You have elected Mr. Day speaker."

Schaefer jumped to his feet. "Having voted on the prevailing side, I move for reconsideration." Copeland, right on cue, was up in a heartbeat. How they'd handle reconsideration was part of the script the coalition wrote at the cabin the night before.

Copeland asked the chief clerk whether the motion was valid. Without hesitation, Holcomb said his authority in presiding over the House was limited to one thing—the election of a speaker. "A speaker has been elected by your vote on the last ballot." Therefore his duty was done. "The motion is declared out of order." With that, Perry and Doc Adams each grabbed a beefy arm and escorted the beaming new speaker to the rostrum.[11]

After congratulating Day, Evans acknowledged that O'Brien had served the House "long and well." But it was obvious that the Democrats were too fractured to elect a speaker. Having come so close to winning an outright majority at the ballot box, Republicans were unwilling to suffer through another session controlled by "radical liberals," Evans added. The coalition was their only choice to set the House on a course toward "a really new era."[12]

At last able to address the House, O'Brien accused the Republicans of "dishonest and immoral" conduct that endangered the very fabric of the two-party system. "There should be a code of ethics, even among legislators," he declared. Henceforth, there should be party loyalty oaths. "I think a price was paid here today and we are going to suffer by it. . . . We didn't like your platform either, and I can tell you people right now you are in for the most interesting 60 days you have ever had."[13]

Adele wrote that "as he continued to rail at the Republicans and the Democrats who'd thwarted him, voices rose and the man who once was king was obviously just another House member talking too long." It reminded her of Nixon's bitter press conference two months earlier after he was defeated in his comeback bid for governor of California.[14]

When they adjourned to their caucus room, several shell-shocked Republicans asked almost in unison, "Now what?" "Redistricting," Slade said with a confident smile. But he had underestimated O'Brien's ire and Bob Greive's wily intransigence. Redistricting would take two more years.

Styling themselves as "the Loyal 43 of '63," the O'Brien Democrats assailed "the appalling perfidy" of the dissidents and their co-conspirators. By choosing "to skirt close to the shores of anarchy" they had "transformed an ordinarily orderly House into a travesty on the traditional two-party system."[15] (Translation: The bastards outsmarted us.)

The coalition hit Olympia's watering holes that night and slept in on Sunday. Come Monday, however, and for weeks to come more delaying tactics stalemated the House. Permanent rules weren't adopted until January 30 and not much got done until they were well into February.

WITH CENSUS TRACTS, MAPS and Magic Markers, Gorton and Mary Ellen McCaffree spent many nights poring over the state's 49 legislative districts, precinct by precinct. It turned out that the maps from Shell service stations were the most accurate. In those halcyon days when a service station actually offered service, the maps were free.

The goal was to create enough strategically placed Republican swing districts to give the party a fighting chance in lean years and a majority in good ones. No mean feat. One squiggly line bisecting a neighborhood could spell defeat or victory.

McCaffree was surprised when Gorton told her she was going to be the bill's sponsor. Huh? A freshman? He explained that he was a lightning rod for the suspicious Democrats, while she hadn't been around long enough to make anyone really mad. Rarely in Washington legislative history has a rookie played a bigger role. "Mary Ellen outworked me," Gorton

Howard McCurdy, the redistricting aide for the House GOP Caucus, draws some lines in 1965. Looking on intently from left are Reps. Joel Pritchard, Damon Canfield and Mary Ellen McCaffree, Governor Dan Evans, Reps. Tom Copeland and Slade Gorton. *Howard McCurdy Collection*

says. "I'd tell her I had to get some sleep, and she'd be at it past midnight. She was tireless." So was 22–year-old Howard McCurdy, a UW grad student Pritchard had recruited to work for the Republicans during the session. McCurdy became the GOP number cruncher, reveling in the black art of district drawing.

On Day 53, the coalition's redistricting bill finally cleared the House and was sent to the Senate. Greive had made it clear to Gorton and Evans that their plan was dead on arrival. The Senate Democrats had ideological fractures of their own but enjoyed a 32–17 majority. Like O'Brien, Greive faced a perpetual power struggle in his caucus and wasn't about to give away the farm. The press marveled at how he always managed to find just enough votes to remain majority leader.

Gorton figured that a divide-and-conquer strategy might work in the Senate, too. That Slade was wooing his enemies made Greive even more determined. With his horn-rimmed glasses, trademark bow tie and enigmatic smile, Greive was an astute politician. Representing a lunch-bucket West Seattle district, he prided himself on "working twice as hard as anyone else." Like Gorton, he rubbed a lot of people the wrong way. Too smart; too ambitious, they said. The crafty Catholic and the cerebral Episcopalian were locked in perhaps the greatest battle of wills the Legislature has ever seen. The stakes couldn't have been higher.

Greive dismissed the Evans bloc as "tennis court Republicans." They were a bunch of politically ambitious rich kids, he said, "from rich parents and a rich constituency that was solidly Republican, and they were going to get themselves re-elected." Gorton was peddling their redistricting plan as more fair to all concerned, Greive scoffed, "just like you launch a new advertising campaign for a soap or for tobacco" when all they wanted was what he wanted—*control.* They were running around telling the press, "We want something where the Legislature truly reflects the vote. It's a bunch of hogwash!"[16]

In crisp sentences that radiated self-confidence, Gorton kept asking why a majority of the people shouldn't be able to elect a majority of the legislators. He was gleeful that he was getting under Greive's skin.

Jimmy Andersen and Tom Copeland—pals since grade school in Walla Walla and decorated World War II combat veterans—scoffed at the tennis court crack. They told Gorton to not give one damn inch. While Copeland viewed Evans and Gorton as rivals for the leadership of the caucus, he harbored a visceral distaste for Greive, who in time drew him into a fleeting alliance that cost him dearly. "Now, let's get something crystal clear," Copeland said years later, jaw tightening. "Senator Greive never, ever came up with any kind of legislative redistricting program that did a damn thing for statewide Democrats. . . . His total emphasis was to take care of 13 to 17 Democrat senators that would vote to maintain him as Senate leader, and that was it."[17]

Gorton worked with his well-liked seatmate, Don Moos, a rancher from Eastern Washington, to ensure that rural legislators weren't shortchanged. They drafted a constitutional amendment calling for automatic redistricting and a special commission to oversee the task. Crucially, the Moos-Gorton "little federal plan" required that the line drawers provide as much representation to rural areas as permissible under the population standards. In other words, the districts with the least population would be the rural ones. Greive, facing pressure from rural senators, began to draft his own constitutional amendment. It was contingent on the Legislature approving his redistricting plan.

GREIVE CONSIGNED the House bill to committee. The sorcerer had a gifted apprentice of his own. Young Dean Foster ran the numbers, tweaked the majority leader's plan and gave him something to shop around on the House floor. Gorton warned that two could play that game.

A lot of people, including some members of his own party, were wary of Slade "because he could just outsmart anybody," Don Eldridge said. But Greive had way more detractors and clearly had met his match in Gorton. "I tell you, the two of them, that was a combination," the GOP caucus chairman said. "I'd liked to have been a little mouse in the corner at some of those sessions."[18] Pritchard said Greive was "Machiavelli on redistricting. He was too smart for everybody . . . until he ran into Gorton," who "knew every jot, diddle, corner—whatever it was."[19]

The combatants were like car salesmen trying to close a deal with a squirrely prospect who didn't want extra undercoat. No one knows his own district like an incumbent. Members of their caucuses squinted at the maps as they traced the new lines. "The worst part," Greive said, "would be that you thought you had everybody satisfied, and then at the last minute Fred Dore would come along and say, 'You've got to do something for Petrich!'"[20] One day, Greive and Senator John T. McCutcheon from Pierce County were looking on as Foster drew boundary lines.

"No, no, no, no," McCutcheon said. "I don't want that precinct. Move away from American Lake."

"What is your rationale about moving away from American Lake?" Foster asked.

"My rationale is quite simple: To save my ass!"[21]

"Slade and Bob understood the numbers equally well," says Foster, who went on to become chief clerk of the House and chief of staff to Governor Booth Gardner in the 1980s. "Slade knew he couldn't write enough Republican districts to win a majority. It all depended on the swing districts."

Foster and McCurdy were getting a real-world education in practical politics that no classroom could provide. They even roomed together for a while. "Greive often said that if they would leave the two of us alone for an evening or two we could have solved the redistricting puzzle," says McCurdy, who wrote a thesis on the experience and became a university professor. He hadn't met Gorton before that memorable 1963 session. "The first thing you noticed immediately about him was that he wasn't from Washington State. He didn't look, walk or talk like the Pritchards, the Moriartys and the Evanses and, for that matter, a lot of people on the Democratic side. He clearly kind of exuded this aura of an Eastern intellectual. He was incredibly smart, and you had to be to understand redistricting. You basically had to memorize all the districts. We didn't have computers so all of this was on paper or in your head."

Hayes Elder, a Greive staffer appointed to the House in 1964, gave Mc-Curdy a lift back to Seattle one day. They immediately began parsing the landscape. "We'd identify the precinct we were in and then tell what the vote had been in the 1960 presidential election and the 1962 legislative elections," McCurdy says, smiling over the memory. "The amount of knowledge you had to store in your head was really astonishing, and Gorton was up to it. That surprised a lot of people because nobody thought there was anybody else in the Legislature with that kind of head for small numbers other than Bob Greive. It had been an enormous source of Greive's power."

Gorton was rarely flustered. Stress made Greive even more emotional. Political lives were at stake, he was reminded daily. Ralph Munro, Washington's former longtime secretary of state, was a classmate of Foster's at Western Washington State College. He well remembers the day Greive sent a State Patrol trooper to Bellingham to yank Foster out of class. The senator needed help with the redistricting maps.

Nerves were frazzled; there were fissures right and left—"old guard," "new breed," conservative, liberal, rural, urban, east side, west side. It all made Big Daddy very nervous. Two days before adjournment, the coalition speaker prodded Gorton to give it another go with Greive. Slade took along Pritchard, Moos and Perry. He and Greive clashed instantly. Greive said Gorton didn't understand the implications of what the courts might do if they failed. "Don't be ridiculous!" Slade barked. Clearly peeved that Gorton was so icily resolute, Greive stormed out. Neither could rustle up enough votes to prevail.

THE BATTLE WAS REJOINED when Governor Rosellini called a special session. He admonished the old-guard Democrats to reject any compromises. Rosellini and Attorney General John J. O'Connell, an ambitious Democrat, felt certain they could stave off court intervention and leave redistricting to the 1965 session. Rosellini expected the 1964 elections to produce solid Democratic majorities in both houses. He was weighing whether to seek an unprecedented third consecutive term. O'Connell was saying he shouldn't run. He wanted Rosellini's job. Big Daddy Day did too.

Gorton and Evans now believed they were likely to get a better deal from the courts, which might redraw the districts, make all the legislators run at large or appoint a special master. Under any of those scenarios Republicans surely would do better than agreeing to a shotgun marriage served up by Greive. Olympia was one seething soap opera.

Greive came up with a stopgap plan. He and Foster unveiled it for Gorton, McCurdy and the other four members of a conference committee. They quickly focused on the 10th District in Eastern Washington, the state's smallest. Greive wanted to save its senator, Dewey Donohue, and Gorton wanted to eliminate the district. They bickered and bargained for an hour, McCurdy recalled. "Finally Gorton agreed to Greive's solution. It was a classic gerrymander, a dumbbell-shaped district one-half mile wide at the middle, but it would elect Senator Donohue. In return, Gorton won the Republican district he wanted for the adjoining Tri-Cities area."[22]

In King County, they were swapping half a scalp here and half a scalp there, Greive seeking to preserve Democratic hegemony, Gorton out to create new opportunities for Republicans. When the plan saw the light of day, the weary conferees got an earful. Bitter accusations reverberated through both chambers.

TWENTY-THREE DAYS OF OVERTIME couldn't break the stalemate. The nastiest legislative session in state history ended on April 6, 1963. Two weeks later there was a biting postscript. Timing his veto so that it couldn't be overridden, Rosellini axed an appropriation to fund interim committees. The move played right into the hands of his opponents and unleashed a torrent of bad press. "Shocking," one editorial said. Another branded it the "childish act" of a fast-and-loose politician—an Italian politician, many said *sotto voce*. Evans said the veto was "the most shameful political act in the last 30 years in this state."

Between the sessions, the jockeying for positions continued, with Rosellini artfully dodging another special session and O'Connell playing political rope-a-dope. The federal court talked a good fight, only to balk when push came to shove. Gorton was more frustrated with the courts than with Greive—and utterly disgusted with the attorney general. "You can't get frustrated with Greive for being political," McCurdy says, "but you can get frustrated when federal judges don't do what their constitutional duties require them to do and the attorney general keeps arguing for more delays" for partisan political advantage.

"Slade had proposed some redistricting legislation in the 1961 legislative session, but he really hadn't been in combat," McCurdy continues. "The '63 session was his first Normandy. He found out what people later acknowledged—that besides being very smart he was very politically capable too." In fact, looking back nearly a half century, McCurdy believes Evans, Gorton and Pritchard—the whole crew of "new breed" Republicans—came of age in that year. They said to themselves, "We're as good as these guys. They're not better than we are." They thought they were but didn't know it for sure. "They hadn't been tested and this was the test—the 1963 session."

Twenty months later, the crucial unfinished business of redistricting would be taken up again in Olympia, with more late-night drama under the dome. The veto was going to change hands.

7 | Taking On Giants

D AN EVANS, CIVIL ENGINEER, was back at work in his office in Seattle when an Associated Press reporter called in the spring of 1963. "What's this about a Draft Dan Evans Committee?" "Draft Dan Evans for what?" he laughed. "Well, governor, of course." Evans said it was news to him. Not that the thought hadn't crossed his mind. Gorton, the Pritchard brothers and C. Montgomery "Gummie" Johnson, Weyerhaeuser's public relations man, were telling him he had little to lose and a lot to gain by running for governor in 1964 even though it was shaping up as a Democratic year.

With his Eagle Scout-family man image, Evans was the handsome young face of progressive Republican politics in Washington State. The press coverage of the fractious coalition session had introduced him to a statewide audience. Herb Hadley of Longview, elected to the House in one of 1962's biggest upsets, was thinking big. He launched the Draft Dan Evans Committee. "Those guys just thought, 'Well, we'll goose this thing along,'" Evans recalls.

The Evans brain trust began meeting weekly. Gorton increasingly believed Dan had a real chance, and if they lost a close one they'd still be looking good for 1968. Joel Pritchard said there was only one way to go— "full tilt." He and Frank maintained that winning the GOP nomination for governor was going to be tougher than beating Rosellini. Gummie, who smoked Churchillian cigars and cussed like a sailor, was always gung ho. Jim Dolliver, the sharp lawyer who functioned as chief of staff for the House GOP caucus, was also enthusiastic. "We all felt like we were on a mission," Gorton remembers. "We were pretty young," Pritchard said, "and we were taking on giants."[1]

The murder of John F. Kennedy in Dallas on Nov. 22, 1963, cast a pall over politics. Most analysts believed Americans were unlikely to want three presidents in the space of 14 months. There were clear signs, however, that Washingtonians were open to electing a new governor. No Washington governor had ever won three consecutive terms, and Rosellini

had an image problem. The Republicans called him "Taxellini" and accused him of cronyism. Still, Attorney General O'Connell opted to run
for re-election rather than challenge the governor. Big Daddy Day stayed
out too, realizing that a chiropractor from Spokane—no less one who'd
conspired with Republicans—was a long shot to defeat a sitting governor
for the Democratic nomination.

The Republican frontrunner was 34-year-old Richard G. Christensen,
a Lutheran minister with fiery eyes and a "family values" platform. Some
members of the Evans camp called him "*Christ*-ensen." He'd given U.S.
Senator Warren Magnuson a too-close-for-comfort race in 1962 by suggesting that the veteran Democrat was soft on communism. Christensen
and Evans were ideological opposites, two young men competing not just
for the nomination but for the opportunity to set the party's course for
years to come. The third contender was Joe Gandy, an old-guard, downtown Seattle Republican.

Although Evans trailed badly in the first polls and the campaign was
often close to broke, the Pritchards were so irrepressible it was infectious.
Joel organized armies of doorbellers; Frank oversaw advertising and polling; Slade worked the rubber chicken circuit; Gummie ordered buttons
and brochures outlining Evans' "Blueprint for Progress." Dolliver did
double duty as the campaign committee chairman and candidate's chauf-
feur. A Swarthmore graduate with a salt-and-pepper beard and infectious
laugh, Dolliver called the committee the Chinese Communists because
"they were always arguing with each other." Joel's nickname was the one
that stuck: They were "Dan Evans' Group of Heavy Thinkers," DEGOHT
for short.[2]

At work, Gorton was walking on eggshells for several months. Gandy
was a senior partner in the law firm. Everyone knew Gorton was an Evans
man but there was never any flak. "As it turned out," Slade says, "the two
best things that ever happened to the Evans' campaign were Gandy getting in and Gandy getting out. When Joe got in, he expected to pick up the
support of the downtown business community lock, stock and barrel. By
that time, however, we'd already picked up a lot of those people. They were
saying, 'Sorry, Joe, but we already committed to Dan.' Gandy gave us a
huge extra motivation: He made us work just that much harder. Then, of
course, when he got out he endorsed Dan."

Frank Pritchard says Slade had a habit that amazed him. "He's the only
guy I've ever known who could sit in a meeting room intently reading a
newspaper and at any point jump right into the meeting without missing
a beat."

A FRIENDLY AUTO DEALER made an in-kind donation of a loaner car. Dolliver drove Evans all over the state. "It was easier to drive Dan than to fly him because Dolliver drove faster than an airplane could fly," Gorton jokes. "There were months in which we raised no more than a couple of thousand dollars." Norton Clapp, the Weyerhaeuser eminence, passed the hat among his friends more than once.

Frank Pritchard had been managing A. Ludlow Kramer's campaign for secretary of state. It was going so well for the swarthy young Seattle City Councilman that Frank moved over to help Johnson, who had gone to the mattresses in a donated room at the Olympic Hotel in Seattle. "Gummie slept there most nights," Pritchard recalls. "Between the primary and the general election I spent practically every day there, and I learned to smoke cigars. One day I did 12. We had a helluva good time!" They were tracking poll numbers, reviewing ads and calling Dolliver a couple of times a day for reality checks from the hustings.

Evans, an engineer to the marrow, tracked the polling data on a graph. Joel Pritchard kept saying, "Just watch—We're going to accelerate."[3] They barnstormed out of the state convention, calculated they were going to catch and pass Christensen around August 15th and apparently did just that, judging from what happened a month later on Primary Election Day. Buoyed by ticket-splitters, Evans crushed Christensen and would never trail Rosellini in the polls. The governor's hopes for a third term hung on President Johnson having long coattails. Rosellini tried to tie Evans to the bellicose Republican nominee, Arizona Senator Barry Goldwater, who once wished out loud that he could just lob a nuclear missile "into the men's room of the Kremlin."

Evans and Gorton were Rockefeller Republicans. Gorton was particularly suspect to the right because he had been a character witness for John Goldmark. Evans, however, was the more liberal of the two. His clean-cut, moderate image appealed to the state's powerful cohort of swing voters.

Hard-core Goldwaterites noisily dominated the GOP's grass roots in Washington State, which left the party in disarray after the 1964 national convention. Many old-line conservatives, embarrassed by the paranoia of the rabid right, signed on to help Evans. The campaign made excellent use of the network of Republican legislators. Four years later, when Gorton was in a tight race for attorney general that pipeline would prove crucial.

Evans' lead legislator in Eastern Washington was Don Moos, Slade's seatmate in the House. Moos drew an important assignment. Goldwater campaigned in Washington State only once after the primary election. "He came to Spokane late in the campaign and Dan had to go, of course,"

Gorton says. "But Moos was there and he had one duty: He always had to be in front of any camera when Dan was near Barry Goldwater because the Rosellini people were desperate to get a picture of Goldwater embracing Dan. They never got it because Don kept it from happening."

ON NOVEMBER 3, 1964, with 140,000 votes to spare, Daniel J. Evans, 39, became the youngest governor in Washington State history. He carried all but five counties. More than 200,000 LBJ voters crossed over to Evans. Nationally, he was one of the few major-office Republican candidates to dodge the landslide.

Having repelled the Birchers in the primary, Gorton handily won a fourth term from King County's 46th District. Another bright spot for the DEGOHT was Lud Kramer's victory. At 32, he became the youngest secretary of state in Washington history and the first Republican to hold that office since the coming of the New Deal in 1932.

Among the state's four new Democratic congressmen—all Magnuson-Jackson protégés—swept into office by the Democratic tsunami, two would become major players in both Washingtons: 35–year-old Tom Foley, a lanky lawyer from Spokane, and 37–year-old Brock Adams, a Seattle lawyer with a boyish smile.

While Gorton and the rest of the Evans brain trust survived, together with the six dissident Democrats who helped forge the 1963 coalition, the Republicans lost nine seats in the House. The Democrats would now have an impregnable 60–39 majority there, as well as a still solid 32–17 majority in the state Senate. When it came to redistricting, however, they were still fractured by fear.

Seattle Post-Intelligencer cartoonist Bob McCausland portrayed the new governor as a noble knight astride a white charger. To joust with a hostile Legislature, Evans had a powerful lance—the veto. As Gorton and Greive girded to resume battle over boundaries, the federal court held the real sword. It ordered the 1965 Legislature to enact a redistricting plan that met the U.S. Supreme Court's landmark "one man, one vote" equal representation mandate before it could take up any new legislation other than housekeeping.[4]

Howard McCurdy was ready. He had spent the summers between sessions drawing lines in Mary Ellen McCaffree's basement.

Greive tried a fast one.

8 | Weird and Wonderful Shapes

T HE WASHINGTON STATE LEGISLATURE convenes at noon on the second Monday in January. By tradition, the governor is inaugurated at noon that Wednesday. The Democrats were out to make the most of those 48 hours and blitz through a redistricting bill for their lame duck governor's signature. The opening prayer beseeched the Lord to protect the state from "discord and confusion; from pride and arrogance." The Lord let human nature run its course.[1]

Drained by the 1963 session, John O'Brien acquiesced to the elevation of his former No. 2, Bob Schaefer, to speaker. O'Brien became majority floor leader. Greive, once again by the skin of his teeth, kept his job as head of the equally dysfunctional family across the hall. Tom Copeland, harboring ambitions of his own, succeeded Evans as minority floor leader. Chuck Moriarty, a charter member of the Evans bloc, was now the minority floor leader in the Senate.

Gorton's heart sank as he scrutinized Greive's new redistricting bill. Even a Republican landslide would generate only a handful of new GOP lawmakers. Greive and Foster had concocted a Democratic masterpiece. McCurdy ran the numbers several times, hoping to find flaws. "It's constitutional," he told Gorton glumly. When the bill passed the Senate on the first day of the session, suspicious Democrats in the House represented the only obstacle between Greive's handiwork and Rosellini's signature. Led by young Gary Grant of Renton, the opponents were a coalition of old dissidents and young turks.

Gorton staged a full-court press to hold Greive at bay. Both sides called in favors, twisted arms and salved old wounds. "If a wavering Democrat was disgruntled with his district," said McCurdy, "Gorton or Pritchard would hint that better things might come from negotiations later." Moos worked on rural conservatives and independents.[2]

Falling just short of a majority at every turn, Greive, O'Brien and

Schaefer kept regrouping, unaware that the Republicans had drawn up a secret play. Gorton discovered there was no specified time for the inauguration of a governor. "Wednesday" was all the statute said. Evans phoned home to Seattle and told his wife, Nancy, to get a babysitter.

It was 10 p.m. Tuesday, January 12, 1965. Gorton, McCaffree and McCurdy knew Greive was running out of time. House Democrats caucused, only to emerge downcast 40 minutes later, still at least two votes short. They repaired to their chamber, bitching among themselves. The Republicans resisted the temptation to cheer this dispirited parade. Schaefer looked exhausted. Copeland took him aside. There's no way you're going to pass a redistricting bill tonight, the minority leader said. Then he dropped the bomb: There was no tomorrow either. If need be, Supreme Court Justice Richard Ott, Bible in hand, and the governor-elect would enter the North Gallery just before midnight for the swearing in of Daniel Jackson Evans as Washington's 16th governor.

"You're not kidding, are you?" Schaefer blanched.

"I'm absolutely dead serious," said Copeland.

"How would it be if we adjourned right now?" Schaefer suggested.

"You've got a deal."3

It was the end of the beginning.

THE NEXT MORNING, Gorton was up early, drafting a paragraph on redistricting for Dan's inaugural address. "I now urge the Legislature to pass promptly a legislative redistricting bill which will obey the mandates of the state and federal constitutions, provide equitable representation for all areas of the state and ensure that the party which wins a majority of the votes will win a majority of the seats in the Legislature," the new governor told a joint session of the Legislature.

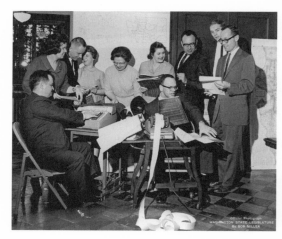

Crunching numbers during the 1960s redistricting battles. Mary Ellen McCaffree is second from left; Don Moos seventh from left. Howard McCurdy, who did much of the heavy lifting for the Republicans, is standing next to Gorton. *Bob Miller/Washington State Legislature*

Evans made it clear that the torch had been passed to a new generation of Republicans. "This administration is not frightened by the word 'liberal,' nor is it ashamed of the word 'conservative.' It does not believe that the words 'fiscal conservative' are old-fashioned, nor will it ever fear to spend money if money needs to be spent."[4]

With the regular Democrats back in control of the House, Lud Kramer invited Gorton to install McCurdy at a large conference table in his spacious new office. There, for several hours a day, Gorton and McCaffree could be found, hunched over maps as the grad student ran an adding machine that spewed paper by the yard. The governor met with his legislative leaders most mornings, invited fence-sitters to his office for a cup of coffee and used his bully new pulpit to generate front-page stories punctuated with indignation at the Democrats. In the basement, Greive and Foster had their own impressive operation.

"The war rooms were at full output, with maps by the billions it seemed . . . all in conflict," said Senator Web Hallauer, a liberal Democrat from the Okanogan. "Everybody was taken in for personal interviews to try and line them up . . . A legislator would go through the Gorton shop and be informed about what was intended for him there and what could be done to him. He would then receive like treatment from Senator Greive." Hallauer's district was a major bargaining chip. "It was like playing Russian Roulette with your friends."[5]

As January wound down, the Democrats pushed through a redistricting bill. Evans immediately announced he would veto it. Compromise talks collapsed when Greive and Gorton got into a shouting match over who got what in Seattle, Tacoma and Spokane. Even amiable Don Moos blew a fuse, telling a cabal of young House Democrats that they were nothing but "a bunch of freshmen and third-stringers." Greive, who attended Mass every morning, was in such febrile condition after one bout with Gorton that friends summoned his parish priest from West Seattle.[6]

Gorton, McCaffree and McCurdy had been secretly preparing an executive request redistricting bill for Evans to submit to the House with bipartisan sponsorship. When it was unveiled on February 8, it produced headlines but only a few Democratic sponsors. Gorton warned that there would be no further compromises. He and Moos were outraged when they discovered that Copeland was working behind their backs, meeting with Greive and Big Daddy Day, their erstwhile ally, in a downtown Olympia hotel room. Copeland had outmaneuvered Moos to succeed Evans as minority leader and resented Slade's ascendancy and closeness to the governor. Greive stepped into the breach. Soon, he and Copeland "were proclaiming that a redistricting settlement was imminent." Gorton was as angry as McCurdy had ever seen him, "convinced not only that Copeland had devastated the strategy for the governor's bill, but that the minority leader, who had entered the negotiations with only an elementary knowledge of redistricting, had surrendered the Republican position."7

Fearing his frustration might make things even worse, Gorton suggested that Joel Pritchard and Moos should be the ones to read Copeland the riot act. They told Copeland he faced a vote of no confidence if he didn't knock it off. He desisted reluctantly and never entirely. Two years later, when the Republicans finally gained a majority in the House, Copeland's decision to consort with Greive was one of the grudges that cost him the speakership.

"One feature of the Evans-Pritchard-Gorton leadership that always impressed me," McCurdy says, "was their ability to 'lock' the House caucus — to convince the minority Republicans to vote as a bloc. It meant that Greive had to deal with Gorton and the Republican leadership instead of building a majority by picking off stragglers one by one. The solidarity of the House caucus in both the 1963 and 1965 sessions was a tremendous source of power for the leadership in general and Gorton in particular. The Democrats were never able to achieve it —but then, they were in the majority. The House Republicans understood that any division in the caucus would doom them to minority status for years to come."

THE FEAR AND LOATHING in Olympia lasted 47 days. One night the Senate was still squabbling at 3 a.m. In the other Washington, Defense Secretary McNamara was testifying that the situation in South Vietnam was "grave but by no means hopeless" and the key testing ground of whether the United States could prevent "Chinese communist aggression throughout Asia." In Selma, Alabama, the Rev. Martin Luther King Jr. led a march of 1,300 Negroes to the courthouse to register to vote.

Humor was the potion that precipitated a brief outbreak of comity between Gorton and Greive. They were invited to address the state's Chambers of Commerce. Greive went first. He launched into a witty standup routine on his relationship with Gorton and how much fun they were having. The audience loved it. So did Slade, who replied in kind. Tension broken, two tacticians at the top of their game proceeded to offer a spellbinding discourse on the intricacies of legislative politics. When it was over they walked back to the Capitol together and talked in Greive's office for a couple more hours. "They had developed a tremendous respect for each other's capabilities," McCurdy says, "so it was sort of a breakthrough." Not that they actually liked one another, Foster makes clear.

To end the stalemate over the Seattle-King County legislative districts, Gorton surrendered any claim to having a corner on piety. He offered Greive "a weird bird-shaped district, with a major Republican stronghold in the beak and a scattering of Democratic outposts in the body." Greive, a connoisseur of gerrymandering, couldn't help but admire Gorton's handiwork. They both laughed at their machinations.

There were five final obstacles to a compromise. One was Gorton's proposed new 21st District, fashioned from the growing suburbs between Seattle and Everett. Gorton and Evans insisted on protecting their favorite Democrat—Jack Dootson of Everett—by moving one of the three Democratic incumbents in his area to the new 21st. Otherwise, Jack was toast.

"Jack Dootson was the most memorable character I have ever known in politics," Gorton says emphatically. In the throes of the 1963 redistricting debate, when the Democrats presented their alternative to Gorton's bill, Dootson had stood to be recognized from his back row seat: "Mr. Speaker, I have examined the two bills before us. I think Representative Gorton's bill is much more objective than my party's bill and therefore I'm going to vote for it."[8] Democrats exploded in outrage. Dootson was unfazed. What happened two years later is one of Gorton's favorite stories. He tells it masterfully, pausing every few paragraphs to shake his head and grin because mere words fail to sum up how inimitable Dootson was:

"A boyhood friend of Scoop Jackson when they were growing up in Everett, Jack Dootson was first elected to the Legislature in 1940 as a member of the left-wing Washington Commonwealth Federation. He was a switch engine engineer in the Great Northern lumber yards in Everett. He served one session in the House in 1941, then went into the Navy and got all the way to lieutenant commander during World War II because he had four university degrees. After the war, he returned to the switch engine job, got elected to the Legislature once more, then lost. His Everett district had one senator and three representatives under the old gerrymandered system. So every now and then Jack would finish third in the Democratic primary and get elected again. He came back to the House as a result of the 1962 election. Jack was still a wild left-wing social liberal but also a huge right-wing fiscal conservative. He had two suits—1940s zoot suits, with wide lapels and baggy pants. He never threw away a piece of paper. You almost couldn't see him behind his desk, way in the back far end of the Democratic side in the House. He stopped going to the Democratic Caucus because its leaders would not brook dissent. He lectured us every now and then on the proposition that the Constitution of the People's Republic of Romania was much superior to the United States Constitution. He admitted that Romania didn't follow it, but nonetheless we should look at it because it is an ideal document."

As the redistricting debate was raging in February of 1965, Gorton continues, "Bob Greive said to me, 'All right, I'll make a deal. You'll get what you want if I can determine which Democratic senators lose.' 'Fine,' I said, though I didn't like it. In the case of Web Hallauer I almost cried tears because he was such a good guy. He had courageously defended John Goldmark and was never a strident partisan. But this was the price for getting the job done. The last unsettled question was the fate of Jack Dootson. Under redistricting, we had to go with 'one person, one vote,' so the districts were going to have one senator and two representatives. We put Dootson in a different district where he'd have a chance of finishing second. But the Democrats wouldn't settle for that. Dootson was going to go. Their position was 'He's a Democrat. You can't protect him. We made the deal. We determine which Democrats lose.' 'Hell no!' say I and Dan Evans. 'Dootson is our guy.'

"This goes on for 24 or 48 hours, though we've never actually talked to Dootson. Then Dootson came to me and said, 'I've got to see you and the governor in the governor's office.' We go down to the governor's office. Jack says, 'I understand you're holding up redistricting over me.' 'Goddamn right, we are Jack! And we're going to keep on doing it.' 'Oh,' Jack says, shaking his head, 'I'm so disappointed. I've always looked at you two as my ideals in principled politics, and you're holding up the people's business over my legislative district? I don't think I can support you anymore.' Gulp. We said, 'OK, Jack.'

"But it gets better!" Gorton declares, mirth in his voice. "Jack Dootson wouldn't accept campaign contributions. He'd buy small ads in the *Everett Herald*. They'd say, 'Jack Dootson, independent Democrat for the Legislature stands for . . .' and then in small print he'd list 20 things that he was for. And so help me, at the end it would say, 'If you disagree, perhaps another candidate would suit you better.' This was long before public disclosure of campaign contributions.

"A year later we're all running for re-election and we aren't going to give up on Jack. I go to Gummie Johnson, who is now the state Republican chairman, and I get a thousand dollars in cash. I also get a good ad agent, someone who will at least write decent ads. I take the money and the ads to Dootson's house in Everett and I say, 'Jack, this is my money. I want you to win. And this is the kind of case you can make that might possibly get you through that primary. Just take this money and buy the ads. They're from me.' And Jack says, 'Well, Slade, you're a wonderful person. You're my ideal in politics, but I can't take campaign contributions. And as for these Madison Avenue kind of advertisements, I'd be *ashamed* to attach my name to them.'

"Down he goes. Jack Dootson is defeated. I don't see him for 15 years. The last time I ever see him he is in front of the Federal Building in Seattle, where my U.S. Senate offices were, carrying placards denouncing aid to the Contras!"

IT WAS FRIDAY, FEBRUARY 26, 1965. John O'Brien was desperately trying to block the bipartisan Gorton-Greive redistricting compromise approved by the Senate. He believed Greive, conspiring with Gorton, had protected his Senate supporters while hanging House Democrats out to dry. Now, however, O'Brien was out of time and short on votes. Yet the former speaker railed on, denouncing Evans as a "power-hungry" dictator who had manipulated his Republican colleagues "like a master puppeteer" while "grossly abusing his veto power."[9]

Gary Grant, who had annoyed the hell out of Gorton and Greive by promoting his own redistricting plan, read a letter he'd received from a Democratic precinct committee chairman: "Dear bum: All of the plans I see in the paper are those of the Senate and of Evans. Neither is good for me. . . . [T]hese kinky redistricting lines will possibly wipe out both you and Evans. Did you ever try to draw straight lines? Is that too much to expect for $40 a day? Well, I hope you finish the job this year so I will be able to start campaigning against you next year." Grant said House Democrats were "about to commit an act of hari-kari." He demanded to know from Dootson how much thought he'd given to the details of the proposal he was backing "besides consideration for your own district? Seventeen seconds, Mr. Dootson?"

Grant clearly didn't grasp that the Senate bill was Dootson's death knell.

In his rambling, courtly way, Dootson said there was the unmistakable scent of hypocrisy in the air, but "it isn't an ill wind that blows no good" if they'd all learned something in the past six weeks.

"With apologies to Robert Service," Hugh Kalich, a Lewis County Democrat, read a piece of doggerel celebrating duplicitous "lawyer guys" like "the great Slade Gorton and his crew."

Copeland called it "a lousy bill . . . a very lousy bill, but the best we can do . . . and the moment of truth is here."[10]

Governor Evans signs the hard-fought redistricting bill in 1965. From left, Jack Dootson, Tom Copeland, John Ryder, R.R. "Bob" Greive (bow-tie), Howard McCurdy, Bob Bailey, Lud Kramer, Hayes Elder, Gorton, Dean Foster, William "Big Daddy" Day, Mary Ellen McCaffree, Jack Rogers, Don Moos, Marshall Neill and Chuck Moriarity. *Washington State Archives*

Gorton had been curiously quiet for three days of bitter floor debate. He knew victory was at hand—and that he was a lightning rod. After the unhappy Democrats had finally talked themselves out, he addressed the House. They had been on a long and winding road for two years, Gorton said, and the process had produced some "weird and wonderful shapes." But perhaps the people had been better served than if one party had been able to dictate the outcome. As for charges of a sell-out, "I can only say of Senator Greive that he has been devoted to a solution of this problem for at least three years; that he has spent more hours on it than anyone else in either house, myself included; that I never noticed that he was anxious to do in his own party, but as a matter of fact I hope I never have to deal with anyone who is tougher in working for his own party . . . It's hard to see how a district that 'saves our senators' doesn't also 'save our representatives.' . . .

"I do commend this bill to you and we say to all of you that if you can't feel joyful, you can feel triumphant . . . in one respect and one respect only: You have done the job. . . . Maybe with practice, we will be better the next time around, but there is always the first time and this will be the first brand-new redistricting bill that this Legislature has done since 1901. And to that extent at least, I believe we can be proud of it."¹¹

With that, they voted. Redistricting was approved, 56–43, with Dootson joining the majority to seal his own fate. That afternoon, Governor Evans, flanked by Greive and Gorton, signed the bill into law. Dootson was there—smiling like all the rest. So were McCurdy and Foster, who had acquired an education in practical politics no university could match.

Greive, who died in 2004 at the age of 84, "had tremendous persistence, and developed about as many enemies as friends," Gorton says. "His enemies wanted his scalp as much as his job, and being majority leader meant everything to him. He was intense, single-minded and very smart. We might still be there in that debate if Bob hadn't figured out a way to outsmart the other Democrats outside his clique of supporters."

McCurdy went on to Cornell to earn a doctorate. He was an intern at the LBJ White House during the summer. "Lyndon Johnson reminded me a great deal of Bob Greive," he says. "They were ultimate political animals. What really characterized Lyndon Johnson, especially in the U.S. Senate, was that he understood what anybody wanted and what you could threaten them with. He also understood which people you couldn't threaten, which people were cheating on their wives, which people needed campaign contributions . . . So he could go to people individually and work out the details on a one-to-one basis and never actually show them the bill. Greive worked the same way. He would single them out one by one and show them only the part of the bill that would influence them. You got the full treatment. Then he'd put together a coalition without anyone having seen the whole legislation.

"Slade was not really a true political animal in the same way Bob Greive and Joel Pritchard were," says McCurdy. "He was the analyst—the Bob McNamara; the intellectual who was able to hold the policy stuff together. That was Slade's role, and a lot of people resented how good he was at it."

POSTSCRIPT: THE REDISTRICTING BATTLE was rejoined after the 1970 Census, with Gorton as attorney general and Greive more aggrieved than ever that he'd met his match. The court ordered the legislators to produce a constitutionally equitable plan by February of 1972. Otherwise, a redistricting "master" would be appointed, which suited the Republicans just fine. Gorton was confident that if it came to that the outcome would be more swing districts. Greive groused that the attorney general's opinions were smokescreens for stalling.

A bow-tied bundle of kinetic energy, Greive came bounding into the senatorial cafe around 10 one night during the 1971 session. He plopped down next to George W. Scott, a young Republican from Seattle, and inhaled a bowl of cream of tomato soup as they talked, "his spoon moving in a tight oval." Then, as abruptly as he had arrived, Greive stood, turned on his heel and galloped back to his maps, taking the stairs two at a time. "His dinner had taken three minutes," Scott recalled.[12]

When the labor lobby entered the fray with an initiative, "the exasperated court appointed demographer Richard Morrill, a Democrat and Gorton's first choice as 'master' to redraw lines for its approval." Greive was outmaneuvered again. "With the court's imprimatur, Gorton and the Republicans—as intended—did better than they could by compromise."[3]

In 1983, voters established the Washington State Redistricting Commission to ensure district boundaries are redrawn through a bipartisan process.

9 | Majority Rules

O N NOVEMBER 8, 1966, Gorton won his fifth and final two-year term in the Washington State House of Representatives, capturing 78 percent of the vote against a faceless Democrat. Better yet, his hard-won victory in the redistricting wars produced a gain of 16 seats and the first Republican majority in the House since 1953. In the Senate, however, thanks in no small part to Greive's artful machinations, Democrats maintained a 29–20 majority.

With their 55–44 majority for the 1967 legislative session, the Republicans elected Mount Vernon's gentlemanly Don Eldridge speaker of the House and Gorton majority leader. Eldridge, an Eagle Scout, had never thirsted for the speaker's job. Years later, he said he believed Dan Evans "and their group would have preferred" Slade as the speaker, "but they knew he couldn't get elected." Eldridge respected Gorton "for his intelligence, enthusiasm and energy." He was also less liberal than Evans, which won him points with many of the old guard. Still, Eldridge observed, "there were a lot of people who just didn't like Slade."[1]

House Majority Leader Gorton in 1967. *Vibert Jeffers/Washington State Archives*

Gorton had played hardball for his party in 1965 and had zero regrets. Being majority leader was no hollow consolation prize to him. He relished the idea of being the governor's right-hand man in the Legislature. He also correctly surmised that Eldridge would be a relatively passive speaker. He was the one who goosed Eldridge to pack his shaving kit and campaign for the job. They spent many weekends on the road, lobbying fellow Republicans to back the Eldridge-Gorton ticket.

Tom Copeland was pissed. He dearly wanted to move up to speaker and had campaigned for two months solid to elect Republicans to the House. When a friend in Seattle told him what Gorton was up to, the Walla Walla farmer sputtered, "You're kidding me?"

Copeland was smart and tough. He'd been a lieutenant with a tank destroyer unit in some of the bloodiest battles of World War II. But he'd ruffled too many feathers in the caucus by trying to usurp Slade's role as lead man on redistricting. Being an east sider didn't help either.

After narrowly winning the speakership, Eldridge, ever the diplomat, enlisted Gorton's support to name Copeland speaker pro tem. They also expanded the job's responsibilities. Copeland unquestionably was an operations and facilities expert. He relished his new assignment. He and John O'Brien teamed up to give legislators offices of their own for the first time in state history. Copeland, in fact, became the architect of the modernization of the entire legislative process. While the disappointment of losing the speakership never went away, he likely left a more indelible mark on the institution of state government by falling short of his goal.

After all the turmoil of the previous two sessions, Eldridge and Gorton held out another olive branch. They made it clear to the Democrats that they would support the re-nomination of Sid Snyder, a popular straight-shooter, as assistant chief clerk, hoping that henceforth the job would always go to a member of the minority party.

THE REPUBLICANS GOT DOWN to business immediately, and any residue of factional rancor was swept away by the excitement of being in the majority. "The governor was feeding us an agenda that would normally choke a horse," Copeland recalled. "Not only were we empowered now, but there was a lot to do. We were ready for the challenge."[2]

Evans' "Blueprint for Progress" was one of the most ambitious gubernatorial agendas in state history. The economy was good but revenues inadequate to the task at hand. (Washington is one of the few states without personal or corporate income taxes.) Schools were bursting at the seams with Baby Boomers. Higher education was antiquated. Besides advocating a limited income tax, the young governor was worried about urban sprawl and highways that were growing more crowded by the day. Evans called for a new Department of Transportation, proposed environment initiatives and lobbied for more effective delivery of social and health services.

Instead of seating himself at front row center, where the majority leader usually operated, Gorton borrowed an idea from Greive and placed himself in the middle of the caucus to be closer to the 26 GOP freshmen. They included some faces that would become familiar in the months and years to come, notably Sid Morrison, Tom Swayze and Tim Hill. The eight freshmen Democrats included Gordon Walgren, John Bagnariol, Ed Heavey and Bob Charette, who'd bounced from Senate leadership to a back bench in the House in the wake of redistricting. Greive was happy to have the independent Aberdeen lawyer out of his hair but Gorton gained a frequent ally across the aisle.

NEXT TO REDISTRICTING, the highlight of Gorton's 10–year career as a Washington State legislator is his relentless effort in the 1967 session to push a dozen "Forward Thrust" bond propositions through the House for Jim Ellis. Forward Thrust was an offspring of Metro, Ellis' program to clean up Lake Washington. In 1956, the Metro speakers' bureau was Slade's first foray into civic life in his adopted home state. Nine years later, he heard Ellis deliver one of the landmark speeches in Seattle history. Appearing before the Downtown Rotary Club, the visionary activist challenged the city's movers and shakers to help him inspire the voters to make a down payment on a vibrant, livable King County for tomorrow. The alternative, Ellis said, was gridlock, smog, clogged storm sewers, farmland succumbing to cookie-cutter subdivisions and a city bereft of greenery, recreational opportunities and affordable housing. Seattle was at a crossroads, Ellis emphasized: It could become one of the world's great international cities or pave paradise and put up a parking lot. His critics called it the full employment act for bond attorneys.

Before they could go to the voters, the proposals needed legislative approval. The push began in the Senate, where Ellis had an ally in his old friend, Joel Pritchard, who'd moved over from the House in the '66 election. Greive, however, was no fan of Ellis and he'd been re-elected yet again as leader of the Democratic majority.

The Forward Thrust bills squeaked out of the Senate in the waning days of a marathon session. Gorton went to work. Directing floor action and telephoning instructions to the speaker's rostrum, "I got every damn one of them passed without change in those three days for my friend and mentor," he says with pride and satisfaction. "Slade was magnificent," says Ellis. "It was a spectacular job."

At the polls in February of 1968, King County voters backed a $40 million bond issue for a multipurpose stadium that came to be called the Kingdome. Another $118 million was approved to boost parks and recreation, including 25 swimming pools and a world-class aquarium. The

voters also supported neighborhood improvements, sewer bonds, enhanced fire protection and $81.6 million for arterial highways. But in
what Gorton calls "the stupidest 'no' vote the people of Seattle ever cast,"
the Forward Thrust rapid transit proposals fell far short of the required
60 percent supermajorities.

Ellis regrouped for another go in 1970, only to be caught out by the
"Boeing Bust," which generated the legendary "Will the last person leaving Seattle turn out the lights" billboard. "By the time the election came
we knew we didn't have a chance," Ellis remembers so vividly. "People
were just scared. Fifty-thousand people had left Seattle. It was just night
and day between 1968 and 1970."

Gallingly, with the failure of the 1970 proposal, the city also lost nearly
$900 million in federal matching funds—three-quarters of the total
tab—that had been earmarked by Senator Magnuson at the height of his
powers. The original rapid transit proposal, if approved, would have been
operational by 1985, Ellis notes, while the last bonds would have been retired in 2006. "You know who got our share of the federal money? At-
lanta," he says, "and they built a beautiful light rail system."

Ellis was down but never out. He knew he could always count on Gorton.
When Slade became a United States senator they teamed up often. The
Mountains to Sound greenway project was a landmark accomplishment.

While Gorton would be at odds with the greens more often than not in
the years to come, he had a solid reputation as a friend of the environment
during his decade in the Legislature. He was a sponsor and floor leader in
the successful push for green belt legislation and energetically promoted
Evans' proposed Environmental Quality Commission, which came to frui-
tion in 1971 as the Department of Ecology. He also backed seashore conservation and was a member of the State Oceanographic Commission.

THE EVENTFUL 1967 SESSION featured the only speech Gorton has never
finished. Sam Smith, a gregarious Democrat from Seattle, was elected to
the House together with Gorton in the Class of 1959. They got along fine,
though frequently at odds philosophically. Their backgrounds couldn't
have been more different. It was hard not to like Sam, even when he
talked too often or too long, because he was a remarkable self-made man,
the son of a Louisiana preacher who turned to sharecropping to feed his
wife and eight kids. Sam Smith was the only African-American in the
Washington Legislature.

About a month into the session, Smith stood to excoriate the Republicans. They weren't giving Democrats their fair share. They were rude and

duplicitous. When Smith sat down, Gorton popped up. "When the gentleman from Seattle has been in a minority as long as we've been in a minority," he began, glancing toward Smith, who began to laugh. Gorton screeched to a halt in mid-sentence, shook his head and turned a lovely shade of red. "Pretty soon all the Democrats were laughing. Pretty soon even the Republicans were laughing. And pretty soon Mr. Gorton sat down. Sam Smith and I told that story on one another for years thereafter."

On the last day of the regular session, the open housing legislation Smith had been championing for years finally won approval. Gorton had been a co-sponsor since 1959. Governor Evans promptly signed it into law. It was a significant start on the long chuckholed road to boosting civil rights in Washington State.

DURING A 52–DAY SPECIAL SESSION, Evans' income tax proposal fell a vote short of the two-thirds majority required to pass a joint resolution. Gorton had done some major arm-twisting to win over conservatives in his caucus.

The legislators' 112–day stay in Olympia demonstrated that the "biennial 60–day session the founding fathers had envisioned was clearly an outdated concept," Don Brazier, a freshman Republican that year, wrote 30 years later in the second volume of his history of the Washington Legislature.[3]

On the whole, 1967 was a productive year for progressive Republicans and their curious collection of ad hoc allies. The Evans-Gorton team pushed through a new Department of Water Resources, together with stricter controls on air and water pollution; established an Office of Community Affairs; boosted the gas tax from 7.5 to 9 cents per gallon to fund highway construction and removed control of community colleges from the local school districts to promote growth and innovation. The Legislature also authorized a new four-year college in Thurston County, which became The Evergreen State College. State employees got a 12 percent raise, teachers 7 percent.

Evans was gearing up for his re-election campaign. Gorton was thinking about what to do next when Mary Ellen McCaffree had an idea.

10 | General Gorton

"**W**HY DON'T YOU RUN for attorney general?" Mary Ellen suggested in 1967. "What a great idea," Gorton thought almost the minute she said it. "I was spending so much time in the Legislature that I wasn't advancing in the private practice of law. I didn't really mind that so much, but I loved politics far, far more and the AG's office combined both." The three-term incumbent, Democrat John J. O'Connell, had already announced he would challenge Evans for governor.[1]

After interviewing a number of hopefuls, a committee of two-dozen Republican attorneys from around the state unanimously endorsed Gorton, who had just turned 40. Evans gave Slade his enthusiastic blessings, although he "would miss him sorely on the House floor and in the caucuses where the big decisions are made," the Seattle *Argus* said that January. "Evans doesn't lack for loyal adherents skilled in parliamentary tactics in the Legislature, but few can match Gorton's adroitness in coping with the Democrats or his knowledge of state government." The Democrats, meantime, had "an almost embarrassing richness of candidates."[2]

John G. McCutcheon, a former Pierce County prosecutor and state representative, was running hard, as were Marvin Durning, an environmental activist, and Fred Dore, a veteran legislator. Durning and Gorton, classmates at Dartmouth, were associates in the same Seattle law firm. Another Democratic hat in the ring was that of Don Abel Jr. ("Elect an Abel Attorney General"), the son of a former State Supreme Court justice. Don Navoni, who headed the Consumer Protection Division for O'Connell, made it a five-Democrat field.

Dore was regarded as the Democratic frontrunner. McCutcheon, however, enjoyed name familiarity. His father, state Senator John T. McCutcheon, had served in the Legislature off and on since 1941. He had a solid base of support from an energetic party apparatus in the state's second-largest county, though he'd lost a bid for re-election as prosecutor two years earlier to an energetic young Republican, Ronald Hendry.

Gorton's only Republican opponent in the 1968 primary was Robert G.

Kerr, a conservative young lawyer from Tacoma. Kerr had withdrawn from the race–too late, however, for his name to be removed from the ballot.

On the first day of an Eastern Washington campaign swing, Gorton and Don Brazier stopped in Waitsburg. Home to about a thousand folks, it's a picturesque burg nestled in rolling amber fields of wheat and barley. After visiting their legislative colleague, Vaughn Hubbard, a local attorney, and paying their respects to the friendly editor of the weekly paper, they surveyed Main Street. Brazier pointed to three locals leaning on a pickup truck, shooting the breeze. "If you really want to be the attorney general," he told Gorton, "you're going to walk across the street, introduce yourself to those guys, tell them who you are and what you're running for." Slade's eyes said he'd prefer lunch. "He knew I wasn't going to let him get away. Finally, he walked across the street and had a chat with them. That is when I decided that Slade really wanted to be attorney general." For his part, Gorton learned there weren't many hicks in Waitsburg, judging from the first question the trio asked when he told them how much he'd appreciate their votes: "What's your position on the price of wheat?"

NINETEEN-SIXTY-EIGHT WAS one of the most gut-wrenching years in American history, beginning with the Communists' massive Tet Offensive across South Vietnam. College campuses roiled with anti-war demonstrations. President Johnson announced he would not seek re-election. Martin Luther King Jr. was assassinated four days later, touching off race riots that came within two blocks of the White House and spread across the nation; Robert F. Kennedy was mortally wounded after winning the California primary, and all hell broke loose on the streets outside the Democratic National Convention in Chicago that summer after Mayor Daley gave his police carte blanche to suppress throngs of young protesters. They tear-gassed and beat bloody hundreds of kids, as well as reporters and bystanders after the protesters got tired of being relentlessly hassled and starting throwing rocks.

Dore's campaign brochure featured his portrait superimposed on a montage of lurid newspaper headlines: "Jail Term in Fire-Bomb Case," "Stabbing on 'Hippie' Hill," "Woman's Scream Routs burglar," "Lawlessness . . . ," "Murder . . . ," "Assault."[3] McCutcheon was only slightly less bellicose. He'd "heard the voices" of those who'd had enough of "violence in the ghettos, riots in the schools and colleges and crime in the streets."[4] Durning, a Rhodes Scholar, called the get-tough talk "the politics of fakery."[5] Gorton agreed. "I have always been for law and order," he told an Associated Press forum that fall, "but too many people today use the phrase when they really mean 'keep the niggers in their place.' "[6]

In an essay published by the Junior League of Seattle, Gorton cited New York Mayor John Lindsay, President Johnson and Governor Evans as three leaders who refused to tolerate racism or stoop to demagoguery. Quoting from Evans' keynote address to the GOP National Convention that August, Gorton wrote that the principle of "equal justice within the framework of law" was paramount. "There is no excuse for weakness and no justification for lawlessness. But we must recognize that strength is no substitute for sound policy and that the rule of law cannot prevail when its foundation is corrupted by injustice and inequality."

The way to win the war on crime was to deploy better-qualified, better-trained, better-equipped and more ethnically diverse foot soldiers, Gorton said. He advocated a new emphasis on community policing to "deter crime before it happens." He concluded, however, that "the only real solution lies in this message: Crime and violence can be most significantly reduced when progress is made in eliminating the conditions that cause a large portion of our society to be alienated from the police, from their government and from their fellow Americans."

Gorton noted that the U.S. Supreme Court had taken enormous flak for its landmark 1966 Miranda ruling ("You have a right to remain silent . . .") and other decisions granting more rights to the criminally accused, but "there can be no denying the fact that parts of our system of criminal prosecution have been unfair, and innocent people have suffered as a result. A man could be arrested and not permitted to talk to anyone until he confessed; his privacy could be invaded without cause, and he could be tried and sentenced without counsel. These abuses had to be corrected."[7]

WITH POLLS IN WASHINGTON STATE indicating a Democratic trend, despite reports that Nixon was leading hapless Hubert Humphrey nationwide, progressive Republicans put together the first, and to date only, effective party ticket in state history—"The Action Team." Each flier, full-page ad and TV spot featured Evans, Gorton, Kramer and Art Fletcher, the first credible African-American candidate for statewide office in Washington State history. They were seen striding forward side by side with clean-cut confidence. The verbiage was a blend of superhero and Sitting Bull. "The Leader," of course, was Evans: "Arrow-straight, disciplined, combining the vigor of youth with the wisdom of experience. . . .

A man of action and a man who doesn't waste words."

Gorton was "The Lawyer with a Cause"—"Young, tough, with a mind like a steel trap and a deep concern for making Washington safe and sane. . . . In the Legislature they call him 'The Leader Who Sits in the Crowd.' Why? Because he likes results, not headlines. And he never walks away from the tough ones. Courage is a rare commodity, but Slade Gorton has it. Lots of it."

Kramer was "The Get-Things-Done Guy" . . . "a rare breed of no-nonsense public servant" who had been "where the action is" ever since he was elected secretary of state four years earlier. For lieutenant governor, Fletcher was "The

The Action Team Evans Fletcher Gorton Kramer

...for an action time

"The Action Team" in one of the full page ads from the 1968 campaign. From left, Art Fletcher, Dan Evans, Gorton and Lud Kramer. *Washington State Archives*

Man With a Plan"—"tall, fluent, with a grasp of problems as broad as his hands"—an ex-pro football player with two college degrees who could "transform the office of lieutenant governor just as he transformed the ghetto of Pasco" where he was a city councilman.[8]

The Gorton campaign blanketed the state with a four-page brochure that featured photos of Slade and Sally leaving for church with their three cute kids, Tod, 9, Sarah, 8, and 6–year-old Becky; Slade in uniform as a major in the Air Force Reserve and at the Capitol conferring with the governor. "Washington is no longer a quiet, secluded state with quiet, secluded problems," the candidate said. "It is growing, urbanizing, changing. The new demands on justice are heavy, reflecting the problems that occur with the influx of people." His platform included legislative reforms to bolster the criminal code, "progressive actions to ensure equal justice, and aggressive steps to protect consumers." Gorton also called for the establishment of a state police training academy, a crime lab and full-time prosecuting attorneys in all but the smallest counties. He promised to hire lawyers who were "doers and thinkers."[9]

What he didn't emphasize in his speeches and ads was that he was also a fervent foe of "tolerance" gambling policies. In King County, tolerance had spawned a network of payoffs that reached from the street to the assistant chief. A beat cop who played along could double his base salary with bribes. Pull-tabs, punchboards, cardrooms and prostitution proliferated. Gorton's problem was that talk of a crackdown wouldn't sit well with the guys rolling dice for coffee in Renton and at church-basement bingo parties in Puyallup.

THE ACTION TEAM ADVANCED intact from the primary. Gorton caught a big break when McCutcheon edged Dore for the Democratic nomination. Gorton and many other observers in both parties had figured Dore was the man to beat. But McCutcheon had the Pierce County Democratic vote locked up while the four other Democrats divvied up King County.

With only 23 percent, Gorton was the top vote-getter in the primary. The Democrats captured fully 63 percent of the vote. Kerr, to Gorton's surprise, finished a respectable fourth overall. The faceless Republican did particularly well in Eastern Washington, carrying Benton, Walla Walla and eight other counties. Gorton obviously needed to shed his Brooks Brothers suit and spend more time making friends in places like Waitsburg— a lesson he learned well that year. "Black Jack Slade" was the desperado of Western dime novel fame, Gorton notes, "so Slade was not a good name to start out with, running for statewide office as an unknown."

There were no Gorton-McCutcheon debates during the eight-week push to the general election. Despite winning the endorsement of 16 daily newspapers and the overwhelming support of the legal community, Gorton knew he was the underdog. Voter apathy for the down-ballot races was one problem. Another was the ideological schism in his own party. Kerr wrote letters to conservative King County Republicans urging them to vote for McCutcheon. The source for the tightly controlled mailing list clearly was the right-wing county chairman, Ken Rogstad. "We're going to get Gorton," Rogstad's good friend, County Prosecutor Charles O. Carroll, was heard to boast. The greatest halfback in America when he played for the University of Washington in 1928, Carroll was in his 20th year as prosecutor and King County's "Mr. Republican." That he could not get Gorton was just one of many signs that 1968 was his last hurrah as a power broker. *Seattle*, the gutsy magazine published by King Broadcasting, and the

Post-Intelligencer printed devastating exposés on his tolerance for tolerance and unsavory friends. Carroll had allies in high places at *The Seattle Times*, but it too was investigating how the perniciousness of looking the other way had poisoned the police force.[10]

IT WAS COMMON KNOWLEDGE in Pierce County that McCutcheon had a drinking problem. Some of Gorton's supporters made sure that news was passed around in swing counties, but Slade balked at exploiting the character issue.[11]

The Evans campaign, meantime, was confident Dan could beat O'Connell but never complacent. While some saw O'Connell as an oily Irish pol, he was also handsome and a forceful speaker, with a dozen years in statewide office. He could point with legitimate pride to the creation of an aggressive Consumer Protection Division in the Attorney General's Office. O'Connell was mortally wounded, however, when it was revealed down the stretch that he was a frequenter of Las Vegas casinos. Evans flatly denied O'Connell's charge that his campaign planted the stories. Democrats would bitterly assert that "Straight Arrow" and his henchmen, Gorton and Gummie Johnson, were holier-than-thou hypocrites.

Gorton and Fletcher hit the road as a pair after the primary. "It was great because Art Fletcher could draw 400 people where I could draw 40," Gorton says. "It was also awful because it didn't matter whether I spoke first or second because I was a complete after-thought to the wonderful orations Art would come through with. He was the son of a preacher, and boy could he preach himself." They became great friends.

Gummie Johnson told Mary Ellen McCaffree he was worried that Gorton—"so bright . . . so abundantly vocabularied"—wasn't connecting with Joe Sixpack. She put together a statewide mailer that went out just a few days before the election.[12]

ABOUT 107,000 ABSENTEE BALLOTS were issued statewide that year. The Gorton campaign cultivated those mail voters. It won him the election. "They always tended to go Republican, and it depended on how hard you worked them. We worked them hard," Gorton recalls. He trailed McCutcheon by some 2,500 votes on the morning after the election—less than two-tenths of a percent—but prevailed by 5,368 when all the absentees were tallied nine days later. King County, despite the divisions in the Republican ranks, gave him a 40,000–vote majority. "Had Fred Dore won the nomination in 1968, he likely would have beaten me," Gorton says, shaking his head at the serendipity of history.

Evans won a second term with nearly 55 percent of the vote. Kramer breezed to re-election. Fletcher—invariably listed in the media as the "Negro city councilman from Pasco"—came up 48,000 votes short against John Cherberg, the veteran lieutenant governor. A right-wing Yakima weekly that backed George Wallace for president produced a racist smear of Fletcher that was circulated in working-class white neighborhoods in the closing days of the campaign. "It was appalling," Gorton says.[13]*

Washington State went for Humphrey by a hair. But Nixon won the presidency, pledging that "bring us together" would be the motto of his "open" administration.[14]

"SLADE GORTON WILL LIGHT SOME FIRES AROUND HERE," was *The Daily Olympian's* six-column headline over a major profile of the new attorney general on Jan. 1, 1969. He didn't fit the stereotype of a politician, the capital city paper observed. "He isn't a glad-handing, backslapping denizen of smoke-filled rooms. Often described as arrogant—'he just doesn't know how to be tactful,' says one long-time acquaintance—he nevertheless skillfully manages to get his way politically without compromising his obvious idealism. His abruptness, however, other friends say, is more an impatience with nonessentials and time wasting than a lack of feeling."[15]

Gorton made it immediately clear that he would be an activist attorney general and that he was more interested in legal talent than patronage, although if you were a brainy young Republican, so much the better. Chris Bayley, a 31–year-old Harvard graduate, was Gorton's pick to head the Consumer Protection and Antitrust Division. Bayley, who grew up in Seattle, and Sam Reed, an activist from Eastern Washington, had founded Action for Washington, a group that included Steve Excell, Jim Waldo, Stuart Elway, Jack Durney and many other young "Dan Evans Republicans." The "Action Team" was their brainchild.[16]

Right after the election, Gorton began evaluating O'Connell's assistants. He concluded many were first rate, including Robert Doran, Ed Mackie, Phil Austin, Charlie Roe, Robert Hauth and the Montecucco brothers, Joe and Rich. Five had been law clerks for State Supreme Court justices. In all, there were some 100 assistant attorneys general. "I resolved that I was going to interview every one of them and decide whether or not to keep them,"

---

* Fletcher went on to serve in the Nixon and Ford administrations and is widely regarded as the father of the affirmative action movement. As executive director of the United Negro College Fund, he coined the slogan "A mind is a terrible thing to waste." He died in 2005.

Gorton recalls. He started with Doran, who had been O'Connell's chief assistant attorney general. They'd been in court together several times in the early 1960s. "I really liked and admired him, so I called Bob and had him set up meetings with all of the assistants. Bob gave me an honest evaluation of each of them." Shortly before Christmas, as they were winding up the interviews, Gorton observed that Doran's own name was conspicuous by its absence from the list. "Does this mean you're leaving—that you want to go and do something else?" Doran hemmed and hawed. "Well," he finally said, "I was number one for O'Connell and I thought you'd want someone else." Gorton said he was going to install his own chief deputy but he wanted Doran to stay on as a key assistant. "Yes!" said Doran. Almost nine months to the day later his wife gave birth. "I always considered myself to be the godfather," Gorton quips.[17]

Brazier, who had been a deputy county prosecutor, assistant U.S. attorney, city councilman and state representative, became Gorton's well-liked chief deputy. He was a Republican, to be sure, but more liberal than Gorton. Slade valued Brazier's penchant for speaking his mind and his common-sense skill as an administrator. Brazier "was a perfect choice," Doran says. "He was great with the staff and a real asset to Slade, but the key thing was that Slade was a lawyer's lawyer and he ran a good legal office. The fact that his first priority was to really get to know people tells you a lot. I don't think he ever asked anyone if they were a Republican or a Democrat. He just wanted talented people. He's somewhat reserved, as people often note, but he was always approachable and friendly to the whole staff."[18] Still, some of the young attorneys at first found it disconcerting when Slade sat behind his imposing new desk doing a crossword puzzle as they offered a briefing—even more so when they discovered he could divide his attention without missing a beat.

"Slade has a brilliant mind that can simultaneously keep the perspective of the big picture and challenging details," Mackie observed. "That enables him to quickly ascertain whether someone briefing him really knows what they are talking about. When he selects someone to do something he has the confidence to let them exercise their judgment in doing the task. . . . The freedom of individuals to make critical judgments does present a problem of foul-ups, so his objective was to minimize foul-ups while encouraging creativity."[19]

Dick Mattsen, an assistant attorney general who had worked for O'Connell and earlier for McCutcheon as a deputy prosecutor, was "pleasantly surprised" by how apolitical the Attorney General's office was under Gorton.[20]

Two years into Slade's first term, at the urging of Gorton and Brazier, Evans appointed Doran to the Thurston County Superior Court bench. In 1977, he handed down a landmark ruling, upheld by the State Supreme Court, that the state was not living up to its "paramount" constitutional duty to provide for the public schools. Doran ordered lawmakers to define, then fund a "basic" education for all students. Whether the state ever actually fulfilled the mandate was still being hotly debated 34 years later.

Recruiting and retaining sharp lawyers was a challenge. High turnover was a fact of life in the office. Bayley accompanied Gorton on an East Coast swing to visit law school campuses. Upon their return, Gorton reported that firms in the East were offering law school graduates $15,000 a year, while his office could barely afford $10,000.

Talented female law school graduates were still finding it difficult to land jobs at major Seattle law firms. They discovered that the new attorney general was gender blind. Being smart was what mattered.

IN THE SPRING OF 1969, King County elected its first county executive under a progressive new home-rule charter. John D. Spellman, who opposed the tolerance policy, had an ally in Gorton. Some of Chuck Carroll's worst fears had come true: "That damn Gorton," one of the Evans gang, was now attorney general and Spellman, a pipe-puffing do-gooder, was rocking the boat in what had been the prosecutor's fiefdom for two decades. Carroll kicked himself for encouraging Spellman to run for county commissioner in 1966, presuming he would toe the line.

Joel Pritchard and another state legislator, R. Ted Bottiger of Tacoma, obligingly requested an opinion from the attorney general on the legality of pinball machines, cardrooms, pull-tabs and punchboards. Gorton pronounced the games illegal—even bingo, although he left some wiggle room for small-stakes games. City or county ordinances licensing gambling activities were in conflict with state law, Gorton said. Tolerance was "very debilitating. It draws in the pros and fosters contempt for the law. Soon it becomes a big-money operation," opening the door to organized crime. Although the State Constitution included an anti-lottery provision, Gorton agreed that "a law that bans a Little League raffle to purchase uniforms or bingo games in a church is a bad law." He warned, however, that if a lodge hired professionals to help manage its raffles it could be subject to abatement proceedings. He backed prison terms of up to five years and fines of up to $100,000, the stiffest in the nation. Opponents, led by Representative John Bagnariol and Senator Gordon Walgren, two up-and-coming Democrats, countered with bills liberalizing gambling.[21]

Although Evans, Spellman and many others of all political persuasions shared his concerns over "Las Vegas-type gambling" and the specter of organized crime creeping into the state through the back door of a Trout Unlimited casino night, Gorton developed a lingering reputation as a bluenose nanny. How and where to draw the line was the problem, said Tom Copeland, the speaker pro tem in the House. Always wary of Gorton, the Republican from Walla Walla nevertheless agreed that "there isn't such a thing as being a little bit pregnant. . . . [W]hat is the definition of gambling? You put some money on the table and you take your chances. Some win, some lose, but the majority loses because the odds are against them. That's gambling. . . . In other words, you're kidding yourself when you think you're sterilizing gambling by saying it's done for non-profit." On the other hand, Copeland noted astutely, "hidden behind this gambling issue was the full knowledge on the part of the legislators that gambling in the State of Washington, if taxed properly, could be a revenue-producing son of a gun!"[22]*

"I have always thought of organized gambling as a vice," Gorton says. "People can be addicted to it. It breaks up families." He pleads guilty, however, to a double-standard tolerance of his own: He loves horse racing. None of his proposals targeted pari-mutuel gambling at racetracks. "The horses are lovely creatures, and the tracks are lovely places. It's a rural thing. And as long as you could only bet at the track there was a certain limitation as to how much money people were going to lose."

THE THOROUGHBREDS RAN at Longacres in Renton. The real action was downtown. The reverberations from a 1967 *Seattle Times* expose of how tolerance had corrupted the Police Department led to a federal grand jury, the tumultuous rise of a new mayor, 34–year-old Wes Uhlman, and the defeat of Chuck Carroll by Chris Bayley in 1970. Gorton's hard-charging former deputy promptly launched a wide-ranging investigation of the payoff network. Bayley impaneled a grand jury that indicted two dozen cops and former political leaders. The case generated more headlines than convictions. Charges against Carroll and some of the others were subsequently dismissed but Carroll's political career was over. Seattle was

---

* Lawmakers were scrambling for revenue when legislation authorizing Washington's Lottery was finally signed into law in 1982 by, ironically, Governor John Spellman. Two years earlier, Bagnariol and Walgren had been caught up in an influence-peddling sting operation dubbed "Gamscam" that many denounced as the handiwork of Governor Dixy Lee Ray. She loathed both of her Democratic rivals.

entering a new era in fits and starts. The *Post-Intelligencer* huffed in an editorial that Bayley was treating church and charity bingo "as though it were a capital crime wave." Uhlman, mindful of a new rival, said Bayley was "creating a tempest in a teapot."[23]

Nor was the war on gambling a winner for Gorton. The bingo ladies hated him "and ultimately the people amended the Constitution to allow lotteries, so now there was more gambling than there ever was before," he notes. When the tribes achieved compacts to open casinos that grew more Vegas-like with every passing year, the Knights of Columbus and card-room operators from Anacortes to Zillah yowled. Ironies were everywhere. In 1969, Attorney General Gorton never imagined that 31 years later contributions from professional gambling interests would help the tribes defeat him in a bid for re-election to the United States Senate.

As for the state lottery, which most voters erroneously believed would be just the ticket to fund education, Gorton denounces it as "a horrendous tax on the poor. I've never bought a lottery ticket in my life, and never will. With each one of these events, legalized gambling has just gotten more extensive. That was one of my crusades that didn't work."

GORTON LAUNCHED ANOTHER CRUSADE a day after the 1971 session, which he denounced as short-sighted and unproductive. The lawmakers had failed to update the criminal code, dropped the ball on consumer protection measures he championed and balked at regulating campaign expense reporting. In a speech to the Seattle-King County Bar Association, Gorton unveiled a sweeping package of proposals to reform the "archaic" legislative system through a series of initiatives and a constitutional convention.[24] The blockbusters were reducing the number of legislators from 148 to 84 and term-limiting legislators and statewide elected officials to 12 consecutive years. He also advocated restricting the Legislature's prerogatives to set its own rules by transferring part of that power to the electorate through the initiative process. Further, he called for open meetings, with recorded votes, as well as precise reporting and policing of campaign contributions and expenditures. Lobbyists would be subject to tighter registration and their campaign contributions and other gifts would be tightly monitored.

Finally, speaking from the experience of trench warfare, he advocated handing the task of redistricting to a bipartisan body. The 1970 Census having plopped the issue back in the lap of the Legislature, Senator Greive had indignantly charged that his old adversary—now ensconced at the Temple of Justice—was using computer data and in-house facilities to assist the Republican caucuses.

In tandem with downsizing, Gorton's plan called for giving the Legislature a much larger professional staff to make it more efficient and "professionalize it." Copeland, who took pride in the facilities reforms he had achieved, dismissed Gorton's program as meddlesome grandstanding. "He's breeding a lot of distrust in the Legislature rather than building confidence in the Legislature," he told reporters.[25] Copeland was also miffed by the Evans-Gorton push for a public disclosure commission. He was still mad decades later when he told an historian that the whole reform proposal was "so very typical of Slade. . . . This is for his political advancement. This is for the enhancement of Slade Gorton; it has nothing to do with the Legislature of the State of Washington." As for the public disclosure commission, "this whole thing sounds so good. Oh, it is beautiful. But what are they doing? They're fining most of the time some guy $1,500 because he was 30 days late on filing his C3 or some dumb thing. Sure, they're finding a couple of big ones and things that are just blatant, but their enforcement ability is so small it's not worthwhile."[26]

Gorton was undeterred. He was clearly an upwardly mobile politician, and a lot of people were intent on stopping him in his tracks. Gorton aggressively defended himself and his office, but he never seemed flustered—all the more annoying. They came at him in waves. The Seattle Liberation Front sued him for libel to the tune of $2 million, claiming it had been defamed by his statement that it was "totally indistinguishable from fascism and Nazism."[27]

Senator Dore, itching to run against him in 1972, suggested that questionable fee-splitting and contingency deals involving outside lawyers serving as special assistant attorneys general had continued on Gorton's watch.[28]

O'Connell's hiring of San Francisco attorney Joseph Alioto for an antitrust action against electrical equipment manufacturers was back in the headlines. Gorton and a dozen utilities had sued to recover a $2.3 million contingency fee Alioto received when he won a $16 million settlement. A prominent Democrat who had gone on to be elected mayor of San Francisco, Alioto gave O'Connell a piece of the action.

McCutcheon, meantime, was indicted by a federal grand jury in 1971, accused of accepting a $39,000 bribe from O'Connell. (The charges were dropped after Alioto and O'Connell prevailed in a civil action.) For Democrats, the plot thickened when it was revealed that Gorton had two White House meetings concerning the case with ex-Seattle lawyers now orbiting the Oval Office. One was with John Ehrlichman, a top Nixon aide; the other was Egil "Bud" Krogh, an Ehrlichman protégé.

Nationally syndicated columnist Marianne Means, exploring "the chummy relationship between the White House and big business," noted that before becoming attorney general Gorton "coincidentally" had been a member of a law firm that represented one of the defendants in the anti-trust case. Further, she wrote, executives of the electrical equipment industry had been major donors to the Nixon presidential campaign in 1968.[29]

Gorton said he had met with Ehrlichman only to see if he could help persuade the Justice Department to delay its own grand jury probe into the fee-splitting case. If the state's case couldn't move forward first, costs would escalate.

Despite Ehrlichman's "sympathetic attention," the feds pushed ahead. And just as he'd feared, Gorton said, Washington taxpayers got stuck with higher bills. The real bottom line, however, was his "firm belief that it is both improper and illegal for an attorney general to take a secret legal fee of more than $500,000 in a case in which he represented the state in his official, salaried position.... The concerted effort on the part of those involved in this fee-splitting venture to make themselves look like heroes is certainly no secret. I can't believe it will succeed. It would be ironic indeed if, by charging 'politics,' elected officials could gain immunity from so much as being questioned about serious conflicts of interest."[30]

Earlier, Dore and Martin Durkan, the heavy-hitting Democrat from Renton, had grilled Gorton during a meeting of the Senate Appropriations Committee. When Gorton lost the fee-splitting case, Dore declared that "the public can only conclude that the attorney general never had a case to start with or that it was not properly handled."[31]

The State Labor Council chimed in, calling for Gorton to resign. Ed Donohoe, the witheringly cantankerous editor of *The Washington Teamster*, called him a man who "only blows the big ones."[32] Joe Davis, the president of the Labor Council, charged that Gorton had also flubbed a consumer-protection suit against Ralph Williams, a wheeler-dealer car salesman. Gorton countered that he had still driven Williams out of business. Davis went on to accuse the attorney general of being in cahoots with a court-appointed geographer to cook up a redistricting plan favorable to the Republicans. A sure sign that it was open season on Gorton came when two members of the old guard took to the floor of the Senate to flay Gorton and the *Seattle P-I's* habitually contrarian Shelby Scates for belonging to the same investment club.[33]

Gorton seemed to be everywhere at once. He was instrumental in the Legislature's enactment of the Shoreline Management Act. His staff was particularly busy on the consumer-protection front. The office moved to ground fly-by-night hearing aid salesmen; targeted warranties that were riddled with loopholes; advocated more rights for car buyers and argued for

Slade and Sally with
President Nixon in 1969.
Happier days were not
ahead. Slade was one of
the first major Republi-
can office-holders to call
for Nixon's resignation
in the wake of Watergate.
Gorton Family Album

expedited payment of judgments in small-claims court. Gorton was active
in organizations to improve the training of police and corrections officers.
Law enforcement became one of his strongest supporters over the years.

The attorney general represents all state agencies and officials—not
just the governor, as many believe. (The governor's own counsel has a
nominal assignment as a special assistant attorney general.) An autonomous office-holder, the attorney general's duty is to protect the public interest by upholding state law. The public interest, naturally, is open to
interpretation. Even Gorton and Evans had their differences.*

"A huge amount of the work is just seeing to it that other people's policies are appropriately represented," Gorton says. He loved delving into
the legal aspects of a case.

Phil Austin was in charge of legal opinions for the office. Once they
were drafted Gorton would test the logic, examine the precedents and
tinker with the wording. He'd call in the office's best lawyers and engage
them in freewheeling debates. The pay wasn't competitive with private
practice—even for Gorton, who was getting $23,000 per year—but it was
one of the most stimulating law offices in the nation.

AS GORTON WAS GEARING UP to run for a second term as attorney general in
1972, the big guessing game was whether Evans would seek a third term as
governor—and if he didn't would Gorton go for it? A poll found Senator

---

* In 2010, Attorney General Rob McKenna, a Gorton protégé, and Governor Chris Gregoire, McKenna's immediate predecessor as AG, found themselves at odds over the constitutionality of the Obama health-care reform package.

Durkan, an old-school Irishman, five points ahead of Evans in a matchup for governor. It also tested the popularity of Kramer and Gorton in a theoretical race with the Democrat. The secretary of state was a way weaker opponent than Evans, while Gorton was weaker yet. "Finishing behind Kramer must have been some kind of hurt," wrote Richard W. Larsen, the influential political columnist for *The Seattle Times*. "Kramer, in his last outing as a candidate, finished fourth in a field of candidates running for mayor of Seattle in 1969."[34] Dore was a deeply disappointed third.

Gorton accepted the poll results philosophically. Being governor was not his cup of tea, although he gave no hint of that at the time. The oldest dictum in politics is "Never say never." His goal was the U.S. Senate. He also knew that Evans was leaning toward a third term. Dan loved being governor—and, as things would turn out, would find the Senate frustrating.

"The issues are sort of mixed," Gorton told Larsen. "Some people are infuriated because they don't get to play bingo." Others admired his aggressiveness. "By his advocacy of consumer protection," the columnist observed, "Gorton makes enemies in the business community. Perhaps a few consumers become Gorton loyalists. When he makes a push for a fair landlord-tenant act, it infuriates the landlords. Few tenants know that anything has been tried."[35]

Gorton seemed curiously serene, Larsen wrote, and likely to seek reelection despite the certainty that the Democrats would swarm at him— "a confident troupe of easy-going, back-slapping, very warm politicians who would like to be attorney general. . . . Week by week, Gorton travels around the state. . . . He plans no image remodeling: It will be horn-rimmed all the way."[36]

Vintage Larsen, the piece stands as one of the most insightful early takes on Gorton's persona:

Some people have called Slade Gorton a snobbish, elitist Ivy Leaguer. Those words came from some of the sweet-talkers. . . . For my part, Slade Gorton often reminds me of Miss Griswold. Miss Griswold was my sixth-grade civics teacher—tall, fiercely humorless. She had icy blue eyes, which peered at the class through thick-lensed glasses. And all the while she had an unnerving smile locked on her face. She labored to excite the class about the dust-covered subject of government. And the more we scuffed our feet and sighed the more shrill Miss Griswold became. . . . Once when the class was studying presidential succession, Miss Griswold asked me a question: Upon the death or incapacity of the president, the vice president, the secretary of state and the secretary of the treasury, who would become president? I replied: Who would care? . . . Miss Griswold kept me at my desk for 20 minutes after school.

Slade Gorton is not a guy you go out and drink beer with. He is stern, politically tough, humorless. When I asked him why he messed up every-body's bingo, he answered with a ferocious, rapid-fire legal soliloquy. For some uncontrollable inner reason, I stayed at my desk for 20 minutes after the interview. . . . He apparently counts on the fact many people had a Miss Griswold back there in their lives at one time. She couldn't have won any class popularity polls day by day during the school term. But, in retrospect, there was something reassuring about Miss Griswold.[37]

IN THE SPRING OF 1971, Governor Evans appointed Don Brazier chairman of the state Utilities and Transportation Commission. Gorton went look-ing for a new chief deputy. He settled on 29–year-old J. Keith Dysart, a University of Washington Law School graduate who had clerked for Washington Supreme Court Justice Robert Finley. Dysart was a Young Republican in good standing. He fairly loved campaigning. Chris Bayley remembers Dysart's delight when he staked out a suburban Seattle li-brary on a rumor that Chuck Carroll would be speaking there during the 1970 campaign for county prosecutor. Dysart called excitedly from a phone booth to say it was true.

"Carroll had refused to debate me, but Keith tracked him down. I was rushed to the library by my teenage driver and sat in the back of the crowd with Keith, who popped up and declared, 'Mr. Carroll, why won't you talk with or debate Mr. Bayley?' 'Any place, any time!' says Carroll, and he proceeded to accuse me of being a tool of the Ripon Society and Nelson Rockefeller."

Dysart had briefly been an assistant attorney general at the University of Washington before joining John Ehrlichman's Seattle law firm. He and Bud Krogh had been junior attorneys there before Ehrlichman was called to the Nixon West Wing and deputized Krogh. Dysart sometimes shot from the hip, but he was smart and fun to be around. He seemed to know everyone. Great wife; two neat kids. They lived not far from the Gortons in Olympia.

Slade would come to rue the day he hired him.

11 | Unhappy Days

E XUDING CONFIDENCE, Gorton announced his candidacy for re-election at the Olympic Hotel, a downtown Seattle landmark, in the summer of 1972. The number of citizen complaints being resolved by the Consumer Protection Division had tripled on his watch. His team had taken down shady car dealers and exposed pyramid schemes, Gorton boasted, punctuating each achievement with an index finger and a flip-chart. Now they were working to reduce motor-vehicle air pollution and preserve public access to the ocean beaches. Federal grants to local police were being expedited. If re-elected, he promised "robust" additional initiatives to protect the public, including more scrutiny of mail-order merchandising, which was gaining in popularity.[1]

It was the calm before a swarm of political tornadoes. Gorton and Evans were about to be immersed in a campaign season that at this writing is rivaled for bitterness only by the 2004 Gregoire-Rossi race for governor. They emerged with decisive victories that were clouded by scandal. Nearly 40 years later, Gorton related his side of the story with uncharacteristic sadness. When he was done, he leaned back in his chair and stared at the ceiling. Finally, his voice sinking an octave, he said, "I think that was the most unhappy period in my life."

Fred Dore was already off and running for attorney general in his slam-bang style, handing reporters a sheaf of Xeroxed press clippings and thank-you letters praising him as a fearless populist. In 1970, for reasons never discerned, someone lobbed a stick of dynamite onto the roof of Dore's home on the periphery of a predominantly black Seattle neighborhood. His wife Mary and four of their five children were at home but no one was injured. Dore's detractors, even some friends, used to josh that he probably put someone up to it. Fred just laughed. He was as feisty as they come. When he was 4, he came down with polio. Two years later he lost his father. His mother told him he could still become president of the United States if he worked hard enough.

In temperament and style, Gorton and Dore were as different as any two men could be. They were both tough guys, though, each in their own way, and fast on their feet. Dore had been a moot court champion at Georgetown Law School, yet he kept ducking debates with Gorton, sending his spouse or a law partner as a surrogate. "I think this debate thing has been overused as a smoke screen by the candidates who are trailing. I feel I'm leading," Dore boasted with a nonchalant grin when a reporter asked why he was often a no-show.

Gorton figured it would be close but never doubted he could win. He began shedding his suit coat on the campaign trail, "hoping the shirt-sleeves would soften his strait-laced appearance," especially since Dore had the look of an old-time, baby-kissing politician.[2]

A FEW WEEKS BEFORE FILING OPENED, 62–year-old Al Rosellini shocked everyone—close friends, longtime supporters, the media and Democratic frontrunner Martin Durkan—by announcing his candidacy for governor. Three years earlier, the former two-term governor had been trounced by an up-and-coming Republican, John Spellman, in a race for King County executive. Most pundits and political pros believed that was the end of a long and colorful political career. Al, however, was still chaffed over his defeat by Evans in 1964. He was also angry and frustrated over the "bloated bureaucracy" wrought by his successor. In a reversal of form, a Democrat was calling a Republican a big spender.[3]

Filing week also produced a surprise for Gorton and Dore—Dore especially. John J. O'Connell, cleared two months earlier on the charges arising from the Alioto fee-splitting case, filed for attorney general just before the deadline. O'Connell never denied pocketing a $500,000 share—upwards of $3 million in 2010 dollars—of Joe Alioto's fees in the anti-trust case against the electrical equipment manufacturers. He insisted he'd done nothing illegal. Now he unloaded on Gorton, accusing his successor of "using the power of his office to pursue narrow and partisan aims." O'Connell said he would neither engage in active fundraising nor wage a "conventional" campaign in the primary. However, if the voters believed in his good name and awarded him the nomination, he was prepared to wage "a full-scale" general election campaign against Gorton.[4]

On one thing at least, Dore and Gorton agreed: For O'Connell to have taken that fat fee while he was still attorney general was flat wrong. Dore said he was confident none of his supporters would jump ship to O'Connell. "They all say he shouldn't have been permitted to receive half a million dollars, which is more than a lot of workmen make in their lifetime, when he had a full-time paying job" as a public office-holder. For his part, Gorton was delighted to have O'Connell in the race. It might be déjà vu all over again if Dore lost and he ended up with a weaker general election opponent, just as he had four years earlier when McCutcheon won the primary.[5]

No such luck. Come September, Dore easily defeated O'Connell to win the Democratic nomination for attorney general. Gorton was the top vote-getter with 33 percent, but the Democrats rolled up nearly twice as many votes. Slade's analysis was that the Dore-O'Connell race had energized Democratic voters while he had only token opposition from a little-known Republican. In any case, the race for AG rated little more than a front-page footnote on the morning after. The banner-headline news was that Rosellini had thrashed Durkan. Al carried 22 counties, including King, Kitsap, Pierce and Snohomish, and was the top vote-getter overall, besting Evans' total by nearly 6 percent. Jim McDermott, a 35–year-old child psychiatrist from Seattle, finished a distant fifth in his first statewide outing. The stage was set for a grudge match between two men seeking a third term in the governor's office. Durkan was so bruised by Rosellini's bare-knuckle campaign targeting "The Two faces of Martin Durkan" that he reserved judgment on whether he would support him. McDermott said he had the same misgivings.[6]

Gorton headed for the stump, leaving Keith Dysart to mind the store. "You are not to engage in any politics," he emphasized, mindful that his young chief deputy was a political junkie. Some people are "all propeller and no rudder," Joel Pritchard once observed. Many remember Dysart as a high-energy, "independent kind of guy" who could be obsessive—at turns confident and moody, upbeat and depressed. Years later, it would be revealed that Dysart had a bipolar disorder, which in retrospect explains a lot. "We didn't know much about bipolar illness in those days," Chris Bayley says.[7]

HUNTER S. THOMPSON'S CLASSIC political travelogue about the Nixon-McGovern race—"Fear and Loathing on the Campaign Trail"—captured the tenor of American politics in the fall of 1972. On October 6, John Ehrlichman, the Seattle attorney who had become one of Nixon's top aides, gave the *Post-Intelligencer* an exclusive interview. He said he was confident that evidence from the Watergate break-in, when fully examined, wouldn't "come within a country mile of the President of the United States." Nixon press secretary Ron Ziegler also hotly denied McGovern's charges that the administration was engaging in dirty tricks: "If anyone had been involved in such activities, they would not long be at the White House. . . . Political sabotage is something we don't condone and won't tolerate."[8]

While Henry Kissinger was telling reporters "peace is at hand" in Vietnam, the gubernatorial combatants in Washington State were engaged in trench warfare. Evans described Rosellini as "one of the most outrageous frauds" the state had ever seen. Rosellini said Evans was stooping to "name-calling generalities when he has no justification for the most extravagant, wasteful and expensive administration in the history of the state." Gorton and Dore traded their own jabs over who was more fiscally conservative and swapped accusations about improprieties. The state Republican chairman, Earl Davenport, charged that the 45th District Democratic Club was using bingo profits to boost Dore's campaign. Dore angrily denied he had received so much as a dime from the club.

It was practically patty-cake compared to the governor's race. With three weeks to go, some polls had Rosellini ahead by 13 points. Then he slipped on his own tongue. Democrats maintain to this day that he also got "wopped."[9]

Seeing no reason to take any chances, Rosellini had been refusing to debate. On Oct. 14, however, the *Post-Intelligencer* reported that a Rosellini campaign spokesman had confirmed that the former governor would be available to take on Evans that very morning during a Candidates Fair at North Seattle Community College. The underdog incumbent arrived with bells on, delighted to see a KOMO-TV crew. Rosellini huffed that he had not really agreed to a debate. As the debate over a debate heated up, Rosellini began to click his teeth—a habit when he was agitated. Then he chided Evans. "Danny," he said, "I wish you'd quit being childish like you have been all during the campaign." Some onlookers booed and one student shouted "Chicken!" Glowering, Rosellini consented to the debate and proceeded to repeatedly refer to Evans as "Danny Boy"—a dozen times, by one count. It was a major mistake, interpreted by many as not only condescending to a younger man but disrespectful to the office of governor. That Monday, Ralph Munro, an Evans aide, cranked out a batch of "I'm for Danny Boy" bumper strips. At their next appearance, before they cut the cards to see who would go first, Evans quipped, "Is it OK with Slade?"—a welcome bit of levity in a relentlessly nasty campaign.[10]

TWO WEEKS LATER, the front pages exploded with double-deck banner headlines and the airwaves crackled when Gorton announced he had suspended Dysart for conducting an unauthorized off-duty investigation of Rosellini's links to Seattle's notorious Colacurcio family. With their network of pinball machines and girlie joints, the Colacurcios had faced racketeering charges for years. The Italian community in Seattle was close-knit. The Colacurcio and Rosellini families were longtime friends. Rosellini, in fact, had defended Frank Colacurcio Sr. in 1943 on a charge of "carnal knowledge" of an underage girl. As recently as 1969 he had put in a good word for the family with police higher-ups in connection with bingo parlors. Rosellini, ironically, had made his name as a young state senator in 1951, emulating the celebrated U.S. Senate Kefauver Committee by investigating organized crime in Washington State.[11]

The Dysart caper not only had the politicians in a dither, Seattle's two daily papers and the best TV station in town, KING, were instantly embroiled, looking for new angles and swapping thinly veiled insults. The *Times* was angry that Dysart had gone to the *P-I* with the Rosellini-Colacurcio story and the *P-I* was annoyed that the *Times* wanted to know what it knew and when.

Dysart was exploring an anonymous tip that Rosellini had helped Frank Colacurcio's brother and a nephew with a liquor license in Hawaii in 1971. He passed along the information to the Evans campaign, which sent a private eye to Honolulu for more sniffing. Dysart had shopped the story to KING Broadcasting as well as the *Post-Intelligencer*. Don McGaffin, KING-TV's ace investigative reporter—a Mickey Spillane character come to life, trench coat and all—loved afflicting the comfortable. He was skeptical, though, that Rosellini would be dumb enough to be the Colacurcios' consigliere and incredulous that Dysart thought a newsman would accept an invitation to fly to Honolulu for an investigation. "He offered to advance the money for plane fare," McGaffin said, adding that Dysart had assured him that Jim Dolliver and Gummie Johnson, two of Evans' most trusted confidants, knew he was investigating Rosellini, as did Jay Gilmour, chairman of the Evans campaign committee.[12]

Station management shared McGaffin's wariness and "urged caution so that KING would not be manipulated to smear Rosellini." McGaffin checked out Dysart's tip with reliable sources in Seattle and Hawaii and concluded the evidence was too flimsy to warrant a story. Then he called Gorton to ask why his chief deputy was busy trying to dig up dirt on Rosellini. "Huh?" said Slade. "I don't know anything about it!" He nosed around that night and, with mounting anger, confirmed it was true. Sally Gorton recalls her husband arriving home at 2 a.m., visibly shaken. He rarely talked politics at home and invariably was in bed before 11, his nose in a book. Dysart was called on the carpet the next morning and immediately owned up, eyes downcast. He said that's what he'd been up to when he took four days of personal leave earlier in the month.[13]

Two ostensibly upstanding Republicans—one an Eagle Scout, the other intolerant of tolerance—now stood accused of political espionage against an ex-governor allegedly consorting with mobsters. It was a circulation manager's dream. Watergate amplified everything.

GILMOUR CONFIRMED THAT DYSART had been working with a detective hired by the campaign committee. Governor Evans knew about the detective, the chairman said, but he didn't realize the attorney general's chief deputy was helping. When reporters caught up with him, the governor said that was quite so. Dysart deserved to be suspended, Evans said. He saw nothing wrong, however, with hiring a private detective to chase down rumors about Rosellini. "We'd be foolish not to," but "there is a difference between spreading rumors and checking out rumors." And why was Rosellini sounding so saintly when he had used an on-duty State Patrol trooper to investigate Dick Christensen when the Lutheran minister was the Republican frontrunner for governor in 1964? "Ask him about that?" Evans said. As for Rosellini's charge that he'd been the victim of anti-Italian innuendo, the governor bristled: "Never have I engaged in racial slurs of any kind." Evans also categorically denied Rosellini's claim that they'd either tapped his phones or obtained his confidential telephone records. Meantime, Evans said, someone had been investigating him, too—and they could have at it; he had nothing to hide. "Our campaign is clean. I gave strict orders at the very beginning to be as clean as we can be." Perhaps not the best turn of phrase.[14]

Evans and Gorton had other assorted loose cannons and wild-hare friends, including a Wenatchee insurance salesman who on November 1 apologized not to Rosellini but to Evans for printing up a batch of "Does Washington Really Need a Godfather?" bumper stickers. "I meant no harm," said Paul C. Meyer. "I thought I had a legitimate message. I was aiming at telling the people about corruption I saw in Rosellini." Meyer said he was a Danish immigrant and a good Republican. How good? Well, he held off on becoming an American citizen until there was a Republican in the White House and only sold insurance to Republicans.[15]

Some saw the Colacurcio story as yet another October surprise cooked up by Evans and Gorton. "Many regular Democrats bitterly believe that the gambling charges" that surfaced just before the 1968 election "were deliberately unloaded" on John J. O'Connell by the Republicans to get Evans re-elected, Dick Larsen wrote. He also observed that Dysart was now "somewhere incommunicado to nearly everyone except selected news outlets." (Translation: the *Post-Intelligencer*, whose executive editor, Lou Guzzo, was not a Rosellini fan.)[16]

BOUNCING FROM PRESS CONFERENCE to press conference with a full head of seethe, Rosellini had a seemingly inexhaustible arsenal of adjectives to describe how "despicable" it all was. He was the victim of a "Joe McCarthy guilt-by-association" "flimsy, fabricated wonderland tale"—a "Watergate West" "Gestapo" operation and a "terrifying type of terrorism" rooted in bigotry and innuendo. It was "an obvious conspiracy" by Evans and Gorton, who would stoop to anything to salvage their sinking campaigns. "It's incredible that Evans and Gorton wouldn't know what the chief assistant attorney general was doing," Rosellini fumed. "Now they have been caught with their hands in the cookie jar and have suspended Dysart in an attempt to cover up their smear tactics." Poor Dysart was just the fall guy for his boss and the governor, Al added, shaking his head.[17]

Well, how about those calls to Hawaii? Rosellini acknowledged he might have phoned an old friend, a Honolulu police sergeant, concerning the Colacurcios but the friend was also celebrating his 25th wedding anniversary and he'd made several calls to offer his best wishes. Pressed for a clearer recollection of whether they had also discussed liquor licenses, Rosellini said, "I don't remember." Then the former governor paused, looked into the air and said nothing for several minutes. Finally, he said, "I would say I did not."[18]

Scoop Jackson, who'd never been chummy with Rosellini, was practically apoplectic during a Seattle news conference. Usually a model of Scandinavian-ness, the senator shocked Larsen and the other reporters by waving his arms in indignation over what they'd done to Al. Jackson pounded the table with his fist, then slammed it hard with an open palm, declaring, "I think it's outrageous that this kind of attack be made against an individual because of his ancestry."[19]

Gorton was also livid, telling the *P-I* that Dysart had acted entirely on his own. "Any candidate certainly has a perfect right to investigate his opponent," Gorton said, but his deputy's activities were "totally inappropriate," even during off-duty hours, and a direct violation of his orders to stay out of politics. Gorton then told the *Times* that Dysart had been working on an investigation with KING Broadcasting and the *P-I*. Spokesmen for both companies bristled. KING's pique was justified but the *P-I*'s protestations rang hollow. Guzzo had found the Rosellini rumor tantalizing, verily steeped in truth. He viewed the Colacurcios as "our own little mafia," the Corleones, Seattle style. Years later, Guzzo recalled that many in Seattle's Italian community refused to believe Rosellini "had trucked with characters like Colacurcio. Something needed to be done, so I wrapped up all the charges against Rosellini and ran my own report under my byline to demonstrate to the Italian community and others that at least some Italian Americans—me in particular—were on the right side of the law."[20]

KING detected in the *Times'* coverage an inference that the station had sat on a juicy story. Having done due diligence, McGaffin "was furious that KING's ethics had been questioned." McGaffin and others at Channel 5 "were convinced that they had been used by Gorton, who they believed knew all along what Dysart had been doing."[21]

Dysart, looking wan, gave Guzzo his exclusive front-page interview on October 30 and accused Rosellini of obfuscating a continuing relationship with Frank Colacurcio. Gorton's suspended deputy labeled Rosellini "a man of questionable integrity." He said the transcript of a trial 10 months earlier in which Frank Colacurcio Sr. had been convicted of conspiracy to violate federal anti-racketeering laws revealed Rosellini's involvement with the family. That said, Dysart added that he deserved to be suspended. "I deliberately kept Slade ignorant of my research activities. Those activities were not brought to his attention until Thursday, Oct. 26. When they were, he acted with characteristic decisiveness . . . What I did I undertook at my own instigation. I am the one who initiated the contact with Mr. Gilmour of the Dan Evans Committee. For Mr. Rosellini to suggest that I am the fall guy is just to demonstrate his ignorance of the facts." Dysart then added unrepentantly, "I confess in front of the *Post-Intelligencer* and William Randolph Hearst if necessary that I'm a Republican. I think that the facts about Mr. Rosellini's relationship with Frank Colacurcio should be known before the people make their choice on November 7." The next day, Dysart finally gave the *Times* an interview. He emphasized that he had not tapped Rosellini's telephones or tried to secure confidential telephone records.[22]

GORTON EMPHATICALLY AND REPEATEDLY DENIED he had been in the loop. "But nobody in the press"—or, for that matter, Fred Dore—"believed me for a minute. It was 'How could your number one guy be doing all this and you not know about it?'" He was, after all, "Slippery Slade." Usually he just accepted that as part of being in the political fish bowl. Now the accusations cut to the quick. Gorton hated it. He felt powerless. "It was awful." Even more galling to Gorton was his discovery that Dysart had been recruited by a fellow charter member of Joel Pritchard's "Dan Evans' Group of Heavy Thinkers." The Dysart caper "is the only gripe I ever had with that wonderful person, Jim Dolliver," Gorton says. "Dan was trailing in the polls and they needed to get some dirt on Rosellini, of which there was plenty to get, so Dolliver came to Dysart and recruited him to go out and dig up information on Rosellini." Despite Slade's warning to stay out of politics, Dysart was champing at the bit to see action and craved attention. "I knew *nothing* about it until Don McGaffin contacted me," Gorton says.

That qualifier—"of which there was plenty to get"—italicizes Gorton's unapologetic contention that Rosellini had been flirting with the dark side for decades. Evans said something similar. His campaign didn't traffic in slurs, rumors and innuendo, the governor said. "We don't have to resort to tactics like that. His record is bad enough to defeat him."[23]

Whether it was his record or the torrent of bad publicity, Rosellini's 13–point lead evaporated. Republican polls had indicated for weeks that the undecideds might be as high as 25 percent. On November 7, 1972, Dan Evans won an unprecedented third consecutive term as governor with 117,000 votes to spare. Gorton trounced Dore. McGovern won Massachusetts and the District of Columbia, Nixon everything else, but the cancer growing on the presidency was metastasizing.[24]

GUMMIE JOHNSON, A POLITICAL LEGEND in his own time, is gone. Dolliver and Dysart are too. Dolliver was appointed to the Washington Supreme Court by Evans in 1976 and defeated Fred Dore to win a full term. Before suffering a debilitating stroke in 1993, he had a robust voice and the dazzling intellectual dexterity to match his gray beard. He was also a deft political strategist and chief of staff whose counsel had been invaluable to Evans for nearly a decade. Neither his oral history nor any of his other public statements address the Dysart incident.

Adele Ferguson, the feisty *Bremerton Sun* reporter, had several sources who suggested that Dysart was telling the truth when he said Johnson was also involved. Evans shares that belief. "I did not know anything about Dysart's activities until the news articles appeared," the former governor said in 2010. "Dolliver told me some of the details but I really don't think he was the chief instigator. Gummie sounds more like the director of this affair. Actually by today's standards it was a pretty tame stuff." Evans remembers Dysart as "a bright young funny guy" who later "went off track mentally and occasionally appeared with some wild story to tell, looking disheveled and lonely." Dysart died in obscurity in 2003, only 61. "He was a wonderful guy in many respects," Gorton says.[25]

Payton Smith, Rosellini's biographer, says the episode underscored the prejudice Rosellini endured as an Italian-Catholic politician. "It is painful for many of us to go back in time and relive prejudices that now seem archaic," he wrote in 1997. "Yet as recently as 1972, otherwise enlightened political figures" such as Evans and Gorton "grossly played on the public's worst fears of Italians in order to achieve their political objectives."[26]

Smith and Gorton first met in the 1950s when Slade was a Young Republican and Smith a Young Democrat. Decades later they were in the same law firm for a couple of years. In a 2010 interview, Smith was asked if he accepted Gorton's denial of any foreknowledge of Dysart's moonlighting. "I don't believe that for a minute," he said. "When Slade gets going on something, especially politics, he can be ruthless. I don't think he was losing any sleep over what those guys were saying about Rosellini." Smith believes, however, that Evans wasn't in the loop on the Dysart caper. "I think Dan is pretty sharp and (would have) said 'I'm not going to go down that corridor with you guys' . . . But his campaign was doing it."

Rosellini's biographer paused for a moment to reflect. Then he allowed that it also should be remembered that "it was sort of dog eat dog in that race" and if Rosellini "had had some stuff" on Evans like the Colacurcio connection he might have gone with it, too. "Al's an old boxer. He would have fought his way out."[27]

When Rosellini turned 95 in 2005, Evans recalled that he and Al had sat together at a Husky football game a couple of months earlier. "I admire him greatly," Evans said. "I hope I'm as active at 95." But time doesn't heal all wounds. Thirty-eight years after one of the most bitterly-contested campaigns in state history, Democrats were still grousing about Evans' Teflon-coated reputation as "Straight Arrow." Dolliver, in fact, liked to tell this story: "One day somebody rose in the (State) Senate and said, 'What would Jesus Christ say about this particular piece of legislation?' And, just like a shot, somebody on the other side of the aisle rose up and said, 'Well, why don't you go and ask him. He has an office on the second floor.'"[28]

As for Gorton, the Democrats figured Slade got what was coming to him when they bounced him out of the U.S. Senate, not once but twice in cliff-hangers. Privately, however, they grudgingly admired his toughness and resiliency. Gorton, who grew up watching the Chicago Cubs, has always maintained that there's no crying in baseball—or politics. When it comes to 1972, however, he's emphatic about three things: He didn't know what Keith Dysart was up to. If he had, he never would have countenanced it. The third thing is that he hates bigotry. "Al Rosellini's ethnicity and religion were immaterial."

While critics snort at the notion that Gorton was oblivious to Dysart's activities, former staffers and campaign workers say it's entirely plausible. After he settled in as attorney general and especially as a U.S. senator, he was a delegator, they say, and largely detached from personnel issues and operational details. "He wanted to be the senator," says former chief of staff J. Vander Stoep. On the campaign trail he'd let the experts develop a battle plan. If he liked it, he was content to be the candidate and stick to the script. Mike McGavick, the son of a good friend, grew up to be the most trusted member of Gorton's inner circle. McGavick had enormous strategic leeway when they were in campaign mode. Slade sometimes was bemused to be "the grown-up" getting prepped and counseled by the kids.[29]

"I THINK HE'S LYING," Fred Dore always said of Gorton's denials in the Dysart affair, which lingered on for another two years after Dysart resigned from the Attorney General's Office following the election. Despite Gorton's denials, rumors persisted that Dysart was still secretly on the AG's payroll. He'd been seen around the Legislature during the 1973 session. Adele determined, however, that he'd been doing "private work for various clients." Dysart soon took a job in Washington, D.C., as counsel to the National Governors' Conference, of which Evans was chairman. "But another reason for the continued interest in Dysart," Adele wrote, "is his longtime friendship, or so it's said, with a couple of principals in that boil on the political process, Watergate," namely Ehrlichman and his protégé, Egil "Bud" Krogh. "Those aforementioned whisperers think it interesting that the Dysart political espionage followed on the heels of the Watergate espionage and some of the circumstances are oddly coincidental." For one thing, Adele noted, Dysart said neither Gorton nor Evans knew what he was up to. "Some of those close to the people involved, however, doubted that Dysart, not a stupid man, would go so far on his own. . . .What they suspicioned was that Jim Dolliver, who is to Evans what Ehrlichman was to Nixon, and ex-state GOP chairman Gummie Johnson persuaded Dysart to use his ability and power to make the investigation, all the while keeping Evans and Gorton in the dark so they could later honestly say they knew nothing about it."[30]

Krogh, who got caught up in the twilight zone of Nixon's West Wing and agreed to direct the infamous White House "Plumbers," told Gorton's biographer in 2010 that he and Dysart were friendly but he could recall no conversations between them about any sort of political espionage in either Washington. Nor could he recall Ehrlichman mentioning that he was in contact with Dysart about politics.[31]

IN THE HEIGHTENED WAKE of Watergate, reporters in Washington State also investigated the activities of a charming young man who had volunteered with the Evans campaign. His name was Ted Bundy. Some tried to couch Bundy's activities as spying, yet the extent of his role was to attend Rosellini press conferences and speeches and report back on what was said, S.O.P. opposition research. Larsen and the AP's Dave Ammons were well aware of what Bundy was up to. He never tried to pose as a reporter. Larsen said it was hardly cloak-and-dagger stuff. Neale Chaney, the state Democratic chairman, agreed. Going to public meetings to monitor the opposition, "That's a legitimate part of the business." Dolliver chimed in that campaigns had to make sure the opponent wasn't saying "one thing in Bellingham and something else in Walla Walla."[32]

In 1973, Bundy landed a plum job as assistant to Ross Davis, the state Republican chairman, and was admitted to law school at the University of Puget Sound in Tacoma. Two years later, the checkered lore of the 1972 campaign would be forever footnoted by the news that Bundy had been arrested in Utah for attempting to kidnap a young woman. His mug shot was soon on every front page, a dead ringer for police sketches of "Ted," a handsome man suspected in a string of disappearances of young women, from Lake Sammamish east of Seattle to the mountains of Colorado. The Volkswagen bug Bundy was driving matched up too. It contained a pair of handcuffs, rope, a crowbar and a pair of pantyhose with scissored eye holes. Bundy would be revealed as one of the most sickeningly prolific psychopathic serial killers in American history. Mischievous Democrats have a good time to this day reminding people that Bundy was such a promising Young Republican.[33]

GORTON SAYS THE NUMBER ONE THING he learned that year was that he "never wanted to be in that situation again." From then on he never had a chief deputy attorney general. After Dysart's departure, Ed Mackie, Phil Austin, John Martin and Mal Murphy were basically equal. One deputy was never in charge of the office in his absence. "And all of the deputies I had after that were strictly lawyers. None of them was particularly active in politics."

He was anxious to see 1972 end, and decided a long trip would be just the tonic for a family that had endured a singularly stressful year.

12 | Riding With History

T HE PARKING LOT WAS CRAWLING with kids on bicycles when Slade and Sally pulled into Tiny's, a regionally famous fruit stand, in the summer of 1972. Heading home from a campaign appearance in Wenatchee, Slade had been intent on lemonade. Now he was mingling with the cyclists.

Fran Call, an intrepid teacher at Mercer Island Junior High, was leading her third group of "Cyclemates" on a coast-to-coast trip. Instantly fascinated, Slade inspected their bikes and gear, quizzed them about their preparations, wanted to know how many miles a day they hoped to cover and where they would be spending their nights.[1]

After moving from Seattle to Olympia in 1969, the Gortons became biking enthusiasts, taking weekend jaunts along Thurston County's beguiling back roads. Slade, Sally, Tod, Sarah and Becky had biked from Olympia to Portland over Labor Day weekend in 1971, collecting $800 in pledges for Children's Orthopedic Hospital in Seattle.[2]

As Tiny's disappeared in the rearview mirror, Slade could see the kids waving. "Wouldn't it be a lot more fun to be doing that than what we're doing this summer?" he said. "Yes, dear," said Sally, who could see the wheels turning.[3]

Five months later, glad to be done with the "awfulness" of the 1972 campaign, he went to see Fran Call, picked her brain and began planning a bike trip from Olympia to Gloucester in the summer of '73. Sally, who likes adventures, signed up as quartermaster, medic and safety officer. It took her months but she finally found everyone matching yellow-and-orange jackets with reflector tape and bright yellow T-shirts.[4] Tod, who was 14, would have been happier playing soccer with his friends but he understood the glint in his father's eye. His sisters—Sarah, almost 13, and Becky, just turned 11—were the most dubious. Then Dad offered a tantalizing bribe: "If you make it all the way across the country you can use your paper route savings and buy horses." They had them picked out before they left—Windy and Shema. "We had their photos and whenever we got discouraged we could pull them out and gaze at them," says Sarah.[5]

Slade, who loves maps, was in his element as a trip planner, securing U.S. Geological Survey maps with contour lines and studying routes that would keep them off heavily traveled highways for most of the distance. He called his brothers and other family members back East and told them they were coming; get the sleeping bags out of the attic. His brother Nat guffawed. "I'll tell you what, Slade: If you get as far as upstate New York I'll do the last week with you." Slade told him he'd better buy a 10–speed and learn how the gears worked.[6]

Next, the Gortons recruited their good friends, Dick and Micki Hemstad, and their four kids to join them. Dick, then director of the State Office of Community Development, couldn't get away for a whole month and ended up staying behind with the youngest Hemstad, who was only 10. On June 6, 1973, the three adults and six kids, ranging from 16 to 11, set out from Olympia. It was Gloucester or bust. Forty-five days and 3,328 miles later, they arrived in Massachusetts after a close call for Slade and Becky.[7]

SLADE HAD LEARNED from Fran Call that if you stuck to the back roads you'd see more of the real America, and it was a lot safer than threading your away single file along a highway, whiplashed by the vortex of semi

The Gorton bicycle expedition on July 3, 1973, outside St. John's Lutheran Church in Sparta, Wis., where they spent the night. From left: Micki, Chris, Jenny and Rachael Hemstad, Sarah, Sally, Tod, Slade and Becky Gorton. *Gorton Family Album*

trucks. Never bike at night, Call said, adding that she and her kids had also discovered that small-town churches were happy to put them up. An active Episcopalian, Slade began making calls. He also pinpointed post offices. About every other day along the way the Attorney General's Office would send him anything he had to sign or review, together with the next set of maps. He'd sign the papers, stuff the old maps into a big envelope and they'd be back on the road again, bisecting every state bordering Canada except Maine.

It took them 11 days to pedal across Montana, from the cool mountains to the sizzling flatlands. Slade routinely brought up the rear with 11-year-old Becky, the youngest rider. When the wind gusted, the sun blazed and rattlesnakes slithered across their path, he'd get her talking about the horse she was going to have. The sights and smells of that trip are still with them all—the trees, the flowers, the crops and critters, including the jackrabbits, prairie dogs, sheep and cattle who observed their progress with curiosity.

With a 25–mph tailwind, they covered 140 miles one memorable day, from Carrington, North Dakota, to Moorhead, Minnesota, whizzing along a road that was as smooth and flat as a pool table. The road seemed to stretch forever, and the only traffic they encountered gave them a wide berth and a friendly beep. At tiny road-stop cafes they feasted on pancakes, fried chicken and homemade pies.[8]

What Becky remembers most—other than the "horrifyingly huge" mosquitoes at a Wisconsin campsite—is the kindness of strangers. "We'd meet someone and they'd say 'You need to stay at our house tonight!' I can still picture us pulling into a Midwestern town with wide, tree-lined streets and Dad knocking on the door of a church to see if we could stay there for the night. It was an amazing way to see America. That whole trip personified my Dad's enthusiasm and eagerness to do everything to the fullest," Slade's youngest says. "There's a great bit of child in him. I'm not saying 'childish'; it's his love of life. The bitter liberals have never been able to grasp that."[9]

Her sister's strongest, not fondest, memory of the trip is that "every darn time we couldn't find a church or someplace else indoors to spend the night, it just poured. We'd be sleeping on picnic tables and we'd try to take cover underneath, only to emerge soaking wet the next morning."[10]

Everywhere they stopped they met people who were amazed at the feat they were attempting. Soon the wire services began tracking their progress. Slade attempted to pull rank only once.

It was a sunny Sunday afternoon in Ohio. As they were leaving Michigan, he called ahead to an Episcopal church in Toledo. One of the priests gushed that the trip sounded exciting, offered to put them up for the night and said he'd meet them a few miles ahead. The expedition was transiting a suburb called Sylvania on a wide street with no traffic when a blue light flashed and a young cop pulled them over. "Don't you know it's against the law in Sylvania, Ohio, not to ride in single file? You're riding double!" Slade was contrite. "Oh, officer, we didn't know." The officer shook his head and began writing a ticket. The laws of Sylvania were not to be trifled with. Gorton decided to flash his attorney general ID card. At that moment, not one but two exuberant priests pulled up and greeted the travelers with hugs and handshakes. The young cop, faced with both church and state, closed his ticket book and departed.

THE RISING SUN was in their eyes on July 12, 1973, as they pedaled east along Lake Erie, just inside Pennsylvania. They were up and rolling at 6 a.m. to avoid heavier traffic along a four-lane highway. Then disaster nearly struck. Slade was riding last, just a bit behind and slightly to the left of Becky, when a car clipped the saddlebag on his bike and punctured his left hip and upper leg with a spear-shaped piece of chrome trim. Slade tumbled onto Becky's bike. Pigtails flying, the 11–year-old was knocked to the ground but emerged with only scrapes and bruises. "Dad crashed onto the cement and his glasses went flying, but he jumped up quickly and asked if I was OK. Then we saw the piece of chrome hanging out of his leg and I screamed. He just pulled it out." Although bleeding profusely, Slade—ever the lawyer—attempted to get the license plate number of the fleeing car. A motorist on the other side of the highway saw it all happen, hung a U-turn, gave chase and returned with the number. The 24–year-old hit-and-run driver was soon in custody and Gorton was en route to the emergency room. "If anyone had a worse day than I did in that part of Pennsylvania it was that driver," Slade quips. Forty stitches later, they were on the way out of town—except that Dad, to his frustration, was confined to a rental car for two days. State police said he was lucky to be alive. The big saddle bags on their bikes absorbed some of the impact, especially for Becky.[11]

Approximately one state and 500 miles earlier, Nat Gorton had realized it was time to buy a bike. "They're going to be in awfully good shape," his wife Jodi noted. "I don't know how you're going to keep up." Etched in family lore is Nat Gorton's rejoinder: "Anything an 11–year-old girl can do, I can do."

The Gorton party was averaging 80 miles a day. "Our cruising speed when we started out from Olympia was in seventh gear," Gorton recalls. "By the time we arrived in eastern upstate New York, where Nat joined us, it was ninth gear. I was back on a bike east of Buffalo and we were *moving*." Nat Gorton had to throw his bike into the car with about 20 miles to go that day, much to his humiliation.

Two days later, at an Episcopal Church in Vermont the locals warned that the next leg of their journey was all uphill. They thanked them and proceeded to pedal to the top of Sherburne Pass. Nat was five minutes behind but too proud to get off his bike and walk. When he finally caught up, Becky deadpanned, "Oh Uncle Nat, is this what you call mountains back East?"

The penultimate leg was an exhausting 95–mile ride from Dartmouth to Nashua to visit New Hampshire's attorney general. Slade and Warren Rudman had become good friends through national meetings and would go on to serve together in the U.S. Senate.

Tired but excited, on July 20 they set out on the final 40–mile leg to Gloucester. Slade's parents drove out to the suburbs to greet them. Sally celebrated her 40th birthday the next day, pleased that she had lost a couple of dress sizes. Becky Gorton was in the *Guinness Book of World Records* for a while as the youngest person to have bicycled across America. When Slade came back to work, he discovered that wags in the office had replaced his office chair with one that featured a bicycle seat.[12]

"When they're 80, my kids will still remember what they did in the summer of 1973 and what they learned about their country," Slade says. For years to come, the slide show of the bike trip was his crowd-pleaser. "That's all the Rotary Clubs wanted to see. They didn't want to hear about my consumer protection efforts." Well, not quite. When he returned from the trip, he made one of the most controversial decisions of his career in politics. He announced it at the Seattle Rotary Club, which eagerly wanted to hear what a leading Republican had to say about the conduct of the President of the United States.

AS THE GORTONS AND HEMSTADS were departing on their cross-country adventure, the other Washington was poised to boil. Woodward and Bernstein were reporting in *The Washington Post* that ex-White House counsel John Dean had told the Senate Watergate Committee he discussed the cover-up with Nixon on least 35 occasions. Claiming executive privilege, the president would neither testify himself nor grant access to presidential documents. Then his former appointments secretary revealed that since 1971 Nixon had recorded all of the conversations in the Oval Office, including his phone calls. Ten days later, the embattled president refused to turn over the tapes to the committee or Special Prosecutor Archibald Cox, who had been appointed by newly named Attorney General Elliot Richardson. In 1952, when Gorton interned at Ropes & Gray, Boston's oldest and most prestigious law firm, Richardson was his boss.[13]

"I had a lot of time that summer to think about my feelings about Watergate and Richard M. Nixon," Gorton recalls.

13 | Gorton Agonistes

B ECKY GORTON WAS 12 YEARS OLD when it hit home that her father was an increasingly influential, controversial politician. A seventh grader rarely takes notice of the morning newspaper, but when she saw the headline splashed across the front page of the *Seattle Post-Intelligencer* on March 21, 1974, it was "burned in my brain."[1]

In Shadow of Impeachment

Gorton to Nixon: 'Quit'

America was awash in Watergate. Nixon had fired Archibald Cox and abolished the office of special prosecutor, which prompted Attorney General Richardson and his deputy, William D. Ruckelshaus, to resign in protest. Headline writers dubbed it "The Saturday Night Massacre." A month later, in a televised Q&A session at the AP Managing Editors' Convention, Nixon famously declared, "People have got to know whether or not their President is a crook. Well, I'm not a crook!"[2] And on December 7, 1973, a date which will live in Watergate infamy, the White House said it couldn't explain an $18\frac{1}{2}$-minute gap in one of the Oval Office tapes subpoenaed by the Senate committee. Alexander Haig, Nixon's Chief of Staff, said one theory was that "some sinister force" erased the segment.[3]

Gorton found it all profoundly troubling: Without legal authorization or any admonition to protect constitutional rights, Nixon had authorized formation of the "Plumbers" political espionage unit. Despite having "all of the power of the federal government at his command," the president had ignored the mounting drumbeat of revelations about the 1972 break-in attempt at Democratic National Headquarters, never bothering to learn the truth. Further, Nixon withheld evidence from the Department of Justice and Congress, urged the IRS to harass his enemies, solicited illegal campaign contributions and countenanced, as Gorton put it, "the two-time selection as vice president of a man who turned out to be a common extortionist."[4]

Quoting Washington, Madison, Hamilton, Shakespeare and Thucydides, Gorton told a hushed Seattle Rotary Club that the president had burdened the federal government with a "moral climate of cynicism and suspicion." The "finest service" Nixon could perform for his country, Gorton concluded, would be to resign and enable the nation to "start afresh." Otherwise, the attorney general added, impeachment was nearly certain because the president had demonstrated "a broad pattern of indifference to and disrespect for the laws of the United States and the expectations of its citizens." In fact, "Richard Nixon, out of the evidence of his own mouth," had given the House of Representatives probable cause to vote Articles of Impeachment when he stated that "In any organization, the man at the top must bear the responsibility." If what Nixon had done didn't merit impeachment, Gorton asked, "What actions of a future president will be? What invasions of your privacy, what violations of your civil rights?"[5]

Gorton's voice was flat—it reminded many of John Dean's testimony when he told the Senate committee about "the cancer growing on the presidency." It was also tinged with sadness and indignation, especially to the handful of those who knew that the 17–page speech had been germinating for months. It stands as one of his most eloquent in more than a half century in politics.

Gorton noted that most Rotarians had generally supported Nixon's progressive foreign policies, as well as his efforts to reduce federal spending and centralization. He liked those things, too. But they'd been betrayed. "It is your attitudes toward government that have been discredited. It is your policies which are being increasingly defeated. It is your voices in Congress who will be stilled in November's elections if events continue to drift as they have for the past year." Gorton said it was clear that the turmoil could grind on for months, even years, if it came down to a trial in the U.S. Senate. "The nation can ill afford that time."[6]

"For most citizens," the attorney general concluded, "either impeachment or resignation is an extraordinary remedy with unknown and fearsome consequences for the future. They agree with Hamlet's dread of an unknown future, which 'makes us rather bear those ills we have than fly to others that we know not of. Thus conscience doth make cowards of us all. . . .' It is our freedom, our rights against an ever-present and increasingly powerful government which are at stake."[7]

When he was done, the Rotarians, who were "predominantly Republican and conservative, as is Gorton, gave him a long applause," wrote Shelby Scates, the *P-I's* political writer. Only "one person—not identified—

walked out of the Olympic Hotel ballroom in protest." Others said Gorton's bill of particulars was devastating to Nixon. John Ryder, a banker and former state senator, said Gorton said what had to be said. "It took courage to come before this audience and make that speech." Gorton told Scates it was precisely the kind of audience he wanted. He took issue with those of all political persuasions—liberals as well as conservatives—"who would avoid taking action against Nixon because of the possible precedent that might be established." That included his longtime friends and political allies, Governor Evans and Congressman Joel Pritchard, the lone Republican in the state's delegation. They had urged him to not give the speech. (Frank Pritchard, however, backed his stand.) They "fail to recognize that the future is always unknown," Gorton said, "and that we will change presidents in any event in 1977. But, most important, they fail to consider that the precedent created by not acting decisively in the face of such overwhelming provocation may well turn out to be far more dangerous than the precedent established by any form of positive action." Warren G. Magnuson, Washington's senior senator, had Gorton's speech entered in the *Congressional Record*.[8]

AT KING COUNTY REPUBLICAN HEADQUARTERS, Gorton's speech started hitting the fan practically before the cleanup crew had retired the Rotary regalia and folded the tables. "People are fit to be tied," a secretary to GOP Chairman Dennis Dunn told Scates the next morning, adding that she had fielded 15 to 20 angry calls. Dunn was vacationing in Mexico with his wife Jennifer, Slade's distant cousin, and hadn't heard the news. "The reaction to the speech ranges from highly irate to very negative," the secretary said. "Mostly they are saying, 'If Gorton thinks he's going to run for governor, I don't know where he'll get Republican support.'" The state chairman, Ross Davis, was more big-tent temperate, emphasizing that Gorton was speaking for himself, not the party. "Those who support the president should speak out," Davis said. "Those who oppose the president should speak out. There isn't any party—or ideological pattern."[9]

Gorton gave the same speech in Bellevue the next day and in Spokane a day after that. He received standing ovations on both occasions. The *Post-Intelligencer* offered an editorial he likely was tempted to frame. Gorton had taken "a courageous stand," the Hearst paper said, adding that he "has always been long on courage in the political arena, and he has always disdained opportunism in public office, despite what his opponents have said. He could have gone along playing a safe role on the Nixon question . . . He could have kept his views to himself and tried to ride out the

Republican storm as many others have—by pretending Watergate and related affairs were Nixonian in context and had nothing to do with the Republican Party. But Slade Gorton is not built that way. He doesn't mind embracing a controversial subject nor speaking up for an unpopular cause, regardless of the consequences. This newspaper has been in disagreement with Gorton on several issues, but it recognizes what most Washington residents readily accept: Gorton is an honest, earnest, brave public servant who acts according to conscience, not political expediency. . . . Above all, Gorton's stand is like a reveille call at the fort for the beleaguered state Republican Party. After a long period of hemming-and-hawing, all the stalwarts who have been ducking the issue now may have to stand up and be counted."[10]

"What is Gorton's future?" the *Post-Intelligencer* posited. "Long considered a logical, exceptional successor to Evans as the head of his party and with excellent potential for the governorship, the attorney general may have put his future on the line. It is possible the ultraconservative wing of the party may write him off. . . .It is also possible, as a consequence, that he may have alienated major contributors to whatever campaign he may project in the future. . . . But we don't think so. On the contrary, we believe Gorton's willingness to stick his chin out and walk where others fear to tread will win him far more support than he might have lost. . . .We are also convinced independent voters and many Democrats will remember his daring, too. Gorton has been one of the most dedicated, hard-working, effective attorneys general in Washington State history. . . . If President Nixon could have had associates at his side of Gorton's caliber instead of the stripe he chose, we're convinced resignation or impeachment would not now be subjects of national concern."[11]

Returning home to find his conservative wing of the party in high dudgeon, Dunn fumed that Gorton's stand smacked of "grandstanding" and derriere-protecting. "I don't feel that to stab a man in the back is an act of courage," the King County Republican leader said. "On the contrary," Gorton's suggestion that Nixon resign made "a mockery" of the presumption that a person is innocent until proven guilty. Gorton's speech had played right into the hands of "a hostile press" and the other powerful "liberal-left forces," Dunn told the Young Men's Republican Club. Given Nixon's plummeting approval ratings, many Republicans were "running scared." Gorton, who "had been talked about seriously" as a possible candidate for governor in 1976, sadly seemed to have joined that crowd, Dunn said.[12] In the argot of the Nixon administration, the operative words there were "had been."

Four Seattle business executives, by coincidence, had telegraphed the beleaguered president the same day as Gorton's speech, expressing support and apologizing "for any weak sisters, turncoats, liberal judges, selfish politicians and journalists." Stiff upper lip, they told Nixon: "Do your job as you see it." (Nixon's bottom line in time would be revealed: "When the President does it, that means it is not illegal.") Henry Seidelhuber, president of an iron-works and one of the signatories, said that if he had known what Gorton was up to, "I would have been there and booed until he left."[13]

THREE DAYS AFTER THE ROTARY CLUB SPEECH, the Republican State Central Committee unanimously adopted a resolution rejecting Gorton's call for Nixon's resignation. However, one party member who asked not to be identified told the Associated Press, "I think I probably agree with Slade, but I don't think he should have said it in public." Another Republican overheard him and nodded.[14]

Pierce County Republican leaders were among the most apoplectic. Their statements underscored the widespread assumption that Gorton would be a candidate for governor in 1976. The senior House Republican, Helmut Jueling of suburban Tacoma, said Gorton was "doing to the president what he was elected to keep from happening to the people of the state—judging a case before the evidence is in. He has tried him and convicted him. It's a strange thing for a candidate for governor to do. Gorton has lost a lot of Republican support." Charles Newschwander, the assistant minority leader in the State Senate, thought it was "the worst thing Gorton could have done." County Prosecutor Ron Hendry, who had ousted Slade's old foe, John G. McCutcheon, said that if Nixon were to step down before all the facts were known it "could ruin the institution of the presidency."[15] Governor Evans was of a similar mind. "I think the president's resignation would be a bad thing," he told reporters. "It wouldn't solve anything" and would set a bad precedent. He was quick to add, however, that he wasn't being critical of Gorton. "The attorney general has the right to say anything he wants. He has his own opinions and has the right to express them. I just happen to disagree with him." Evans also flatly disagreed with Dunn's characterization of Gorton's statements. "It was not 'a stab in the back' and he didn't mean it that way at all."[16]

On the Monday following the round of speeches, Gorton was unfazed. "Of course I'm sticking by my statements. A lot of people are asking for copies of the speech. It is a very popular publication right now." The attorney general said his office had received 212 letters—137 opposing his suggestion and 81 supporting it. The phone callers were more supportive—81 out of 119. "This is about what we expected. The people who call or write generally have their minds made up in advance . . . The speech, however, was aimed at persons who did not have their minds made up."[7]

Five months later, in a dramatic televised address from the Oval Office, Richard M. Nixon announced his resignation. To leave office before the end of his term was "abhorrent to every instinct in my body," he told the nation. But "as president, I must put the interests of America first. . . . By taking this action I hope that I will have hastened the start of the process of healing which is so desperately needed in America."[8]

That was precisely Gorton's point. Protracted blood-letting in an impeachment trial would polarize the country all the more. In any case, he never wanted to run for governor. Urged on by the National Republican Senatorial Committee, he flirted with challenging Senator Magnuson that fall. The old lion looked vulnerable in 1974.

Gorton concluded the time wasn't yet ripe. He'd be patient.

14 | The Jolt from Boldt

MORNING DAWNED GRAY, AS USUAL, along the Washington coast on September 11, 1971. Joe DeLaCruz, the 34-year-old business manager for the Quinault Indian Nation, crouched defiantly on the Chow Chow Bridge, which was blocked by an old pickup truck. A sign next to him said too many hillsides and creeks had "died for your stumpage." The tribe's logging units were now closed. The Quinaults had had enough of the incompetent paternalism of the Bureau of Indian Affairs and the sweetheart deals offered by the state Department of Natural Resources. The agencies had allowed logging companies to pay below-market rates for Indian timber and clog rivers and streams with debris.

A charismatic leader with piercing eyes and a mane of swept-back hair, DeLaCruz posed for photos before talking with reporters. He said his people were taking back the land where their ancestors had lived for the thousands of years before the white man floated in with his beads and disease. The timber companies had driven pilings into stream beds without permission from the tribe, eroding spawning beds and polluting waterways. The 190,000-acre reservation was the most savagely logged area in the state. "The damage to our fisheries is as bad as the big stump farm" they've created, he said, and the broader issue could be summed up with one word: "Sovereignty."[1]

DeLaCruz and Gorton, tough, resourceful politicians from different worlds, were destined to collide repeatedly. DeLaCruz went on to lead the National Congress of American Indians and World Council of Indigenous Peoples. One of the last things he did before he died was order a batch of "Dump Slade" buttons.

NORTHWEST INDIANS' PUSH for treaty rights hit the front page in 1964 when Marlon Brando, the acclaimed actor, joined a fish-in on the Puyallup River near Tacoma and was promptly arrested by state Fisheries Department officers. For the Indians, fisheries regulation in Washington State was a bifurcated quagmire. The Fisheries Department regulated salmon, a staple of Indian life for nutritional and spiritual sustenance, while the Game Department controlled fishing for steelhead, a sea-going trout prized by the non-Indian anglers whose fees largely funded the agency. Indians were not allowed to net steelhead, which traditionally had helped sustain them during winter months. They were also prohibited from selling any they caught on their reservations.[2]

The tribes believed the white man was the real "Indian giver," breaking promises since the 1850s when the territorial governor, Isaac Stevens, signed treaties covering some 8,000 natives from Neah Bay at the tip of the Olympic Peninsula to the Nisqually along Puget Sound. In return for surrendering their claims to much of their land and agreeing to live henceforth on the reservations the Great Father had set aside for them, the Indians would receive payments over the next 20 years, plus assistance in learning agriculture and other help "becoming civilized." Further, Stevens said, they would be protected from the encroachments of the "bad" white men who had tried to harm them.

"The importance of the fish to the Indians seems to have impressed Stevens," a dynamic 35-year-old frontier bureaucrat. "He did not intentionally reserve to the Indians any more rights than he thought necessary, but he understood that the one indispensable requirement for securing agreement of any kind from Pacific Northwest Indians was to assure their continued right to fish." Each treaty he signed contains this provision: "The right of taking fish, at all usual and accustomed grounds and stations, is further secured to said Indians in common with all citizens of the Territory." For the next 120 years, "in common with" was translated by the courts as "no different than." Indians, in other words, were subject to state laws governing the resource. In particular, they were barred from net fishing on rivers and streams.[3]

State enforcement agents and Indian fishermen clashed often in the early 1960s. Willie Frank, the Nisqually elder whose magnificently wizened face belonged on a quarter, filed a petition with the federal court, accusing state enforcement agents of brutality. Frank asked for an independent investigation.

Warren G. Magnuson, Washington's senior senator, attempted to produce clarity with two Senate joint resolutions in 1964. The first recognized the tribes' treaty rights but stipulated that off-reservation fishing would be subject to state regulation. The second called for a federal buy-out of the off-reservation fishing rights. The state supported both; the tribes, increasingly emboldened, neither. The proposals died in committee. Five years later, Governor Evans embraced a ruling by the U.S. District Court in Portland that gave the tribes that fished the Columbia greater leeway. Evans ordered the Fisheries Department to make available a greater volume of fish to Indian fishermen and allow nets in some rivers. The Game Department, however, was beyond his control. Its management was adamant that there would be no net fishing by Indians.[4]

The federal Justice Department, under a Nixon Administration sympathetic to the tribes, zeroed in on a "much bigger target: the regulatory system for all fisheries of western Washington—Puget Sound. . . ."[5]

The lawsuit filed by the U.S. attorney for the Western District of Washington State in September of 1970 was *U.S. v. Washington,* but when the judge who presided released his ruling some 3½ years later it would be forever known as The Boldt Decision.

Bald, bow-tied and upright, George Hugo Boldt of the U.S. District Court in Tacoma was nearing 70. Earlier in his career he had dressed down Teamsters Union boss Dave Beck before sentencing him to McNeil Island federal penitentiary for corruption. A few weeks after the fishing rights case was filed, several members of the radical anti-war Seattle Liberation Front were being tried in Boldt's courtroom on charges of inciting a riot at the Federal Courthouse in downtown Seattle. One of the defiant defendants accused the judge of being "a lying dog." Outraged at their disrespect for the court, Boldt admonished them for their "contumacious" remarks. One day he summoned 20 federal marshals to restore order. When a mace-spraying melee ensued, Boldt declared a mistrial. He found the defendants in contempt of court, sentenced them to six months to a year in prison and refused to grant bail.[6]

Hank Adams, a DeLaCruz protégé who was a key strategist for the tribes, was so worried about the possible outcome of a decision by Boldt in the fishing rights dispute that he flew to Washington, D.C., to ask the government to drop the case. The tribes' attorneys had deep misgivings of their own. But to Gorton's surprise and the outrage of white fishermen, Judge Boldt gave the tribes far more than they expected.[7]

IT TOOK NEARLY THREE YEARS for the case to come to trial. Judge Boldt's initial utterances from the bench were classics in jurisprudentialese—100–word sentences that defy diagramming. He appeared to listen intently, however, and from time to time offered sympathetic observations. When a salt-of-the-earth Indian witness confessed that he "couldn't make it past the eighth grade without cheating," the judge allowed, "I wouldn't be surprised if the rest of us had that same problem."[8]

Boldt seemed particularly impressed by the testimony of Dr. Barbara

Lane, a scholar who had studied Chinook Jargon, the trade language used to translate the treaty language for the tribes in 1854. Also familiar with the minutes kept by the white negotiators, the professor testified that the U.S. government "had intended, and the Indians had understood, that Indians would continue to fish as they always had, selling their catch as before." The phrase "in common with" the white citizens of the territory "was intended and understood to mean simply that the Indians could not exclude whites and that both peoples would share equally in the fishery."9

On February 12, 1974, as Gorton was weighing his speech suggesting that Nixon should resign and preparing to argue a reverse discrimination case before the U.S. Supreme Court, he was jolted by the news that Judge Boldt had handed the tribes a landmark victory.10 Boldt knew it was Lincoln's birthday, and some would say his ruling was to Northwest Indians what *Brown v. Board of Education* was to the integration of public schools.11 "In common with," Boldt said in a 203–page decision, meant the Indians were entitled to up to 50 percent of each run of fish that passed through their usual and accustomed fishing grounds. Further, he said the treaties made no distinction between salmon and steelhead. He ordered the state to take action to limit fishing by non-Indians to ensure the tribes got their share, emphasizing that "off-reservation fishing by other citizens and residents of the state is not a right but merely a privilege which may be granted, limited or withdrawn by the state as the interests of the state or the exercise of treaty rights may require."

The director of the Game Department was "extremely disappointed," the chairman of the Steelhead Committee of the State Sportsmen's Council "flabbergasted." The outdoor editor of *The Seattle Times* said it seemed like "an extreme manifestation of the nation's guilt pangs over centuries of shoddy treatment of its native people."12 Indians, who comprised less than one percent of the state's population, were going to get half the fish, angry steelheaders and worried commercial fishermen fumed. It was a highly volatile situation. Everyone worried about the hotheads, of which there were plenty. Judge Boldt was burned in effigy and received death threats. He was also accused of having an Indian mistress and, later, of being senile.13

THE STATE AGENCIES MET with Gorton and quickly resolved to appeal the decision. As his point man, Gorton picked 29–year-old James M. Johnson. A tall, athletically slender Harvard man, with a reedy, chin-first style of speaking, Johnson was dubbed "Son of Slade" by DeLaCruz. When a contingent of angry fishermen descended on Olympia to protest the Boldt Decision, Johnson assured them the Attorney General's Office would file an appeal and declared he was confident the decision would be reversed. To the Indians and their attorneys it was a "disgraceful episode."[14]

Johnson says he was just doing his job. Fresh out of the military, he "wasn't looking for another war. In those days I got shot at more in the AG Office than I ever did in the Army." Over the next four years, Johnson appeared before Judge Boldt more than 200 times, seeking injunc-

An editorial cartoon in *The Seattle Times* in 1974 after the Boldt Decision on Indian treaty fishing rights. *Alan Pratt/The Seattle Times*

tions to halt on-reservation fisheries after runs had been exhausted. Someone fired shots at his car on more than one occasion, he says.

Johnson maintains that the five tribes Boldt subsequently barred from sharing in the treaty harvest weren't just grasping at straws when they filed a post-mortem challenge to the judge's mental competency. Boldt was suffering from Alzheimer's disease in 1978, a year before he ruled against the five tribes, according to his 1984 death certificate. "Anybody in the courtroom should have known that well before," Johnson says. "He used appalling judgment. . . . Not only would he not listen to my complaints at all . . . on many occasions Boldt would remember he didn't like me but he couldn't even remember who I was."

An avid fisherman since boyhood, Johnson was outraged when Boldt jailed a hundred protesters and made "contemptuous comments" about white fishermen. Johnson says the tribes hated him because he wouldn't be intimidated, and their lawyers were steamed when he succeeded in denying them what he characterizes as "millions in attorney's fees."

The tribes campaigned against Johnson and Gorton with a vengeance in the decades to come as Gorton moved to the U.S. Senate and Johnson to the Washington State Supreme Court after representing non-Indian property owners in a battle over shellfish rights.

Often forgotten in the choosing up of sides is that while Magnuson and Jackson enjoyed good relations with the tribes, in 1978 "even those supposed friends asked Interior Secretary Cecil Andrus to consider 'less than full implementation of the Bodlt Decision.'"[15]

WHILE GORTON AGGRESSIVELY LED the Attorney General's Office in resisting the Indians, his clients—especially the state Game Department—were of the same mind, says Al Ziontz, who represented the Makahs, Quileutes and Lummis. The Game Department's constituents were the sports fishermen, "and I don't think I'm exaggerating or slandering them when I say they were fanatics. When it comes to steelhead these guys couldn't accept the idea that anybody could take a steelhead except a sportsman. They were almost a government within the government. The Game Department had its own director, who was not appointed by the governor.... The board was made up of representatives of the major sportsmen's organizations and they were armed with police power. They had patrol officers who could arrest Indians. The sad result was that for 80 years Indians were forced to sneak at night in order to fish and to take a chance on being arrested. Many of them were arrested and ended up in jail. Their catch was confiscated and their boats were confiscated. Their nets were confiscated."

For all his warts, Ziontz says, President Nixon was a solid progressive on Native American self-determination. Suddenly the State of Washington found itself on the defense. "Instead of the state apparatus prosecuting the lone Indian who was not equipped financially or with expert witnesses to contest the testimony of biologists and fisheries management specialists, now they faced the full force of the federal government."

The Boldt Decision "hit like a bombshell," Ziontz says. The tribes' attorneys were as stunned as their adversaries. Gorton could have advised his clients "that federal treaties were supreme under the Constitution of the United States. They couldn't be ignored. But the Game Department turned a deaf ear to that. I don't know what he told them," the tribal lawyer says. "I wasn't there. But they certainly acted as though they were prepared to fight it to the death."[16]

The U.S. Court of Appeals for the Ninth Circuit upheld the Boldt Decision in 1975. Gorton was thwarted again the next year when the U.S. Supreme Court refused to review the case. "I'll get this case in the U.S. Supreme Court," Johnson says he declared "to considerable laughter around the office" because once a case has been denied review it's rare to succeed the second time around. "I think I'm the only guy who's ever done that,"

Johnson adds, savoring the memory of being Gorton's key assistant in such a high-stakes legal battle so early in his career.[17]

A group of commercial fishermen who asserted that the state had no authority to apportion fish for any purpose other than conservation prevailed in Superior Court. Next up, the Washington State Supreme Court "not only held that the state had no authority to enforce the Boldt Decision, but that recognizing special rights for the Indians would violate the Equal Protection Clause of the U.S. Constitution!" Ziontz, incredulous, wrote in his memoirs. Boldt's reaction was "breathtakingly audacious," the retired Seattle attorney adds: "He put the entire fishery under federal supervision and ordered federal agencies to take over enforcement." Now the U.S. Supreme Court was intensely interested.[18]

EACH MORNING THE U.S. SUPREME COURT is in session, clerks see to one of its oldest traditions: Quills similar to those used as ink pens in days of yore are placed on the attorneys' tables. Framed on Gorton's office wall are 14 quills, each one a souvenir of a case he argued before the court. Half of them involved Indian issues, including the pitched debate over taxing cigarette sales at reservation smoke shops. Chief Justice Warren Burger observed that Gorton made "the best arguments before the Supreme Court of any attorney general in America."[19] Justice Byron "Whizzer" White, a Rhodes Scholar and fierce questioner, concurred. One of the ones he lost, however, was the Boldt Decision—6–3 in the summer of 1979. Burger joined Justices Stevens, Brennan, White, Marshall and Blackmun in voting to affirm. The dissenters were Rehnquist, Powell and Stewart.

Writing for the majority, Stevens said the language of the treaties was as unambiguous as the high court's decisions in six previous fishing treaty cases. Footnoted is the appellate court's scathing opinion that the state had engaged in "extraordinary machinations" to resist enforcing treaty fishing rights. "Except for some desegregation cases . . . the district court has faced the most concerted official and private efforts to frustrate a decree of a federal court witnessed in the century."[20] Justice Powell, writing for the dissenters, asserted however that "nothing in the language of the treaties indicates that any party understood that constraints would be placed on the amount of fish that anyone could take, or that the Indians would be guaranteed a percentage of the catch. Quite to the contrary, the language confers upon non-Indians precisely the same right to fish that it confers upon Indians, even in those areas where the Indians traditionally had fished. . . . As it cannot be argued that Congress intended to guarantee non-Indians any specified percentage of the available fish, there is neither force nor logic to the argument that the same language—the 'right of taking fish'—does guarantee such a percentage to Indians."[21]

Gorton's opposition to the Boldt Decision helped propel him to the U.S. Senate. Over the next 20 years, the tribes viewed his repeated efforts to limit their sovereign immunity as an attempt to settle the score. He was often cartooned as "The Last Indian Fighter," a frontiersman in buckskins, six-guns blazing as he dodged arrows, tomahawks and spears.[20] Talking about revenge, Gorton said, was an easy way for people to avoid arguing the merits of his assertion that non-Indians living on reservations were being deprived of their right to have their disputes heard by neutral courts. The tribes are not separate nations "like France or Germany," but dependent nations with limited sovereignty, he maintains.[22]

"My views on Indians and other minorities are simple and consistent," Gorton said some 36 years after Boldt. "The 14th Amendment mandates that 'no person' shall be deprived of the equal protection of the laws by reason of race. Nothing could be clearer—except to six members of the Supreme Court. In the case of Indians, the court avoids the dilemma by saying that the rights derive from treaty status, not race, a distinction without a difference; a distinction that allows Indian casinos that can't be matched by non-Indians and that can't be affected by the state's policies on gambling, good or ill. In the Boldt Decision, the Supreme Court had to distort the plain meaning of the Stevens treaties, which gave the Indians equal rights to fish, not 50 percent."

Hands clasped behind his head, Gorton mused: "Ironically, my first brush with Indian law, in my first term in the Legislature, was on the side of the Indians in a dispute over state jurisdiction on reservations. . . . The view of the state from a time long before I became attorney general was that the fundamental phrase at issue in the Boldt Decision and in the whole case of *U.S. v. the State of Washington* was 'in common with the citizens of the territory.' And what does that mean? The Indians' view and the United States' view was that it meant the Indians get half of the fish. The state's view, which I still think is absolutely correct as a matter of law, was that it meant that they have the same rights that the citizens did—because Indians weren't citizens at the time the treaties were signed in 1854. What Governor Stevens and everyone meant was that there'd be no distinction between Indians and non-Indians. The Indians would have rights 'in common with' the citizens, which of course meant that 50 or 60 years later when fish began to get scarce and you began to have some kind of conservation laws, the same laws applied to everyone."

Gorton takes some satisfaction that the Supreme Court didn't com-

pletely agree with Judge Boldt and the Ninth Circuit, which "gave the Indians all the fish they wanted for their personal and ceremonial use. So
it's probably five or 10 percent more. The U.S. Supreme Court ultimately
said no; 'in common' meant in common, and everything came out of that."

What Gorton really rues is losing a crucial footnote—literally—that he
believes could have changed history. "It was the biggest mistake in the
practice of law I've ever made in my life," he says, and *prima facie* evidence
that some things are better left alone.

The Supreme Court decision in the fishing rights case was first reported in a "slip opinion"—one not yet formally published. "Of course
you have a right to petition for reconsideration, which is almost never
granted. But the slip opinion made it very obvious that the Supreme Court
didn't know what it was talking about. Boldt's jurisdiction was called the
'case area.' The Indians were to get this 50 percent in the 'case area.' But
there was a footnote in which the Supreme Court majority indicated its
belief that the 'case area' was roughly 40 percent of the waters of the State
of Washington, which was an error. It was *everything*. So the Supreme
Court, in our view, thought it was giving the Indians not 50 percent of the
fish, but 20 percent of the fish. We stewed over that in the office and decided to petition for reconsideration on the grounds that they had made
this mistake. Of course we would have been happy to accept 20 percent,
even though we certainly didn't think it was the law. We got our reconsideration without arguing it. They struck the footnote, however, so the published opinion does not include that footnote about the 'case area.' If we
had let it alone, there it would have been! Later, in other cases, there was
precedent, and it could have been brought up. But it was a terrible mistake because we were being so tough-minded."

Gorton scoffs at the persistent accusation that his opposition to Indian
sovereignty is rooted in racism. "I find racism appalling. But I do have a
profound difference with the tribes. I don't think they should be treated
differently than anyone else. I think the same laws ought to apply to everyone. . . . Discrimination on the basis of treaty status is allowed by the
Constitution, which gives Congress plenary authority. The Indians call
themselves sovereigns. The courts call them quasi-sovereigns, and there's
a difference in that because the Congress of the United States could have
abolished every reservation in the United States of America with one statute. And the Congress of the United States could create that equality. Now
to the extent that it takes property rights, like these fishing rights, we'd
have to pay for them. But it would be a condemnation and there would be
a judgment as to what the value was, and they would receive that value.

"Congress has full authority over relationships with Indian tribes, and Congress has abolished reservations and created new reservations. I think it's very divisive as far as society is concerned to have these rights that really depend on race, even with or without the treaties. For the federal government as trustee and the Indian tribes and other tribal authorities, that's a fundamental difference. As long as they can portray themselves as discriminated-against minorities they're going to create a tremendous amount of sympathy. I think that it has actually been hurtful to Indians because they have not had the same motive to integrate and to get an education and to go to be a part of the wider world that every other minority has. Vietnamese refugees who have been here for only 40 years are higher in economic status than most Indians. Indians isolate themselves because that brings some immediate benefits. But if you're an Indian living on an Indian reservation you don't own your home. It's trust property. It's built by the federal government, and you don't have title to it."[23]

Al Ziontz says Gorton still doesn't get it, but he's not a bigot—just intellectually stubborn. "I know Slade personally. I've gone on a long bike ride with him and his wife. He's a very principled guy. He's not a racist. But his principles don't include a society in which Indians have a separate existence.[24]

ATTORNEYS FOR THE TRIBES exulted in 1973 when the Supreme Court affirmed tribal immunity from state taxes.[25] The arguments of the Attorney General's Office in a 1975 hunting rights case—with assistant AG Larry Coniff at bat—also were rejected.[26] But to the Indians' chagrin, Gorton's persistent genius as a litigator was italicized in one of the last cases he argued before the high court. While the state was still barred from directly taxing Indian merchants, the court ruled in 1980 that it could tax non-Indians purchasing cigarettes on the reservation.[27]

The outcome of *Oliphant v. Suquamish Indian Tribe* in 1978 was also "a severe blow to tribal authority" nationwide. In a 6–2 decision, the U.S. Supreme Court backed Gorton's assertion that the tribes had no criminal jurisdiction over non-Indians.[28]

Unresolved issues spawned by the 1974 Boldt Decision, including the scope of the state's obligation to protect fish habitat and other environmental concerns—"Boldt II"—made their way through the courts for decades and were still percolating well into the 21st Century. In 2007, the U.S. District Court in Seattle ruled that the Stevens treaties imposed a duty on the state to fix thousands of highway culverts—from Neah Bay to Walla Walla—that hinder fish passage.[29]

For several years, Gorton maintained that Congress should buy back the Indians' rights to off-reservation salmon through condemnation proceedings, much like the government acquires land for a new freeway. After achieving condemnation for public necessity, a court could determine the dollar value of the treaty rights and send the bill to Congress, the attorney general told the 1976 Pierce County Republican Convention. "Redress is the duty of all the people in this country, not just a few fishermen in a handful of Western states." Two years earlier, they had practically expelled him from the party for urging Nixon to resign. This speech met with rousing applause.[30]

Ramona Bennett, the leader of the Puyallup Tribe, was outraged. "Rights aren't for sale," she said. "When you sell your rights, you have sold yourself, and the Indians are not for sale. Fishing is our identity. It's our future, our sense of history. Indian children can't grow up to be white people. If they can't find an Indian future for themselves, they're dead. Taking our fishing rights would be genocide. . . . Would Gorton sell his children, or his law degree or his citizenship?"[31]

Nor was Governor Evans impressed by the idea. Purchasing the Indians' fishing rights would be "very, very expensive, and very, very difficult," he said. Evans advocated expanding propagation programs to provide enough salmon for commercial fishermen, anglers and the tribes. That was a lot easier said than done, he acknowledged, especially given international pressures on the resource.[32]

Justice Johnson says it was no secret that Evans and Gorton disagreed over Indian fishing issues, but it was always philosophical, not personal. "Slade had a longstanding close relationship with the governor. Governors do not have authority over the AG; that's true, but they can (exert influence)." Johnson's predecessor as chief of the attorney general's Game and Fisheries division, Larry Coniff, was reassigned in 1975 for criticizing the Fisheries director, Thor Tollefson, at a Fisheries Department Christmas Party.[33] Tollefson shared Evans' view that the resource should be divided equally among the sports, commercial and Indian fishermen. An outspoken ideologue, Coniff was a holdover from O'Connell's days as attorney general. His indiscretion gave Gorton an opportunity to install Johnson. It certainly wasn't a sop to Evans. The tribes would come to view Johnson as a greater threat than Coniff because he was so shrewd.

Gorton always "had my back," Johnson says. When the bumptious Dixy Lee Ray became governor in 1977 Johnson says she tried to get him fired more than once—the first time over a case that stemmed from a major salmon kill on the Columbia. The Washington Public Power Supply System had the river drawn down in the middle of a fall Chinook run to check the intake structure for a nuclear power plant at Hanford. When WPPSS officials denied culpability, Johnson moved to have their license revoked, which effectively put a red-tag on the bonds for their nuclear plants. Soon, a limo-load of Wall Street lawyers arrived in Olympia and asked for an audience with the attorney general. Gorton guffawed and sent them down the street to plead their case with Johnson, who boasts that he "beat 'em big time" and ultimately secured a spawning channel and a hatchery.

Incensed by Johnson's swagger, Governor Ray wrote Gorton to say he had to go. "I'm the attorney general," Gorton replied, "and the assistant attorneys general serve at my pleasure, not the governor's." The governor fired off another letter, to which Gorton tersely replied, "After your next election, your successor may discuss it with the attorney general."[34]

THE REVERSE DISCRIMINATION CASE Gorton argued before the U.S. Supreme Court in 1974 was the year's most explosive civil rights issue: To what extent could state colleges and universities reach out to admit racial minorities at the risk of excluding qualified Caucasians?

Marco DeFunis, 22, a Sephardic Jew, sued the University of Washington Law School in 1971. Although he had higher scores than more than a dozen black and Hispanic applicants who were admitted, DeFunis was rejected. "If he had been black, he would have been in. He was kept out because he was white," his lawyer told the high court. Gorton countered that DeFunis was in fact only "marginally qualified." His scores lagged behind numerous other white applicants also denied admittance. The twist was that a local court had ordered the university to provisionally admit DeFunis. The state Supreme Court reversed the ruling but U.S. Supreme Court Justice William O. Douglas intervened, issuing an order that kept DeFunis in school.[35]

The case drew huge national attention, with more than 30 *amicus curiae* briefs filed by interested parties on both sides. Archibald Cox, the renowned Harvard Law School professor, offered to argue the case on behalf of the University of Washington. The former Watergate special prosecutor had already written a friend-of-the-court brief supporting the university's stand. Gorton politely but firmly declined the offer, telling reporters, "We're going to argue it ourselves. Specifically, I am." Asked about speculation that he was just after publicity to boost what the media viewed as a likely campaign for governor in 1976, Gorton laughed and observed that defending racial quotas likely would cost him votes, not burnish his image. The truth was that he "wasn't about to sit back and let someone else have all the fun" of arguing cases before the highest court in the land. He didn't run for attorney general to push paper at the Temple of Justice.[36]

"Welcome to the big leagues! You've got nine of the smartest people in the country asking you questions," Johnson says, recalling the six times he helped Gorton prep for the Supreme Court and his own appearances in the years that followed. "It's a real high. Slade was very good at that, in part because he had prepared so thoroughly. We got former U.S. Supreme Court clerks and the National Attorney Generals' Office to do moot courts for us, so that was great preparation."

For the DeFunis case, Gorton followed his usual routine, arriving in Washington, D.C., five days early. He holed up in a modest room at the Quality Inn within shouting distance of the Capitol. A reporter from *The Seattle Times'* Washington Bureau found him there, plopped on the bed in socks and shirt sleeves, surrounded by mounds of documents. Several pairs of tennis shoes were piled in a corner. Gorton confessed he'd taken a break for a round of tennis with one of Congressman Pritchard's legislative aides, but mostly it was all work and no play. He'd spent most of Sunday in a moot court staged by the Lawyers Committee for Civil Rights Under Law, which included a number of former Supreme Court clerks. "They grilled me!" Gorton grinned. "It may well be tougher than what will happen before the Supreme Court justices." Preparation, he said, was "everything." Surprisingly, he revealed that he was nervous before any public appearance, "whether it's the United States Supreme Court or the Davenport Kiwanis Club. You tend to get very keyed-up. . . . The buildup of adrenalin is of great assistance in doing an adequate job."[37]

After all that work, things ended in a fizzle. The high court ruled the case was moot. DeFunis was nearing graduation, magna cum laude, no less.

NO ONE CAN EVER RECALL seeing Slade Gorton sweat in a courtroom. But a rash act of Evergreen pride in 1977 could have spelled trouble. Gorton was poised to argue a case on behalf of the Washington State Apple Advertising Commission, challenging a North Carolina law stipulating that containers of out-of-state apples had to be labeled with a U.S. Department of Agriculture grade. The core of Gorton's argument was that Washington State's standards were demonstrably superior. "In other words, an extra fancy USDA apple won't necessarily be an extra fancy under Washington's grading system." To protect its growers, North Carolina had passed

THE JOLT FROM BOLDT

a law saying state grades couldn't be used in advertising out-of-state apples. Gorton asserted that North Carolina was violating the interstate
Commerce Clause of the federal Constitution. "That was an easy win.
What was not an easy win was whether we had any business in the federal
courts with this case. My client wasn't a bunch of apple growers, who are
private parties. It's the Washington State Apple Advertising Commission,
which doesn't own any apples at all." The major issue, then, was what's
called "standing"—whether a party has the right to be in court.

A week before the high court was to hear the case, the American Bar
Association's annual meeting happened to be in Seattle, with Chief Justice
Burger on hand to deliver his State of the Judiciary speech. The new U.S.
attorney general, Griffin Bell, was also there to meet and greet. Gorton
was the president of the National Association of Attorneys General, so
attendance was obligatory. Sally insisted he take her "because all he did
was talk about the Supreme Court."

The reception afterward featured a cornucopia of Washington products—Chateau Ste. Michelle wines, WSU's Cougar Gold cheese, smoked
salmon and whole pyramids of certifiably extra fancy Washington Red
Delicious apples. The Gortons dutifully made their way through a long
receiving line. After the chief justice offered a cordial "Good afternoon,
Mr. Attorney General," Sally whispered to Slade, "You should have given
him a Washington apple." He'd had a couple glasses of wine and thought
"Why not?!" He strolled over to the hors d'oeuvres table, selected one of
Washington's finest, got back in line and handed it to Burger, saying,
"Mr. Chief Justice, this is an extra fancy Washington Red Delicious apple.
Remember it a week from tomorrow!" When it hit him—quickly, too—
that this act amounted to an attempt to prejudice the chief justice of the
United States, he imagined the first words out of Burger's mouth a week
hence would be "Marshal, take that man away in chains!"

The court unanimously struck down the North Carolina law, with
Burger delivering the opinion. Gorton framed another quill.[38]

15 | Designated Hitters

O NE OF GEORGE CARLIN'S GREATEST RIFFS compares baseball and football: "Baseball is a 19th century pastoral game. Football is a 20th century technological struggle. Baseball begins in the spring, the season of new life. Football begins in the fall, when everything's dying. . . . Football has hitting, clipping, spearing, piling on, personal fouls, late hitting and unnecessary roughness. Baseball has the sacrifice."[1]

Though he has a reputation for playing tackle, Gorton laments that politics today is more like football than baseball. He loves baseball. Although he intervened decisively three times over a quarter-century to save big-league baseball for Seattle, his heart belongs to those lovable losers, the Chicago Cubs. He can close his eyes and see himself as a 10-year-old at Wrigley Field in 1938; hear the roar of the crowd and the whack of a bat launching a triple into left field. He can smell the peanuts and remember the snap of the casing when he took his first bite of a ball park hot dog slathered with mustard and relish. He keeps a meticulous scorecard. Don't interrupt him. It's serious business.

Before Gorton helped Seattle acquire the Mariners, Seattle had a big-league team for one not-so-golden year. The Seattle Pilots' hapless 1969 season is immortalized in Jim Bouton's *Ball Four*, one of the best books—many say *the* best—ever written about baseball. The Pilots traded the future American League Rookie of the Year, a lippy kid named Lou Piniella, to Kansas City at the end of spring training. You can look it up.[2]

WITH NO ASSURANCE of a prime tenant if a domed stadium was built, bond issues had failed in 1960 and 1966. Facing strike three, stadium boosters enlisted American League representatives and heavy hitters, including Boston outfielder Carl Yastrzemski, to campaign for the new proposal that was part of the 1968 Forward Thrust package Gorton had championed as a legislator. Voters backed the $40 million stadium proposal and Seattle got the Pilots.

Old and undersized, Sick's Stadium would be their home until the

Kingdome was erected. The site selection process proved controversial, which mattered little in the larger scheme of things because unfortunately—or maybe not—the Pilots were one and done. The club still holds the dubious dual distinction of being the only team in Major League Baseball history to move after one season and the first to declare bankruptcy. At the end of spring training in 1970 the franchise was sold to Bud Selig, a Milwaukee auto dealer destined to become commissioner of Major League Baseball. Lock, stock and balls, the Pilots landed in Wisconsin and were reborn as the Brewers.[3]

"The Pilots were financed in such a way that they would have gone bankrupt even if they had sold every seat in that ratty old minor-league field," Gorton says. "So all that fall and winter of 1969-1970 we were worried about whether they were going to leave. Dan Evans was governor; John Spellman was King County's new executive and I was the new attorney general. We went looking for a new owner. But this was pre-Gates; pre-Allen; pre-Microsoft. There was no enormous wealth here then—no angel to buy the team, keep the club in Seattle and do it right. Eddie Carlson, the civic booster who had headed up the Seattle World's Fair, and some others advanced the idea that the Pilots should be community-owned, an idea the Major League Baseball owners *detested*."

In January of 1970, Gorton, Evans, Spellman, Carlson and Seattle's new mayor, Wes Uhlman, made a pilgrimage to Oakland where the owners were having their winter meeting. "They assured us the Pilots were going to stay in Seattle," Gorton recalls. Not to worry. "We'll find a way to do it. We don't want to move them. Thank you, gentlemen, for all your hard work on behalf of baseball!" After the delegation departed, the owner of the Washington Senators in essence declared, "Well, I hope we gave those guys enough rope to hang themselves."

When the moving vans were loaded a few months later, Gorton realized he was on deck. "Isn't there something we can do?" he said to himself. Then he answered his own question: "Well, if there's somebody who is going to do it, it's going to be the attorney general."[4]

TO TAKE ON MAJOR LEAGUE BASEBALL, Gorton sent to the plate a designated hitter destined for the Bar Association's Hall of Fame. "Bill Dwyer was perhaps the greatest trial attorney I've ever known," Gorton says. It was Dwyer who dazzled him when they squared off as young lawyers in an antitrust case in 1958; and it was Dwyer who asked him to testify as a character witness for John Goldmark in 1963 after the Okanogan Democrat was smeared as a Communist and lost his seat in the Legislature.

Major League Baseball has enjoyed an exemption from the historic
Sherman Antitrust Act since 1922 when the U.S. Supreme Court held
that "the national pastime" is a monopoly meriting special protection.
Recognizing he'd never get to first base by challenging the federal exemption, Dwyer's strategy was to sue the American League in a state court,
seeking $32 million in damages resulting from the loss of the Pilots. The
Kingdome was finally under construction but the taxpayers had lost their
prime tenant. Skeptics observed that even if the state prevailed the verdict
would be monetary. What Seattle wanted was a replacement team.

"Dwyer's idea was to get the case in front of a jury, then put on the witness stand some of the club owners who approved the move of the Pilots,"
Art Thiel recounts in *Out of Left Field*, a lively history of the Mariners.
"Gorton felt Dwyer's strategy had a shot. He figured the jury would find
the owners as loathsome as he did." Gorton had concluded "that if an
American League owner moved into your neighborhood, he would lower
property values."[5]

"Since Washington had recently passed its own antitrust statute, our
state courts were not obliged to follow federal precedent," says Jerry Mc-
Naul, a Seattle attorney who was Dwyer's co-counsel. "That made it imperative that we get the case into our state court system and prevent it
from being removed to federal court. The way we did that was by adding
the concessionaire for the Pilots, Sports Service, as a defendant. It also
gave us an additional argument that even if there was an exemption, it was
lost when the league conspired with a non-exempt party—Sports Service.
We sued for fraud, breach of contract and violation of Washington's new
antitrust statute. That strategy worked. Not only did it accomplish our
objectives, but we also ultimately settled with Sports Service for an
amount that pretty much financed the state's litigation costs in the case."[6]

The owners bobbed, blustered and bunted, using every angle to try
and get the case moved to a federal court. Dwyer, Gorton and Spellman
persisted, attending several Major League winter meetings to ask for a
new team. "We were given five minutes, maybe, after we'd waited around
for two or three days—just treated contemptuously," Gorton recalls.
There was talk that the Giants might move north from San Francisco. It
was all lip service, Gorton says. Delaying tactics. The plaintiffs refused to
fold. They had nothing to lose.

In January of 1976, after six years of wrangling, the trial in *State of
Washington, et al. v. The American League of Professional Baseball Clubs, et
al.* got under way in Snohomish County, north of Seattle. The trial came

to Everett on a change of venue because every prospective King County juror had a financial stake in the case. McNaul has vivid memories of the club owners arriving in the old blue-collar town "with their major egos on their shoulders and their white bucks on their feet and lots of gold necklaces."

The first owner Dwyer put on the stand was heaven sent for the home team. Charley Finley was a micromanaging maverick who ran the Oakland A's with an iron hand and kicked sand in the face of baseball traditionalists. A Damon Runyon character come to life, "Charlie O" alienated the other owners in the league, as well as the majority of his players, managers and employees, despite presiding over three world championship teams in the 1970s. After Dwyer and McNaul took his deposition in Chicago prior to the trial, Finley asked what they were doing for entertainment that night and offered to rustle up a pair of call girls. The offer was declined.

"Finley treated the jury as he had treated Gorton and other Seattle inquisitors over the years: He arrogantly talked down to them, and he repeatedly disclosed strategies baseball didn't want revealed." It didn't take much prodding to get Finley to admit the league did zero to keep the Pilots in Seattle. Jerry Hoffberger, the owner of the Baltimore Orioles, conceded that he and other owners should have done a better job of investigating the finances of the Pilots' ownership. When he left the witness stand during a recess, Finley sauntered past Dwyer and said under his breath, "You've been doing your homework, haven't you, pal?"[7]

"Bill Dwyer just shredded the American League owners," Gorton recalls with awe and satisfaction. "We were about 20 days into the trial when the American League lawyers realized that the jury was going to vote for capital punishment. (Media interviews with several outraged jurors attested to the sentiment in the jury box). Almost overnight, they agreed to expand and give us a team if we'd drop our lawsuit." Shrewdly, Dwyer and Gorton didn't dismiss the case immediately. "We provided in the agreement that the trial would be recessed and continued for a little over a year—until the opening of the 1977 baseball season, to make sure a team was out there in uniform, playing baseball," Dwyer recalled.[8]

The expansion of the American League gave Seattle the Mariners and Toronto the Blue Jays. Major League Baseball returned to Seattle on April 6, 1977, when the Mariners played the California Angels before a Kingdome crowd of 57,762. The M's were skunked, 7-0, and finished their inaugural season with a 64-98 record. There's always next year. Seattle was back in the big leagues.

"We got a wonderful deal," Gorton says. "The new owners only had to pay the same franchise fee the Pilots' owners paid—$5,250,000. There were several minority owners from the Seattle area, but Danny Kaye, the entertainer, was the principal owner of the new Seattle Mariners. He was the first of a series of successive owners whose eyes were bigger than their stomachs. Danny loved the idea of owning a big-league baseball team but they didn't have enough money to build a really competitive team. And they were playing in the Kingdome, which turned out to be an awful place to play baseball and an awful place to play football, for that matter."

It took the franchise another 14 years to post a winning season and eight more after that to acquire a real ball park. But they were safe at home, at least for the time being.

16 | Bicentennial Follies

THE COVER OF *TIME* MAGAZINE on February 17, 1975, did a lot more than pique Gorton's interest. "Scoop Out Front," it declared. There was Henry M. Jackson, looking decidedly presidential. Only 15 years earlier, Washington's squeaky-clean Scandinavian senator was his friend Jack Kennedy's first choice for vice president. There had been so much water over the dam it seemed like a century. Jackson now had "by far his best and certainly his last bona fide opportunity to win the presidency and reinvigorate" the centrist wing of the Democratic Party, *Time* said.

In politics as well as temperament Gorton and Jackson had much in common, even more, in fact, than Gorton realized at the time. Scoop was the wild card in Washington State politics in the bicentennial year. If he won the Democratic nomination for president, the political power grid would be energized by a whole series of job opportunities, from the county courthouse to the state capital, U.S. House and Senate.

Jackson declared his candidacy for president nearly two years out, hoping to foreclose the competition. President Ford was an "honest and honorable man," Jackson said, "a decent man" who had nevertheless failed to meet the challenge of a deepening recession, mounting inflation, the energy crisis and pressing foreign policy issues. Unlike 1972, when he began as a virtual unknown, Jackson was immediately the frontrunner. Ralph Nader's Study Group pronounced him the most effective

Jackson on the cover of *Time*.

member of the U.S. Senate. His name recognition was at 60 percent nationally and rising. Jackson was strong on national defense; an unwavering friend of Israel and foe of détente, appalled by the Soviet Union's oppression of human rights. That he was an unapologetic Cold Warrior earned him the hostility of antiwar liberals in the McGovern wing. Another liability was his charisma deficit. Still, a Gallup Poll ranked him as one of the 10 most admired people in the world. His rivals for the nomination included a little-known, under-funded, one-term former governor of Georgia—a born-again Baptist peanut grower named Jimmy Carter.[1]

In Olympia, Governor Evans was weighing whether to seek an unprecedented fourth term. Although many observers kept the notion percolating, Evans had no interest in running for the Senate in the event Jackson won the Democratic presidential nomination. Gorton, despite what the same pundits and papers were saying, had zero interest in running for governor if Evans didn't. However, he definitely would be a candidate for the Senate if the seat fell open. A Citizens for Slade Gorton Committee was being formed. Seattle Congressman Brock Adams—a tough guy to beat—would be the Democratic frontrunner if Scoop was out of the picture.

Jackson, however, was once again a star-crossed presidential candidate. "As nice a man as Scoop Jackson was, he could put an audience to sleep faster than anybody I have ever seen," a reporter for ABC observed after Jackson's candidacy faltered on the grueling primary trail. The thoughtful man with the engaging smile—as opposed to the abstemious square—got lost in the klieg lights. Carter, the outsider, was the clean breeze in a spring of discontent over the battered domestic economy and international tension. Carter's victory in the Pennsylvania primary in late April was the end of the line for Jackson. Exhausted and frustrated, he flew back to Seattle and bowed out gracefully. "I am a realist," Scoop said. "I gave this campaign everything I had." Still, it was good to be home and there was important work yet to be done. "No state has done more for its native son than the State of Washington has done for me." He would seek re-election to the United States Senate in 1976.[2]

Gorton joked that he was the real loser of the Pennsylvania primary. It was actually a lucky break. His chances of winning a seat in the Senate would be much stronger against Magnuson in four more years. He promptly announced his candidacy for a third term as attorney general. Evans had already concluded with deeply mixed emotions that it was time for something new, although he wasn't sure what it would be. King County Executive John Spellman, an affable pipe smoker, was the favorite for the GOP nomination for governor, while Seattle Mayor Wes Uhlman faced Dixy Lee Ray, an intriguing new face. Never married, the marine biologist was 62, fascinatingly frumpy in her knee socks and

Pendleton skirts, with a pair of dogs for best friends. The former chairman of the Atomic Energy Commission was undeniably brainy, yet also a political naïf with a short fuse. What did she want to change in Olympia? "Everything!"[3]

GORTON AND HIS DEMOCRATIC OPPONENT, J. Bruce Burns, a little-known attorney from Tacoma who had served three terms in the Legislature, were unopposed in the primary. "I'm running against a fellow who knows every dirty trick in the book," Burns said. He vowed to "remove partisan politics" from the office and scolded Gorton for hiring outside attorneys when there were 200 lawyers on the state payroll. Gorton countered that the taxpayers were his client and he was making sure they got their money's worth by deploying the talent to win when a case required special skills. He pointed to Dwyer's home run against the haughty American League owners. The office had aggressively pursued antitrust and consumer-protection litigation, winning cases against the asphalt industry and antibiotic drug manufacturers. With claims filed by more than 80,000 families, the latter was a source of particular pride to Gorton since "literally every citizen in the state was a beneficiary." He had championed Congress's decision earlier that year to amend federal antitrust laws to permit state attorneys general to recover damages on behalf of individual citizens in price-fixing cases and was itching to file more consumer-protection lawsuits. He was unapologetic about his vigorous opposition to the Boldt Decision as "both bad law and bad social policy." Gorton promised to continue being "an activist attorney general."[4]

Burns' charge that Gorton was practicing partisan politics stemmed from the attorney general's headline-making disputes with his predecessor, John J. O'Connell, and Karl Herrmann, the pugnacious state insurance commissioner who famously once issued "NO SMOKING" signs that featured "By order of KARL HERRMANN, Insurance Commissioner and State Fire Marshal" in letters nearly as big as the warning. Gorton also sued Seafirst Bank and state Senator August P. Mardesich, a powerful Democrat from Everett, over a retainer to Mardesich's law partner that was largely passed along to the redoubtable "Augie." It amounted to bribery, Gorton charged.[5]

"Slade and Augie were the two brightest guys in the Legislature in all the years I was there," says Sid Snyder, who began his political career as an elevator operator at the Capitol in 1949 and retired as Senate majority leader a half century later. They relished strategy; their command of seemingly small details inspired awe. It was Mardesich who finally deposed their mutual longtime rival, Bob Greive, as Senate majority leader. The fallout from that struggle led to Mardesich being charged with extortion and tax evasion. The lawyer turned commercial fisherman won an acquittal from a federal jury in 1975 but his political career was all but over. A pair of pros, Mardesich and Gorton rolled with punches. "Slade is a hell of a sharp cookie," Mardesich observed 20 years after their last dustup. The feeling was mutual. "Augie had one of the greatest one-liners I ever heard," says Gorton. "He was a fairly conservative Democrat, and when we were young legislators in the House some liberals excoriated him for abandoning the Democratic platform. Augie stood up and sort of looked at the ceiling, gathering his thoughts. 'Well,' he finally said, 'I always understood that the platform was the place from which you mounted the train. And when the train left the station the platform was left behind.'"

Between Herrmann and Gorton, however, there was absolutely no love lost. The hard feelings dated back to the redistricting wars when Herrmann was a state senator. The insurance commissioner's downfall was actually precipitated by a fellow Democrat, State Auditor Robert Graham, who issued a scathing report detailing irregularities and questionable practices in the agency. Gorton promptly filed a civil suit seeking $500,000 in damages. He accused Herrmann of using his office for personal gain, including "misfeasance, nonfeasance and malfeasance." Herrmann responded with an indignant flurry of countersuits demanding $3.2 million in fines and damages. "He is out to get my political hide," the commissioner told reporters, asserting that the attorney general had hired a convicted "shake-down artist" as an investigator and conspired with "high officials in the Nixon Administration" in a "vicious and vindictive" political vendetta. King County Prosecutor Chris Bayley, a former Gorton deputy, was part of the plot, Herrmann said.[6]

KING-TV, which aired four documentaries highly critical of Herrmann's performance in office, was served with a $1.3 million libel suit. Herrmann also threatened to charge Gorton with malfeasance if he refused to pursue the auditor's recommendation that members of the State Liquor Control Board, including Evans appointees Don Eldridge, Leroy Hittle and Jack Hood, be held accountable for thousands of bottles distributed for "taste testing" and "routine business purposes." The grand jury indictments were tossed out in 1973, but the auditor issued a new finding in 1975. It was particularly discomforting to Evans and Gorton to have Eldridge, their old legislative ally, accused of wrongdoing. Evans had appointed the highly regarded former House speaker to the Liquor

Board in 1970 as part of his effort to reform the system. Evans halted the practice of using "samples" for official entertaining at the Governor's Mansion.[7]

Gorton finally filed a civil suit against the board members. Many viewed the charges as a tempest in a cocktail shaker. The Thurston County Superior Court dismissed Gorton's case. He appealed, pro forma, and was handed a 9-0 defeat by the State Supreme Court. "That was one occasion when I was delighted to lose," Gorton says. "I was forced to bring that lawsuit. Jack Hood was a friend of mine, too. Unfortunately, the episode generated some resentment by Don Eldridge that I regretted and, in retrospect, was justified on his part."

COME NOVEMBER, GORTON HANDILY WON a third term as attorney general and Dick Marquardt, a gentlemanly moderate Republican, bounced Herrmann. Jackson won re-election to the Senate with nearly 72 percent of the vote and Carter edged Ford, who might have profited from having Evans as his running mate rather than the acerbic Robert Dole. A Ford stalwart during the president's bruising battle with Ronald Reagan at the Kansas City convention, Evans had been on the short list of vice-presidential possibles. The Evans delegation headed home deeply disappointed that Dan wasn't on the ticket. Evans chose his words carefully but his body language betrayed his feelings. He took being passed over as a sign that his decision to take a break from politics was a good one. Jackson, meantime, was miffed when Carter picked Walter Mondale rather than him as his running mate and in any case felt better qualified than Carter to be president. Carter had seriously considered Jackson but concluded, correctly, that he and the congenial Fritz Mondale were more compatible. To have had Washingtonians on both national tickets would have been an interesting twist of fate.[8]

Dixy Lee Ray thumped Spellman to become Washington's first female governor. Eighteen months earlier she wasn't even sure whether she was a Republican or a Democrat. Her aide and confidant, Lou Guzzo, former executive editor of the *Seattle Post-Intelligencer*, coaxed her through the minefield of political realities to the expedient conclusion that she was "a conservative Democrat." Shelby Scates, Senator Magnuson's biographer, wonderfully characterized Guzzo as "the Henry Higgins to this unfortunate Eliza Doolittle." Dixy's first foray into politics nevertheless was loverly. Spellman and Ford had the misfortune of facing two quintessential outsiders in a year where the inside seemed upside down.

Gorton and Evans took cheer in two victories for the old team. Joel

Pritchard, the lone Republican in the state's congressional delegation, breezed to re-election with numbers as impressive as Jackson's. And in a race for the state Supreme Court, Jim Dolliver scored a hard-won victory over Fred Dore in the most partisan nonpartisan judicial race in memory.[10]

EARLY IN THE 1977 LEGISLATIVE SESSION, Gorton's enemies cooked up a peculiar little stew that few could swallow. Sponsored by Mardesich and wily old Slim Rasmussen of Tacoma, among others, Senate Bill 2213 purported to increase the quality of legal counsel by allowing state agencies to hire their own lawyers. Gorton thus would be divested of some 130 assistant attorneys general. One wag dubbed it the "Pierce County Bar Relief Act of 1977." The media coverage of the bipartisan outcry that ensued provides a fascinating snapshot of how Gorton was perceived at a crucial juncture in his political career. David Brewster, founding editor of *the Weekly*, Seattle's year-old alternative paper, dissected the brouhaha in a story that displayed his trademark style, a blend of erudition and political savvy:

> Gorton, always admired by the press, rallied the media to his side. After they had finished exposing the bill as the ill-considered ploy it was, its chances sank by the end of the week. . . .The odd episode brings certain realities into daylight. First is the diminishing popularity of Gorton, one of the brightest men in government. Gorton's problems with the Legislature stem back to the redistricting fights of 1965 when he and Bob Greive fought a long battle that left several politicos cut out of a job (including Rasmussen). Gorton was elected attorney general in 1968, and he became a political strategist for Governor Evans, which brought him more enemies. His willingness to file seemingly very political suits . . . brought him more grudges; and his unwillingness to socialize with the legislative crowd (Gorton is a devoted family man) gave him a reputation for haughtiness. Indeed, he does not suffer fools well and there are plenty of fools in Olympia. And so, during the Sawyer-Mardesich years Gorton virtually gave up trying to push any legislation, since his sponsorship was virtually a kiss of death with that gang. That dismal period, combined with the moody inertia of Dan Evans in the last term, caused Gorton's performance to languish. . . . Meantime, Gorton drifted apart from Evans, splitting with him on the Boldt Decision and over what to do about State Parks Director Charles Odegaard's overexpenditures. Gorton said he would have fired Odegaard, and Evans was furious. (Parks, naturally, is one of the departments gunning for Gorton in the present dispute.) Politically isolated, targeted by labor, realtors, Liquor Board allies and the Herrmann machine, Gorton limped home over a weak challenger this last election.

A good Democrat clearly could have beaten him. . . .White-hatted, courageous (for taking on Seafirst), a practitioner of political hardball, brilliant
and candid Gorton remains. But somehow he has failed to develop a core
issue or much deep loyalty.

And so the Democrats pounced, clumsily. . . . The measure is amazingly stupid. Mardesich's signing up as a sponsor is a political blunder
that is difficult to fathom. Why the office should be plundered when
Gorton is admittedly in his last term and numerous Democrats aspire to
it and wish its power is also hard to figure. . . . And then there is the matter of Governor Ray. It is to be expected that Dixy would be wary of Gorton, since so much of her advice is coming from the Pierce County wing
of the party that loathes and suspects him. But she never made any effort
to examine this for herself. . . . [A] single, three-minute accidental meeting is all Gorton and Ray have had since her election. Thus Dixy quickly
joined in support of the dismemberment bill even though it is costly and
would lead to still more departmental autonomy free from executive control. It seems part of her excessive desire, verging on political paranoia,
to fire or emasculate all vestiges of Evansism. To turn the well-informed,
ambitious and scathing Gorton against her for four years is a political
blunder of immense proportions . . .

Whatever the outcome, it has done Gorton a world of good. If the bill
passes, a referendum would be likely—a moral crusade to restore his political stock. The bill, even in failing, has given Gorton a needed kick in
the pants . . . Had lawyerly John Spellman been elected, I'm afraid Gorton would have lapsed into a deeper lethargy in his overrated job. Now he
can see that his office really will be a shadow government and restraining
force on a naïve new executive branch. Ironically, Gorton's real allies are
the new Democratic leadership, who are also rapidly forming an alternative government to the embarrassing Dixy. Given this new mission and
finally out from under Evans's shadow, Slade Gorton might emerge at last
as the state leader (and U.S. senator) he has always wanted to be. Maybe
S.B. 2213 is a good idea after all.[11]

The bill died an embarrassing death after O'Connell and Smith Troy,
another former Democratic attorney general, testified that it was wrong-
headed. Senator Durkan consigned it to the round file. Slade had performed a long-forgotten favor for him years before and Durkan never
forgot.

By April, Bruce Brown of the *Argus* found "The Unsinkable Slade Gorton" in an expansive mood. Gorton did his best to sound beleaguered,
deadpanning that "it has been a struggle just to stay alive." However, "the
assertion is immediately undone by Gorton's broad, infectious laugh. . . .

It is clear that the Legislature has failed to either curb the power of the attorney general's office or derail Gorton's seemingly inexorable progress toward the higher office that he has long confessed an interest in. 'Slade Gorton is a political time bomb,' said one Democratic representative last week, 'and I'm sorry to say it but I think we've laid the bomb right on our own doorstep.' . . . [T]his sort of legislative hassling is exactly what his political career needs. With the Democrats playing a scruffy Sergeant Garcia to his sleek Zorro, he may be able to turn the nearly impossible trick of making his involvement in state government a political asset, and in so doing make his mark exactly where he chooses . . . the cloak of progressive, clean government wrapped around him as a defense against the rabble."[12]

It was not for nothing they called him slippery.

Brewster and Brown were spot on. Whatever ennui was lurking as Gorton began his ninth year as attorney general dissipated in the controversy over the half-baked bill. When they tried to dismember him, he emerged not only in one piece but reinvigorated. The next four years passed in a blur, with Gorton flexing the legal muscle of the new antitrust law to seek damages for the taxpayers in price-fixing cases, including one against the major oil companies operating on the West Coast. He relished arguing several cases before the U.S. Supreme Court. While they largely affirmed the Boldt Decision, the justices were again impressed with his preparation and presence. He was at the top of his game. The 6-2 verdict that the tribes had no criminal jurisdiction over non-Indians was a particularly galling defeat for the tribes. Liberals saw Gorton's opposition to Boldt as "refined demagoguery" and environmentalists in the Evans wing gossiped that he was not a true believer.[13]

Gorton, however, robustly defended a state law that banned supertankers from Puget Sound and was entertained by the fallout from Governor Ray's escalating petulance. Dixy had "an abiding faith that technology could prevent environmental disasters" and scoffed at opposition to a super-port and pipeline at Cherry Point in Whatcom County near the Canadian border. Senator Magnuson, who had championed legislation to protect the marine environment, was incredulous that a marine biologist could endorse such a plan. She branded him a "dictator," which Maggie took as an honorific. In private, he referred to her henceforth as "Madame Zonga," a nod to a tattooed lady who was once one of the lurid attractions on Seattle's First Avenue.[14]

ASSISTED BY NORM DICKS, his former aide, and three other Washington congressmen—Don Bonker, Jack Cunningham and Pritchard—Magnuson sent a bipartisan congressional torpedo into Dixy's hull in the fall of 1977. Twenty-four hours after he introduced it, Congress passed an amendment to the Marine Mammal Protection Act that barred federal approval for expansion of Cherry Point or any other oil port in Washington east of Port Angeles on the Strait of Juan de Fuca, the gateway to Puget Sound. President Carter immediately signed it into law.

Later that month, Gorton went before the U.S. Supreme Court to defend the state law that prohibited oil tankers of more than 125,000 dead-weight tons from entering Puget Sound. The law was struck down in federal District Court after a lawsuit by Atlantic Richfield, which operated the refinery at Cherry Point. Gorton told the justices that without the ability to regulate supertanker traffic, the state's ability to protect Puget Sound from a disastrous oil spill would be dramatically compromised. Dicks, who was on hand for the arguments, praised Gorton's performance and predicted a victory for the state.

Four months later, the high court handed down a decision that was a mixed bag for Washington. Gorton did better than he had expected. The court held that since Congress had already mandated uniform design standards for oil tankers, the state law mandating higher and different standards and banning supertankers from Puget Sound violated the federal Supremacy Clause. However, the state's tug-escort requirements violated neither the Commerce Clause nor the federal government's attempt to achieve international agreement on regulation of tanker design. The lower court had also over-reached in entirely invalidating the state's prerogative to impose pilotage requirements on vessels entering and leaving its ports.

The upshot of the Magnuson Amendment has been to limit the size of tankers that transit Puget Sound. While not super, they carry more oil than the *Exxon Valdez* spilled and they still make hundreds of trips a year through the Strait of Juan de Fuca.[15]

LATER IN HIS CAREER Gorton's environmental record would be characterized as odious. Critics rarely acknowledge his role in establishing the state Department of Ecology, his efforts to protect Puget Sound or his intervention in concert with Magnuson to prevent its magnificent killer whales from becoming circus animals condemned to doing trained-seal tricks in tanks. Ralph Munro, Washington's former longtime secretary of state, maintains that Gorton is "the absolute hero" of that story, aided by the *P-I's* ace Olympia reporter, Mike Layton, who stoked the outrage. Magnuson's enormous clout proved crucial.

It was February of 1976. Munro and his wife Karen were out for a Sunday sail on Budd Inlet at Olympia when they encountered a SeaWorld capture crew. In a scene that seemed like *Apocalypse Now* meets *Free Willy*, aircraft buzzed overhead and depth charges exploded as speedboats herded six terrified orcas toward nets. After frantic calls to several newsrooms went unanswered, Munro reached Layton at home. Soon he was watching from the shore, outraged. Nearby was John Dodge, an Evergreen State College student who went on to become an award-winning reporter. "I'm haunted to this day by their plaintive, eerie cries," he says. So too the Munros, who became whale conservationists overnight. "It changed our lives," Ralph says. "It was horrifying and heartbreaking."

Munro, then working as an aide to Governor Evans, arrived at work outraged Monday morning, brandishing the front page of the *P-I*. Evans, unfortunately, was skiing in Utah. "Our chief of staff thought I was over reacting, so I called Slade. His secretary caught up with him in Walla Walla and he soon called me back. He was so mad over the capture that he said he almost wanted to go out and cut the nets himself. He told me to go to his office at noon and there would be a group of attorneys assembled to help." Gorton's deputies were initially skeptical. "They all started teasing me: 'You want us to do *what*? Save the whales! Give us a break!' But they had orders from Slade and we all went to work."

With a U.S. marshal and the biggest, meanest-looking fisheries officer they could find, they served papers on a SeaWorld official late one night next to the capture raft. Layton and KING-TV's Don McGaffin spotlighted the story as the drama moved to a series of courtrooms. Testimony revealed that about a dozen whales died during the capture of 45 Southern Resident orcas at Penn Cove off Whidbey Island in the 1970s as trappers herded them out of Admiralty Inlet with cherry bombs and separated calves from their mothers. "One of SeaWorld's guys threw down his papers and moved across the courtroom to our side," Munro recalls. "He muttered, 'I'm tired of lying' loud enough for the judge to hear." SeaWorld soon wanted to settle. Munro looked on as Gorton stood in the hall outside federal district court in Seattle and told SeaWorld's attorneys there would be no deal until they agreed to never again seek permits to capture whales in Washington waters. "No way," they said. "OK," Gorton said with a shrug. "Let's go back to the courtroom." They folded. SeaWorld complied with the court's order to relinquish its permit. The orcas it had captured were set free. It was the last orca capture in U.S. waters.[16]

Magnuson, the architect of the Marine Mammal Protection Act of 1972, had been pushing to declare Puget Sound an orca sanctuary. After the Budd Inlet capture, he and his staff whipped up an amendment. "We worked at breakneck speed on the act for two days," says Gerry Johnson, the Seattle attorney who was then an administrative assistant to the senator. "Still, it wasn't fast enough. Time was running out on the restraining order. The senator said, 'Get me Mo (Judge Morell Sharpe) on the phone. I was surprised and told Magnuson, 'You can't interfere with a federal judge.' But he insisted. Magnuson told him, 'I've got this little bill on marine mammals but I need just a few more days to work it out.' When he hung up, Magnuson said, 'He's going to extend the order.' We passed the bill through Congress a few days later."[17]

Magnuson and Gorton were politicians who got things done—each in their own way. Maggie, however, was clearly in decline. By the fall of 1978, Gorton was bored with being attorney general. The wind was also blowing the right way, with the recession deepening and Carter floundering. Bob Moore, executive director of the National Republican Senatorial Committee, came to Olympia to sound out the prospective candidate and reconnoiter.

"Did he give you any encouragement?" reporters wanted to know.

"The fact that he was here makes it obvious they're interested," Gorton said. "I'm going to spend the next year making a decision."[18]

He was already 90 percent decided.

17 | A Gold Watch for Maggie

Mount St. Helens in Southwest Washington erupted like a hydrogen bomb at 8:32 a.m. on May 18, 1980, shedding its summit in a cataclysmic landslide. A mushroom cloud rose 15 miles and a pall of ash rolled east at 60 mph, drifting down like gritty gray snow. It turned day into night in Yakima and Spokane.

The eruption killed 57 people and countless creatures, laid waste to 230 square miles of forest, clogged lakes, rivers and bays and wiped out highways and bridges. Magnuson, the Senate Appropriations Committee chairman, went to see his friend Daniel Inouye, a ranking member. "I've had a volcano go off in my state," Magnuson advised. "Maggie," said the senator from Hawaii, "I've got them going off in my state all the time." "Danny," Magnuson replied with a smile and a pat, "your time will come." Washington state's senior senator had decided to be "scrupulously fair with federal funds," Vice President Walter Mondale once quipped. "One half for Washington State, one half for the rest of the country."[1]

As usual, Maggie brought home the bacon: Nearly a billion dollars in emergency relief. But when he accompanied President Carter on an inspection tour three days after the eruption, TV cameras caught him stumbling as he attempted to navigate the stairs from Air Force One to the tarmac at Portland. A diabetic, the 75-year-old senator had a sore foot that wouldn't heal. Opinion polls indicated early on that it would be risky for him to seek a seventh term. He was president pro tem of the Senate, the realization of a dream. "Go home. Rest on your laurels. You have nothing left to prove," trusted advisers said. "But he couldn't imagine himself not being a senator," said Gerry Johnson, a top aide who resigned at the beginning of 1979. He had clashed with Jermaine Magnuson, the senator's protective spouse. She wanted one last term for her old lion, once the most raffishly handsome man in Congress.[2]

Gorton also couldn't imagine himself not being a senator. It was what he'd wanted to be ever since he was 14 when future congressman Walter

Judd told a wartime assembly at Evanston High School that public service was the highest calling.

In politics, timing is often everything. While most of his brain trust and many potential donors were skeptical, Gorton felt in his bones that 1980 was his year. He believed Maggie was vulnerable and that Carter was an albatross for the Democrats. The president seemed impotent, even whiny. All the charm had evaporated from his Georgia drawl. On the Fourth of July, 1979, lines at gas pumps stretched for blocks. Eleven days later, responding to a bleak memo from his strategist and pollster, Patrick Caddell, the president gave his famous "malaise" speech. Carter lamented "a crisis of confidence" that "strikes at the very heart and soul and spirit of our national will." It was a thoughtful speech laced with candor, just not what the doctor ordered. Americans were disillusioned and pessimistic, out of gas, literally and figuratively. Carter's bracing Baptist sermon wasn't going to pump them up.

That November, Iranian revolutionaries stormed the U.S. Embassy in Tehran and took hostage 66 Americans. The conservative tide that swept Margaret Thatcher into 10 Downing Street was also buoying Ronald Reagan. "Government is the problem, not the solution," Reagan said, adding that the nine most terrifying words in the English language were *"I'm from the government and I'm here to help."*[3]

Washington hadn't elected a Republican senator since former Tacoma mayor Harry P. Cain in 1946, and he was evicted by Scoop Jackson after one controversial term, even in the teeth of the Eisenhower landslide.

Gorton vs. Magnuson was shaping up as one of the most dramatic races in state history, with national implications. The Republicans were counting on Gorton to help them gain a majority in the U.S. Senate. First, however, he needed to win the Republican nomination.

Gorton had invited Howard Baker of Tennessee, the Senate minority leader, to headline his first fundraiser. When other Republicans joined the race, Baker sent his regrets. The only other volunteer for a pre-primary visit was Rudy Boschwitz, an ebullient freshman senator from Minnesota. Slade called to let him off the hook. "I said I'd be there," Boschwitz replied, "and I'll be there." He became one of Gorton's best friends.

VOTERS A GENERATION LATER would be accustomed to hearing Gorton characterized as a movement conservative. In 1980, unless you happened to be an Indian, he was viewed as what he is—an intellectual centrist with libertarian tendencies. During his 22 years in Washington politics, Gorton had evolved as less liberal than Evans and Pritchard (opposition to the Boldt Decision being Exhibit A), but he backed the Equal Rights Amendment and opposed a constitutional amendment banning abortion "because we live in a pluralistic society." His environmental record was also praiseworthy.

Gorton's first hurdle was defeating a self-styled "real Reagan conservative," Lloyd Cooney. A paratrooper in World War II, Cooney was sort of a Mormon Barry Goldwater. In June, he resigned as president and on-air editorialist at Seattle's KIRO, the broadcasting company owned by the LDS Church, to challenge Gorton for the Republican nomination. Emmett Watson, long the sage of three-dot journalism in Seattle, once described Cooney's TV persona as "an unseasoned platter of elbow macaroni . . . [T]he quintessential stuffed shirt: bland, preachy and too self-righteous for comfort." Cooney delivered his pungent management editorials five nights a week, often right from the hip. He had a strong base of support in the resurgent fallout shelter wing of the party, true believers who sported "Impeach the media" buttons during Watergate. To them, Slade Gorton was a highly suspect commodity.[4]

"Cooney was someone you couldn't take lightly," says Paul Newman, the political consultant who worked with the Gorton campaign in 1980. (And not to be confused with the popular actor, although he has some Butch Cassidy bravado—as well as Brooklyn bluntness—in his voice.) "The religious right was emerging and they loved Lloyd. That was the year I became aware of a quantum leap in power they had taken. We couldn't be the enemy. So right from the get-go, even though we knew we couldn't get them on our side, we were nice to them; we respected them. Anything we could do not to be the enemy we did. They never totally unified behind Lloyd."

Gorton bested Cooney by 84,000 votes, ironically making better use of TV. With only 36.6 percent of the primary vote, Magnuson was as vulnerable as they'd believed. Gorton, Cooney and two little-known Republicans accounted for 59 percent. The outcome also illustrated the impact of Washington's blanket primary (now morphed into a regardless-of-party "top two"), which allows voters to cross party lines and vote for whomever they choose. Gorton might well have lost to Cooney in a party-registration primary, such was the strength of the conservative bloc. Cooney, in reality, was less intransigent than his flock. "I found him to be a nice guy, without a trace of meanness," says Gorton. "He endorsed me the day after the primary."

Newman, it was abundantly clear, knew his stuff.

The Gorton-for-Senate campaign was now fully energized, collecting $180,000 from the National Republican Senatorial Committee. They'd already spent most of it, however, and Gorton borrowed $200,000 from his father. Magnuson already had $800,000 and expected his war chest to top $1 million. Slade's supporters sported buttons that said "I'm a Slade Gorton skinny cat."

It was crucial to unify the party behind Slade. "As it turned out we didn't have to do a damn thing," Newman says. "It was done masterfully for us by Jennifer Dunn, the state Republican Party chairman. In the beginning I thought that nobody who looked that good could be that sharp, but she was. She was everything a state chairman should be. And the party came together seamlessly. I became a Jennifer Dunn fan. It was no surprise to me that she later made her mark in Congress."[5]

Gorton's brothers, Mike and Nat, raised $6,000 for the campaign at "Another Tea Party" in Boston, touting him as a potential "third senator from Massachusetts." They fudged, however, in billing him as "a native son who went West." When news of the event trickled back to Seattle, Slade told reporters, "I was born in Illinois and grew up in Evanston. I've never lived in Massachusetts. I chewed Mike out royally when I saw it. I was mad as hell." But he kept the money.[6]

"THE FIRST TIME I MET SLADE," Newman recalls, "was after I got a call, probably from his old pal Joe McGavick, inviting me to a meeting with his brain trust. I told them right up front, 'I think you're going up against Goliath without a stone in your sling.' I was impressed, however, that Slade didn't care. His attitude was 'We're going to do this regardless of how tough it is,' and even later on when we were really sucking for money he was always determined. He was putting it all on the line. Everybody understood that Slade was smart and that his arrival would raise the average IQ in the Senate by probably five points, but I don't think people realized how tough he is. He's the equivalent of an intellectual alley fighter— willing to mix it up. I told them, 'We've got to take Warren Magnuson's greatest strengths and use them against him—jujitsu them. And we've got to use Scoop Jackson as our weapon.'"

They developed a survey to gauge how deeply the issue of seniority resonated with the public. One choice was this: "To protect its future, a state needs one senior senator with great influence and one junior senator who is building seniority, even if that means less influence in these difficult times." The response crossed all lines—age, gender, race, political

Slade Gorton

Washington's Next Great Senator!

You're Slade's special interest.

Slade cares about your family as deeply as he cares about his own.

Vote Nov. 4

Slade knows how to produce a balanced budget and create a surplus...because he's done it!

He's earned the chance to serve us in the Senate!

A "Next Great Senator!" flier from the 1980 campaign. *Washington State Archives* leanings. The junior senator and senior senator choice was overwhelming. They had a stone for the sling: "Slade Gorton, Washington's Next Great Senator!"

"For one of our first TV commercials, we got big pictures of Slade and Maggie and made jigsaw puzzles out of them," Newman says. "The voice over was, 'While we have Scoop Jackson let's build more seniority.' That was the zinger! Jackson was our fail-safe. We'd pull one of the pieces off Maggie's face and replace it with a piece of Slade. It looked as if Maggie was morphing into Slade."

Inflation was a huge issue in 1980. Newman scouted up newspaper ads from the 1930s, reviewed the prices and filmed a commercial outside the little grocery store beneath Gorton's campaign headquarters in Seattle: "When Senator Magnuson went to Congress, $10 would buy you this. Here's what $10 will buy you today!"[7]

"Paul's theme was brilliant," says Gorton. "The key thing was to not disrespect Magnuson. He'd been a great senator. Now, after 44 years in Congress, Maggie deserved a gold watch."

HELEN RASMUSSEN, a veteran volunteer for moderate Washington Republicans, was the unsung hero in 1980, according to Newman. "Nobody thought Slade could win, so it was hard to find someone to commit to taking the campaign manager's job, and we didn't have any money to pay them anyway. We needed someone who knew the state, knew how to mobilize the volunteers; someone who was a hard worker. Several said that was Helen, so I went to meet Helen. Well, she was incredible— smart, tough, a good sense of humor to be able to take all the crap thrown at campaign managers and still laugh it off. I came back from our meeting and said, 'She's the one.' That probably was as good a strategy choice as any I made."

Gorton's driver during the campaign was Joe McGavick's politically precocious 22-year-old son, Mike. They'd first met when Mike was 8, towing a wagon filled with brochures boosting his dad's campaign for the Legislature. "Driving those long stretches in Eastern Washington, you're the only person he's talking to," McGavick recalls, which is precisely why he jumped at the chance.

After a few days, Gorton began asking, "What would you change in what I just said?" The college kid's suggestions soon began finding their way into his speeches. With his ruddy Irish cheeks and mop of curly hair, some took "Mikey" for just another go-fer. But not for long. He ended up running Gorton's campaign in a large chunk of the state. McGavick would become an influential aide, indefatigable campaign manager, chief of staff and "second son"—someone Slade counted on to tell the truth, even when it hurt.

IN 1968, WHEN MAGNUSON faced the first of two challenges from state Senator Jack Metcalf, a rustic conservative from Whidbey Island, he was already looking long in the tooth. He'd barely avoided an upset in 1962. George Lois, a wild hare New York ad man, came up with a memorable ad campaign based on the fact that Magnuson was the architect of some of the most progressive consumer protection legislation in U.S. history: "Keep the Big Boys Honest."

Magnuson was not nuts about his nickname but Lois loved it.* He styled his client as a champion of the average Joe and Jill. Buttons and bumper strips declared "I've got kids. I'm for Maggie!" and "I'm a House-wife. I'm for Maggie."

To offset the notion that Magnuson was dod-dering, Lois cooked up a 30-second commercial that's included on a list of the 100 greatest TV spots of all time: Voice over as Magnuson looks into the camera: "Senator Magnu-son, there comes a time when every young senator shows that he's putting on years. Senator Magnuson, there comes a time, sure as fate, when slim sena-tors assume a more im-pressive stature. So, once

Warren G. Magnuson—"Maggie" to millions— deserved a gold watch after 44 years in Con-gress, the Gorton campaign said. *Washington State Archives*

youth is gone, once dash is gone, what can you offer the voters of Wash-ington?" Magnuson reflects for a moment, then taps his noggin. Voice over: "Let's keep Maggie in the Senate!"9

---

* At a White House dinner during World War II, Winston Churchill heard FDR call his poker-game buddy "Maggie" and advised, "Well, young man, don't mind it at all. I think the reason I'm prime minister of Great Britain is that I'm known as 'Winnie' in every pub in the country."8

Metcalf's boast that he was "Jack the giant killer" really was a sling with no stone. Magnuson trounced him. For good measure, he did it again in their 1974 rematch.

Six years later, TV would play a decisive role in both campaigns. But Magnuson was now 75 and Gorton was no Metcalf. Newman's masterstroke was another commercial inspired by that first survey on seniority. It opened with a portrait of Jackson. The voice-over intoned, "Did you know that Scoop Jackson, our *junior* senator, is 68 years old?" Jackson was so vigorous that no one realized he was 68, but everyone knew Magnuson was older. Shuffling along, he looked all of 75, while Jackson could have passed for 58 and was recently rated as America's most effective senator. "But he will probably retire in six or 12 years," the unseen announcer suggested. "Isn't it time to start building new seniority while we still have Scoop Jackson in the Senate? That's why now is the time to honorably retire Senator Magnuson and replace him with an energetic, experienced, intelligent public servant—Slade Gorton."

Jackson was furious, telling reporters the ad made it seem as if he was endorsing Gorton. "It's deliberately misleading!" he shouted. Privately, Scoop reportedly remarked, "That's the greatest ad I've ever seen. How do we force it off the air?"[10]

WITH SIX DECADES OF SENIORITY, "Scoop and Maggie" were one of the most formidable tag teams in Senate history. Ensconced at Appropriations, Commerce, Interior, Energy and Armed Services, they greased the skids of Washington's postwar emergence as a progressive American state. They built dams that transformed the Northwest economy and pushed Washington to the forefront of aviation, consumer protection, cancer research, fisheries and international trade. In his biography of Magnuson, Shelby Scates observes that "They played to separate sides of the voter psyche: Maggie, the earthy, carousing, good guy to have a drink with; Scoop, the sober, up-at-daybreak, home-in-the-evening citizen." Magnuson, though, "had never enjoyed as broad or as deep a base of support" as Jackson, notes Robert G. Kaufman, Jackson's biographer. By 1980, Magnuson's infirmities "contrasted starkly with the vigor of his opponent."

The Gorton campaign featured photos and footage of Gorton jogging, "Imagine a senator with 22 years of public-service experience who is still in the prime of his life." And imagine two candidates spending nearly $1 million on advertising, most of that on TV. It was a stunning sum at the time. In terms of media-buy sophistication and total expenditures, the

Gorton-Magnuson race was a watershed event in Washington State politics. The game would never be the same.

A spot the Magnuson campaign ran after the primary attempted to blunt the age issue with droll humor. Magnuson, in fact, was making it more of an issue than Gorton. An invisible announcer observes that the senator had slowed up some in recent years. "Sure, I walk a little slower," Maggie says. Then, with a twinkle in his eyes and a craggy grin, he adds, "But the meeting can't start till I get there."

Refusing to debate, Magnuson took the unusual step for an incumbent of running attack ads. He warned labor union members that "if you elect Ronald Reagan and a Republican Congress, you can put the Exxon sign on the White House." As for being a "big spender," the senator said he would plead guilty to being the guy who brought billions in federal money to the state. "Would they send back the money for the West Seattle and Hood Canal bridges? For the cruise missile? For Hanford and the Columbia Basin? How many Columbia River dams do they want to tear down?"[11]

THE DEMOCRATS HAD THREE CROSSES to bear—Iran, inflation and interest rates. Still, a mid-October poll for *The Seattle Times* found Magnuson with a 10-point lead. The Gorton camp was confident it was eroding. Jackson could sense it, too. He stumped the state tirelessly, declaring "We need Maggie!" The Gorton campaign detected desperation when Magnuson reached back to the 1960s to blast Slade's legislative record, claiming he was a flip-flopping Scrooge who had even voted against funds for kindergarten. Evans and Pritchard immediately cut radio spots saying it wasn't so.

The campaign coverage was also hurting Magnuson, who looked lumberingly ancient on the 6 o'clock news, especially when they cut to his lean, athletic 52-year-old opponent. Magnuson's statements were "gruff homilies." Gorton answered questions with rapid-fire details and bounded confidently onto stages. New commercials softened Gorton's reputation for aloofness by showing him mingling tie-less in small groups of just-folks admirers. At the Spokane Democrats' Autumn Festival, two men helped lift Magnuson, who "managed to ascend two stairs onto the platform." His legs seemed "barely able to support his chunky body" and his hands often trembled.[12]

Ron Dotzauer, who went on to become a sought-after political consultant, was Clark County's young auditor in 1980, running for secretary of state against Ralph Munro. Twice during the campaign, he found himself on stage with Jimmy Carter, Jackson, Magnuson and a host of other Democratic poobahs and hopefuls. "Maggie's staffers sat me right next to him. My orders were to grab him by the back of his pants and help him stand up whenever there was an applause line. You couldn't tell it from the front," Dotzauer cackles, "but I had him by the back of his britches."

Howard Baker stumped with Slade in Seattle and Spokane after the primary. The campaign hoped he would allude to Maggie's appetite for alcohol, but the minority leader flatly refused. The epitome of a Southern gentleman, Baker loved the Senate. Later, Baker explained to Gorton his conviction that a senator could appropriately campaign for any candidate of his party in any state. However, he could never make negative comments about a colleague. "He taught me something about the United States Senate as an institution," says Gorton. Baker is one of his political heroes.

IN THE WANING DAYS, Ted Kennedy jetted to Seattle for a fundraiser and gave one of his patented tub-thumpers to several thousand of the faithful. "Maggie can achieve more in six minutes than other senators achieve in an entire six-year term!" Kennedy thundered. In a twist, Magnuson was also hoping for coattails from Jim McDermott, the young state senator who had settled one score by depriving "Madame Zonga"—the despised Dixy Lee Ray—of renomination and was thought to be leading John Spellman in the race for governor.

Magnuson spent upwards of $1.25 million; Gorton about $900,000, but he nearly matched the incumbent on advertising buys. Newman's ads for Gorton, produced by David Stern's Seattle agency, were clever and well timed.[13]

The Seattle Times endorsed Gorton, saying he had "the vigor, vision, experience and grasp of today's realities to give Washington State a fresh, effectively different voice in the Senate." The *Post-Intelligencer* said Magnuson's seniority was too valuable to lose but "Gorton, we think, would make a first-class senator." *The Spokesman-Review* in Spokane praised Gorton's "stamina and vision." The *Weekly,* striving to offer Seattle a cliché-free zone, gave a worldly shrug: "Senator Magnuson is out of political fashion; his staff isn't what it used to be; if he serves out the next term that will be 50 years in Congress, which is too long for anyone's brain. Senator Gorton is smooth, quick, up with the political trends, a cunning legislator, master of the data. It adds up to an irrational choice: vote for Maggie."[14]

Barnstorming 6,600 miles across America on election eve, hapless

Jimmy Carter ended up in a crowded hangar at rain-swept Boeing Field with Jackson, Magnuson, McDermott, Tom Foley, Norm Dicks, Mike Lowry and a cheering throng of loyal Democrats whistling past a grave-yard. Magnuson introduced the president. Carter took his hand. Motor-ized Nikons captured Maggie smiling bravely as the president poked the air with a clenched fist. Carter knew from his number-crunchers that it was all over. When Scoop saw Patrick Caddell's last tracking poll that af-ternoon he sensed a tsunami. Gorton's trend line mirrored Reagan's. He'd caught Magnuson 10 days earlier and gained every day.[15]

ON NOVEMBER 4, 1980, Ronald Reagan carried 44 states, including Wash-ington. Gorton won going away, capturing 54 percent of the vote to end Magnuson's storied career in Congress. Another high-profile Democratic casualty was the party's 1972 presidential candidate, George McGovern of South Dakota. He was crushed by another Newman client, Congressman James Abdnor. The "Reagan Revolution" gave Republicans a Senate major-ity for the first time since 1954. Spellman handily outpolled McDermott.

Magnuson complained that national TV projections of a GOP sweep almost two hours before the polls closed in the West cost him votes. His advisers conceded, however, that it didn't alter the outcome. "It's like be-ing in a plane crash," said Eric Redman, a Magnuson strategist. "Every-body gets killed regardless of their merits."

Rather than thinning out as the returns grew increasingly gloomier, the crowd at Magnuson's campaign headquarters got bigger as the night wore on, anticipating the senator's valedictory. With Jermaine at his side and a phalanx of loyal aides and admirers, Magnuson arrived just before 11. "We were subject to some sort of tidal wave that swept into the State of Washington," the old campaigner said, eyes sad but upper lip stiff. He'd never before lost an election. "There is a time to come and a time to go. And I guess after 48 years they decided to turn me out to pasture."

"No!" came a shout. Others, many of them weeping, began to chant, "We love you, Maggie!" Magnuson gave them a smile and a wave. "I wish my successor well. In a way, he's probably done me a favor."

"No! No!"

"Well," the senator concluded, "maybe he's doing you a favor." Then he turned fondly to his partner since 1952. "I don't know what I'm going to do without you, Scoop." Jackson, voice quavering, put a hand on his shoul-der. "Maggie, it's the other way around. I don't know what I'm going to do without you."[16]

A few blocks south, Gorton, as is his wont on election nights, was squinting at the numbers, county by county. He refused to be excited by the early returns, despite congratulatory calls from vice-president-elect Bush and Strom Thurmond and the whoops that greeted two network projections that he was the sure winner. He remained in a curtained-off room, checking returns with his county chairmen. Finally, he plopped himself edgily in front of one of the four TV sets in his cramped head-quarters and "impatiently switched channels just as his 21-year-old son, Tod, got the picture adjusted. His daughters, Becky 18, and Sarah, 20, flanked their father, while Sally stood behind him and smoothed his hair." When his lead in King County was confirmed, he at last emerged to cheers.[17]

"It's important for all of us to remember that Senator Magnuson has served our state extremely well. He has been a great senator," Gorton said, promising to work tirelessly to keep the faith. "It's a wonderful and euphoric evening, and I'm beginning to be in awe of what we have wrought." Finally he flashed a triumphant grin.[18]

A study in wounded grace, Magnuson phoned to offer congratulations, "and if you need any help setting up your new office, just let me know." A few minutes later came another call. "Congratulations," Scoop said. "We're the senators from Washington State. I want to have lunch with you next week."[19]

18 | The Giant Killers

THE GREAT COMMUNICATOR was having a difficult time communicating with the freshman senator from Washington State. The aura of the Oval Office and the president's charm usually did the trick. But Gorton had been spending too much time with Pete Domenici, the stubborn Budget Committee chairman, worrying about the deficit, insisting some tax increases were necessary. Gorton had a "Yes, Mr. President, but . . ." comeback for every argument. Finally, Ronald Reagan threw down his pencil and muttered, "Damn it, I can't listen to all this!" Afterward, Gorton tried not to smirk. "I must say I did speak rather sharply." Being a U.S. senator was wonderful.[1]

Steeped in seniority, wrapped in marble and fastidiously decorous, some say the U.S. Senate is the world's most exclusive club; others describe it as the world's greatest deliberative body, while cynics dismiss it as "the place where bills go to die." Gorton's knowledge of the institution allowed him to hit the deck running. He relished its traditions. Why was Daniel Webster's desk assigned to the senior senator from New Hampshire when Webster represented Massachusetts? Gorton knew. He enjoyed the banter in the private dining room where the senators could let their hair down. He quickly absorbed the rhythms of the place, the strategy sessions and committee hearings, the 19th-century, third-person etiquette on the floor.

The 97th Congress could have been called The New Faces of 1981. Most senators were in their first terms and few members of the House had served longer than six years. Reagan's coattails carried 16 freshmen to the Senate. Ten of them, like Gorton, had no prior service in Congress. The freshman class also included 33-year-old Dan Quayle of Indiana, Chuck Grassley of Iowa, Al D'Amato of New York, Arlen Specter of Pennsylvania and Slade's friend Warren Rudman, the former attorney general of New Hampshire. Chris Dodd of Connecticut, Irish, ambitious and the son of a former senator, was one of the Democrats' two freshmen. "Only 10 states have the two senators they had six years ago," Dodd observed. "Of the 20 committee chairmen in the Senate, 14 of them are in their first terms or the beginning of their second terms. I left the House after six years. I ranked in the top 50 percent in seniority out of 434 people. It's an incredible phenomenon."[2]

Gorton made the most of the opportunity, quickly emerging as the leader of the self-styled "Giant Killers" who had bounced the likes of Magnuson, McGovern, Herman Talmadge, Gaylord Nelson, Frank Church and Birch Bayh. Old hands chafed at their impatience. William Proxmire, the quirky Democrat from Wisconsin, said they were undermining the collegiality of the institution, especially that Gorton. With the exception of Gorton and Rudman, *The Wall Street Journal* said, the Giant Killers were more like a "Popsicle Brigade."[3]

GORTON'S PROUD PARENTS—both would be gone within two years—looked on with his siblings, spouse and children as Vice President Mondale administered him the oath on January 3, 1981. Mary Ellen McCaffree, who'd helped him win the redistricting wars in the Legislature, was busy setting up the office. She was Gorton's first chief of staff, the administrative assistant, or A.A. as they say on the Hill. Chris Koch, a University of Washington Law School graduate who had worked for Magnuson, agreed to stay on for a few months to help them learn the ropes.

The legislative assistants—L.A.s—included Marianne McGettigan and Creigh Agnew. McGettigan was in law school at Boston University when Gorton came through on a recruiting trip as attorney general in 1974. He snapped her up. She joined the office right after graduation and quickly advanced to senior assistant attorney general. McGettigan was the only member of his AG staff Gorton brought East. Agnew, who handled energy and natural resource issues, was an Everett girl who had worked for Bremerton Congressman Norm Dicks. She was well versed on timber issues. Ritajean Butterworth, a friend, campaign organizer and adviser since 1959, became Gorton's state director, setting up offices in Seattle, Spokane and Vancouver.

McCaffree, McGettigan, Agnew and Butterworth are four of the hundreds of talented women Gorton attracted to public service. Their ranks include a governor and a state Supreme Court justice. Others became influential attorneys and corporate executives. McGettigan became chief lobbyist for the Major League Baseball Players' Association, Agnew a vice president at Weyerhaeuser. Anna Perez, Gorton's communications director in 1982, went on to become press secretary to First Lady Barbara Bush. Invariably characterized as a chilly geek, Gorton is in fact kind and thoughtful, according to female former staffers. They call their sorority "The Gorton School of Public Affairs"—as opposed to "The Clinton School of Affairs that Have Become Public."

Flirtation or any sort of sexual harassment? "You're kidding?" says former legislative assistant Cassie Phillips, laughing out loud. "The underlying reason Slade has hired so many women is that he doesn't know the difference. He's utterly gender and color blind."

Perez says, "Slade didn't think of me as black; he thought of me as Anna. The only judgment he made about me was the quality of my work. I think Slade's attitude toward gender and race is like Ella Fitzgerald singing Ira Gershwin."[4]

McGettigan marveled that Gorton's brain was always working overtime. When the Equal Rights Amendment was about to expire in the summer of 1982—three states short of ratification—Slade asked her to draft a simple-majority bill that would by statute provide women the same rights. McGettigan ran it by a law professor Gorton admired. The opinion was that it would pass constitutional muster, "but women's groups opposed it, which I thought was shortsighted," the former legislative assistant says.

Avoiding the corps of professional staffers who pop from office to office on Capitol Hill, Gorton rarely hired anyone without Washington State roots. He wanted people who understood the issues back home. Painstaking competence was his expectation. He also fostered a casual atmosphere. On the day Agnew joined the staff, she greeted Gorton with a cheery yet deferential "Hello, senator." When the staff meeting began, Gorton announced, "Creigh just made the most serious mistake any of you can make. I want all of you to call me 'Slade,' not 'senator.'" He also gave them leeway and courtesy that many other staffers on the Hill envied, according to Koch, who succeeded McCaffree as chief of staff in 1983 and went on to become chairman of the Federal Maritime Commission. "He was a delight to work around. Slade Gorton was never an asshole to his staff, and that doesn't sound like a big deal until you've seen the way many other politicians treat their staffs."[5]

Gorton is so single-minded, however, that he can be oblivious. The Butterworths have a summer place next to the Gortons' on Whidbey Island. Sometimes Slade would open a window or door at 8 a.m. on a day ostensibly dedicated to leisure and yell out to Ritajean "as though we were in the office and he wanted me right now, like I worked for him 24 hours a day, regardless of where." No shrinking violet, she would shout back, "Not now, Slade!" He'd be chastened until the next time. No one on the staff knew or understood him better. He trusted her implicitly.

·

J. Vander Stoep, who was elected to the Washington State Legislature at 23, became chief of staff during Gorton's second term in the Senate. The button-down young Republican from Chehalis was a classic Gorton find. Heading Gorton's staff "was the best job in D.C. by far," Vander Stoep says. "He wanted no part of the day-to-day operations. When it came to the management of his organization all he would say to me—and this was very rare—was 'This staff person can't keep up.' And I would proceed from there. But if I was hiring competent people, that's all he wanted. His philosophy has always been 'Hire talent; don't hire experience.' Not that experience is bad, but we're not looking for 20-year Capitol Hill veterans in defense or education or what have you, because you can learn the subject matter very quickly if you have talented people. 'What we want,' Slade always said, 'is energy and commitment.'"[6] It was no surprise, then, that Mike McGavick dropped out of college to follow Gorton to D.C. He became Slade's legislative assistant for foreign and defense policy, immersing himself in the arcane details of weapons systems. "He was a college senior but he had a complete grasp of the issues," Gorton recalls. "He had general officers calling him 'sir.' That's how impressive he was."

Gorton's staff had a bipartisan reputation as one of the best in Congress, says former state legislator Max Vekich, an activist with the Longshore Union and cradle Democrat. The Vekiches were frustrated at every turn as they attempted to get a family member out of Croatia at the height of the strife in 1993. "So who do you call in Washington, D.C., at 4 a.m. when you desperately need help? You call Slade's staff." Vekich apologized to Vander Stoep for rousting him out bed. "This isn't politics," the chief of staff said. "This is family."

ON INAUGURATION DAY, Iran finally freed the 52 American hostages after Carter released several billion dollars in frozen Iranian assets. Carter had been an indefatigable lame duck but Reagan's people maintained that Iran's grand imam, the steely-eyed Ayatollah Khomeini, gave in because he was worried about dealing with a tough new president. Others saw the timing as one last insult to Carter.

On the domestic front, the challenges faced by Reagan and the new Congress were the most daunting since the 1930s. High inflation, high interest rates and high unemployment had pushed the "Misery Index" to record levels. Inflation averaged 13.6 percent during 1980. The Fed kept interest rates high, with the prime around 20 percent, for much of 1981. It would take two years to tame inflation. Reagan's approval rating sagged to 35 percent at the beginning of 1983. Yet the president's Norman Rock-well optimism never waned. He had the role of a lifetime. Promising to prime the pump by slashing taxes, Reagan also wanted to cut federal pro-grams and boost military spending to combat communism. Gorton only years later came to see him as an exemplar of big picture greatness.[7]

Howard Baker led the Republicans' first Senate majority in 27 years. Democrats still held the House, 244-191, with Tip O'Neill, a master of the legislative minuet, hunkered down as speaker.

"COMMITTEES ARE THE HEART of Congress, where much of the work is done, policy formulated, reputations made, power wielded."[8] Fortunately for Gorton, the Senate Republicans were democratic—the most demo-cratic, in fact, of the four caucuses in Congress. In the other three, leader-ship weighed applications and decided who got what. Senate Republicans chose committee members in a set of rounds, like the National Football League draft in reverse, with the senior member picking first. Freshmen who had served in the House got to choose in the order of their seniority. The next rung was former governors, who ranked below even the most junior former House members. When it was Gorton's turn to pick, it was down to alphabetical order. That made him fourth of the 10 GOP fresh-men with no prior experience.

Gorton had boned up on the committees, asking Jackson and other old hands for advice. Having secured spots on Commerce, Science & Trans-portation and Environment & Public Works, he was pleased with his good fortune.

The 53-member caucus had a festive dinner before the third round. Gorton button-holed Domenici: "Pete, this was a fascinating day. It looks to me like there might be a Budget Committee seat avail-able when they get to me in the third round. Would you advise that I take it?" Do-menici was impressed. "I watched you today," the sena-tor from New Mexico said. "Today you made two good picks for your state. Tomor-

Gorton and Domenici: Deficit hawks.
Gorton Family Album

row if you want to pick for your country, pick mine." Gorton picked Budget. It would put him in the thick of things for most of his career in the Senate, with Domenici as mentor and friend.

The son of Italian immigrants, Pietro Vichi Domenici worked in his father's grocery business after school. A smart, athletic boy, he earned a degree in education from the University of New Mexico and pitched one season for the Albuquerque Dukes, a Brooklyn Dodgers farm team. "I had a great fast ball but walked way too many. Every now and then the manager, who was the catcher, would get so mad he would tell them what I was going to do so they could hit me and give me a lot of shit." Domenici pitched it right back, a lifelong trait. He taught math at a junior high before attending law school. Afterward, he quickly became active in politics, heading the Albuquerque City Commission before winning election to the Senate in 1972. Domenici managed to be a loyal Republican while remaining tenaciously independent. "His collegial, bipartisan approach belied a fierce determination to get his way and won admiration from all quarters"—grudgingly from the White House.[9]

Gorton shared Domenici's concerns over deficit spending. Gorton was for a strong military, having been a colonel in the Air Force Reserve, but he was against giving the Pentagon a blank check. During his first term, Gorton was frequently at odds with his president over budget priorities. The White House found him to be an annoyingly independent thinker. "Slade was articulate. He liked to be part of getting things done, and he already had legislative acumen," Domenici says. "He quickly became a player. If I had to choose five people to bring into the back room with Bob Dole—where 50 percent of the business is done around here—I wanted this guy with me."

Gorton also won a slot on the Small Business Committee and the chairmanship of the Merchant Marine Subcommittee. Gallingly to the tribes, he was named to the Select Committee on Indian Affairs. Early on, he successfully sponsored an amendment to the Lacey Act, which was enacted in 1900 to prevent transportation of poached fish and wildlife across state lines. Gorton's amendment elevated violations of state or tribal fisheries laws to federal felonies. The move filled a law enforcement gap but the tribes were wary. The Washington State Department of Fisheries and the National Marine Fisheries Service had already launched a sting operation that in 1982 led to the arrest of 72 Indians for illegally catching or selling salmon and steelhead. David Sohappy Sr., a longtime fishing rights activist from the Yakama Tribe, and his son, David Jr., were sentenced to five years in prison by Jack Tanner, the first African American federal judge west of the Mississippi. Earlier in his career, Tanner had championed Indian fishing rights but he said the law was the law. The Columbia River Inter-Tribal Fish Commission observed with disgust that the "Salmonscam" defendants stood accused of damaging fish runs by illegally taking 2,300, fish while ocean fishermen legally caught 129,000 from the same run of upriver spring Chinook. The Sohappys became martyrs to the cause and the tribes grew unhappier yet with Gorton. A year later, their lobbying derailed his attempt to push through a bill to ban gillnetting of steelhead by Indians. Anglers asserted that the commercialization of the prized game fish sanctioned by Judge Boldt was threatening its survival, a notion the tribes hotly contested.[10]

AFTER SIX MONTHS IN WASHINGTON, D.C., Gorton was exhilarated and exasperated. He felt instantly at home in the Senate; there just weren't enough hours in the day. "We are assigned to so many committees that we can't become experts on much of anything," he told *The New York Times*. "I'm a member of five committees and more than half a dozen subcommittees. It's very frustrating to have to miss at least 50 percent of the meetings of committees of which you're a member because of scheduling conflicts; you can only be in one place at a time. . . . Another impression is the inability to delegate. As Attorney General, I had 205 attorneys working for me. Obviously, I did the things I found most interesting . . . but the overwhelming bulk of the work of an office like that was delegated. I was primarily a recruiter and an administrator."[11]

Dodd was the other senator the *Times* asked to size up the new Congress. New to the Senate but not to Congress, the liberal from Connecticut complained, "This town is so narcissistic that all we talk about is each other. . . .I think this Congress is far more political, far more partisan, than anything I've ever seen before. Whatever else any Democrat may have to say about the Administration, the Congressional Republicans' discipline and cohesiveness far outstrips anything I've ever seen in the Democratic Party."[12] Gorton had to smile. Congress was the big leagues, but Dodd clearly had never been in combat with the likes of Bob Greive and Augie Mardesich.

"One pleasant surprise," Gorton said, "has been the fact that I've found the Senate to be less partisan than the Washington State House of Representatives, where I spent 10 years. (In Olympia) the majority party caucus often met as frequently as three times a day. Everything was determined by the party caucus. Members of the minority party rarely got to contribute to debate. Here, the equivalent of the caucus meets very rarely. The ability of an individual to contribute something to the ultimate process is much greater." That said, Gorton observed that his party was not nearly as unified as Dodd thought. "We have no more agreement now within the party on many of the social issues which we may be dealing with later this year or early next year than the Democrats do, and perhaps even less. So, again, what is that direction? I'm pleased with the direction as far as economics is concerned. To the extent that we have a party platform which takes very, very rigid positions on some of the social issues, I don't like it particularly."[13]

Gorton was one of six GOP freshmen on the Budget Committee. The others were Grassley, Quayle, Steve Symms of Idaho, Mark Andrews of North Dakota and Bob Kasten of Wisconsin. All but Gorton had served previously in the House. The most junior "Giant Killer" quickly became one of the most influential.

HAVING PROMISED NOT TO DO SO and, at 70, certainly old enough to know better, Ronald Reagan put both feet on the third rail of American politics in the spring of 1981. At the urging of David Stockman, his wunderkind budget director, Reagan endorsed raising the full retirement age for Social Security from 65 to 68 and dramatically reducing benefits for those who opted to take early retirement at 62. The plan would have saved $50 billion over the next five years while shoring up the trust fund. Jubilant Democrats, seeing their first break in the political clouds, vowed to protect the mother of all entitlements and basked in the public's outrage. Speaker O'Neill called the plan "despicable." Claude Pepper, the 80-year-old chairman of the House Select Committee on Aging, stopped just short of pronouncing it the most infamous attack on Americans since Pearl Harbor. Reagan beat a hasty retreat. A resolution condemning any attempt to "unfairly penalize early retirees" was unanimously approved by the Senate.[14]

When in doubt, appoint a commission. As commissions go, however, this one had some bipartisan moxie, with Alan Greenspan as its chairman.

Gorton said he wished they hadn't all chickened out. They should have just done it and endured the flak. Stockman was right, Gorton said. Adjustments to the full retirement age and penalties for early retirement were imperative. Sooner or later—and sooner was better—Congress would have to make tough choices. Otherwise the Baby Boomers reaching retirement age in the 21st Century would find the system bankrupt. "What's lacking is the will," Gorton said. "Everybody knows what that study will recommend."[15]

Reforms were enacted two years later, yet Gorton said more long-term repairs were needed. He continued to push for scaled back cost-of-living adjustments. And it cost him.

19 | Deficit Hawks

THE CENTERPIECE OF SUPPLY-SIDE REAGANOMICS was a combination of spending cuts totaling $41.4 billion and across-the-board tax cuts for individuals and business—some 25 percent over the next three years. The largest tax cut in American history cleared Congress largely intact in July of 1981, costing the treasury $750 billion. O'Neill warned that the plan risked huge deficits, runaway inflation and unconscionable gaps in the safety net for the less fortunate. Howard Baker conceded that it was a "riverboat gamble."[1]

Domenici's Budget Committee was mowing a wide swath through the Democrats' social programs as Thanksgiving approached. Although most of the cuts were actually just reductions in the growth of federal spending, battle lines were drawn—right, left and center—over billions in alphabet soup: AFDC, Aid to Families with Dependent Children, the basic welfare program; CETA, the Comprehensive Employment and Training Act that subsidized a wide array of entry-level public jobs; UDAG, the Urban Development Action Grants, and WIC, the nutrition program for Women, Infants and Children. Revenue Sharing with the states was also on the chopping block, together with food stamp expenditures. Liberals said the cold-hearted Republicans even wanted to reclassify ketchup as a vegetable to save money on subsidized school lunches for poor kids.

Domenici, Gorton and the other Republicans on the committee, with the exception of Dan Quayle, wanted to move more quickly than the president to rein in domestic benefit programs. In the bigger picture, however, they were moderates. Reagan definitely wasn't buying their plan to raise taxes to help balance the budget by 1984. Theoretically, slashing spending and revenues would tame inflation and jump-start the economy.

Reagan was also intent on winning passage of his proposal to boost the Pentagon's budget, which would double the deficit, already $45 billion. Surprisingly, that troubled the president a lot less than Domenici, Gorton and a number of other Republicans, not to mention conservative Democrats. "You can tell me don't worry about deficits," said Ernest Hollings of

South Carolina, who lost his job as Budget Committee chairman in the Reagan Revolution. "We didn't worry about deficits and that is why we're the minority party."[2]

The Reagan brain trust believed the Domenici plan was unlikely to be approved by the House and worried it would jeopardize Republican re-election prospects at mid-term. Domenici, who skillfully worked both sides of the aisle, polled the committee on how it wished to proceed. The Republicans were resolute, the Democrats diffident. J. Bennett Johnston, a conservative Democrat from Louisiana, warned, "We're not going to be able to do it without the active involvement and leadership of the Great Communicator himself." Gorton was undeterred, saying, "The flag of leadership is passing from the White House to this committee."[3]

Domenici and Gorton had asked the administration to submit more detailed economic assumptions underlying its proposed cuts. Stockman and Treasury Secretary Donald Regan made back-to-back appearances before the budget committees to plead their case. When Gorton defended the Export-Import Bank, which helped finance sales of Boeing jets, Stockman insisted that its funding should be cut by $220 million. The pain had to be shared. Gorton found an ally in Nancy Kassebaum of Kansas, already a senior member of the committee after only two years in the Senate. Boeing had a plant in her state, too. They pushed through a motion to restore half the funds for the bank, substituting cuts in subsidized housing and community development to offset the move.[4]

While the Budget Committee backed federal spending cuts of $34.6 billion in fiscal year 1982, it also approved Gorton's amendment to add $18 million to help Public Health Service hospitals in Seattle, Baltimore and New York City comply with federal fire safety codes. That enabled them to qualify for Medicare and Medicaid reimbursement and made it easier for them to survive on their own. Magnuson was pleased. Maggie had championed the hospitals, out-foxing President Nixon to keep them open. Gorton also helped save the Urban Indian Health program in 1983 when Reagan wanted to kill it.[5]

IN THE WAKE OF THE ASSASSINATION of Egyptian President Anwar el-Sadat by Muslim fundamentalists in October of 1981, Gorton and Bob Kasten sponsored a resolution to veto Reagan's $8.5-billion plan to sell Saudi Arabia five Boeing-built Airborne Warning and Control System planes, nearly 1,200 Sidewinder missiles and upgrades for its F-15 fighter jets. Some critics of the AWACS deal called it a dangerous, cynical swap to protect access to Saudi oil and give the U.S. a military foothold in the

Mideast. Gorton shared Jackson's view that the sale could compromise a major U.S. defense system and threaten Israel. On the other hand, the AWACS deal would keep 1,500 Boeing workers in Seattle busy for the next six years. The Boeing lobbyists knew it was hopeless to woo Scoop. They kept making runs at Slade. A week before the AWACS vote, employees at the Renton plant were told over the PA system that if they wanted to let their new senator know how they felt they could dial his local office. Hundreds of calls poured in to Gorton's offices.[6]

Reagan and his congressional allies asserted that the assassination emphasized the importance of reaching out to all moderate governments to help secure a peace in the Mideast tinderbox. Four months earlier, Prime Minister Menachem Begin had the Israeli Air Force take out Saddam Hussein's nearly completed nuclear reactor in Iraq. Now Begin's partner in the Camp David peace accords was dead, and Reagan was pushing ahead with the largest single arms sale in U.S. history. It was "Reagan or Begin." The Israelis were outraged. The Saudis, with their own army of lobbyists, had agreed to many of the U.S. conditions. Gorton noted, however, that they had their own eight-point peace plan and were showing little willingness to cooperate in the Camp David accords to phase in a settlement that offered any hope of lasting peace.

Gorton, Kasten, Quayle, Frank Murkowski of Alaska and Mack Mattingly of Georgia were summoned to the Oval Office for persuasion. A vote against the AWACS sale would be perceived as giving Israel too great a say in U.S. affairs, the wavering and recalcitrant were told during a tense meeting with the president. Gorton bristled: "Prime Minister Begin doesn't control my vote." With one of his trademark head shakes, Reagan replied, "You may not think Israel is controlling your vote, but the world will." During a meeting with another group of opponents, the president had warned, "You're going to cut me off at the knees. I won't be effective in conducting foreign policy."[7]

William Safire, the influential *New York Times* columnist, admired Gorton for showing spine but was outraged by the tenor of the debate. "Missing from the reaction to the assassination of Anwar el-Sadat is the element of outrage," Safire wrote after the White House arm-twisting session. "In radical Arab headquarters in Beirut and Tripoli, the reaction is glee; in Moscow, the party line is a smug he-brought-it-on-himself; in Israel, there is concern for its treaty with an Egypt without Sadat, and in Washington there is sadness, resignation and calculation about how the tragedy can be exploited to rally support for the sale of AWACS to the Saudis. It is as if the world were taking for granted this triumph of terrorism. The only genuine anger detectable at the White House today is directed at those Republicans who dare to defy the President on the sale of our most guarded technological military secrets to the power whose blackmail payments supply weapons to the P.L.O. . . . Should the United States base its national security decisions on what others mistakenly 'perceive' to be our motives? Are we so afraid of 'world opinion' that we must cater to its perception even when we know it to be wrong? . . . When the un-Reaganlike . . . pitch failed to persuade his fellow Republicans—some of whom did not take kindly to the threat that they would be labeled anybody's stooges—Mr. Reagan stressed party discipline and finally used the Sadat assassination as evidence of the need to build a new bastion."[8]

Gorton, Kasten, Quayle and the others proposed that Reagan guarantee the Senate that he would press the Saudis to cooperate in a Mideast peace effort and agree to follow U.S. guidelines on operation of the radar planes.

Reagan's desperate jawboning was winning conversions and collecting stragglers. A week before the final vote, Gorton extracted White House support for another $26 million to renovate the Public Health Service Hospital in Seattle. Still, on October 28, the day of the vote, he was holding out for more. Gorton's feisty mother—"Her name was Ruth, but sometimes it was more like 'ruthless,'" Slade quips admiringly—had died two weeks earlier at the age of 83. Her senator son arrived at the weekly Senate prayer breakfast and deduced from the attention he received that many were attempting to divine which way he'd vote. Around 10 a.m. Gorton finally "got what neither the lobbying efforts of Boeing Company Chairman T.A. Wilson nor the charms of Ronald Reagan were able to give him"—the written promise from the president: The U.S. would extract from the Saudis a signed agreement to protect the AWACS technology and not use the new weaponry to threaten Israel. Smiling broadly, Gorton navigated a gantlet of reporters as he headed for the floor. "That did it for me," Gorton said of the letter before providing a key vote in a hard-won 52-48 victory for Reagan. "I was convinced three weeks ago that the president would win. The whole dynamic is on the side of the president. He has the ability to make a deal if a deal is necessary."

Gorton insisted that the hospital money and his vote were "entirely separate" but also conceded with a grin that any lawmaker who had made an agreement with the administration would not admit it. Deal-making aside, Gorton said he concluded that "in foreign policy initiatives, there should be a presumption in favor of supporting the President of the United States."

John Glenn, the astronaut hero turned politician who was on the losing side, summed up the intangibles. "Some of it is party loyalty," the Ohio Democrat said, "and some of it is sitting down with the most powerful single person in the free world, maybe the whole world. When the president says, 'I need your help,' that's a rather potent argument."[9]

GORTON TEAMED UP with Jackson in 1982 to hand Reagan a rare—but as it turned out, temporary—defeat on a defense-rated issue. The Defense Department's budget request included 50 new Lockheed C-5B *Galaxy* troop transports at $182 million apiece. Jackson and Gorton offered a bargain-basement alternative that also benefitted Boeing and the commercial airlines, which were being battered by the recession. The C-5's were way too pricey, the Washington senators said, also pointing to the aircraft's troubled lineage. They asserted that the country could save as much as $6 billion by instead acquiring "the most cost-effective commercial wide-body cargo aircraft," namely surplus Boeing 747s at $44 million each. In the battle that ensued, Jackson and Gorton faced off against two powerful members of the Armed Services Committee, John Tower, the Republican chairman from Texas, and Sam Nunn, the ranking Democrat from Georgia, as well as Defense Secretary Caspar Weinberger. Despite his nickname—"Cap the Knife"—Weinberger argued forcefully that the expenditure for the C-5's was well justified since the *Galaxy* could use rough landing strips and discharge cargo from both its nose and tail. Jackson and Gorton countered that the C-5 was unreliable and more costly to operate and maintain. But Senator Nunn wanted those 8,500 jobs for Lockheed's plant at Marietta, Georgia.

"The whole establishment was against us," Gorton says, marveling at the memory of Jackson in action. Drawing on his encyclopedic knowledge of the issues and legislative moxie, Jackson tailored their case to winning over "the broad coalition of senators either alarmed by the cost of the Reagan buildup or representing districts with economically distressed industries hoping for similar help from the Reagan buildup."

Boeing's powerful lobby shifted into high to help, buoyed by bankers, subcontractors and the airlines. Jackson and Gorton won a bruising victory when the 747 amendment was approved 60-39 in May of 1982. "That was our first, almost equal partnership we had on a major issue in the time I was there," Gorton says, "and it was all kinds of fun, between Scoop's reputation and authority in the field of defense, and my being one of the new majority and pretty outspoken." Then Gorton learned another fact of life in Congress: The lower house often has the upper hand. The Pentagon and the defense establishment wanted the new plane and generated a landslide of votes in the House to scrap the 747 amendment. "When they went to conference, we had no chance," Gorton says. Weinberger did agree to buy and test three used 747's, a puny consolation prize but better than nothing.[10]

THE MOUNT ST. HELENS National Volcanic Monument established by Congress in 1982 was a bipartisan victory for the Washington delegation, including Gorton, Jackson and Congressman Don Bonker, the ambitious Democrat from Vancouver who represented the area around the volcano. Underwhelmed by the Forest Service response, Bonker and his staff developed the preservation legislation. Environmentalists pushed to have the area declared a National Park, which would have been more restrictive than the deft compromise Reagan signed into law.

The Forest Service now manages 110,000 acres for research and recreation, while Weyerhaeuser retained some 45,000 acres within the blast zone, trading the rest of its holdings to the Forest Service for other land. Company foresters nurtured 18 million Douglas fir seedlings on an ash-covered wasteland that once looked as it might never produce another tree. Inside the national monument, logging is prohibited. Dr. Jerry Franklin and other Northwest forest ecologists have learned important lessons from one of the world's most unique biological laboratories. Nature proved to be remarkably resilient—more so by far than Uncle Sam. Chronic budget shortfalls have compromised Forest Service maintenance of the visitors' centers, roads and trails. The debate over access and development is ongoing.[11]

THE SEATTLE SCHOOL BOARD's hotly debated program to achieve desegregation by busing children out of their neighborhoods generated a statewide ballot measure that found 66 percent of the voters opposed. In 1982, as Ken Eikenberry, Gorton's successor as attorney general, was prepping to defend the initiative's constitutionality, Gorton introduced legislation that would have prohibited any arm of government—including the U.S. Supreme Court—from using busing to promote integration of public schools. Even the adamantly anti-busing Jesse Helms of North Carolina voted no, worried that Gorton's plan would be too vulnerable to a court challenge. It was defeated, 49-42. Flayed by liberals, Gorton made no apologies. "I felt then and feel today that assignments by race for whatever reason are blatant violations of the plain language of the 14th Amendment," he said three decades later.

The Supreme Court narrowly disagreed, ruling that the initiative, not busing, violated the Equal Protection Clause. Eikenberry, following Gorton's example and encouragement, had resolved to argue his own cases before the Supreme Court. The former FBI agent and state legislator won three terms as attorney general and lost a close race for governor. In the courtroom, however, he was no Slade Gorton, at least on that day. His nervousness was palpable, the justices impatient. He lost 5-4. If Eikenberry took home a quill, it's unlikely he had it framed.[12]

WITH THE DEFICIT ACCELERATING toward a record $100 billion for fiscal year 1982 and the Treasury growing another year older and deeper in debt, Gorton proved a disappointment to many conservatives. But so did Barry Goldwater. Orrin Hatch of Utah and Dennis DeConcini of Arizona were pushing hard to muster the two-thirds vote required for a constitutional amendment mandating a balanced budget. They were getting little but lip service from the president, who had backed away from his campaign promise to balance the budget by 1984. The defense buildup was too important; new taxes unthinkable. Hatch emphasized that the amendment was flexible, allowing deficits in time of war, national emergencies or major recessions.

"I'm a strong partisan of balancing the budget as quickly as we can," said Gorton, "but having made that decision in 1982 doesn't give me the feeling that I'm wise enough to make that decision for the year 2082, or 50 years from now, or for that matter even 10 or 12 years from now. To put an economic theory into the Constitution is too long a jump for my taste." Goldwater agreed. "If we haven't been able to balance the budget any more than we have in the last 40 or 50 years, a constitutional amendment isn't going to help," the conservative icon said.

The amendment finally passed, only to fail in the House. Four years later, it fell one vote short in the Senate. Gorton was still opposed, offended at the "cut and paste" job its proponents wanted to do on the Constitution: "Compare the elegant language of the preamble. Compare the soaring positions adopted by the Congress in the 14th Amendment. . . . The Constitution is no place for congressional graffiti."[13]

As the Senate began debate on the 1983 budget, Republicans were also split on how to fix Social Security. House GOP leaders said the $40 billion in savings advocated by Domenici and Gorton was dead on arrival. They suggested removing Social Security from the budget entirely, an expedient the gun-shy president pronounced "interesting."

Domenici lit another Merit, inhaled deeply and allowed that the president's comments "were not terribly helpful." It was imperative to include the $40 billion in savings. Otherwise the solvency of the system was in jeopardy. "I consider it to be truth in budgeting, nothing more." Gorton chimed in, "This is a good budget, because it is a fair budget" that faces up to the long-range problems of Social Security.[14]

Fall found Jesse Helms licking his wounds over a succession of defeats at the hands of Gorton and the other centrists. They'd scuttled his plans to ban abortion and legalize school prayer. "Conservative it ain't," he said, "Republican it is."[15]

GIVEN HIS ROOTS and rapidly growing reputation as a comer, *The Boston Globe* took a keen interest in the Yankee who'd wandered West. It published a front-page profile that shows how the quotable new Republican senator was perceived back East early on:

> U.S. Sen. Slade Gorton was eating grapefruit—or was he on his puffed rice?—and talking about the family fish business, which he never did want to go into. . . . He retains the looks of a New England Yankee, though: a preacher, perhaps, with his long face and tall forehead and pale eyes. . . . Gorton thinks of himself politically as a "moderate to liberal in the context of the Republican Party," but confesses to not being sure what those labels mean. . . .
>
> Gorton is described by those who know him as a sophisticated and calculating politician with the somewhat inscrutable ways of a man from a faraway state where partisan politics is not the rule. He projects a "Gee, whiz" Midwestern kind of enthusiasm. . . .
>
> By the time his single scrambled egg arrived, the senator was well into explaining his political philosophy. He felt trapped by labels, and inclined toward lengthy explanations. To oversimplify: Economically, Gorton adheres to a traditional conservative philosophy—balance the federal budget and limit government. However, he wants to emphasize that he is not in favor of dismantling it. At the same time, he is inclined to be protective of the environment, supportive of the Equal Rights Amendment, and a believer that the government should remain neutral about abortion.
>
> Gorton does not wish to be identified with many of his New-Right classmates, or their leader, the President. . . . As a member of the budget committee, he was an early supporter of the Administration's spending-cuts proposals, but now finds himself put off by, among other things, its "unwillingness to deal with (reductions in spending for) defense and an unwillingness to deal with the fact we'll need more revenues." . . .
>
> Gorton says he enjoys the entree that being a U.S. senator provides, but misses the climate of Washington State and its informality. He also feels safer there. He runs every morning. . . .

Other than Alaska and Hawaii, the state of Washington is farther away from the nation's capital than any other place in America, and it feels that separateness, according to Sen. Gorton. He will tell you that the political psychology of the state is such that its citizens are more concerned with matters state and local than national. They are neither fazed, nor do they seek actively to faze, the ways of Washington, D.C. With a smile, Slade Gorton says, "That's probably one of the reasons senators from Washington tend to serve so long." Of course, this was entirely all right with him.[16]

20 | Ship Shape

ORTON DESCRIBED HIMSELF as a budget groupie but Commerce was his No. 1 committee. With broader jurisdiction than any other substantive committee in the Senate, Commerce covers science and transportation, including aviation, space exploration and shipping by land and sea, as well as fisheries and telecommunications.

The last chairmanship available to the freshest of the freshmen was the Merchant Marine Subcommittee, about which he knew nothing. He immersed himself in the intricacies of maritime regulation and global competition. A billion dollars' worth of federal subsidies dating back to World War I added up to "giving free dope to a junkie," one critic wrote. "The situation is so bad that the government now has to pay public money to have privately owned ships built in noncompetitive domestic shipyards. But even worse, despite all this gravy, the industry still has trouble staying afloat." The American Merchant Marine was burdened with both the highest operating and the highest construction costs in the industry, as well as whirlpools of red tape. Foreign carriers were handling three-quarters of all goods entering or leaving the U.S. by ship.[1]

Through myriad court cases and bureaucratic turgidity, one of the major facets of U.S. maritime law, the Shipping Act of 1916, had evolved into a convoluted regulatory regime that met neither the carriers' nor the shippers' needs. It was an arcane field of law with few political rewards, especially for a freshman senator. "The politically tricky part was that shipping conferences existed in every trade lane in the world by virtue of having antitrust immunity," says Chris Koch, an expert on maritime law. "Slade was no great fan of antitrust immunity," his former aide notes. "He was, however, a pragmatist, and international shipping conferences were not going to be abolished as a political matter in the 1980s by a bill in the U.S. Senate eliminating their antitrust immunity. Nor was a political coalition to support an outright abolishment of shipping conferences going to get the support of carriers, ports or maritime labor."

In 1982, Senator Howard Metzenbaum scuttled Gorton's first reform proposal by threatening a filibuster. The intransigent liberal Democrat from Ohio asserted that the Gorton plan would ultimately produce higher prices for consumers. "Metzenbaum took the dogmatic and politically easy approach of simply saying antitrust law should apply," Koch maintains. "Slade had a more challenging task: 'How do I write a bill that would correct the problems with the existing law, and get the support of shippers, U.S. carriers, ports, and maritime labor unions?'"

Gorton regrouped, assembling a coalition of supporters. It included the Port of Seattle, freight forwarders and the Washington State Horticultural Association, which represents Washington's tree fruit industry. They were all eyeing expanded opportunities along the Pacific Rim. The Ocean Shipping Act that won unanimous approval of the Commerce Committee in 1983 granted cargo carriers limited antitrust immunity and a predictable, efficient regulatory regime. Groups of individual shipping companies could set common rates and coordinate sailings without the approval of the Federal Maritime Commission. Gorton added an important limitation: Shipping conferences could not prevent one of their members from deviating from the conference's common rates. Any shipping line could agree with a customer to provide service for a lower price than the conference. Gorton believed this right of "independent action" would undermine the pricing effectiveness of shipping conferences.

Time and tide would prove him right. Metzenbaum and other critics fumed, however, that Congress was poised to "solve" a problem by creating monopolies that would only make it worse. Gorton countered that the United States was the only country in the world that enforced antitrust laws in the shipping industry. "My strong feeling is that attempts to enforce American concepts of antitrust law on an international business are unworkable and wrong. The net effect is to penalize American workers."

It was Gorton's first major victory as a U.S. senator. At a signing ceremony at the White House, Reagan pronounced it a "remarkable achievement" culminating "more than 50 years of effort to make these laws more understandable." Gorton had taken on an issue that more timid souls had demurred on, mastered arcane subject matter and patiently assembled a political coalition of divergent interests to enact a challenging piece of legislation. While the bill was significant to the maritime industry, it also demonstrated the legal, political and legislative talents of Washington's new senator. Gorton thanked Senator Jackson for his support, but Scoop said the achievement was overwhelmingly Slade's.[2]

SIXTEEN YEARS OLDER THAN GORTON, Henry M. Jackson was the studious son of Norwegian immigrants. He grew up in the gritty smokestack city of Everett, north of Seattle. When his third grade teacher asked her students what they wanted to be when they grew up, Henry confidently declared, "President of the United States." Early in their careers, Jackson and Gorton were both seen as spoil-sports, Gorton having earned the enmity of bingo players by cracking down on tolerance gambling. Jackson got his start in politics as a crusading young Snohomish County Prosecutor, targeting gambling and bootlegging. He was disgusted that "school children were spending their lunch money on pinball games" while their fathers squandered their paychecks on slot machines and booze. They started calling him "Soda Pop Jackson."

Gorton was more the intellectual but Jackson was also an avid reader. Both were policy wonks with a remarkable command of detail and nuance and given to encyclopedic answers. While Slade famously suffered from a warmth deficit, neither did Scoop suffer fools gladly. When a press conference or interview grew tedious both were known to observe that a reporter had just asked a particularly dumb question. Jimmy Carter considered Jackson a brilliant yet "pompous" know-it-all. (Gorton and Jackson, in turn, considered Carter weak and naïve in his dealings with the Soviets.)[3]

Anti-war liberals loathed Jackson, the unrepentant hawk, while movement conservatives and the New Right were wary of Gorton's libertarian streak. Both staunchly supported Israel and a strong military. What was good for Boeing was invariably good for America, and vice versa. Jackson admired Reagan as a Cold Warrior but agreed with George H.W. Bush's pre-vice-presidential dismissal of his supply-side strategy as "voodoo economics." At heart, Jackson was still a New Deal/Fair Deal Democrat. When Gorton endorsed a one-year freeze on Social Security benefits, Jackson blew his top. Sometimes they just agreed that they disagreed. Gorton always listened intently to "one of the greatest senators in U.S. history."[4]

They first met in the early 1960s when Slade was representing a Seattle forestry investment firm before Jackson's Interior Committee. Jackson's advocacy proved decisive. "Scoop went far out of his way to help this young guy. When I was a senator I tried to act accordingly. I tried to remember how disappointing it was to work like hell for weeks over testimony and have one senator show up." In 1970, however, they had a falling out. Jackson took offense when Gorton introduced his Republican opponent—Teddy Roosevelt look-alike Charlie Elicker—in a PBS

Sally and Slade with Scoop and Helen Jackson in 1982. *University of Washington Libraries, Special Collections, UW28890*

meet-the-candidates spot. The race was never in doubt. GOP strategists had recruited Elicker in large part to keep Scoop from spending more time boosting other Democrats.

Jackson won re-election with an astonishing 84 percent of the vote, but he shunned Gorton for the next decade. Gorton was mystified and disappointed. "All I said was, 'This is a great guy, and he'd make a great United States senator.'"

Peter Jackson, Scoop's son, also points to some unflattering remarks by Gorton concerning his father's sponsorship of the Indian Self-Determination Act. In any case, Jackson's congratulatory call on the night Gorton ended Magnuson's career in Congress was unexpected, gratifying and a huge relief. In the 32 months they were seatmates, Jackson and Gorton forged a partnership based on mutual respect and shared goals. Absent party obligations, it also bloomed into a genuine friendship.[5]

AFTER THEIR WELCOME-TO-WASHINGTON LUNCH, the Jacksons hosted a reception for the Gortons. Helen Jackson, 21 years younger than her spouse, and Sally Gorton bonded immediately. They were the same age, outgoing and unpretentious. Sally had a degree in journalism; Helen was an English major. "She was beautiful, gracious and smart," Sally recalls. "She looked like Grace Kelly. Just a lovely person. And Scoop was a dear." Sometimes when her freshman spouse was busy, he'd take her to lunch and give her books and articles to read and pass along to Slade. When Peter Jackson, then a boy, was shopping for a bike he turned to Slade for advice. The spitting image of his dad, with his large Scandinavian head and infectious smile, Peter says his parents enjoyed the Gortons' company.

Many were surprised that Gorton and Jackson got along so well. Slade, though, grasped early on "that very frequently the two senators from the same state get along better when they're from opposite parties simply because they don't share constituencies to a great deal. They aren't both sort of maneuvering to be the number one guy in the party when they're home." Jackson and Magnuson had a subtle rivalry, Gorton says. "I probably got along with Jackson better than he got along with Maggie. Now, it wouldn't have been as close, because they were together all the time, and each of them was always the honorary campaign chairman for one another, but their views on issues and their personalities were radically different."[6]

THE MIDTERM ELECTIONS in 1982 found the economy still struggling to climb out of a brutal recession. Joblessness was a record high 10.8 percent by November. Reagan's approval ratings were in the low 40s. Not much had trickled down. The Republicans lost 26 seats in the House, greatly strengthening Tip O'Neill's hand, but held on to their majority in the Senate.

Shaken by Magnuson's defeat, 70-year-old Henry M. Jackson had run harder than ever. He hired hard-charging young Ron Dotzauer as his campaign manager and took seriously pollster Peter Hart's warning that his base had eroded, particularly on the left, which hammered Jackson for supporting Reagan's defense buildup and backing the Bonneville Power Administration's alliance with the Washington Public Power Supply System. Few acronyms in American history have been as apt as WPPSS (pronounced "Whoops"). The Supply System's ambitious nuclear power plant program was having a cost-overrun meltdown. Gorton, Dan Evans and practically every other member of the political establishment in Washington State were also being tarred by irate ratepayers.

Jackson's Republican opponent was Doug Jewett, Seattle's young city attorney and a Gorton disciple. Slade made some uncomfortable appearances at his campaign rallies, hoping Scoop would understand they were obligatory. This time their relationship was so strong that he did. "Selfishly, I was very fortunate that it wasn't a real campaign," Gorton says. Jackson won his sixth term with 69 percent of the vote.[7]

On August 28, 1983, Jackson returned from a grueling two-week tour of China with a deep chest cold and hacking cough. Antibiotics helped, and he resolved to go into his Seattle office on September 1st. He called Gorton to brief him on the trip. Daybreak brought the appalling news that the Soviets had shot down Korean Air Flight 007 when it strayed into their airspace. All 269 people aboard the Boeing 747 perished. It was a

"dastardly, barbaric act against humanity," an outraged Jackson told reporters, and fresh evidence that Reagan was right earlier that year when
he called the Soviet Union an "evil empire." Afterward, Dotzauer told
Jackson he'd never sounded better. Scoop smiled. "You know, I was pretty
good, wasn't I?"[8]

Unable to shake the cough, Jackson went to the doctor, then to bed. He
died that night of a ruptured aorta. The Gortons called Helen to offer
their condolences. Slade and Sally, together with Ritajean Butterworth,
also went to visit Scoop's grieving staff. "He wanted to comfort them,"
Butterworth recalls, "and he wanted to tell them he'd do anything they
needed."

The president, who'd lost a staunch supporter of his defense and for-
eign policy agendas, praised Jackson as "a wise and revered statesman."
Henry Kissinger said America had lost "a true patriot." George Will, the
Pulitzer Prize-winning conservative columnist, said Scoop was a hero for
all seasons. Ted Kennedy and Bob Dole agreed that he was a giant in the
Senate. And Warren G. Magnuson, who never imagined he would outlive
his abstemious younger friend and colleague, was stunned and sorrowed.
"So much for clean living," a former Magnuson staffer cracked with sad
irony at the reception following the funeral.[9]

The new senator from Washington State would be Daniel J. Evans.

AFTER THREE TERMS AS GOVERNOR, Evans took on the politically challenging job of heading The Evergreen State College in Olympia, the innovative school he helped establish. "Greeners" designed their own degree
paths and received evaluations instead of grades. Critics, including Evans'
successor, Dixy Lee Ray, viewed it as a haven for hippies and their leftist
profs.

Evans was the perfect choice for president of the fledgling college,
deftly navigating the legislative minefield and shoring up Evergreen's
academics. By 1983, his sixth year, the kids still had long hair, wet dogs
and wild ideas but it was rated one of the best liberal arts schools in the
West.

The week before Jackson's stunningly unexpected death, Evans made
an appointment to meet with the chairwoman of the Evergreen trustees.
He was going to tell her he would stay on for 10 more months. He wanted
to finish the autobiography he'd been pecking at for years, then do something else.[10]

Gorton urged him to seek the appointment to Scoop's seat. They'd be a
great team, he said, thinking back to their first meeting during Dan's

1956 campaign for the Legislature. Evans was conflicted. Secretary of State Ralph Munro, a former aide and good friend, prodded him to call Governor Spellman. The Korean Air tragedy was all over the radio as Evans drove to the Governor's Mansion. "Good God," he said to himself, "with this many problems and the challenges that we're facing . . . how can you *not* want to really get involved?"[11]

Once appointed, Evans was instantly in campaign mode to serve the last five years of Jackson's term. With Slade joining him on the stump, Evans handily outpolled Lloyd Cooney in a primary barely a month later, then took 55 percent of the vote against Congressman Mike Lowry. Jim Waldo and Steve Excell, the leading strategists in the Evans campaign, had deftly contrasted Lowry's bearded rumpledness and hot rhetoric with Evans' senatorial mien.[12]

GORTON AND JACKSON had conducted hearings in Spokane, Seattle and D.C. on their proposal to protect from development an additional 1.6 mil-

The Washington State congressional delegation in 1982: sitting, from left, Gorton, Pritchard and Evans; standing, from left: Rod Chandler, Al Swift, Norm Dicks, Tom Foley, Sid Morrison, Mike Lowry and Don Bonker.
Gorton Center

lion acres of National Forest land in Washington State under the umbrella of the Wilderness Act. As chairman of the Interior Committee, Scoop had shepherded the act through the Senate in 1964. Tom Pelly, a Republican from Seattle, was one of its champions in the House. The act set aside 9.1 million acres across the nation—land "where the earth and its community of life are untrammeled by man; where man himself is a visitor who does not remain."

With another 52 million acres designated for further consideration, what remains to this day is the contentiousness of deciding which roadless tracts should stay open to logging, mining and grazing and which merit protection from encroaching urbanization. The Roadless Area Review & Evaluation process—"RARE"—rarely failed to provoke controversy. Timber companies, oil and gas interests, miners and ranchers, offroaders and snowmobilers squared off with conservationists. One critic lamented that environmentalists had gained control of the debate over public-lands policy, parlaying the Wilderness Act "into a vehicle for indefinite expansion of a system of ecological museums—and few in Congress seem to mind. . . . [S]omething far more potent than an unadorned conservation ethic is at work, with more serious implications. That something is partly a romance, partly a morality play. The romance is with the notion that land is sacred to the degree it escapes human touch. The morality play involves the conviction that economic pursuits are vulgar."[13]

Gorton is of the strong conviction that economic pursuits are not vulgar. Loggers, miners and irrigators loved having him in their corner. To Earth First!, the environmental equivalent of the Viet Cong, he was the enemy incarnate. Pragmatic environmentalists, however, welcomed Gorton warily as a collaborator whenever the planets were in alignment and concede that he helped them achieve some major victories. One is the Washington State Wilderness Act of 1984.

Led by Senator Evans, a hiker since boyhood, the Washington delegation produced a bipartisan plan that protected a million acres—a compromise, to be sure, and one that hardly ended the debate, but a victory nevertheless for earth and man. Evans, Pritchard and Lowry, who found common cause as conservationists, wanted more; Gorton and Spokane Democrat Tom Foley less. Sid Morrison, the Republican congressman from the Yakima Valley, helped broker a pivotal compromise for Eastern Washington. "[A]fter five intense hours, the delegation emerged from Foley's office, arm-in-arm and smiling."

Evans and Gorton pushed the bill through the Senate. Scoop, sadly, wasn't there to help celebrate its passage on the Third of July. The bulk of

Mount Baker, was protected, 118,000 acres in all. Five new wilderness areas bracketed the western and southern boundaries of the Olympic National Park. Morrison staked out the 150,000-acre Lake Chelan-Sawtooth Wilderness, while Bremerton Democrat Norm Dicks championed the Clearwater Wilderness along the northern boundary of Mount Rainier National Park. The Cougar Lakes area backed by Pritchard and Lowry became part of the William O. Douglas Wilderness.[14]

Jackson had blown a gasket when Reagan's Interior Department, under the ham-handed James Watt, set out to open vast tracts of wilderness to development and limit new additions. After Watt boasted that his coal-leasing commission was diversified with "a black, a woman, two Jews and a cripple," Gorton denounced him from the Senate floor as "a failure on his own terms, a destructively divisive force in American society, an albatross around the neck of his own president."[15]

When Congress honored Everett's most famous son by establishing the 100,000-acre Henry M. Jackson Wilderness in the headwaters of the Skykomish, Watt was gone, but the White House still balked at a Rose Garden signing ceremony. Gorton, Evans and other members of the state delegation, together with Helen and Peter Jackson, assembled at a spectacular overlook in the North Cascades to dedicate the new wilderness. Before the ceremony, Gorton, Evans and the Jacksons hiked to a serene alpine lake to give the wilderness an even more fitting baptism.

With the Washington delegation aggressively honoring Scoop's legacy as a conservationist, the 98th Congress ended up putting more wilderness in the 48 contiguous states under federal protection than any of its predecessors.[16]

21 | The Year of Living Dangerously

RONALD REAGAN AND TIP O'NEILL, two old Irishmen who guffawed for the cameras, quickly found that familiarity bred contempt. O'Neill described Reagan as "a cheerleader for selfishness" and, in a tactical masterstroke, gave him enough rope early on to hang himself in deficits as the recession persisted. Yet after Reagan narrowly survived an assassination attempt two months into his presidency, the speaker was the first outsider admitted to his bedside. Eyes brimming with tears, O'Neill knelt and took the president's hand. Together they recited the 23rd Psalm. Two years later, the mid-term elections answered O'Neill's prayers, not Reagan's. The Lord works in mysterious ways.[1]

Gorton summed it up: "1981 was the Year of the President. 1982 was the Year of the Senate Republicans. 1983 is the Year of Living Dangerously."[2]

In his budget for Fiscal Year 1984, Reagan called for a 10 percent boost in military spending and ratcheted up his rhetoric offensive against the Soviet Union. Reagan noted that the Pentagon's share of federal spending had plummeted from nearly 50 percent in 1960 to less than 24 percent in 1980. The president also envisioned American knowhow developing a space shield against strategic ballistic missiles. Domenici rolled his eyes. God only knows what that would cost. O'Neill chortled over this disarray in the ranks: The deficit was heading for the moon and Reagan wanted to play "Star Wars."

Gorton backed the president but was underwhelmed by Weinberger's stewardship of Defense. He winced when it was revealed that Boeing was charging the Pentagon $1,118.26 apiece for the plastic caps fitted to stools in AWACs planes—and procurement paid it. Snafus like that provided more ammunition for persistent Pentagon critics like Senator Grassley, who asked, "Why should we dump huge sums of money into the Defense Department when it is rotting with bad management?"[3]

House Democrats offered the Pentagon a 4 percent boost and proposed

$30 billion in tax increases to trim $15 billion from the deficit. They were also out to restore some of the funds Republicans cut from child nutrition, food stamps, welfare, day-care and Medicaid. Nor was Reagan going to get anything approaching 10 percent from Domenici if the Budget Committee plowed ahead on schedule. More like 5, maybe 6. The president beseeched the chairman to give him some breathing room, saying, "I can't promise you anything but we may find some flexibility on defense." Reagan's brain trust was telling him the leading economic indicators were perking up. The recession in fact was over; much of the media just hadn't noticed. Reagan was stalling for time on the ides of March, 1983.[4]

Gorton and Grassley said Reagan was wrong to ask for the delay, and if they complied it would be even "more wrong" because they were members of an independent branch of government. "Each time the president has intervened in the budget process here he has been wrong," said Gorton, and "he's wrong now. This uncertain trumpet is going to harm the budget process."[5]

The Democrats on the committee warned that the White House would attempt to set in motion "a public relations steamroller" for Reagan's military budget while members of Congress were in their home districts the week before Easter.[6]

Reagan met with the Republican members of the Budget Committee on April 5, with Howard Baker as the broker. The majority leader suggested a 7.5 percent boost for defense; Domenici offered 5. The meeting broke up when Weinberger was nowhere to be found. Domenici's committee was poised to vote when he was summoned to the "Senators Only" phone booth outside the meeting room. It was the White House calling. Reagan and Weinberger wanted him to hightail it over for a chat. "It's too late," Domenici said through clenched teeth. "I'm the president," Reagan barked, "and I want you to hold off for a while. People in that committee are up for re-election. They're going to be coming to me for help." The chairman was undeterred.[7]

"Reagan asked me three times to postpone it because Cap needed more time," Domenici recalls. "But Weinberger was playing games with us. They said they supposed Gorton agreed with me, and I said, 'Mr. President, we've got to do our job. All the senators are here and there's a statute. The law says we're one branch of government and you're another.' Reagan got very upset. We did not have a friendly goodbye. That was the way that year was. We couldn't conceivably continue on that path with defense in terms of real growth. Slade captured that from the get-go with me and joined me every way he could."[8]

Old friends promoted
to the other Washing-
ton: Congressman Joel
Pritchard and U.S.
Senators Dan Evans
and Slade Gorton.
*Washington State
Archives*

Gorton and Lawton Chiles, the Budget Committee's ranking Democrat, put together a middle-ground plan that finally broke the impasse.
Domenici and Chiles, a gentlemanly moderate from Florida, were good
friends. With Domenici in the White House dog house, Gorton's role as
the chairman's chief strategist took on new importance. Steve Bell, the
Budget Committee's staff director, sat about six feet from Gorton during
every committee meeting. "Although a lot of Republicans got mad at him,
I thought Slade was engaged in a real act of statesmanship as he tried to
put together a budget resolution that could be bipartisan in nature when
we had run into an absolute stone wall," Bell says. "When I would talk to
his staff and heard that people back home perceived him as (divisive) it
was amazing to me that a guy who is so constructive could be seen as so
polarizing."

The fallback Gorton-Chiles plan advocated $9 billion in tax increases,
sparing some social programs from deeper cuts, and a 6 percent increase
in military spending. It squeaked out of the Senate, 50-49, and headed to
reconciliation. The House wanted $30 billion in new taxes and 4 percent
real growth in military spending. Reagan vowed that he would veto any
tax increase and held tight on 10 percent for the Pentagon.

By fall the economy had moved from recovery to expansion and the
Dow Jones Industrial Average posted back-to-back records, closing at
1,272. Senate and House budget conferees compromised on a plan calling
for $12 billion in additional revenues and a 5 percent real increase for the
Pentagon. No veto was forthcoming but deciding who got gored was tor-
tuous. Reagan was never reconciled to reconciliation. Gorton said the president and Congress better face the music: "We can't balance the budget

of the United States on the basis of defense or discretionary programs."
Even though 1984 was going to be an election year, Gorton insisted that
any serious deficit-reduction program had to deal with entitlements.[9]

GORTON'S GROWING REPUTATION AS a deficit hawk was cemented in 1984
by the hand-to-hand combat, on all flanks, over the Fiscal Year 1985 budget. Gorton, Kassebaum and Grassley "favored debate in order to forge
consensus on bigger defense reductions; yet they feared delay even more,
endangering the Finance Committee bill, given their conservative colleagues' suspicions. Moderate Republicans and Democrats wanted quick
action as well because the financial markets were getting skittish," Joseph White and Aaron Wildavsky write in *The Deficit and the Public Interest,* their compelling analysis of the 1980s budget wars. But delay there
was, as filibuster threats, recriminations and internecine squabbling over
a deficit-reduction package created gridlock. The Republican-controlled
Senate nearly handed the White House a major defeat when a budget
proposed by Democrats came within a vote of passage.[10]

Gorton's new compromise plan put him at odds with his friend Domenici, as well as senior citizens and federal pensioners—in an election
year no less. Slade wanted to attack the $200 billion-and-still-climbing
deficit with an assortment of tax hikes and by limiting increases in Social
Security and federal and military retiree benefits to 3 percent below the
rate of inflation. The Pentagon would get a 5 percent real-growth boost.

In an emotion-charged debate on May 8, 1984, fellow Republicans attacked Gorton's plan. Domenici warned that cutting Social Security
would put the burden of deficit reduction on "a lot of people who are hurting in this country. . . . [T]his is a $28.5 billion reduction in Social Secu-
rity, $2.8 billion in reduction for military retirees, $3.5 billion in civil ser-
vants." Gorton countered that it was time to be "more daring," time to
face the fact that reining in the entitlements represented the only way to
make a significant dent in the deficit. The next day, his plan crashed and
burned, 72-23, mustering support only from Dan Evans and a few other
Republican moderates. "It was in the middle, crushed by two extremes.
Ironically, this is almost certainly a precursor of what is going to happen
next year," Gorton predicted. The irony was that there was so little risk
he'd be proved wrong.[11]

IN THE MIDDLE OF THE BUDGET IMPLOSION, Gorton ensnared himself in
another white-hot issue—school prayer.

Ronald Reagan was operating at the peak of his conservative avuncularity in his regular Saturday morning radio address on Feb. 25, 1984: "Sometimes I can't help but feel the First Amendment is being turned on its head, because ask yourselves, 'Can it really be true that the First Amendment can permit Nazis and Ku Klux Klansmen to march on public property, advocate the extermination of people of the Jewish faith and the subjugation of blacks, while the same amendment forbids our children from saying a prayer in school?' . . . (Consider) the case of the kindergarten class reciting a verse before their milk and cookies. They said, 'We thank you for the flowers so sweet. We thank you for the food we eat. We thank you for the birds that sing. We thank you, God, for everything.' But a Federal court of appeals ordered them to stop. They were supposedly violating the Constitution of the United States."

Howard Baker asked Gorton and Rudman—two heavy thinkers, one an Episcopalian, the other a Jew—to draft an alternative to Reagan's proposed constitutional amendment on school prayer, one that might be more acceptable to Democrats and moderate Republicans. Rudman respectfully declined. Gorton plunged right in. Believing the Reagan amendment smacked of state sponsorship of school prayer, his solution was this: "The accommodation by the United States of the religious speech of any person . . . shall not constitute an establishment of religion." The key word was "accommodation," Gorton said. "The goal should be to treat religion equally with other forms of free expression." His amendment would permit voluntary prayer, whether spoken or silent, so long as it was not mandated or otherwise directed by school officials. Religious groups would be permitted to use public school facilities on an equal extracurricular basis with the gay and lesbian league or chess club. Neither proposal—Reagan's or his own—would have any impact on Washington State, Gorton pointed out, since the state constitution bans "virtually any kind of religious activity in public schools." Evans was opposed to a constitutional amendment, as were Lowry, Pritchard and Bonker, a devout Christian who said that when prayer becomes institutionalized "it loses its spiritual meaning and it is in danger of becoming a mockery."[12]

Reagan's amendment made it to the Senate floor where it was rejected 56-44, eleven votes short of the necessary two-thirds majority. Gorton, Evans, Hatfield, Packwood, Rudman, Goldwater, Kassebaum and Boschwitz were among the 18 Republicans voting no. Jerry Falwell, president of the Moral Majority, prophesized, "Like those in ancient Israel who cried out to their oppressors, 'Let my people go!' those of us who are oppressed by our political leadership today are also crying for them to let us go or we plan to let them go in November."[13]

Gorton and Evans won praise from the ACLU, not exactly an answer to their prayers for an understanding Republican base back home.

GORTON WAS AMONG THE OUTRAGED when the owner of the Baltimore Colts, one of the NFL's iconic franchises, loaded the team's gear—everything from shoulder pads to memorabilia—into a fleet of moving vans under cover of night and decamped to Indianapolis. Gorton and his staff drafted a bill that would have required the NFL to create two expansion teams by 1987, one of them guaranteed to Baltimore. More importantly, the legislation also stipulated that no major professional sports league, including baseball, basketball and hockey, could sanction shifting a team to a new city without weighing profitability, facilities and fan support. Then, if a league voted to move a franchise, the final decision would have to pass muster with a board that included a community representative and a member appointed by the American Arbitration Association. NFL Commissioner Pete Rozelle, who was lobbying for immunity from antitrust laws, vehemently opposed Gorton's bill. It cleared the Commerce Committee but was bogged down by more intrigue.

The budget mess, meanwhile, got messier.

As fall approached, debates still raged, left and right, over Social Security, defense and the deficit. Congressmen Dick Cheney of Wyoming and Trent Lott of Mississippi, the minority whip, said Reagan and Weinberger were on a collision course with Congress over their sky-high military budget request. If Reagan "doesn't really cut defense, he becomes the No. 1 special pleader in town," said Cheney, a future secretary of defense. Aid to the anti-communist Nicaraguan Contras, which Gorton supported early on, also poisoned relationships.

"Day in and day out the toughest, most emotionally draining issue was aid to the Contras," says Rich Ellings, who in 1984 became Gorton's legislative assistant for foreign and defense policy. "Anti-war and pro-Sandinista activists from Washington State called me incessantly and wrote Slade accusing us personally of genocide, maiming and killing babies and siding with evil rich landowners, while Seattle liberals had Sandinista leaders visit the city with much fanfare. Congress put time limits on Contra aid and changed its mind several times on the strings attached, which meant the issue would be reviewed again and again." Gorton wanted to be constantly up to speed on every development.

Ellings was a young Ph.D. who had come highly recommended by professors at the newly named Henry M. Jackson School of International Studies at the University of Washington. When he interviewed for the job with Gorton, he said he wanted "real policy world" experience to prepare himself for a career as a teacher and researcher. Exhilarating and exhausting, the job was everything he'd hoped for and a lot more. The man widely viewed as arrogant was a great boss and mentor. Age didn't matter to Gorton; smarts did. He loved to regale the staff with insider stories. Late one night when Slade was still on the floor of the Senate, they were eating pizza in his office, with Ellings plopped in the senator's chair. When the phone rang, he answered "Rich Ellings" on autopilot as if he was in his own cubicle. It was Mrs. Gorton, who mused that he must be the "acting senator."

ONE MONTH FROM ELECTION DAY, as he prepared for his first debate with Walter Mondale, Reagan shut down "nonessential" government services.[14] Surprisingly, in light of the final outcome, some polls indicated Mondale was within striking distance, so the amiable former vice president came out like Sugar Ray Leonard, throwing uppercuts when the bell rang in Louisville on Oct. 7, with Barbara Walters as the referee. Recalling a decisive moment in one of the 1980 debates, Mondale said, "When President Carter said you were going to cut Medicare, you said, 'Oh, no, there you go again, Mr. President!' And what did you do right after the election? You went out and tried to cut $20 billion out of Medicare. And so when you say 'There you go again' . . . people will remember that you signed the biggest tax increase in the history of the United States . . . You've got a $260 billion deficit. You can't wish it away." Reagan's rejoinder was that his program was working. The budget would be balanced by 1989, he promised. America was on the rebound. Then he vowed, "I will never stand for a reduction of the Social Security benefits to the people who are now getting them . . ."[15]

Congressman Lowry thought Mondale had scored some points. The Republicans were promising what he called "Voodoo Economics, Number 2"—no new taxes, no cuts in Social Security or Medicare, a massive military buildup and Star Wars gismology. "I think there's still a chance—an outside chance—that Mondale can pull this off," Lowry told Dick Larsen, *The Seattle Times'* political columnist, two days before the election. He conceded that the deficit was boring. Larsen said that was an understatement. "On a scale of thrilling things to read about," it ranked somewhere between the Tacoma phone directory and the Department of Agriculture's "Abstract of Soybean Production Trends, 1958-1968." For all the time he'd spent and the damage it had done to his relationship with Reagan, Gorton had to sadly agree. "Nearly everywhere it's a yawner."[16]

If there was any deficit anxiety in the electorate, the Gipper had the elixir. Reagan could have reprised the defining moment of the 1980 debate when he looked the TV camera square in the lens and asked Americans, "Are you better off now than you were four years ago?" But this time he didn't need to ask. The economy was sizzling, generating four million new jobs. Inflation had declined to 3.2 percent, the lowest in 11 years.[17]

Reagan was re-elected with nearly 59 percent of the popular vote and the largest Electoral College margin in history. The flip side was his surprising lack of coattails—a gain of only 14 GOP seats in the House and a loss of two in the Senate. Tennessee elected Democrat Al Gore Jr. to succeed the retiring Howard Baker. The election "left the ideological divisions in Congress more raw than ever."[18]

Gorton had voted with his president a "whopping" 85 percent of the time, *The Seattle Times* declared, noting that only a handful of staunch conservatives—including Ted Stevens and Strom Thurmond—had been more loyal. This was lost on Ronald Reagan, who should have been more appreciative, but not on Mike Lowry or Brock Adams. The two ambitious Seattle liberals never missed a chance to style Gorton as a right-wing Reagan lapdog. Adams had been out of politics since 1979 when Jimmy Carter requested his resignation as secretary of transportation in a general Cabinet housecleaning that largely testified to the disarray in the White House.[18]

Adams believed he alone could beat Gorton.

AFTER THE ELECTION, Bob Dole edged Alaska's Ted Stevens, the assistant leader for eight years, in a tense contest to succeed Baker as Senate majority leader. Domenici was eliminated on the second ballot. Gorton, despite a spirited campaign, lost the race for the No. 2 leadership post, majority whip, to genial Alan Simpson of Wyoming. "It was a great adventure," said Slade. "I learned more about the Senate and more about myself. But I had the misfortune of running against a man who may be the single most popular individual in the Senate." He was upbeat as usual, though, certain he had gained from the loss because people recognized that he was a go-getter.[19]

Gorton and Evans voted for Domenici, but his bipartisanship and zeal for a balanced budget combined to undermine his bids for leadership spots during his 36 years in Congress. One of Pete's keepsakes was a framed drawing of Sisyphus, the Greek condemned by the gods to pushing a huge boulder up a hill, only to have it roll right back down the minute he got to the top. Domenici couldn't win for trying. Democrats claimed he was in Reagan's hip pocket, which was patently untrue, while conservatives questioned his loyalty. Stockman labeled him "a Hooverite" for harping on the deficit. As a Domenici protégé, Gorton carried most of the same baggage.

Never a brooder, Gorton's response to a loss is to remind himself that while many things happen for a reason, being Zeus is the best state of mind—never Sisyphus.[20]

22 | Déjà vu All Over Again

EXIT POLLS CONFIRMED THAT MONDALE got very little traction on the deficit. What resonated—and backfired—was his unapologetic acknowledgment that if elected he would raise taxes. When the budget battle was rejoined in the winter of '85, the president wanted 6 percent more for defense and deep cuts in domestic spending. The Social Security cost-of-living adjustment, however, was now off limits. Domenici and Gorton kept plugging away. The Senate countered with an inflation adjustment for defense in Fiscal Year 1986 and 3 percent real growth in both FY 87 and 88, plus a one-year freeze on the COLAs. Domenici's goal was to trim the deficit by some $60 billion.

Come spring, the White House and the Senate were still entrenched, bobbing up periodically to exchange grenades. The Senate won a temporary victory at 1:30 a.m. on May 10 when "a pale and weak" Pete Wilson was pushed slowly into the Senate Chamber in a wheelchair to a standing ovation. The Republican from California, who had undergone an emergency appendectomy the day before, brought the house down when he looked up at Dole before he voted and deadpanned, *"What was the question?"* Wilson's vote pushed the Senate's FY1986 budget resolution into a tie that Vice President Bush promptly broke. In the House, however, O'Neill's majority Democrats flatly rejected any compromise on the COLAs. Reagan took to the airwaves to declare everyone should read his lips. "I'll repeat it until I'm blue in the face: I will veto any tax increase the Congress sends me."[1]

The guns-and-butter debate got even hotter in July after Gorton and Chiles came up with another bipartisan plan to put a bigger dent in the deficit. It called for $59 billion in new taxes stretched over three years, less for defense and no Social Security cost-of-living increases. To soften the blow, the plan advocated investing 20 percent of the overall savings in programs to help needy old folks.[2]

The president hosted a cocktail hour at the White House. Gorton and Chiles were invited, together with Dole and O'Neill. Congressman Lowry even made the guest list, but Domenici was snubbed. The usually charming Reagan dropped a dead mouse in the punch bowl by offering a sermon against tax increases. Gorton and Chiles spoke up for their compromise. "We marched up the hill and looked deficits square in the eye and then we've blinked," Gorton asserted. "That's bad policy." The president blew his top.[3]

William H. Gray III, the Pennsylvania Democrat who headed the House Budget Committee, was asked for his take on the feud between the White House and the Senate Republicans. "In North Philadelphia," he said with a chuckle, "we learn you don't get involved in somebody else's fight. You might get shot."[4]

The reality on the street, so to speak, was that Ronald Reagan was now a lame duck, but Gorton and 21 other Republicans in the Senate were up for re-election in 1986. "A very substantial number of Republican senators regard the budget deficit as the greatest challenge facing the country, and we feel that the failure to deal with it really threatens economic growth," Gorton said. In the long haul, "good policy will be good politics," he added, because reducing the deficit would goose the economy and re-elect Republicans.[5]

GORTON AND HIS GOOD FRIEND, Rudy Boschwitz of Minnesota, cleared out their heads and lungs by running together many mornings. When Rudy wasn't up for jogging, he'd still stop by the Gortons so they could walk to the Capitol together. Sally Gorton would say, "Would you like something for breakfast, Rudy?" He'd say, "No, no, no, nothing at all. Well, maybe a cup of coffee. Well, how about a piece of toast?" Rudy became family.

The descendant of Pilgrims and the self-described former plywood peddler whose family fled Hitler's Germany when he was 3, walked and talked, trying to figure out how to get Reagan to see the light on the deficit. It was a fascinating era, with a complex cast of strong-willed characters, Boschwitz says. "Pete Domenici is very calculating, and I don't mean that as a pejorative at all. He was very smart, very focused, and he had a great impatience with colleagues who didn't agree with him. Reagan was like Domenici. Slade had a much better touch. I think he improved Domenici. He made Domenici think about elements of the budget in a different way. And, oh God, is he such a quick study, which was why he was so effective so quickly. Not only that, he understood the legislative process better than I did. Better than most people. He'd be reading *Time* magazine as he walked through the halls, or reading memos. He was so focused he could do that. In a way, he's an automaton. . . . He was very good to have on your side."[6]

Ted Stevens was madder than hell when he discovered Gorton was not on his side. A senior member of the Appropriations Committee, Alaska's powerful, often petulant senator was intent on securing an unprecedented $7 million "experimental technology" grant for a Sitka pulp mill. Gorton was having none of it. To meet the same Environmental Protection Agency mandate Alaska Pulp Company was facing, the ITT-Rayonier mill at Port Angeles in his state had installed new pollution-control equipment at its own expense, Gorton said. Why should the taxpayers foot the bill in Sitka?

One foot plopped on a chair, Stevens twirled his glasses in frustration and glared at his upstart Republican colleague. Alaska Pulp's problems with the EPA all began when Gorton got involved, Stevens fumed. Gorton simply wasn't listening to him. He had violated senatorial courtesy. The vote would reveal who his "real friends" were. The implication was clear: Anyone who opposed him on this one better understand that their own projects would be DOA at Appropriations. Gorton insisted the subsidy was grossly unfair. He won.[7]

Reagan was as stubborn as Stevens. He wouldn't budge on his budget, insisting that big deficits posed no real threat to the economic upswing. Domenici and Gorton made another run, suggesting a tax on oil imports, slower increases in Social Security benefits and a delay in adjusting income tax brackets for inflation. The plan was flatly rejected by the White House. "I regret to say that the president has sold us down the river again," Gorton said. The stick didn't work, so he offered a carrot a few days later, saying, "He's the greatest political asset we have and he remains that asset."[8]

Then it came to pass that "two things happened that never could have if the ordinary logic of politics had applied"—tax reform and the Gramm-Rudman-Hollings Act. Gramm-Rudman or GRH for short, mandated automatic across-the-board spending cuts if the president and Congress failed to reach established targets to balance the budget. Foley, the House Democratic whip, summed it up with a Tom Clancy metaphor: Gramm-Rudman was "about the kidnapping of the only child of the president's official family that he loves" (think Defense) "and holding it in a dark basement and sending the president its ear." But the hostage game worked two ways. "Democrats could slice defense's ear only by doing the same to their own 'children.'"[9]

Phil Gramm, the former Democrat whose Texas drawl disguised a doctorate in economics, had teamed up with Gorton's centrist friend, Warren Rudman of New Hampshire, and Fritz Hollings of South Carolina, a conservative Democrat with a sharp tongue. "Gramm was smarter than most everyone except Slade," Boschwitz says. "Rudman was a bulldog like Gramm, but sometimes ran a little roughshod over people." Hollings could be a tough guy, too.

Gorton pronounced Gramm-Rudman "one of the rare examples I've seen since I've been here of a truly new idea. There's a tremendous inertia under the present system in favor of the status quo. The genius of GRH . . . is that it profoundly changes the consequences of inaction."[10]

The House and Senate approved their versions of Gramm-Rudman in November. The president signed the act into law in December, but Congress got a lump of coal in its Christmas stocking. Reconciliation was still stalemated. Domenici said the deficit-reduction numbers produced by the White House Office of Management & Budget were "patently absurd." Tip O'Neill called OMB's plan "crazy and nonsensical."[11]*

OREGON'S BOB PACKWOOD, who had ascended to the chairmanship of the Finance Committee with Dole's promotion to majority leader in 1985, was at odds with his committee over tax reform, the centerpiece of the president's domestic agenda. In markup, committee members had inserted so many loopholes—Packwood himself was looking out for timber industry interests—that the proposal bore no resemblance to the revenue-neutral original ideal. Gorton, Boschwitz and Grassley were among the 50 senators who said tax reform should take a back seat to agreement on reducing the deficit.[13]

Finally, Packwood rallied a core group of supporters, consulted tax experts, surrendered some feathers from his own nest and brokered a bipartisan bill that emerged from his committee on a unanimous vote and endured a thousand tweaks to become law that fall. Reagan had asked for a tax code that was "simpler and fairer." Roughly revenue neutral, it was simpler for individuals but more complex for companies doing business overseas. As to fairness, it comforted more of the afflicted, afflicted more

---

* Gramm-Rudman's automatic cuts were declared unconstitutional in 1986. The Supreme Court said they violated the separation of executive and legislative powers. A revised version was enacted in 1987. In the final analysis, Smith and Wildavsky assert in their book on the deficit, Gramm-Rudman not only failed to force a solution, "it actually paralyzed the system." Two years out, Senator Domenici agreed that it wasn't perfect, but he denied it was a failure. An exercise in exasperation yes, futility no.[12]

of the comfortable and reduced rates for the middle class. It also shifted some of the tax burden from individuals to businesses and, in retrospect, even the IRS now concludes that "some of the over-reaching provisions of the act also led to a downturn in real estate markets, which played a significant role in the subsequent collapse of the Savings and Loan industry." In other words, a horse designed by a committee encountered the Law of Unintended Consequences.

Gorton and Evans praised the Senate for "rising above special-interest groups," but felt let down by Packwood. With Gramm as an ally, they wanted citizens of states like Washington and Texas with no income tax to be able to deduct sales taxes from their federal income tax returns. Packwood promised to support them, in return for their votes to defeat an amendment on Individual Retirement Accounts. Then he laid low when the Gorton-Gramm-Evans proposal was rejected.

"We were furious," says Gorton. "So much for neighborly help," says Evans. In floor debate they pushed Packwood to fight for it in conference. He agreed to make it a priority and put together a compromise that restored 60 percent of the deductibility. In the end, the members of Congress from big states, "for whom state income tax deductibility was life or death," prevailed.[14] The sales tax deduction ended up on the cutting room floor. Brock Adams picked it up and had a field day asserting that Slade and Dan were a pale imitation of Scoop and Maggie. Worse, all that haggling, from spring to fall, left Gorton with little time for campaigning back home. The red-eye weekend flights took their toll.

23 | Gorton v. Zappa

M ILLIONS OF MUSIC FANS who didn't give a rip about the budget deficit were introduced to Slade Gorton in 1985 when Frank Zappa came to Capitol Hill. A brilliantly oddball musician and record producer, Zappa's progeny include Moon Unit and Dweezil and more than 50 albums, including "Burnt Weeny Sandwich" and "Weasels Ripped My Flesh." He was the father of The Mothers of Invention, a seminal art-rock band.

Drugs, sex and violence in rock 'n' roll worried Tipper Gore, the spouse of Senator Al Gore, and Susan Baker, the wife of Treasury Secretary James Baker. They founded the Parents Music Resource Center—PMRC—whose goal was to convince the music industry to offer parents guidance on the content of records. Nineteen record companies had agreed to put "Parental Guidance: Explicit Lyrics" labels on their albums. The Senate Commerce Committee, featuring Gorton, Gore and James Exon, a home-spun Nebraskan, resolved to hold a fact-finding hearing on "porn rock."[1]

Hair cropped short, mustache neatly trimmed, Zappa wore a conservative suit and a brittle air of indignation at the machinations of "bored Washington housewives." Beginning with a recitation of the First Amendment, he denounced their proposal as "the equivalent of treating dandruff by decapitation." It was "an ill-conceived piece of nonsense that fails to deliver any real benefits to children, infringes the civil liberties of people who are not children, and promises to keep the courts busy for years. . . . No one has forced Mrs. Baker or Mrs. Gore to bring Prince or Sheena Easton into their homes. Thanks to the Constitution, they are free to buy other forms of music for their children. . . ."[2]

"Taken as a whole," Zappa continued, "the complete list of PMRC demands reads like an instruction manual for some sinister kind of 'toilet training program' to house-break all composers and performers because of the lyrics of a few. Ladies, *how dare you?* (Your) shame must be shared by the bosses at the major labels who, through the Recording Industry Association of America, chose to bargain away the rights of composers, performers, and retailers in order to pass H.R. 2911, the Blank Tape Tax, a private tax levied by an industry on consumers for the benefit of a select group within that industry."[3]

Zappa had told reporters he was suspicious the hearing was merely a front for the proposed tax: "A couple of blowjobs here and there and Bingo! — you get a hearing." The major record labels wanted the bill to "whiz through a few committees before anybody smells a rat," Zappa added, denouncing the proposal as something "whipped up like an instant pudding by The Wives of Big Brother."[4]

For a man whose wife had been told by Zappa "May your shit come to life and kiss you on the face," Gore's remarks at the hearing struck Gorton as pathetically obsequious. "I found your statement very interesting," Gore told Zappa, "and although I disagree with some of the statements that you make and have made on other occasions I have been a fan of your music, believe it or not. I respect you as a true original and a tremendously talented musician.... The proposals made by those concerned about this problem do not involve a government role of any kind whatsoever. They are not asking for any form of censorship or regulation of speech in any manner, shape, or form. What they are asking for is whether or not the music industry can show some self-restraint . . . Your suggestion of printing the lyrics on the album is a very interesting one. . . . You are very articulate and forceful."[5]

Then it was Gorton's turn: "Mr. Zappa, I am astounded at the courtesy and soft-voiced nature of the comments of my friend, the senator from Tennessee. I can only say that I found your statement to be boorish, incredibly and insensitively insulting to the people who were here previously; that you could manage to give the first amendment of the Constitution of the United States a bad name, if I felt that you had the slightest understanding of it, which I do not. You do not have the slightest understanding of the difference between government action and private action, and you have certainly destroyed any case you might otherwise have had with this senator. . . ."

"Is this private action?" Zappa shot back.[6]

Gorton warned Zappa he might be held in contempt of Congress for his defiant attitude. "Go ahead Senator," Zappa snarled. "I already hold you in contempt."[7]

Zappa's bravura performance made him a sought-after public speaker on freedom of expression. Not long before he died of prostate cancer in 1993 at the age of 52, he observed, "Since 1985 I'm probably more famous for having Slade Gorton tell me I didn't know anything about the First

Amendment than for any song I ever wrote." Zappa even released an
album featuring excerpts of his exchanges with Gorton and Gore.[8]

"I went after this guy really hard as just being totally and completely
outrageous," Gorton says. "As a result, I've heard people who were teenagers back then cuss me out over that 25 years later—all kinds of correspon-
dence about how I was insulting Frank Zappa. A good part of my outrage was that Al Gore would not defend his own wife in an open hearing.
I developed such total contempt for that man that it has never left me to
this day. And of course he and Tipper eventually changed their minds
and went all-Hollywood for campaign donations. But Tipper did say
something very nice to me about it afterward."

GORTON WAS BACK in big-league sports in 1985, introducing a bill to regulate the transfer of franchises from city to city. Drafted by Marianne Mc-
Gettigan, it also required Major League Baseball to add two expansion
teams. Baseball's new commissioner, Peter Ueberroth, was unhappy; the
Players Association pleased. "I don't think the owners understand this is
a serious issue for us," said Donald Fehr, their acting executive director.
"It means jobs."

Gorton was rooting for the fans. "We had these no-good absentee
owners and there were always rumors the Mariners were going to leave
Seattle in one of those bidding wars. But I was never going to get the
bill passed. The chairman of the Senate Commerce Committee was Jack
Danforth from St. Louis. The Budweiser people were never going to let
him undercut the value of their sports franchises. I was still a threat,
however, and we had some very good hearings."

Fresh from his triumph as president of the organizing committee for
the 1984 Los Angeles Olympic Games and the cover of *Time*, Ueberroth
decided it was time for a private chat to get the senator squared away.
McGettigan greeted Ueberroth and his lobbyist at the door, ushered them
to Slade's office and took a seat next to the senator. "Slade, it's wonderful
to meet you!" Ueberroth declared. "I've been looking forward to this for
so long. I know how interested you are in baseball. We're going to sit
down here right now and we're going to settle all these problems. This is
just going to be a great relationship." Suddenly he shot a finger just inches
from McGettigan's nose and commanded, *"COFFEE! Black."*

Gorton all but fell out of his chair. "I saw Marianne's life pass in front
of her eyes in about two-tenths of a second. I saw the catatonic expression
on the face of the lobbyist." McGettigan, a feisty Irish redhead with a
first-class brain and a law degree, took a deep breath and went to fetch

what Gorton calls "the most expensive cup of coffee Peter Ueberroth is ever going to have in his life." She returned forthwith, politely handed over the steaming cup, sat down and began to take notes. Slade had yet to get a word in edgewise. At one point, however, Ueberroth interrupted himself, leaned in, guy to guy, and said, "Got a good joke. Can't tell it in mixed company."

Finally they departed. The second the door closed, Gorton fell to the floor, laughing so hard he couldn't get up to scrape McGettigan off the ceiling. "Well, Marianne," he finally managed to say, "one thing we've learned today is that Peter Ueberroth is never going to be president of the United States."

A few minutes later, the lobbyist poked his head back in sheepishly to say he was sorry. When word of the incident made its way around the Hill, Ueberroth called Slade to apologize for insulting his "secretary."

Gorton was proud of the fact he had women in positions of authority and offended that there were so many men "out there who still didn't get it," says McGettigan, who in 1992 became chief lobbyist for the Major League Baseball Players Association.[9]

GORTON WAS ALWAYS in the thick of something. He promoted bills to de-regulate cable TV and ban "cop-killer" bullets. He also found himself sparring with farmers and religious fundamentalists and ended up disappointing the National Confectioners Association. In the end, he accomplished something no one in Congress had been able achieve in a decade of trying: He pushed through a bill to lengthen Daylight Saving Time by three weeks.

Backed by a coalition of barbecue and briquette-makers, convenience stores, fast-food chains, sporting goods manufacturers, garden-supply outlets and amusement parks, Gorton's bill was the most popular of several in the hopper. His original plan called for four more weeks of Daylight Saving Time, from the first Sunday in April to the first Sunday in November. The coalition represented some 8,000 companies. "From a political standpoint, at least some of these companies were represented in virtually every congressional district," David Prerau notes in his history of Daylight Saving Time. "And many had an indirect effect—increased sales at McDonald's, for example, led to greater demand for Kansas beef and Idaho potatoes." Washington State in fact produces 22 percent of America's potatoes.[10]

The usual opposition was lined up against Gorton. Farmers said it confused their cows; Bible thumpers said man was playing God with the heavens. But President Reagan strongly supported the plan. Backers in the House prevailed in October of 1985. Gorton, however, was stymied by opponents on the Commerce Committee. After six months of frustration, he hit on an end-around, attaching his measure to a benign proposal to boost federal fire prevention efforts. He also made an important concession by jettisoning the one-week extension into November. Greatly disappointed were the candy manufacturers, who had counted on extra hour of daylight for trick-or-treaters, all the better to sell more M&M's. The coalition was more excited by the prospect of an extra three weeks in the spring. The Fire Prevention Bill with Gorton's rider sailed through the Senate on a voice vote and won overwhelming approval in the House. Reagan signed it into law on July 8, 1986.[11]

Gorton would need those extra hours of daylight for his re-election campaign. Brock Adams, the former six-term Democratic congressman from Seattle, formally announced his candidacy on March 20 after nearly two years of "tiptoeing around the notion, surveying, scoping—like a big-game hunter at the edge of the jungle." When Lowry bowed out of the race in January, the man Tom Foley thought of as "the young prince of politics" was off and running. He had a long way to go. Adams' own polls agreed with Gorton's and one conducted by Elway Research for *The Seattle Times*: He was at least 23 points behind—48 percent to 25 percent. The undecideds—27 percent—offered optimism.[12]

At 59, Adams was a year older than Gorton, yet he seemed perpetually youthful. The first student body president in University of Washington history to graduate at the top of his class, Adams went on to Harvard Law School. He and Gorton first met early in their careers when their law firms were on the same side in a protracted antitrust case. Adams' first foray into politics resulted in the only electoral setback of his career. In 1958, he lost to the entrenched incumbent, Charles O. Carroll, in a race for King County prosecutor.[13]

While Gorton was making a name for himself in the Legislature, Adams was busy campaigning for John F. Kennedy. At 34, he was rewarded with an appointment as America's youngest U.S. attorney. Seattle sent him to Congress three years later. Serving in the Carter cabinet was an unhappy two years, as it was for most. Being senator had always been his goal. Now Scoop and Maggie were gone.[14]

"We had no money," Adams' campaign manager, Ellen Globokar, recalls. "We didn't have momentum. But we had a great candidate, someone who really knew the state and had great political instincts."[15]

Adams' effusiveness—like Gorton's professorial air—could be grating. One reporter dubbed him the "Yappy Warrior." They both talked too much, an Adams admirer observed. Their campaign managers would cringe "as the eyes of the audience glaze over as dazzling explanations go on and on and on."[16]

Unquestioned was their status as leading contenders. Now on tap was the race everyone was anticipating a decade earlier before Jackson lost the Pennsylvania presidential primary. For starters, they exchanged insults. Gorton said Adams was a carpet-bagger who hadn't really lived in Washington State since being elected to Congress in 1964. Adams said that with Gorton "we've got a senator who talks and no one listens."[17]

24 | Let's Make a Deal

G ORTON AND EVANS ignited a right-wing firestorm on March 4, 1986, when they nominated William L. Dwyer to a vacant seat on the U.S. District Court in Seattle. Before it was over, the left was also mad as hell at Gorton, and Adams had another juicy issue to exploit.

Characters from past dramas—friend and foe alike—keep popping up on the changing sets of Gorton's life. It was Dwyer who won a libel verdict in 1964 for John Goldmark, with Gorton as a character witness for the liberal legislator falsely accused of being a communist. And it was Dwyer whom Gorton sent to the mound against the American League owners in 1976 to secure a new ball club for Seattle. A proud member of the ACLU, Dwyer went on to represent a Black Panther, pro bono; won a state Supreme Court decision overturning a Seattle movie censorship ordinance and defended a controversial children's sex-education book at the Public Library. Dwyer, in short, resoundingly flunked the Reagan Administration's litmus test for prudent jurisprudence. "This man is not even a Republican!" huffed State Senator Jack Metcalf, demonstrating remarkable powers of observation. Ashley Holden, one of the defendants in the Goldmark case, was a hero to the state's unreconstructed Republican right. Noisily alive and well at 92, he said he still knew a pinko when he saw one. "Dwyer is a left-wing liberal and a Democrat, and why would a Republican senator want to nominate a man like that?" Because he is extraordinarily well qualified, said Gorton and Evans. Dwyer "exemplifies what a judge should be," King County Prosecutor Norm Maleng, another Republican, said later as the debate intensified.[1]

When Reagan and Attorney General Ed Meese stonewalled Dwyer's nomination, Gorton informed the White House that he would vote against Daniel Manion, an Indiana lawyer the president desperately wanted on the federal bench. The son of a John Birch Society director who was the Rush Limbaugh of his day, Manion was characterized as a "barely literate" conservative ideologue by his foes. Forty law school deans asserted that he was a mediocre lawyer. Even the Senate Judiciary Committee, which had a Republican majority, deadlocked on his nomination to the Seventh Circuit of the U.S. Court of Appeals in Chicago. Gorton said Manion's qualifications were "no more than marginal." *Seattle Post-Intelligencer* columnist John De Yonge wrote, "The fact is, Gorton, when he was state attorney general, wouldn't have hired Manion as a 99th assistant attorney general in charge of writing clam laws."[2]

Scrambling for votes to avoid having to cave in on Dwyer, the Justice Department made a deal with David Durenberger, a Republican from Minnesota who had balked at Manion. If he'd vote for Manion, his own nominee for a federal judgeship would get the go-ahead after 10 months in limbo. Democrats agreed to a roll call, believing that with Gorton and Evans on their side and some other tricks up their sleeve they still had enough votes to defeat Manion. The Durenberger deal hadn't escaped Gorton. He was more determined than ever to see Dwyer on the bench.

It was June 26, the day of the vote: Evans, Gorton, Bob Dole and several other senators were plopped on the old leather sofa in the Republican cloakroom just off the Senate floor. Quayle came charging in, saying he needed more votes for Manion. "Why should I support Manion," Gorton said, "when I can't get Dwyer's nomination out of the damn Justice Department?" Dole grabbed the phone. "Get me Ed Meese!" he barked to the operator. The attorney general wasn't immediately available, but the majority leader left a blunt message: Tell him they'd better get the lead out on Dwyer if they want Manion.[3]

As the roll call was getting under way, Gorton received a call from the White House: Vote for Manion and we'll stop blocking Dwyer. Gorton's vote made it 47-47. Vice President Bush had the tie-breaker. Senator Byrd,

The Reagans
and the Gortons.
*Gorton Family
Album*

the old pro from West Virginia, quickly changed his vote to "yes" so the Democrats could move for reconsideration. Dole craftily called up other business and prevailed in a parliamentary chess match that stretched over the next four weeks. Evans, who had never wavered in his opposition to Manion, voted against the pivotal procedural motion to reconsider. It was unfair, he said, to make Manion undergo another roll call on the merits of his nomination.[4]

Dan Manion was headed for the federal bench.

As quids pro quo go it was classic D.C. horse-trading, except that the stakes were higher than usual: a lifetime appointment to the federal bench. Democrats railed at Gorton's perfidy. "Slade Gorton couldn't deliver without selling out on his principles," Adams said. Gorton was unrepentant. Absent the Dwyer dustup, he would have supported Manion, he said, because Indiana's Republican senators, Quayle and Richard Lugar, assured him their nominee was no right-wing lapdog. Further, the American Bar Association rated Manion as qualified, albeit marginally. Gorton resented being characterized as insensitive to the bedrock principle of an independent judiciary. He said Dwyer's appointment was in fact a victory in the battle to counter Reagan's single-minded push to install conservatives on the bench. "I regret I cannot do it across the country."[5]

Gorton's deal-making was analyzed and editorialized from Seattle to Savannah. "Deals are made all the time in Congress," The Washington Post said. "But Mr. Gorton took it too far. . . . Judges aren't pork." Eric Pryne of The Seattle Times' Washington Bureau wrote that the episode illustrated "an important distinction" between Gorton and Evans, "who are so alike in so many other ways. Simply put, the difference is this: Gorton has fewer qualms about engaging in the give and take, the wheeling and dealing, the horse-trading that is an essential but sometimes unpleasant element of political life. Evans, while not averse to compromising and negotiating, doesn't play the game as readily or with as much relish."

"Slade has always loved the give and take, the rough and tumble," Jay Fredericksen, a former Evans press secretary, told Pryne. "He knows how to use it. He's very good at it. Dan is a different kind of guy. Slade will do what he has to do. Dan doesn't like to bend." One of Gorton's press aides agreed, though his metaphors were less flattering to the boss. "This is not a perfect world," said David Endicott. "If people want to play that game, Slade will play it. . . .He will get down in that trough with them." Evans took pains to dispel the notion that he disapproved of what his friend and seatmate had done. "I think all of the furor and the talk about Sen. Gorton

212   SLADE GORTON: A HALF CENTURY IN POLITICS

selling out or doing something inappropriate is just pure hogwash." On the other hand, he wouldn't have made the swap.[6]

The political calculus of the Manion-Dwyer deal was tricky. While conservatives and liberals berated Gorton, some analysts said he might have scored important points with the middle. The Adams campaign played the integrity card. "There has always been an underlying question of the true motives of Senator Gorton," said Governor Booth Gardner, Adams' campaign chairman. "An almost subliminal question that the Manion situation clarified is that he does what is in the political and not the public interest. 'Slippery' is back." Ashley Holden pronounced the deal "outrageous." He planned to hold his nose and vote for Gorton as the lesser of two evils, "but not all conservatives are like me."[7]

Other conservatives were angered by Gorton's efforts to help Evans protect a national treasure while still preserving property rights. Slade couldn't win for trying.

FOUR MILES WIDE AND 85 LONG, the Columbia River Gorge is one of the scenic wonders of the world. On a clear day and even in the mist, the vistas sculpted by cataclysmic Ice Age floods are breathtaking. Flanked by rimrock cliffs, the semi-arid eastern portion features rolling beige hills, farms, ranches and plateaus that seldom see people. Then, as the Great River of the West makes its way past the Cascades, Washington and Oregon view one another from steep bluffs lush with Evergreen forests and a profusion of waterfalls. From the Washington side, Mount Hood is a picture-perfect ancient volcano snoozing in a white blanket.

Gorgeous as all this is, the river itself is a far cry from what Lewis and Clark saw. Dammed for electricity and irrigation, beginning with the New Deal and boosted by Scoop and Maggie, the march of progress along the Columbia dispossessed Indians, strangled salmon and set the stage for a battle that was heating up when Jackson died: Should the Gorge be protected as a federal park? To environmentalists, the answer was an unequivocal yes. However, upwards of 70 percent of the 41,000 residents of the Gorge were opposed. They were represented by 24 local governments fearful of federalization. So too the Grange and the National Association of Counties.

A bill introduced by Oregon's Republican senators, Mark Hatfield and Bob Packwood, proposed a two-state commission to manage land-use in the Gorge, designating it a national scenic area to be managed by the Forest Service. Evans, Gorton and most other members of the Washington and Oregon delegations backed a commission largely composed of residents and autonomous of state and federal authorities. Washington Governor John Spellman and Oregon's Vic Atiyeh hatched a compromise that emphasized self-governance, with preservation efforts largely funded by Uncle Sam. Locals on the Washington side dismissed both plans as "nothing more than urban snobbery" that would kill jobs, shrink the tax base and create "virtual ghost towns." Bob Leick, the Skamania County prosecutor, headed the Gorge Defense League. He defended the county's lack of a zoning ordinance and argued that new housing would not necessarily detract from the scenic value of the Gorge. "We're not going to knuckle under just because somebody doesn't want to look at one of our homes."[8]

The final bill was the handiwork of Evans and his staff. Emerging from the Energy and Natural Resources Committee on which Evans served, it authorized a three-tier management plan. At Gorton's insistence, 13 "urban areas" within the Gorge were exempt from the legislation: North Bonneville, Stevenson, Carson, Home Valley, White Salmon, Bingen, Lyle, Dallesport and Wishram in Washington and Cascade Locks, Hood River, Mosier and The Dalles in Oregon. A compact between the two states established a 13-member commission to develop land-use regulations. Each governor would name three members; each of the six Gorge counties would have a seat and the Forest Service would have a non-voting representative. Evans said they had taken special care to solve any economic impacts, including low-interest loans from EDC grants to the states. The bottom line, Evans said, was to prevent "erosion of the spectacular beauty of this national treasure."[9]

A month before the 1986 General Election, Congress approved the Columbia Gorge National Scenic Area, authorizing up to $40 million for land acquisition and protecting Forest Service land from logging or development. Gorton took pains to emphasize that the bill barred the Forest Service from using condemnation to acquire residential homes, farm land and grazing land, as well as "lands used for religious, educational or charitable purposes."[10]

Unimpressed was the Skamania County Republican Central Committee. Charging that Gorton had sold them down the river, it urged voters to support Adams. Reagan signed the bill into law two weeks after the election.[11]

25 | Trick or Treat

THE GORTON CAMPAIGN was riding high on April Fools' Day and scared stiff by Halloween. Paul Newman and Helen Rasmussen, key players from the triumph of 1980, were back on board for 1986. The re-election war chest was brimming and A-list advice from the East was also plentiful—too plentiful, if you asked Newman. Roger Ailes and his inventive assistant, Larry McCarthy, were among the experts enlisted to help with Gorton's TV advertising. Ailes, the future creator of Rupert Murdoch's Fox News Channel, was a hot commodity after coaching Reagan to his landslide victory over Mondale. "Slade now had a palace guard, all the money in the world and Roger Ailes offering advice," Newman says. "I admire Roger, but it was the full employment act for consultants. No one thought Slade could lose."[1]

Steve Excell, former chief of staff to Governor Spellman and Congressman Pritchard, was back in Seattle, doing opposition and issues research for the Gorton campaign in a run-down house they called The Gulag. What he saw made him nervous, too: "The Beltway people didn't understand what was happening out here. Paul saw it immediately. We needed to be on the attack."

"These people were tremendously loyal to Slade and had the best of intentions," Newman says. "They'd helped their senator accomplish a lot, but they'd lost sight of my message: The campaign had to be run from the state." As Tip O'Neill often observed, "All politics is local." Others note, however, that besides Rasmussen, Slade had a strong advisory committee in Seattle that included Walt Howe, Bob Storey and other stalwarts from his previous campaigns. The notion of a palace guard raises hackles, as does the assertion that the campaign wasn't being aggressive. Early on it publicized a letter signed by a number of prominent Democrats who were endorsing Gorton, including Jerry Grinstein, one of Magnuson's former top aides. "It was a challenging time for everyone and differences of personality and opinion were inevitable—as they are in any political campaign," says Chris Koch, Gorton's chief of staff in that character-building year. Koch joined the campaign team after the primary.

John Carlson, a Republican pundit and future candidate for governor, observed later that the Gorton campaign featured two consultants "who hate each other's guts" and 2½ campaign managers. Gorton, he wrote, came across as "an imperious viceroy grudgingly tolerating his leather-faced constituents with Brylcream-spackled hair."[2]

Newman says he smelled trouble and told Gorton so as early as spring. "But nobody believed me. Even Slade was a little snippy. My big error was that I should have resigned right away. My influence and involvement in the campaign steadily waned throughout the summer. All of a sudden Brock caught fire."

Adams had loads of kindling. Yet for much of the spring Democrats and pundits were muttering "Where's Brock?" The Adams campaign was caught up in problems of its own. Ellen Globokar, Brock's 31-year-old campaign manager, was an outsider from Michigan. She was getting the cold shoulder from Lowry partisans and outright second-guessing from Karen Marchioro, the mercurial, intimidating state Democratic chairwoman. Globokar pushed ahead with stoic tenacity. "A lot of people viewed it as a kamikaze mission. I had meeting after meeting with

people who would tell me Brock Adams couldn't win. I felt powerless for a large portion of the campaign." She took a calculated risk to challenge Gorton's effectiveness and went in hock $100,000 before the primary to start buying ads.[3]

Boosted by a noisy senior citizen group, Adams began to hammer away at Slade's support for scaling back the Social Security cost-of-living adjustments. Gorton dismissed the group as "a

Brock Adams on the campaign trail, 1986. *Brian DalBalcon/ The Daily World* wholly owned subsidiary of organized labor and the Democratic Party," adding that when Adams left Congress the Social Security system was hemorrhaging $1 million an hour. Gorton insisted that every vote he'd cast was to help make the trust fund solvent and reduce the deficit. Adams responded with a rally featuring Congressman Pepper, who celebrated his 86th birthday in Seattle by declaring that if Reagan and Gorton had their way seniors would be eating Alpo. Democrats also alleged that Gorton had over-stated his role in securing passage of the wilderness bill. The Manion-for-Dwyer hostage swap helped create more doubts about his integrity. Hanford was the game-changer.

WHEN THE FEDERAL DEPARTMENT OF ENERGY named Hanford as one of three finalists for a national nuclear waste repository and wanted to drill an exploratory shaft deep into the basalt caverns beneath the Columbia, polls found the citizenry overwhelmingly opposed. Scoop and Maggie had "real clout," Adams said. Where was Gorton when the feds wanted to dump on his state? In 1982, Adams noted, Gorton said a nuclear waste repository was "a national responsibility from which no state should be allowed to remove itself unilaterally." True, said Gorton, but he also helped write an amendment mandating a second repository so that Hanford, if selected, wouldn't have to carry the whole load. "My opponent doesn't tell you that." Adams shot back that Scoop had favored an amendment calling for a national survey of potential sites and delaying the whole process until 1987. Gorton opposed it. Gorton said the process was now being politicized, the administration having shelved studies for a second repository in the East. The process should be turned over to an independent board, he insisted.[4]

It was radioactive tit for tat. Adams had the best one-liner. When Gorton urged his constituents to write letters to Energy Secretary John Herrington, a Reagan appointee, Adams snorted, "It's time to fight, not write. He couldn't deliver for the state, so he's asking the Post Office to deliver for him."[5]

Governor Gardner was busy ginning up a referendum on the issue to help energize the Democratic base for November. Adams also denounced a proposal by Gorton, Evans and Congressman Morrison to investigate converting one of the mothballed Washington Public Power Supply System plants to produce less-radioactive weapons-grade fuel so the old "Chernobyl-style" N Reactor could be decommissioned. They said the plan offered the added advantage of helping the struggling Supply System. Among the proletariat, sympathy for WPPSS was in short supply.

When seven workers for a Hanford contractor were dismissed for mishandling plutonium, the specter of a deadly accident or the contamination of the Columbia aquifer grew more menacing, with the WPPSS bond debacle thrown in for bad measure.

In June, an energized Adams gave the speech of his life at the State Democratic Convention in Spokane. "In the past, our Northwest senators fought our tough battles in the Senate," he thundered. "We won when California tried to take our water. We won when others tried to put supertankers in Puget Sound. But what do we win now?—the DOE nuclear lottery! The East gets the power and we get the garbage. Maybe we should call the site the Slade Gorton Memorial Dump!" The delegates leapt to their feet, cheering and chanting "Brock! Brock!"[6]

WITH CONGRESS STILL IN SESSION, Gorton was a red-eyed weekend warrior. A mid-August poll for the Adams campaign showed the Democrat closing the gap to 4 percent, with 20 percent of the likely voters undecided. Although Gorton's tracking polls around Labor Day indicated Slade still had big lead, low-turnout primaries are a crap shoot. Newman and Excell were worried. Confirmation arrived in the form of a lightning bolt on the night of September 16 when the primary election ballots were tallied. Adams nearly outpolled Gorton. The turnout was 27 percent, and fewer than 20 percent of the voters showed up in King County's traditionally Republican suburbs. Every headline hailed the upset. What Adams most needed now was money to match his momentum, and Democratic donors opened their checkbooks. With a net gain of four seats, the party could regain control of the Senate. Frank Greer, one of the country's top Democratic consultants, came on board.

Team Gorton called for reinforcements and regrouped, shifting its focus from Gorton's record to Adams' record. Evans loaned much of his staff to the campaign. All of Slade's competitive juices kicked in. They interspersed their attack ads with more positive, senatorial messages and quickly regained the lead. Excell warned, however, that things could turn on a dime if they made any mistakes. Adams certainly wasn't making any. Whenever he landed a solid punch, the gap would close.[7]

While Reagan had helped Gorton raise $2 million, the administration was doing Slade more harm than good, sending mixed signals on the waste dump and dragging its heels on its end of the bargain over the judges. Manion had been on the bench since July. Dwyer was in limbo. Such was Attorney General Meese's disdain that the Seattle attorney wasn't even nominated by the White House until late September. When

Meese's deputies learned that Dwyer and his wife had attended a Mondale fundraiser, they urged Gorton to forward three names for consideration. "I will send them three names," he replied icily: "William L. Dwyer, William L. Dwyer and William L. Dwyer."[8]

Intent on punishing Gorton, Democrats on the Judiciary Committee stonewalled a vote on Dwyer. There was no hope of confirmation before the general election—more red meat for Adams. Gorton was under fire left and right. "The question in terms of the general public is why it is that a Republican senator would be blocked by a Republican Department of Justice and a Republican White House and require him to engage in this type of behavior," observed Arval Morris, a professor at the University of Washington Law School. Prodded by a *Post-Intelligencer* reporter, Gorton snapped, "I can't understand why you and your newspaper have failed to appreciate what I achieved in getting (Dwyer) nominated to the federal bench."[9]

The campaign attempted to defuse the issue with a commercial that emphasized Gorton's access and independence. The president and the senator are seen conferring intently in the Oval Office. "Slade and I don't agree on every issue," Reagan looks up to say, "but you can always count on Slade's dedication and care for the people of Washington State. I urge you to re-elect my good friend Slade Gorton."

THE 1986 CAMPAIGN, from Seattle to Sarasota, is remembered by veteran reporters and politicos as "the year of the 30-second war." Reporters were galled to find themselves covering commercials—"free media," in campaign lingo—laced with exaggerations and emotional images. When Gorton called a press conference to preview three new spots set to air during the last two weeks of the campaign, R.W. "Johnny" Apple Jr., the bigger-than-life correspondent for *The New York Times,* was on hand, sizing up one of the nation's tossup congressional races. As the videotape began, he rolled his eyes and exchanged weary glances with the local scribes. Had reporting really come to this? "For most senators, incumbency is a tremendous electoral asset," Apple wrote, "but for Mr. Gorton it has proved a mixed blessing. It has helped him raise a lot of money for television advertising, more than any candidate in this state's history. He will probably spend $3.3 million overall, as opposed to $1.7 million for Mr. Adams.* But it has also kept him out of the state while Mr. Adams . . . rebuilt his networks of supporters here."[10]

---

* Roughly double that to get 2010 dollars.

Jim Kneeland, a former Gardner press secretary who had become a political consultant, was critical of the media's role as enabler by spending "a disproportionate amount of time" focusing on the commercials. But that horse was already so far out of the barn trying to lasso it was futile. "Truth Squad" sidebars designed to help viewers and readers survive barrages of negativity became a staple of political coverage.[11]

The Adams campaign relentlessly styled Brock as a principled fighter. Adams' most memorable, and likely most effective, commercial posed him in front of a giant diesel locomotive hauling out-of-state nuclear waste to Hanford. "I'm stopping these trains from making Washington state a dump!" Adams vowed.[12]

Before he headed West to cover the race, Joel Connelly, the *Post-Intelligencer's* Washington correspondent, pored over internal documents detailing how the Department of Energy was ignoring the views of its own scientists on whether the basalt beneath Hanford could safely contain radioactive material. Gorton pointed to the revelation as more evidence that the administration needed to find another site.[13]*

WHEN CONGRESS FINALLY WRAPPED UP WORK on the tax reform bill and adjourned on October 18, Gorton dashed to the airport. He had 16 days to try and save his seat. Adams had been at it every day for months. He and the governor were practically joined at the hip, an inspired decision. In public affection, a columnist marveled, Booth Gardner ranked "somewhere between Donald Duck and fresh-baked bread." One of the TV spots ordered up by Globokar and Greer paired portraits of the two that were so strikingly similar it almost appeared they were brothers—two happy warriors against a first-termer with high negatives. Joe Biden, the ranking Democrat on the Senate Judiciary Committee, and Ted Kennedy came to Seattle to flail Gorton as a flip-flopper on the Manion vote. Kennedy passed the hat, sang a few verses of "My Wild Irish Rose" and took off the gloves to emphasize his colleagues' "antipathy toward Slade Gorton." The breach of Senate etiquette was denounced on both sides of the aisle. Slade summed up his disgust with his favorite adjective, "ludicrous," which he could imbue with sub-zero disdain. Kennedy had spent years futilely pushing the judicial nomination of one of his father's pals, a man rated

---

* In the margin of one critical report an expert had penciled a succinctly unscientific translation of what the study said about Hanford's suitability: "It sucks." Connelly had to wait 24 years for a more liberal editor before he could share that tidbit.[14]

by the ABA as "lacking in intellectual capacity." "We are all horse-traders here," said Rudy Boschwitz.[15]*

The consensus was that Gorton won all three of the debates, two of which were televised statewide. He had prepped by recruiting Phil Gramm to play Adams in a mock debate, complete with rostrums and a TV camera. "It is the worst humiliation I have ever suffered," Gorton recalls, "and a great lesson that Gramm is one of the smartest guys who ever came down the pike. Here was a conservative Republican mopping the floor with me with a dead-on performance as a liberal Democrat. I beat the real Brock Adams at least that badly in our debates." But how many votes did he win? Seattle's KOMO TV, one of the sponsors, selected a panel of undecided voters and asked them to rate the candidates' performances. Gorton was clearly the better debater, the real people agreed, yet he came across as "too cold, too tight, too forced," with a smile that seemed pasted on. They were "more inclined as a result of the encounter to vote for Adams," who was chirpy but likable. Gorton's people told him he had to work at being more charming. They aired a commercial featuring the engaging Sally Gorton. "Sometimes he doesn't let it show," she told voters, "but he cares so much." Evans, the sure-fire surrogate, cut several radio and TV commercials denouncing the attacks on his friend in his rich baritone.[16]

Unchastened, Adams asserted that the Republican plan to convert a civilian commercial reactor to produce weapons-grade plutonium would violate the 1968 nuclear proliferation treaty. A new commercial aired in the last days of the campaign featured Adams standing in front of one of the mothballed WPPSS plants, charging that if Gorton had his way it would become "a nuclear-bomb factory." Slade was outraged. "If political hypocrisy were a crime, Brock Adams would go to jail!" Calling Hanford a bomb factory, Gorton said, "is sort of like calling a rope manufacturer a hangman." An aide handed reporters copies of a speech Adams had made in 1966 when he was a member of Congress. In it, Adams called the N Reactor "a valuable asset which has served us well in building our defenses."[17]

Gorton charged that Adams missed key votes as a congressman and was an ineffective Transportation Secretary. Further, he was a "foreign agent" during his lobbying days, representing Japanese fishing companies competing with Washington fishermen and Algerian oil and natural

* In 1992, however, Kennedy graciously agreed to grease the skids for the Senate confirmation of Slade's brother Nat to the federal bench in Massachusetts.

gas interests. The ads clearly hurt, Globokar glumly admitted, adding that some voters even called their campaign headquarters wanting to know if Adams was a spy. The *Post-Intelligencer's* Shelby Scates wrote that "two talented guys are behaving like a couple of turkeys, allowing the campaign to degenerate into a shabby travesty of the real qualities of these two people."[18]

THE GORTON CAMPAIGN was conflicted over a White House offer to send in Reagan down the stretch. Most Republicans were going to vote for Slade regardless, Excell and Newman said at a strategy session. Having his back slapped by Reagan wasn't going to win him more votes from Democrats. "But many on the finance committee said they needed the president to raise big dollars to ensure we were ready for anything down the stretch," Excell says. Others were worried about the "base." Having Reagan appear with Gorton would help solidify his standing with conservatives—and they shouldn't forget his appeal to "Reagan Democrats." National polls indicated that fully 8 percent of those who described themselves as likely Republican voters weren't going to show up on Election Day. Ralph Munro, Washington's secretary of state, projected the turnout at a sluggish 55-60 percent, well below the previous comparable midterm. The election could turn on the turnout.

"With the waste dump such a hot potato, Paul and I were worried about what Reagan might say," Excell recalls. "The Senate staff said it was impossible to guarantee a positive announcement on Hanford. So as advice goes, it was a fine mess. The campaign team was Balkanized." Gorton listened intently. Finally, he sided with the majority: Bring the Gipper to Spokane. "There comes a time when you have to turn mother's picture to the wall," Newman sighed. At least Reagan would be appearing in a smaller media market.[19]

The Adams campaign was craftily amping up expectations, predicting Reagan would try to rescue Gorton with an "October surprise" by announcing a halt to the dump-site testing process and ordering a fresh start on the whole process. Gorton said that was ridiculous. "We are simply going to be getting to the president with some information he doesn't have. . . .There's no way we'll get a decision on the spot, but we'll get his ear." Hoping to steal some of the thunder from Reagan's visit, Adams and Gardner also headed for Spokane for a Labor Council rally with hometown Congressman Tom Foley.[20]

On October 30, a chartered jet carrying 130 members of the national press touched down at Geiger Field just west of Spokane minutes before

Air Force One. So much for a small media market. Slade and Sally went aboard the president's plane. Before long, the threesome emerged in the doorway with smiles and waves for the photographers. Dan and Nancy Evans joined them on the cold, wind-whipped tarmac. Then Gorton and Evans piled into the president's limo with Donald Regan, the top White House aide, for the ride to the Spokane-Sheraton. The imperious chief of staff had complicated things for Gorton with a recent remark that Washington State was likely to be the final choice for the nuke-waste site.

They were all tired, Reagan having made 54 appearances in 22 states. Still, the president seemed curiously preoccupied. They would soon learn why. Aid to the Nicaraguan guerrillas was the single most controversial issue of his presidency. Reagan called them "freedom fighters." Tip O'Neill said they were a "ragtag army of racketeers, bandits" and nun-rapers. Gorton had supported the administration early on, calling that "the greatest mistake" he'd made as a first-term senator. He had opposed the most recent Contra-aid proposals—"thank God before it brought Americans into a conflict in that country." Adams said Nicaragua smacked of Vietnam and charged throughout the campaign that Gorton's change of heart was just election-year politics.

In Spokane, protesters outside Reagan's hotel were shouting, "Prepare for the arrival of the chief Contra!" Reagan was worried that the issue was about to morph into a crippling scandal. The story broke the day before the election: His National Security Council had engineered a covert arms deal with Iran to secure the release of American hostages and generate funds for the Contras. Lt. Col. Oliver North, a swashbuckling National Security Council operative, famously thought it was "a pretty neat idea."

Gorton and Evans, however, had no inkling of all that. Reagan handed them a copy of what he planned to say about Hanford. It was a noncommittal disaster. Mr. President, they said, you can't say this. They spent the rest of the ride and another hour in the president's 15th floor suite emphasizing that what he said about Hanford the next day could make or break Slade's campaign. The president rejected a chance to feast on Northwest quail with Regan and Communications Director Pat Buchanan and went right to bed.[21]

Downstairs, Gorton was telling reporters he'd had "a more detailed discussion" with Reagan about Hanford than ever before. "We now have a much more informed White House." He said he didn't ask the president to drop Hanford from consideration, just to follow the site selection policies laid out by Congress: No exploratory drilling in Fiscal Year 1987. "If the law is followed, as far as I'm concerned, Hanford will be dropped. . . .

I do not know what's going to be in the president's speech tomorrow. I certainly hope he says something on the subject. But we don't expect any tremendous announcement."[22]

Evans and Gorton also met privately with Connelly and his *P-I* colleague, Neil Modie. Connelly says the senators implied that Reagan would say something to defuse the issue.[23]

Adams was working overtime to pump up expectations: "If Gorton doesn't get from him a commitment to stop the dump process and start over and fire Herrington . . . then I think the visit may backfire on him."[24]

A ROARING CROWD OF 5,000 filled the Spokane Coliseum on the morning of October 31, with Joel Pritchard as master of ceremonies, exhorting the faithful to welcome the president with a rolling wave. Reagan dutifully saluted the Washington State University Marching Band, the Central Valley High School Band, the Eastern Washington University Collegians and "three members of Washington State's A-Team in Washington, D.C.: Senator Dan Evans and Representatives Sid Morrison and Rod Chandler—and of course the State Chairman of the GOP . . . *Dunn Jennifer!*" That gaffe was especially embarrassing because Dunn adored the president. She had named one of her sons Reagan.[25]

"Slade Gorton is a man of principle and integrity," the president declared. "You know, every time Slade walks into the Oval Office, I can't help thinking of another great senator from your state—Scoop Jackson. And like Scoop, when Slade sits across a table from you he has the courage and honesty to tell you what he believes, whether he agrees with you or not. I've seen him in action, making a reality of Scoop's longtime dream of a home port for the Navy at Everett, and believe me he's about the most effective fighter any state has on Capitol Hill."[26]

Gorton was holding his breath. "A perfect example," Reagan continued, "is the issue of selecting potential sites for a nuclear waste repository. Slade has told me about his deep concern for the health and safety of Washingtonians, particularly as it relates to this issue. On this point, Slade has gotten the ears of everyone back in the nation's capital." Someone in the audience yelled, "Way to go, Slade!" Reagan nodded. Slade kept smiling. "Now, as you know, there were plans to begin work at Hanford this fiscal year. Well, Slade, working with Dan Evans and Mark Hatfield, persuaded the Congress to adopt a provision that stops the drilling of an exploratory shaft for 12 months. And Slade has alerted me that some people have suggested that this administration might intentionally circumvent the law. Well, that's the kind of thing that touches my temperature control (laughter). And let me

President Reagan with Slade and Sally on Halloween 1986 in Spokane.
The Gipper did not win one for the Gortons or "Dunn Jennifer." *Kit King/*
The Spokesman-Review

tell you I will see to it that the law on this issue is followed to the letter, and
let no one tell you differently. . . . So when you go to the polls, win one for
Slade Gorton; win one for your future, and win one for America's future.
And I can't resist saying it: Win one for the Gipper!" With that, thousands
of balloons descended from the rafters.[27]

The Gipper had just fumbled on the 5-yard line. Slade was still grin-
ning on the outside as Reagan clasped his hand and held it high. Somewhere in the Adams war room high fives were being exchanged. Halloween was no treat for the Gorton campaign. Around the state and across
the nation, Reagan's muddled statements about Hanford led every newspaper story and newscast.

Adams crowed that Reagan's "terribly disappointing," ambiguous statement about following the law was proof positive that Gorton had zero pull
with the White House. Governor Gardner charged that the Department of
Energy had already violated federal law by beginning tests at the proposed
waste dump site. When a White House spokesman replied that the president didn't agree, he went on to make matters worse by emphasizing that
Reagan had no plans to overrule any decisions by the Energy secretary.

Gorton had "a tremendous downside risk" from the Reagan visit, Ad-

ams said, "and the downside risk came true. . . .We hear all these statements about Mr. Gorton being in the Oval Office and see these television
commercials showing him talking to the president. It makes me wonder,
whatever were they talking about?" Still, Christine Gregoire, an assistant
attorney general handling the state's lawsuits over Hanford, said she was
encouraged by Reagan's promise to obey the law.[28]

Gorton's pollsters told him he was eight points ahead when Reagan
arrived and six behind the day after he left. Stu Elway's Oct. 31 snapshot
gave Adams a three-point lead, 47-44. However, after a lively internal debate, *The Seattle Times* decided against printing the results, explaining a
week later that "we don't think such election-eve or Election Day horse-
race poll results serve any good purpose." Like projections based on East
Coast exit polling, late polls also tend to anger readers who believe they
alter the outcome, wrote Alex MacLeod, the paper's managing editor.[29]

All of the polls agreed on one thing: 8 to 10 percent of the likely voters
hadn't made up their minds, doubtless turned off by the raging negativity. Ron Dotzauer, who had engineered Gardner's 1984 gubernatorial victory, said the seat of his pants told him the race was dead even and whoever had the best finishing kick would win.

In the Tri-Cities, where Hanford's reactors emerged ghost-like from
the cold morning fog on the last day of the campaign, the reporters on the
plane peppered Gorton with questions about why he hadn't been able to
convince Reagan to review or reverse his Energy Department's stance on
Hanford. Connelly listened intently while Gorton did his best to change
the subject as they hopped from Pasco to Yakima, then to Vancouver and
finally back home to Seattle. A large man with a walrus mustache, inquisitive eyes and a voice that sometimes betrays a hint of weary incredu-
lity at the things politicians do and say, Connelly asked the question one
more time. Gorton cleared his throat and furrowed his brow. "Last Thursday night was the first time he had heard anything about the subject, as
far as I could tell. He was not going to overrule a Cabinet department the
first time he heard something about it."[30]

As the campaign plane passed over Mount Adams, Gorton gazed for a
moment at a peak he had summited. He told Connelly that a tracking poll
conducted the night before showed him back up by six points. He dis-
counted a KIRO-TV poll that found Adams ahead by the same margin,
conceding, however, that there was "a fairly substantial undecided vote
out there—well over 20 percent, which could decide the election."[31]

"One of those polls is full of beans," Sally Gorton piped up. They all
laughed.[32]

NINE MINUTES AFTER THE POLLS CLOSED in Washington State, ABC News announced Adams was the likely winner based on exit polls. The puncturing of the first balloon went largely unnoticed at Gorton's election-night party at the Westin Hotel since hardly anyone was watching TV. At 8:35, they paid attention when the first returns gave Adams a 10-point lead. "It can change in a hurry," someone said reassuringly. It could and it did. By 10:20, a huge cheer of relief went up as Gorton pulled even. He made an appearance at 11:40. "The reports of our demise were greatly exaggerated," he declared with a hopeful grin before brushing past a crowd of reporters en route to the back door. He was worried. By 1:30 a.m., buoyed by the last returns from King County, Adams had a cushion the absentees couldn't erode. The party was over. A reporter found Pritchard waiting for an elevator. Why was Gorton losing? "More people in this state are Democrats than Republicans," Slade's old friend said. "It's a tough state" for a Republican.[33]

A big man wearing a Ronald Reagan mask and a sign that said "loser" brought down the house when he strolled into the Adams campaign headquarters.[34]

Brock Adams was victorious by 26,540 votes, 50.66 percent of the total cast. He carried King County by 34,000, 54 percent, and posted solid margins in the other traditionally Democratic counties on the west side of the Cascades—notably Grays Harbor, Pierce and Cowlitz. That offset Gorton's advantage on the East Side, although Adams ran him a surprisingly close race in Spokane County. Skamania County, where the Republicans were furious with Slade over his support for the Columbia Gorge protection plan, went for Adams 2,312 to 602.

Five other Republican senators elected with Reagan six years earlier were also defeated. The president's coattails were gone. He was now a lame duck with a Democratic Congress that could subpoena Iran-Contra players to its heart's content. Adams would be joining a new Democratic majority in the U.S. Senate, together with Harry Reid of Nevada and Tom Daschle of South Dakota. One of the Republicans' few new faces was former POW John McCain, succeeding the retiring Barry Goldwater in Arizona. On Seattle's Queen Anne hill, Warren and Jermaine Magnuson were euphoric. Tip O'Neill, retiring from the House, declared, "If there was a Reagan revolution, it's over."[35]

Losing was an experience Gorton had difficulty intellectualizing. He had been 9-0 at the ballot box. On the morning of November 5, he strode into a storefront office on Seattle's Denny Regrade to take his place in front of a semi-circle of cameras and reporters. A campaign aide had warned the media, "He doesn't want to answer any questions analyzing the election, so be sensitive, OK?"

Slade was flanked funereally by Sally and their two daughters. Their eyes were swollen. Sally found it hard not to hang her head. It was so painful to watch her guy concede. The Senate was his life's ambition. His chin was up but his smile was thin and his words, though gracious, had a distant quality, as if he was reading from a prepared text. Blinking into the glare of the TV lights, he read a letter of congratulations to Adams: "You ran a skillful and effective campaign which peaked at exactly the right time. You begin a Senate career at an exciting and challenging time in our nation's history. You have my best wishes for a satisfying and successful term." He thanked his family, his campaign workers, his Senate staff and the people of Washington for "28 magnificent, challenging, exciting years." No regrets. "I would not give up the past six years for anything in the world."[36]

"Senator," a TV reporter cried out, "what went wrong?"

"Analyzing elections is for winners and for pundits," Gorton replied crisply.

What about the future?

Gorton said he would never again seek elective office, but he said it in such an abrupt way that someone asked it again a few minutes later.

"That's what I said," he said.[37]

26 | Post-mortems

I F VICTORY HAS A THOUSAND FATHERS and defeat is an orphan, this waif was left with a footlocker full of second-guessing. Paul Newman, the genius of 1980, was now the goat of '86, according to one post-mortem. Phil Watkins, the campaign's communications director, told a forum that poor polling decisions early on played a big role in Slade's loss.[1]

"Stuff like this comes with the territory when you're a consultant," Newman says, flatly denying his polls were flawed. "I didn't have any traction in that campaign for most of the summer. After the primary, all of a sudden it's like somebody playing a game of checkers. They've got four checkers left and they say, 'OK, tell me how I can win this game?' What you want to say is, 'The way you can win this game is to call me when it starts.'

"The truth is highly overrated," Newman quips, but one thing is for sure: "The Reagan visit was a stake in the heart. We had a lead when Reagan showed up. We lost the lead literally the day after. And we still almost came back."[2]

Chris Koch, Gorton's chief of staff, agreed with those who were calling Hanford "Gorton's Iran," a reference to Jimmy Carter's travails with the ayatollah. "The Hanford issue was a mess for us," Koch said. "In a logical world, people shouldn't have held Slade responsible for it. But Brock did a good job of capitalizing on it. They ran a picture-perfect campaign, once they got going."[3]

Elway's polling on the Sunday and Monday before the election revealed that Adams voters were overwhelmingly motivated by Hanford, Social Security and Medicare. The referendum on Hanford as a dump site found 82.6 percent in favor of telling the feds to take a hike. Further, 55 percent of Adams' vote came from women. He projected more warmth than Gorton. "He just didn't do the 'little touch' things that make a difference, particularly for a guy whose strength isn't one-on-one," one Gorton supporter told *The Seattle Times* on condition of anonymity. "He needed to have someone

who'd take the magazine out of his hand when he needed to talk with people" rather than surrounding himself with policy-oriented staffers. Dave
Adams, a spokesman for the state GOP, noted that Gorton had worn sweat-
ers and gone tie-less during the 1980 campaign against Magnuson. Dark,
senatorial suits on his lean frame now made him look stiff.[4]

GORTON LEFT IT TO THE PUNDITS, and they had no shortage of opinions.
Lou Cannon, the White House correspondent for *The Washington Post*,
said it was bogus to blame Reagan for Gorton's defeat. The president
wasn't about to say anything more about Hanford than he did, Cannon
said, and the Gorton campaign had only itself to blame for fanning the
flames by inviting him to the state. David S. Broder, another widely read
columnist, said the broader issue was the damage to civility. "All across
America voters have been inundated in a tidal wave of negative TV ads
which have polluted the atmosphere, cheapened the dialogue of democracy and guaranteed that whoever wins office this year, the public has
been cheated of its chance to hear its would-be leaders address the issues
they must face." Broder pointed to the "essentially unconstrained flow of
cash into congressional campaigns" and the ascendancy of consultants
and their pollsters.[5]

Newman believes, however, that "if something is important, the American people know it, regardless of what campaign professionals advise.
The tail does not wag the dog."

As a lifelong baseball fan, Gorton had to chuckle if he saw Martin Nolan's analysis in the *Boston Globe*. The 1986 campaign reminded Nolan of
Mickey Mantle's next-to-last home run. In the twilight of his career, legs
aching, the Yankee slugger stepped to the plate against the Detroit Tigers
in September of 1968. Denny McLain was on the mound for the Tigers.
With a 6-0 lead, he was feeling mischievously magnanimous toward the
future Hall of Famer making his last appearance in Detroit. McLain
strolled to within a few feet of the plate and in a stage whisper told Bill
Freehan, the catcher, "Let's let him hit one." Mantle turned to Freehan
and asked, "Is that right?" Freehan nodded. When McLain delivered a
juicy fastball down the middle, Mickey sent it soaring for his 535th homer.
The Detroit crowd cheered.

When their eyes met as Mickey rounded third base, McLain winked.
Watching intently from the on-deck circle was Joe Pepitone, who strode to
the plate, waved his hand in the middle of the strike zone and said "Right
here!" McLain promptly knocked him down. The explanation to the puz-
zled Pepitone was simple: "You ain't Mickey Mantle."

"As they brushed off Tuesday's dust from their uniforms," Nolan wrote, "Mack Mattingly, Jim Broyhill, Jeremiah Denton, Ken Kramer, Jim Abdnor, Mark Andrews, Ed Zschau and Slade Gorton all have discovered that they ain't Ronald Reagan."[6]

Actually, you could make a case that Ronald Reagan wasn't even Ronald Reagan any more.

27 | The Comeback

RETURNING TO THE CAPITOL in defeat was devastating. Outwardly, though, at least around his wife, Gorton was neither melancholy nor brooding. "Just quiet," Sally says. And she knew what that meant: He was trying to come to grips intellectually with what he felt viscerally—profound disappointment and a sense of loss. Being a senator was his life's ambition.

"He simply would not talk about it. So I was quiet, too." On the morning he had to go back to his office on the Hill, he dithered. "I knew he couldn't bear the thought of facing the staff he loved so much. When he finally left, I went to see the good soul of the neighborhood. I called at her door, unannounced, went in and sat down at her kitchen table and poured out the whole horrible story for the whole afternoon—all the dirty tricks; everything that went wrong that shouldn't have. And at the end of the afternoon—and I mean three or four hours—she walked me back to my garden gate and we stood there laughing. I'd gotten it all out of my system to a wonderful friend who would just listen. Otherwise I don't know what I would have done. Slade didn't need to know how badly I felt—how badly our girls felt. But the truth is I'm sure he did because he's often said he could let all of those attacks—'the Ivy League lawyer,' as if that was a derogatory statement; 'the cold, calculating patrician politician'—just roll off his back. He always said it's much harder on the spouse and the children. And he's right. When he lost, he didn't make anyone else feel badly. He didn't blame anybody. He kept it all inside."

Gorton got busy writing letters of reference and making calls to help his staff land new jobs. He told them how great they were and said it was going to be all right. As for himself, he planted a seed that a seat on the 9th U.S. Circuit Court of Appeals would be palatable. Five judges on the 28-member court based in San Francisco had offices in Seattle's Federal Courthouse. Dan Evans told reporters he would "enthusiastically support" his nomination.[1] With a vacancy to be filled, Reagan had an opportunity to move the left-leaning court to the right, or at least toward the center. But Gorton was not on his short list.

What Slade sensed at the time was fully documented in 2007 when Reagan's diaries were published. The dyspeptic entry for May 27, 1987, says: "Last subject was a group of our Sens are demanding we appoint former Sen. Slade Gorton (Wash. defeated in 1986) to court of appeals. We might settle for a district judgeship if there's an opening—but he has been an opponent of everything I've tried to do."[2]

Attorney General Ed Meese—Reagan's dark side alter ego—also mistrusted Gorton, and the feeling was mutual. Senator Orrin Hatch of Utah and many other conservatives who wanted Gorton to get the seat were unhappy when a "Meese man," San Diego law professor Bernard Siegan, was nominated. An ad hoc coalition of liberals and conservatives soon derailed his nomination. By then Meese was on his way out on the heels of multiple scandals and Gorton was weighing other options.[3]

Reporters were pressing Evans on his own future. Would he seek re-election in 1988? He was mulling, and he wasn't in a hurry. One thing was clear: He still hated passing the hat, describing as "an abomination" the "incessant" fundraisers that were already nightly events almost two years before the next election.[4]

AS SLADE AND SALLY crossed the Potomac and headed home to Seattle through the middle of America in their Renault Alliance, they listened to the Iran-Contra scandal unfold on the car radio.

Slade accepted an offer to join Davis Wright & Jones, one of Seattle's leading law firms, after a therapeutic overseas business trip financed by his brother Mike, who knew getting away would do him good. Never much of a traveler and a critic of junkets, he enjoyed making calls on customers and suppliers of Slade Gorton & Co. in New Zealand, Australia, Singapore and Hong Kong.

That March, while Jennifer Dunn and 13 other members of the Republican National Committee were lunching at the White House, Dunn told the president and his new chief of staff, Howard Baker, that Gorton "would make a great FBI director." William Webster was leaving the post to become director of the CIA. Baker said "there'd be nobody better" than his former Senate colleague. Dunn's suggestion caught Slade by surprise. "With friends like that, I don't need any enemies," he laughed. "No one has talked to me about taking that job, and I have no background in that kind of law enforcement . . . so I will not be offered that job." In fact, he'd

had no job offers of any kind from the administration, "and I'm not hanging on every ring of the phone."[5*]

Gorton was the law firm's lead lobbyist for a $1 million federal study on
the merits of having the Department of Energy acquire a mothballed
WPPSS reactor to produce nuclear weapons material—the project he had
championed in Congress together with Morrison and Evans, who were
still staunch supporters.

BILL DWYER'S NOMINATION to the federal bench was still on ice in June of
1987. Gorton and Evans were furious. Slade told Howard Baker that a deal
was a deal. He'd paid a heavy price for putting Manion over the top; now
it was time for the president to tell the Justice Department to get off the
dime. Asked if he thought the president was behind the delay, Gorton
said, "I think he's so disengaged he doesn't know of it. I doubt that the
question has even gotten to him."[7]

The White House equivocated, then said it was the Democrats' fault.
Underestimating his adversary, Meese gave Dan Evans the runaround.
Often on icy terms with Reagan when they were governors, Evans demonstrated he too could play hardball. Gorton cheered as his friend threatened to block every Reagan judicial nomination on the West Coast if the
Justice Department continued to stonewall Dwyer. Brock Adams, who
never suggested Dwyer wouldn't be a fine judge, volunteered to help.[8]

Dwyer was finally sworn in on Dec. 1, 1987. "He will bring such moral
courage and enlightened wisdom to the bench that all who sit in judgment before him—no matter how unpopular—will receive just treatment," Evans predicted. When Dwyer succumbed to cancer 15 years later
at the age of 72, he was mourned as a towering figure in Northwest law.
Gorton and Evans had given the nation one of its foremost trial judges.
Philosophically, however, Gorton and Dwyer were often at odds. The future held a monumental clash.[9]

DAN EVANS WAS NOT A HAPPY CAMPER. In fact, a long hike in the Cascades
would have done him a world of good. At 62, not only was he a junior

---

* It wasn't the first time an admirer had advanced Gorton as a candidate for director of the
FBI, although the original notion didn't come to light until 1991 with the release of a batch of
Oval Office tapes from the Watergate era. Nixon is heard talking with John Ehrlichman
about his fervent desire to be rid of J. Edgar Hoover. The crafty old G-Man was Nixon's equal
when it came to ruthless duplicity. As they're kicking around possible successors, Ehrlichman suggests Gorton—"a young attorney general in my state who's a very classy guy."[6]

member of a minority party, being a senator was nothing like being a governor. In public life, "not much beats the opportunity a governor has to be in control of the agenda," he said almost wistfully. "You may not control the decision, but you control the agenda." Alan Simpson observed, "Dan has an engineering mind. It's precision and it's putting link on link on girder on girder, and in this place the sand comes along every four days and washes out the foundation."[10]

The sulfurous debate over Reagan's nomination of Robert Bork, a divisive conservative, to the U.S. Supreme Court, was one of the last straws for Evans. During a three-day swing around the state, reporters asked if his re-election campaign was officially under way. Evans said he was still waiting "for that bolt of lightning from above." It arrived without thunder around midnight on October 20, 1987, more like a germinated epiphany than a bright flash. Evans told his wife he'd had enough and announced his decision before the day was out at a packed news conference. In an eloquent essay for *The New York Times Magazine,* Evans summed up his feelings:

> I came to Washington with a slightly romantic notion of the Senate—perhaps natural for a former governor and civil engineer whose hobby is the study of history—and I looked forward to the duel of debate, the exchange of ideas. What I found was a legislative body that had lost its focus and was in danger of losing its soul. In the United States Senate, debate has come to consist of set speeches read before a largely empty chamber; and in committees, quorums are rarely achieved. I have lived though five years of bickering and protracted paralysis. Five years is enough. I just can't face another six years of frustrating gridlock. . . .
>
> Consider the filibuster—speaking at length to delay and defeat a bill. This legislative tactic has an honorable past, but recently its use has grown like a malignant tumor. . . . Now merely a "hold," or threat of filibuster, placed by a senator is sufficient to kill a bill. Senator Jesse A. Helms's bitter feud with the State Department provides a classic example of this. The Republican from North Carolina has shown himself particularly adept at using the rules to further his own foreign policy agenda. . . . Only rarely is the Senate willing to go through the pain and time necessary to stop this bullying. The dramatic decline in discipline helped to stretch out legislative sessions interminably, and thus eliminated the extended periods of time that legislators used to spend among their constituents. Most of us have been forced to become only Tuesday-through-Thursday senators, squeezing in brief weekend visits to avoid feeling like exiles from our own home states.[11]

Evans' decision created the state's first wide open U.S. Senate race since 1944 when Magnuson defeated Harry Cain.

Possible successors, the media reported excitedly, included every member of the state's congressional delegation except Foley, who was on track to become speaker of the House. The Democratic nomination—and election, too—was practically Governor Gardner's for the asking, everyone agreed, but he was a shoo-in for re-election in 1988.

Lowry and Don Bonker, the seven-term congressman from Vancouver, soon emerged as the Democratic frontrunners. Lowry's King County base was formidable and he'd run statewide in 1983. Bonker had name familiarity problems outside his district, but he was less liberal than Lowry. He was also an expert on international trade and an evangelical Christian. Bonker felt certain he could beat Gorton by co-opting the middle if he could get past Lowry.

Norm Dicks, a Magnuson protégé who turned out to be a lot like Jackson, was reluctant to risk his growing seniority on the House Appropriations Committee. Congressman Al Swift of Bellingham, a former TV commentator, had been poised to challenge Evans. Now he had cold feet because he knew winning the primary would be dicey. "My reading of the field is that there's one I can beat, one I can't and one that's a toss-up." It was easy to deduce he was talking about Dicks, Lowry and Bonker, in that order.[12]

Sid Morrison, the four-term Republican congressman from the Yakima Valley, immediately formed an exploratory committee. Ralph Munro, who loved being secretary of state, wasn't interested. Just to be certain his message was clear, he said so three ways: "No. Hell no. Absolutely no." Joel Pritchard had his sights set on becoming lieutenant governor. The much-admired Bill Ruckelshaus, Gorton's old friend, was back in Seattle after a second tour of duty heading the federal Environmental Protection Agency, making some real money as a lawyer. John Spellman was definitely interested, saying, "This can and should be a Republican seat." However, after the thumping he took from Gardner four years earlier, he was damaged goods. Jennifer Dunn would run only if no other viable candidate emerged.[13]

The Seattle Times' coverage of the shadow boxing failed to even mention Gorton. Hadn't he said only 11 months earlier that he would never again seek elective office? The *P-I* at least bothered to ask. "I have no intention of getting into a race for the U.S. Senate that lasts 54 weeks," Gorton told Connelly. On the other hand, if he bided his time and the others fell by the wayside it might be 20 weeks shorter. He didn't say that, of course. What he did was call Mike McGavick.[14]

MCGAVICK LOOKED YOUNGER THAN 30. In campaign years, though, he was an old pro, having started at 8, doorbelling with his dad in Seattle's Wallingford neighborhood. From his post at the pro-business Washington Roundtable he'd watched Gorton's 1986 campaign from the sidelines with escalating frustration. Now he had a chance to run the show and help his mentor return to the Senate.

Gorton unhesitatingly placed his fate in McGavick's hands. "It's been said that a lawyer who represents himself has a fool for a client," Gorton said, ruminating on the mistakes he'd made in the last campaign.[15] "I didn't mind losing control of the Senate in 1986 if we could get rid of him, he was so arrogant," said Eddie Mahe, a political consultant from New York.[16] One of Gorton's favorite writers, Arnold Toynbee, explored patterns of "departure and return," concluding that a defeat, followed by a second chance, can be transformative. Creative personalities often emerge "with new abilities and creative powers."[17]

"Right after Slade lost in '86, I don't believe he had any thought he would run again," McGavick says. He'd heard how hard Gorton was taking the loss, so he flew to D.C. a few weeks after the election to offer moral support. Over lunch with the Gortons "it was nearly physical how down he was—his sense of loss of the career he'd most dreamed of having. He wasn't to the point yet of asking 'What went wrong?' He was more trying to sort out what he'd do to make a contribution now."

A year later when Evans made his announcement, "it was very quickly clear that if Slade really wanted to run he could have the nomination," McGavick continues. "He was also clearly interested in self improvement, and not just from a political standpoint, which I honestly believe is one of his most remarkable characteristics. I'll never forget him coming around to a bunch of us and saying, 'What could I have done better?' It was really quite astonishing and humbling."

McGavick organized a luncheon. "There were about eight of us, including Walt Howe, Ritajean Butterworth and Bob Storey—old, old friends of Slade's. It amounted to an intervention around what we felt Slade had lost track of. For one thing, we felt he had become a lousy listener. He's so smart and confident that he just didn't communicate to other people that he was listening to them. People would go back to Washington all excited to be meeting their U.S. Senator and they'd leave feeling they got lectured at. We told him that listening requires confirmation of being listened to. It was a painful session. These were all his oldest and dearest friends and they really ripped into him." Howe was struck by the fact that "Slade simply was not defensive. He was humble and receptive."

Afterward, McGavick and Gorton walked back to their offices together. "How do you feel?"

"I feel like crap."

"Well, that had to be awful, Slade. I'm sorry I contributed to it."

"No, I get it. I think I just need to work on this."

They met again a couple of weeks later. "Look," said McGavick, "you're just too damn smart—so smart that you can't let people finish their sentences. What you need to start doing is to pause for two seconds after the other person finishes before you answer them. It'll do two things for you: One, you'll quit finishing their questions for them and, two, it will appear as if you actually had to think about what they said. That'll really impress people and make them feel good about themselves. Remember, they don't ask a question just because they want to know the answer; they ask a question because they think it's important."

Gorton smiled. "Thank you," he told his young friend.

The Gortons mailed 18,000 Christmas cards in December of 1987, as many as when he was a senator. Inquiring minds wanted to know if his sleigh was in the race. He said he was still undecided. There was money left over from the 1986 campaign, "and there were very few things it could be used for, so it was quite appropriate to tell people what my new address was."[18]

ON JANUARY 8, 1988, Slade's 60th birthday, Sid Morrison bowed out in large part for a reason that would dog Gorton. A statewide poll commissioned by the 4th District congressman found voters with strongly negative feelings about Hanford, either as a waste repository or weapons supplier, the specter Adams had raised so effectively. Morrison was also discouraged that so few were enthusiastic about having a senator from Eastern Washington. "I will not apologize for my support of the good people who work at Hanford," he said, "but I have come to recognize intellectually, if not emotionally, that it would be extremely difficult to run statewide when an opponent's reference to 'that guy from Eastern Washington who represents Hanford' would count as two strikes against me." Gorton was now unquestionably the leading contender. Morrison said his poll indicated Slade could win, "but he will have some barriers as well." Bonker was on it instantly, flatly predicting Hanford would cripple Gorton's candidacy because "it now goes beyond his earlier position of supporting conversion. He has a direct investment in that project by way of his law firm." Lowry's administrative assistant, Don Wolgamott, agreed. Privately, he told Lowry they couldn't let Bonker project himself as the more aggressive challenger.[19]

The planets were aligning. McGavick was busy putting together the campaign staff and working on a strategy to contain Hanford's radioactivity. Some conservative Republicans who would never forget or forgive Gorton's apostasy over Goldmark and Dwyer were promoting a McCainesque newcomer named Leo Thorsness. A former Vietnam POW and Medal of Honor recipient, Thorsness had lost to McGovern in the 1974 U.S. Senate race in South Dakota. He would opt to run for a seat in the Washington State Legislature. Gorton's opposition from the right would come from Doug Smith, a little-known Everett lawyer who called Gorton a big spender, and Bill Goodloe, a former state senator and newly retired Washington Supreme Court justice who said frustrated conservatives viewed Gorton as definitely "on the liberal side of center." Gorton, they said, had deserted his president on school prayer, abortion and a balanced budget amendment. Goodloe's candidacy was potentially much more worrisome than Smith's.[20]

HE SEEMED SO RELAXED that many did a double take. With less geeky glasses, an engaging grin and a heavy dose of contrition, Gorton made it official in mid-April. The message was the same at every stop on the kick-off tour: During "the unhappy days of 1986, I must confess I lost contact with too many people in the State of Washington. I was not listening. That will never happen again." He never should have voted for aid to the Contras, he said, or swapped his vote to get Dwyer confirmed. Above all, he regretted voting to freeze the cost-of-living increases for Social Security recipients. "I *really* wasn't listening then." He condemned the Reagan Administration's "current so-called policy of 'benign neglect'" toward "a larger and larger underclass of people who are at or near the minimum wage." It was shameful, Gorton said, for America to have so much "homelessness, undertrained and under-educated young people." He really meant it. "Slade really went through a conversion," said Eddie Mahe, who signed on as a consultant to the campaign.[21]

Gorton said he had developed his new "Evergreen Vision" by talking to people from all walks of life all over the state for the past four months. He promised "a fierce counterattack" in the war on drugs and advocated using the military to interdict drug shipments because the kingpins were growing bolder and more sophisticated by the day. He vowed to champion better schools and universities, find innovative new ways to meet social needs and promote a healthier economy. His version of "read my lips" was a promise to oppose "any tax increases on working American men and women." In Everett—proposed home of the Navy base Lowry had de-

Slade with Betsy Nortz, his first grandchild, on Primary Election night 1988. *Gorton Family Album*

nounced as "homeporking"— Gorton's welcome was especially warm. He said a strong military was essential to promoting peace and protecting America's strategic interests. In this, he said, he and Sally had a new stake: A five-week-old granddaughter whose father was a bombardier/navigator with an A-6 Intruder squadron on the carrier *Enterprise* in the thick of things in the Persian Gulf.

Peace activists outside one of Gorton's press conferences parted like Moses at the Red Sea when Sarah Gorton Nortz arrived with baby Betsy in her arms. Gorton commercials soon featured Slade giving Betsy her bottle. He was hugging, high-fiving or jogging across the tube to the soaring strains of the theme from "Chariots of Fire" or emphasizing that adversity can be character-building. "We lost some tough cases while I was attorney general," Slade told the camera, "but the Senate loss was even more personal. I needed to listen more and the voters made that point crystal clear. But my parents taught me that you can come back from a loss and be even stronger." McGavick was really in the driver's seat this time, leaving no detail to chance.[22]

Marchioro, the Democratic chairwoman, allowed it was too bad the Academy Awards were handed out the week before. Lowry gave his patented little incredulous chortle, and his campaign manager, hard-charging Rose Kapolczynski, said she doubted the voters were gullible enough to buy an old wolf in a new Mister Rogers cardigan. Though still professionally wary, some reporters couldn't help but note the change in Gorton. Bob Partlow, the political writer for *The Olympian* and the other Gannett papers in the state, had covered Gorton's first public appearance after his loss to Adams, a speech at The Evergreen State College in Olympia early in 1987. At a reception afterward, Gorton studiously avoided him. Partlow finally cornered him and asked if they could talk. "I'm not in public life anymore," Gorton snarled. "I don't have to talk to you." With that, he turned on his heel and walked away. A year later, Partlow went to Seattle for Gorton's first interview about the Senate race. "He could not have been friendlier. We went to a nearby restaurant, just the two of us sitting there on a mid-morning weekday, chatting like long lost friends at a ta-ble with a red-and-white checkered tablecloth. It was like right out of the 1950s." After Partlow wrote about the new Gorton, Mike Oakland, the political editor, hooted that he had gone in the tank for Slade.

With McGavick in tow, Gorton even had dinner with Joel Connelly, his on-again, off-again bête noire. Before the salad arrived, Slade and Mickie Pailthorp, an activist lawyer who was the love of Connelly's life, became absorbed in a free-wheeling discussion on the fine points of all things legal, as well as U.S. policy in the Balkans and dog-training, leaving Con-nelly and McGavick to talk politics.[23]

"McGavick was right. I was a lousy listener," Gorton says. Losing something he valued so dearly had a salutary effect. "I learned a lot."

THERE WAS ALSO A NEW Lowry—a makeover even more striking than the kinder, gentler Gorton. Bob Shrum, a sought-after Democratic consul-tant and speechwriter, told Lowry to lose the scraggly beard that the Se-attle version of *Saturday Night Live* said made him a leading contender in the Yasser Arafat Look-Alike Contest. And he couldn't pound the table or wave his arms like a cross between Huey Long and Joe Cocker or deliver his bug-eyed battle cry—"We're right and they're wrong!" That wasn't senatorial.[24]

In the course of one summer's day, Gorton could be seen driving a miniature Model T at the Pacific County Fair while Lowry was giving a staid speech in Aberdeen in a handsome pinstripe suit. Like an awkward Irish step dancer, he kept trying to remember to keep his arms at his sides. But he was still the same small-town guy who grew up among the amber waves of grain on the Palouse, Lowry stressed; still a passionate supporter of "all those working-class folks" depending on Social Security for their retirement. Gorton wanted to balance the budget on the backs of senior citizens, Lowry said, and now he's making $250 an hour as a lob-byist—"a total of $60,000 of taxpayers' money to push conversion of a WPPSS plant into a weapons-production reactor." As Lowry got the hang of being more dignified, it served him well. He was an engaging, natural-born politician with a solid base in the state's largest, increasingly blue county. Gorton and McGavick never once underestimated him.[25]

McGavick and Gary Smith, the campaign's communications director, were pleased to see Bonker beating up on Lowry, although they also worried that if he managed to win the primary he would be harder to beat. By August, Bonker had no choice but to style Lowry as an unelectable liberal ideologue, using the same themes the Gorton campaign hoped would resonate with voters. Bonker railed that "when almost the entire Congress worked hard to pass a major anti-drug bill, Mike Lowry said no." He also "consistently backed radical budget proposals that would slash defense spending $300 billion over a three-year period. . . . Scoop Jackson and Warren Magnuson would be appalled to hear someone say just what Mike said about being against farm programs and the Everett port . . ."

McGavick and Smith carefully indexed all those nuggets. When Bonker also took a strong poke at Gorton, claiming better bona fides with the agricultural community, the campaign immediately responded with radio and TV spots, but only in Eastern Washington. Bonker's claim was "hogwash," the ads said. "We didn't want to draw the attention of the Seattle media because we were afraid we'd set up an unwanted dynamic,"

McGavick says. "It was amazing how much affect that had on the outcome of the primary. I think if that hadn't happened we would have faced Bonker, and I think we would have lost."

Gorton was in good hands. His campaign manager was pursuing victory with the agility of an old pro and the single-minded determination of youth. With the primary looming, McGavick's wife went

The "new" Slade at the Pacific County Fair in 1988. *Brian DalBalcon/ The Daily World*

John McCain campaigns for Gorton in 1988. Slade is greeting Henry Chamberlin, like McCain, a former prisoner of war. *Thomas Donoghue for the Gorton Campaign*

into labor with their first child. He told her he needed to attend a campaign event on Whidbey Island. "If you get on that ferry," she counseled, "you're going to miss out on things here." He stayed, she recalled, but "he was on the phone as the baby was being born."[26]

FOR A CAMPAIGN MANAGER, Washington's open primary can be like herding cats. Worried by tracking polls showing Gorton voters migrating to Bonker, McGavick aired radio and TV spots featuring Slade urging his supporters to stand pat: "Let's not start out in a hole." They needed a strong showing to convince financial backers he was a likely winner in November.[27]

Gorton finished first, with 36 percent of the total, and Lowry swamped Bonker in King County to win the Democratic nomination. Smith and Goodloe could manage but six percent between them. The Democrats had 58 percent of the vote but this definitely was not 1986 all over again. Gorton carried 30 of the state's 39 counties; Lowry only two. Bonker swept Southwest Washington, including the smoke-stack counties where Scoop and Maggie were icons. An Elway poll found that 43 percent of Bonker's backers would now support Gorton. Lowry's opposition to a home port in Everett and the buildup of the Trident nuclear submarine base at Bangor across Puget Sound cost him two big, traditionally Democratic counties. When McGavick crunched the numbers he knew his strategy was a winner: They were running against the Space Needle. Gorton declared Lowry was "more liberal than Ted Kennedy, and more liberal than even Seattle can support. . . . I will be a senator for all the people of the state, not just for a handful of liberals in downtown Seattle."[28]

On paper, Gorton and Lowry—polar opposites with negatives in the 40s—appeared virtually unelectable statewide. The task was to win the undecideds, get out the vote and make the other guy look even less palatable. McGavick and Kapolczynski soon had them surfing snark-infested waters. About the only thing lacking in this campaign until September finally came through was a sex scandal.

It was revealed that Kari Tupper, 24 at the time of the alleged assault, had told police in March of 1987 that Senator Adams slipped a drug in her drink and raped her. Lacking physical evidence, the district attorney in D.C. found the complaint "totally meritless." The incident lay dormant and undetected for months until Adams feared it was about to surface in a D.C. magazine. He called a preemptive news conference to proclaim his outraged innocence. "My family and I have been harassed by this woman for over a year," he declared. In retrospect, the phrase "this woman" sounds eerily Clintonesque. Many said Tupper's statements had the ring of authenticity. Her parents and Adams had been friends since their days together at the University of Washington. The senator had helped Tupper land a job as a congressional staffer. She told police he began pressuring her for sex when she was a college student in Seattle, perhaps out of un-requited lust for her mother, whom he had dated 40 years earlier. Rebecca Boren of *The Weekly* wrote presciently that the next phase of the news coverage would be "the search for another woman claiming to be an Adams victim."[29]

Mike McGavick and Slade during a lighter moment on the campaign trail in 1988. *Thomas Donoghue for the Gorton Campaign*

Lowry and Gorton on the campaign trail in 1988 as seen by David Horsey, the Seattle P-I's two-time Pulitzer Prize winner. *Seattle Post-Intelligencer*

Adams made things worse when he refused to answer any questions, instructing his subordinates and friends to do likewise—"a modified limited hangout" in Watergatespeak. It didn't work any better for Adams than Nixon. While the senator stonewalled, Tupper granted long interviews that enhanced her credibility. "All you do when you don't take questions is you raise questions," said Ron Dotzauer, by then a leading Democratic consultant in Seattle. "Containment is implied deceit." Kapolczynski groused that political reporters "all seem to be on the sex and drug beat," while another Lowry campaign aide suggested, "Maybe Brock could find a trade mission in Europe until this election is over." McGavick gave strict orders to not comment on the controversy. "The word was very quickly put out: Chortle in private," said one Republican insider. The story took Adams out of play for the Lowry campaign and likely prompted some voters to rethink their decision to oust Gorton two years earlier.[30]

HEADING INTO OCTOBER, polls indicated Gorton had a five- to seven-point lead. The campaign had aired a series of 30-second spots hammering Lowry for voting against a sweeping anti-drug bill. "Apparently the drug problem doesn't scare Mike Lowry," Gorton warned, "and that's a frightening thought." The candidate and his retinue were sporting "War on Drugs Booster Club" buttons. "The single most salient issue" in this campaign is drugs, McGavick said.[31]

Kapolczynski told Lowry he had to get tougher. Shrum and his partner, David Doak, rolled out a flurry of body blows: "There's a reason Slade Gorton isn't in the Senate any more. While he was there he voted to deny low-income senior citizens a Social Security cost-of-living increase. Not once but nine times Slade Gorton voted against Social Security benefits. And then he voted 13 times to cut Medicare and health services for seniors." As columnists clucked their tongues at the "wretched" nastiness, lamenting that campaigns had been reduced to "he hit me first" schoolyard spats, McGavick observed, "Just saying this guy's a nice guy is not going to make any difference. You can only move numbers when you have a message that affects the (voting) decision." Gary Smith noted that while voters always claim they like positive ads, they're more heavily influenced by negative ones.[32]

With Congress working overtime, Lowry was the frequent flier in this campaign while Gorton was canvassing the state, appearing to actually enjoy watching Rotary Club members fork over "happy bucks" in honor of new grandchildren and WSU football victories. Wearing a flannel shirt at the Columbia County Fair, he awarded blue ribbons to a pair of FFA kids and patted their pigs on the butt. McGavick's strategy was a combination of old-fashioned grass-roots politics and well-funded modern marketing that could respond quickly to new developments. Smith dealt with the press and helped make sure Slade was relentlessly on message. Gorton's only job was being the candidate. "This is the most fun campaign I've ever been in," he said. His new glasses, augmented by contact lenses, were a big improvement. The old Coke-bottle bifocals either had him with his chin up, appearing aloof, or looking down as if condescendingly. Unfortunately, the contacts made him blink a lot, especially in the glare of TV lights.[33]

IN THE EARLY-MORNING HOURS of Monday, October 3, Lowry arrived in Chicago on United's red-eye from Seattle and collapsed while awaiting a connecting flight to D.C. Battling successive bouts of bronchitis, the flu and a bad cold, Lowry had been self-medicating with aspirin and a coffee chaser. Doctors in the intensive care unit at Chicago's Resurrection Hospital diagnosed a bleeding ulcer. He was lucky they caught it early. They wanted him to stay longer than two nights, but he needed a cash transfusion. Lowry was back at the Capitol in time for a fundraiser at the home of Pamela Harriman, Georgetown's grande dame of Democratic politics. The haul was $260,000, and sorely needed to keep pace with McGavick's couterattacks.[34]

On Oct. 7 Lowry got a hero's welcome at SeaTac airport. He was also cheered by two new polls that calculated Gorton's lead was now within the margin of error. Sympathy for Lowry's illness apparently diluted any disgust over the attack ads. McGavick was right: They worked.

Even Evans gave the Democrat a boost by opposing conservative amendments to allow warrantless searches in drug cases and the introduction of illegally obtained evidence. Like Lowry, Evans also opposed Gorton's call for the death penalty to deter "murderous drug lords" and civil fines as high as $10,000 for simple possession. See, Lowry said, liberalism in defense of the Constitution is no vice.[35]

Three days later, McGavick responded with the most controversial ad of the campaign. It accused Lowry of favoring legalization of marijuana. The charge was based on a nine-year-old article in the *Daily*, the University of Washington student newspaper. The article said Lowry "told a small group of people he would support their quest to legalize marijuana." Disagreeing with their request that alcohol be prohibited instead of pot, the congressman was quoted as saying, "Prohibition of anything doesn't work." Fast forward to 1986, Gorton's commercial added, and there was Lowry, as liberal as ever, voting against "the biggest drug-fighting law ever passed." And now, in 1988, he had opposed another crackdown "because it had penalties on drug dealers Lowry thinks are too tough."[36]

"This really crosses the boundary into misstatement," Lowry complained bitterly, adding that he favored "stiff, strong penalties on drug dealers" as long as the Constitution wasn't trashed in the process. He surmised that the comment attributed to him in 1979 might have stemmed from a question about a Seattle city ordinance decriminalizing small amounts of marijuana. "I do not support legalization of drugs, including marijuana, and I have not," Lowry said. Reporters who had covered him for years knew that was true. McGavick was unrepentant. "He's disputing his own words," Gorton's campaign manager insisted. "I am surprised that Mike is claiming a misstatement. It absolutely is in the record." To a reporter who kept challenging the spot's veracity, McGavick said, "You guys can never catch up to an ad." The campaign promptly issued a new press release accusing Lowry of "yet another attempt to obscure his very liberal record."[37]

Pressed for documentation, Gorton's people said that when they couldn't find the former student reporter, Kelly Smith, to double check the story they conducted a thorough search for corrections or clarifications. Finding none, they aired the ad because they said it was such an important issue. After Lowry's people went ballistic, the Gorton campaign found Smith in California. He "stands by the story," they said. "He's prepared to sign an affidavit." However, when the UW *Daily* interviewed Kelly Smith, he said Lowry spoke against prohibition of alcohol "but he never came out and said, 'I support legalizing marijuana.'" Smith told *The Seattle Times* the same thing, but admitted his memory of the 1979 meeting was "pretty shaky." Smith doubtless was being pressured by Democrats to support Lowry's version of the story, the Gorton campaign said.[38]

Reporters asked him to explain how Lowry's comments got screwed up. "Maybe it was the copy editor." Who was that? "Sharon Kanareff," now none other than Gorton's press secretary. Kanareff pleaded innocent to any creative copy editing. Conspiracy theorists had a field day and the press began mumbling about "the same old Slade."[39]

DAN EVANS WAS DISGUSTED by the marijuana ad, but he kept silent for the time being. Others decried the Republican "demagoguery" of portraying Democrats as soft on crime, a theme the Bush campaign was using to great effect against the Democratic presidential nominee, Michael Dukakis. The hapless Massachusetts governor had supported "rehabilitative" weekend passes for hardened criminals. Willie Horton, a murderer who committed a rape on his days off, became a household name in 1988, thanks to the masterful mischief of Lee Atwater, Bush's campaign manager.[40]

The marijuana ad backfired, Lowry maintained, "because it reminded people of why they originally voted Gorton out of office. The new Slade Gorton is as untruthful as the old Slade Gorton." On the contrary, McGavick said, the ad halted a slide in Gorton's poll numbers and italicized the notion that Lowry was too liberal to represent anyone but Seattle. Another Gorton ad, in fact, said Lowry was "a liberal even Seattle can't afford." Images of the Ayatollah Khomeini and Libyan dictator Muammar Gaddafi flashed on the screen to highlight Lowry's votes against an Iran trade embargo and criticism of U.S. bombing raids on Libya. "I will be a senator for all the people of the state," Gorton promised.[41]

David Stern, who produced upbeat ads for Gorton earlier in the campaign, said after the election that he had no role in the negative ads that dominated the closing weeks. The designer of the yellow Happy Face that achieved ubiquity in the late 1960s, Stern was unhappy that candidates now seemed "concerned only with winning, not with how you play the game."[42]

In 2002, McGavick told the Greater Seattle Chamber of Commerce, "We clearly need to raise the level of civil discourse in our community. If I see one more of those negative 30-second ads, I'm going to throw up—and I used to make them!" When he was running for the U.S. Senate himself in 2006, McGavick said, "We let the (marijuana) ad finish its week-long run. Though we never raised it again, we should have pulled it once evidence mounted that the *Daily* article was not an accurate reflection of his views." In 2010, McGavick told Gorton's biographer, "Happily, I finally had a chance to apologize to Lowry personally about that ad, sometime after my own campaign. He was hugely gracious. The odd thing is that our camp in '88 always admired Lowry. He was, like Slade, a serious policy guy, and he believed in what he said."[43]

THE BLOWBACK ON THE MARIJUANA AD prompted the Gorton campaign to go positive, using Evans to testify to Slade's environmental activism. Abundantly clear was that campaign managers and image makers were running the show. Lowry was practically tongue-tied when Joel Connelly asked why he had agreed to only one debate. He turned to an aide and asked, "Tim, do you know how I'm supposed to answer on this one?" If anyone deviated from the script Kapolczynski was in their face. The next day, Gorton seemed startled when asked about a fundraising piece that featured his signature. "Latest Washington state opinion polls show my lead slipping away," the letter said. "In less than two weeks, Lowry's vicious smear campaign has made this race a dead heat." Gorton's brow furrowed. "I would say we are modestly ahead."[44]

He was modestly behind, according to some polls. One thing they knew for certain was that they didn't want Reagan's help, which angered some state party officials and business bigwigs who argued that the president would boost the party's morale and coffers, as well as GOP candidates in other races around the state. Shades of 1986. Eddie Mahe, counseled against a visit and got no argument from McGavick or Gorton. Slade could close his eyes and conjure up practically every moment of that awful Halloween in Spokane.[45]

The Gorton campaign then performed what some saw as a sanctimonious pirouette, mailing a "Biblical Scorecard" to 40,000 foursquare conservatives. Most were fans of TV evangelist Pat Robertson, whose supporters had stormed the GOP precinct caucuses and state convention. The flier said Lowry had voted "100 percent against family-moral-free-

dom issues," backing gay rights, abortion and the Equal Rights Amendment, while opposing "Star Wars" and following the ACLU line on anti-
drug laws. Gorton in fact also voted pro-choice, backed the ERA, the
National Endowment for the Arts and had been endorsed by the gay Log
Cabin Republicans. He too received a zero on the scorecard, but the campaign said that was because he didn't respond to the questionnaire. Gorton said the flier was "simply an opposite side of the coin" from ratings by
the ACLU and the Americans for Democratic Action. "Mike tends to be a
zero or close to a zero on any conservative rating . . . I tend to be a 50 or
70 on any conservative group rating. It's simply another illustration that
I'm in the middle of the political spectrum, perhaps a little to the conservative side, and Mike is in the extreme." The flier included testimonials
from Idaho's Steve Symms and other archconservatives. Electing Lowry
would be "to hand Mike Dukakis, Teddy Kennedy and Jesse Jackson a victory on election day," they warned.[46]

Lowry's misgivings about negativity prompted him to question the
wisdom of a last-minute ad reprising the Hanford "bomb factory" theme.
But Kapolczynski and adman Steve McMahon were gung ho to hit Gorton hard. Hanford had been just what the doctor ordered for Adams in
'86. The new commercial featured a big semi rolling toward the camera.
A yellow sign on its side said "Caution Nuclear Waste." Voice over: "The
congressional record shows while Slade Gorton was in the Senate he
voted with the nuclear industry to make it easier to dump the nation's
nuclear waste in Washington State. And after he was defeated, Gorton
went to work as a Seattle attorney on a new project—to turn WPPSS into
a factory producing highly radioactive fuel for nuclear bombs. . . . Slade
Gorton's been working for the nuclear industry for years. Do you really
expect him to stop now?" As the truck rumbles past, the camera pans to
a group of kids standing by the road.[47]

The Gorton campaign was indignant. Lowry said the truth merely hurt.
"Of course it's a bomb factory," he told reporters. "What do you think you
use tritium for—flower pots?" In a 2008 interview, however, Lowry said
he "absolutely should have nixed" the ad. "It was negative, but not compared to today's." A videotape excavation of the mud of yesteryear confirms
everyone was doing it, the harbinger of even stronger stuff in the years to
come. As zingers go, however, Bomb Factory Redux and Gone to Pot, complete with a scruffy stoner lighting a joint, still hold their own.[48]

DAN EVANS, WHO HAD CHAMPIONED converting the unfinished WPPSS
plant No. 1 at Hanford to produce tritium, was "really ticked" by the Lowry

ad, especially the kids watching the truck roll by. Branding it "outrageous and sleazy," he says it reminded him of the infamous commercial LBJ ran briefly against Goldwater in 1964: A little girl is plucking petals off a daisy, "1, 2, 3 . . ." as the image morphs into the countdown for a nuclear blast. The Lowry ad also insinuated that Gorton bilked the taxpayers by accepting $60,000 in legal fees to work on the conversion proposal, Evans added, when "he earned it." Asked if Gorton's marijuana ad wasn't also over the line, Evans told reporters he would have publicly chastised his friend if "Slade had brought up that ad three days before the election."⁴⁹

Evans phoned McGavick. He wanted to do "something powerful" to respond. McGavick and Gary Smith came up with what became one of the most memorable political ads in Washington State history. Gorton's young handlers worried, however, that Evans might think their visual punch line was over the top. So they sent him into the studio with Mike Murphy, a producer who had done solid work for the GOP Senatorial Committee. Murphy's job was to see if he could subtly sell Evans on a zinger.

Evans gave the script a read-through as Murphy sized up the lighting and camera angle. "Come on, Mike Lowry, clean up your act," Evans said, delivering the line with a disgusted, give-me-a-break lilt that was spot on. "Your negative TV ads distorting Slade Gorton's good record embarrass this state. You'd have us think that Slade opposes all environmental legislation and that he would sink Social Security. Actually, he's passed more environmental legislation than you have. And when Social Security faced bankruptcy, Slade helped to save it."

Excellent, Murphy said. But he had an idea for a punchier ending. It might be corny, but it was worth a try.

"I'm game," Evans said.

The accessories were conveniently at hand, borrowed from McGavick's grandfather. They rolled film. "Mike, you've been spreading so darn much stuff I've had to change my shoes," Evans declared, senatorial in suit and tie. Then the camera pulled back. Evans lifted a leg to reveal he was wearing hip boots.⁵⁰

He nailed it on the first take. Looking back, Evans muses, "If I'd had 24 hours to think about it, I probably wouldn't have agreed." Smith believes "Hip Boots" was *the* pivotal moment of the campaign. Evans is dubious: "A good many people had already voted. I doubt very much that there was a significant shift towards Slade because of the ad alone." McGavick and Smith say that's just Evans being modest.⁵¹

For whatever reason, a large bloc of undecideds swung Slade's way

The famous Dan Evans "Hip Boots" TV commercial from the 1988 Gorton-Lowry campaign. *Ian Stenseng/Washington Secretary of State*

over the final weekend. McGavick predicted they'd win "by an eke." On November 8, 1988, Washington's habitual ticket-splitters returned Gorton to the U.S. Senate by 40,000 votes out of 1.85 million cast, 51.09 percent. They favored Dukakis over Bush—an easy winner nationally—by about the same margin. McGavick's strategy worked flawlessly. To offset Lowry's 50,000-vote margin in King County, Gorton carried 27 of the state's 39 counties, rolling up nearly a 32,000-vote margin in the Tri-Cities, home to 12,000 Hanford workers. Gorton posted a 14,000-vote victory in Yakima and decisively won the war in the "defense" counties: Kitsap, home to the Bremerton Navy Yard and the Bangor sub base; Snohomish, hoping for a home port, and Pierce, home to Fort Lewis and McChord Air Force Base. For good measure, Gorton also carried Clark, Bonker's home base. With Ritajean Butterworth as field director, McGavick had established an energetic, well-funded campaign organization in every county, big or small. And for playing hardball he had no apologies. "We were helped by it. Absolutely."[52]

11 p.m. Nov. 8, 1988: A glum Mike Lowry watches Slade on TV as the returns make it clear Gorton is headed back to the U.S. Senate. *Alan Berner/The Seattle Times*

The bottom line, Stu Elway's polling confirmed, was that the Gorton campaign convinced just enough voters that Lowry was too liberal. Slade was the safer choice. "The drug problem" was a major factor for two-thirds of the respondents. They backed Gorton 46 percent to 38 percent. Gorton led 46-39 among independents.[53]

The American Association of Political Consultants named McGavick a finalist for campaign manager of the year. He lost to Lee Atwater. Heady company for a Republican. His next job was Gorton's chief of staff.[54]

Among the new faces to emerge from 1988 was Patty Murray, a pint-sized school board member from North Seattle. The former preschool teacher had mobilized opposition to cuts in educational programs after a legislator dismissed her as just "a mom in tennis shoes." Murray upset Bill Kiskaddon, a two-term Republican, to win a seat in the State Senate. She aimed a lot higher four years later.

28 | Who Gives a Hoot?

O N THE MORNING OF JANUARY 19, 1989, Gorton and McGavick were settling in, assembling the senator's staff. George H.W. Bush was polishing his inaugural address, trying to find the best place to reprise the "thousand points of light" he'd talked about on the campaign trail. In the heart of the Olympic Peninsula, 2,400 miles away in the other Washington, it was still dark when Jim Carlson headed for a meeting at the Quinault Ranger Station. Carlson owned two mills. One produced lumber, the other shakes and shingles. He also sold logs. Like most of the hundred workers he employed, he'd been at it since he was a teenager. Guys like Carlson loved the smell of sawdust in the morning. It was hard, dangerous work, but you were outside with a plug of snoose in your cheek, working with your hands and wits, not sitting in some office in a monkey suit. Carlson's business smarts gave him what he considered the best of both worlds.

Loggers on the peninsula were mostly the offspring of Dust Bowl refugees or old country immigrants—Swedes, Finns, Germans and Croatians. Werner and Marzell Mayr's father came to America from Bavaria in 1905 and soon made his way to Grays Harbor where the mills hummed and screeched 24-7, processing a seemingly never-ending supply of great-girthed timber. Schooners lined up stem to stern at their docks. The Mayr brothers began logging in the depths of the Depression with a horse named Maude to haul the 12-foot sled they stacked with pulp wood. The Dahlstrom boys were chips off the same block.

In 1970, when Ed Van Syckle, the retired editor of *The Aberdeen Daily World*, set out to write a definitive history of logging on the Olympic Peninsula, he'd had a title in his head ever since his own days in the woods as a teenager decades earlier: "They Tried to Cut it All."[1]

About two dozen mill owners arrived at the Ranger Station on the day everything changed. They expected to be told the U.S. Forest Service would offer for sale approximately 90 million board feet in the district in 1990—enough to keep them all going. But just before Christmas, when the staff at the Quinault District of the Olympic National Forest got its first look at the new habitat protection circles mandated for the Northern Spotted Owl, they crunched the numbers and braced for a shock wave.[2]

"They told us the cut would be only 42 million board feet," Carlson recalls. It got very quiet for what seemed like minutes. The room was thunderstruck. Tom Mayr, who was running the family sawmill in Hoquiam, had heard about the spotted owl a couple of years earlier at an industry meeting, and "it was kinda like, 'yeah, yeah, yeah.'" Now he realized that the future would be "survival of the fittest." Then Rex Holloway, a Forest Service official, told them 42 million was the good news. The bad news was how low it could go. Within the next few years they'd probably be lucky to get 20 million board feet.[3]

Monte Dahlstrom departed with his mind reeling, anger and frustration mounting with every mile as he headed back to town. "This will be economic devastation for Grays Harbor," he told editors at *The Daily World*. "It will be a different place to live." For a while, they thought he was exaggerating.[4]

Gorton was caught off guard, too. He was campaigning to reclaim his seat when federal Judge Thomas Zilly ruled that the government's decision to not list the owl for protection under the Endangered Species Act, as environmentalists were demanding, was "arbitrary and capricious."[5]

Two weeks after the Forest Service broke the news to the mill owners, a delegation from the Grays Harbor Chamber of Commerce arrived in D.C. to deliver petitions signed by 5,000 locals who believed the Forest Service plan would decimate timber country. Gorton, McGavick and Heidi Biggs, the senator's legislative assistant for natural resources, listened intently for more than hour, which impressed LeRoy Tipton, the Chamber president. "Slade wasn't even in his permanent office yet. They went around and scrounged chairs for us from other offices. We told him we stood to lose thousands of jobs when you factor in the multiplier from each job dependent on timber dollars. Slade was shocked that they were just pulling the rug out from under us. It was clear to me—to all of us, I think—that he was going to be our champion."[6]

"There is no way to overstate the way in which this issue radicalized Slade," says McGavick. "And the environmentalists had made it easy for him by attacking him in the '86 campaign after he did so much to increase the wilderness. It seemed like spotted owl issues took up most of every day for many of us. It changed the dynamic for Slade in a very positive way, though as the state drifted more urban it limited his upside and made each election a fight from the start."

IN MARCH, BILL DWYER, whose controversial appointment to the federal bench contributed to Gorton's defeat by Adams, emerged as the owl's champion. He issued a temporary restraining order barring the Forest Service from proceeding with 135 timber sales in spotted owl habitat areas. Gorton was outraged. It struck him as "anti-human." Environmentalists said he was giving people false hope and populist claptrap when what they needed was straight talk. Loggers and mill workers needed to recognize that their way of life was simply unsustainable, and automation was as much to blame as decades of greed and disrespect for the environment.

The Dahlstroms and Mayrs filed suit, asserting that the set-asides violated the Grays Harbor Federal Sustained Yield Act, approved by Congress in 1949. When some 1,500 timber supporters staged a protest that briefly blocked traffic on the Riverside Bridge in Hoquiam, a main artery of Highway 101, an annoyed motorist in a Volvo station wagon stuffed with camping gear shouted at one burly logger, "Hey fatso, if you hadn't flunked sixth grade, you could get a real job!"[7]

Time magazine put the owl on its cover. Inside was a breathless anthropomorphic eulogy that infuriated timber country:

"[A] lumberjack presses his snarling chain saw into the flesh of a Douglas fir that has held its place against wind and fire, rockslide and flood, for 200 years. The white pulpy fiber scatters in a plume beside him, and in 90 seconds, 4 ft. of searing steel have ripped through the thick bark, the thin film of living tissue and the growth rings spanning ages. With an excruciating groan, all 190 ft. of trunk and green spire crash to earth. When the cloud of detritus and needles settles, the ancient forest of the Pacific Northwest has retreated one more step. Tree by tree, acre by acre, it falls, and with it vanishes the habitat of innumerable creatures. None among these crea-

The spotted owl makes the cover of *Time* in 1990.

Gorton meets with Glen Ramiskey, left, of the Longshore Union and other
Grays Harbor labor leaders during the spotted owl controversy in 1991.
Brian DalBalcon/The Daily World

tures is more vulnerable than the northern spotted owl, a bird so docile it
will descend from the safety of its lofty bough to take a mouse from the
hand of a man."[8]

Some environmentalists said the owl was the proverbial canary in the
coal mine, an indicator species. Others called it the tip of an iceberg. Andy
Stahl of the Sierra Club Legal Defense Fund admitted it was heaven sent.
"The Northern Spotted Owl is the wildlife species of choice to act as a
surrogate for old-growth protection," he told an environmental law conference in Eugene, Ore., in 1988. "I've often thought that thank goodness
the spotted owl evolved in the Pacific Northwest, for if it hadn't, we'd have
to genetically engineer it," he chuckled. The videotape of that speech became Exhibit A in timber country.[9]

"I'd been Slade's natural resources/environment staffer for six weeks
when the owl controversy went national," recalls J. Vander Stoep, who was
fresh out of law school. Although only 33, he had spent six years in the
Washington Legislature. "I wish I'd have known what I was getting into,"
he told McGavick, only half-joking. A few months later, McGavick gave
him his report card: "You're my ticket back to Seattle!" By 1991, Vander
Stoep was Gorton's chief of staff.

McGavick's legacy included a subtle but important course correction. It was his observation that they'd been staffing to Slade's strengths. He didn't have many weaknesses, but McGavick saw to it that they were addressed with the new hires. Vander Stoep had the same philosophy, as well as attention to detail that McGavick admired. One of the new staffers was Curtis Hom, an American-born Chinese with a law degree from Columbia. "Slade loves give and take," Hom says. When they descended on him one day with armloads of documents, he looked up with a grin: "Three at once! But that's OK. I hire you to challenge me."

A witty, tech-savvy guy, Hom went on to spend 15 years with Microsoft. By encouraging talented young people to go back to Washington State after a couple of years learning the ropes on Capitol Hill, Gorton was building an indispensable Rolodex. "The system was modeled after Scoop's office," McGavick says. "He had the business and legal community at home loaded with successful former staffers, and we wanted a similar network of alums."

If you were smart, it didn't matter how old you were. Gorton loved it when they talked back. As a committee hearing got under way one day, he whispered to Cassie Phillips, a sharp young attorney, that Wendell Ford of Kentucky had a thicker briefing book. "Senator Ford appears to be better prepared than I am." "That's because he needs it more than you do," Phillips replied.[10]

They all marveled at Gorton's ability to focus. "You can have conversations with Slade Gorton in 35 seconds that could take other people half an hour," Vander Stoep says.

The conversations about owls took longer.

WHEN GORTON CAME TO ABERDEEN to meet with worried loggers, mill operators and business leaders, Jim Carlson brought along his daughter Kellie, a spunky little blonde who was a junior at Lake Quinault High School.

"I hope you don't forget us in Grays Harbor," a millworker in the back of the room told Gorton. "All we have is you."

"I can't promise success," the senator said, "but I can promise a fight."

From Port Angeles to Omak, every crowd looked and sounded the same. A 9-year-old boy from Forks carried a handmade sign that said "What about my future?" Another said "Spotted owl tastes like chicken." Someone even dummied up a box of Spotted Owl Helper. Houses and businesses sprouted signs affirming they were "Supported by Timber Dollars."[11]

Gorton announced he planned to introduce a bill to permanently guarantee Northwest loggers at least 3.3 billion board feet annually from federal forests. "Owls are important," he said, "but people are more important than owls." It was risky business for a politician who won a second term in the Senate by the skin of his teeth. Despite an environmental record that was creditable by any objective measure, dating back to his days in the Legislature pushing Jim Ellis's Forward Thrust legislation, Gorton was now the greens' public enemy No. 1. Polls suggested strong support statewide for preserving old-growth forests, even if that left timber towns in dire straits. The job loss from spotted owl set-asides was estimated at 35,000 in some reports, although environmentalists said that was hyperbole. Gorton acknowledged that decades of wanton clear-cutting had decimated ancient forests. Those errors were being corrected by modern, sustained-yield forestry that respected biodiversity, he said, but the bulk of the new plantations wouldn't be mature until the 21st century. "The 1990s are crucial. To get to that sustained harvest, we have to make it through the 1990s." Environmentalists, abetted by the liberal media, are elitists who "don't really believe in the realities of reforestation," Gorton said. "They don't connect timber with the realities of housing, paper and furniture . . . with real people and real families."[12]

Timber families took their cause to downtown Seattle. Aleda Dahlstrom held her 8-year-old daughter tight and told reporters her husband's Hoquiam sawmill was just one of many that provided family-wage jobs. "We want people to realize we are people. By shutting off the log supply they are hurting our families."[13]

A Seattleite who watched Gorton being huzzah'd at one such demonstration called it a "diesel Chautauqua" in a letter to the editor. It reminded him "of nothing so much as those antebellum Southerners put forward by Jefferson Davis to economically justify slavery. 'Think of the jobs that will be lost,' they cried, 'consider the economic devastation to

James Neel, a 9-year-old from Forks, with his aunt, Bev Larson, at a timber rally in Olympia in 1991. *Brian DalBalcon/The Daily World*

the South.' . . . As for the notion of Gorton as populist, let's give the trees and spotted owls a vote; even at a 3/5 discount, Slade may have to rethink the nature of his constituency."[14]

Larry Mason, the enterprising leader of the Clallam County delegation, said timber country was hugely unimpressed with Brock Adams' response to the crisis. Adams promised that in trying to find a compromise he was "carefully listening to all sides of the issue—something the responsible members of the Northwest congressional delegation are trying to do." That was unmistakably a dig at Gorton, who was arguing that a report by Jack Ward Thomas, a respected Forest Service research biologist, and other federal scientists, was heavily biased in favor of the owl. Environmentalists were pleased the report called the owl "imperiled," but many of them said it still didn't go far enough. "Human beings are also imperiled," Gorton insisted.[15]

Adams signed onto a plan drafted by Senator Mark Hatfield and his fellow Oregonian, Democratic Congressman Les AuCoin. Catching the environmentalists at loose ends, their bill did an end-around on Judge Dwyer, unlocking a billion board feet he had placed off limits. The plan, Section 318, also mandated the sale of an additional 8 billion board feet by the fall of 1990. It was appended to the 1990 funding package for the Forest Service and Bureau of Land Management. Outmaneuvered—at least temporarily—the environmentalists waived their right to appeal. They called it "The rider from hell."[16]

The Hatfield-Adams legislation was enacted on Oct. 23, 1989. A few days later, Dwyer lifted his preliminary injunction. He did not, however, relinquish his jurisdiction over the case and demanded a recovery plan. Indiana Congressman Jim Jontz, the bane of the timber industry, warned that their victory would be short-lived, saying, "I personally consider the ancient forests as much a part of our nation's heritage as the Grand Canyon or the Everglades." As an effigy of Jontz was consigned to a bonfire in Hoquiam, Bill Pickell, general manager of the Washington Contract Loggers Association, shouted "May he burn in hell!"[17]

IN THE SUMMER OF 1990, as the Fish & Wildlife Service rule designating the owl as a threatened species went into effect, Gorton negotiated with Bush's chief of staff, John Sununu, to convince the president to convene a task force. To the distress of environmentalists, the secretaries of the Interior and Agriculture—both Bush appointees—announced that timber sales would continue for the remainder of the year. By September 1, they hoped to have a less restrictive plan for harvest levels in Fiscal Year 1991, as well as modifications to the Endangered Species Act. The alternative, Gorton said, was "complete devastation of those communities." Some environmentalists "are moving toward a goal of complete elimination of the timber industry in the Northwest."[18]

Congressman Dicks said Gorton was making a risky gamble. He sympathized with timber communities, but warned that any plan that fell short of the habitat protection advocated in the Thomas report could be thrown out by the courts. That could end up reducing the harvest to zero. Judge Dwyer's temporary injunction was ample warning, the Bremerton Democrat said. Jim McDermott, the Seattle liberal who had won Lowry's seat in Congress, said Gorton knew full well that any plan that fell short of the Thomas report "doesn't have the chance of a snowball on a Washington, D.C., sidewalk." It was 90 degrees on the day he said it.[19]

Win or lose, Mason said timber families would have long memories. "Gorton is the only strong advocate of reasonable timber harvest in the State of Washington. If Brock Adams had his way, we'd all be on welfare."[20]

At Gorton's urging, the administration also prodded Congress to jump-start the process to convene the "God Squad," a Cabinet-level committee vested under the Endangered Species Act with the responsibility of weighing whether the economic impact of saving a species was simply too high for society to bear. George Mitchell of Maine, the Senate majority leader, had helped write the act 17 years earlier. It would be "a dereliction of duty," he said, for Congress to expedite the process. To Gorton, that was fresh evidence that the Democratic Party "stands nakedly captive to the wine-and-brie urban special interests attacking the prospect of saving even some of the 35,000 jobs now imperiled in the Northwest." Gorton said Scoop Jackson "would have found this moment a horror" for "he understood, as I do, that the people of those towns are the very definition of what it is to be American." Congressman Peter DeFazio, D-Ore., shot back, "I think it would be news to me and news to all of the working class, wage-earning people of the Pacific Northwest that . . . 'special-interest Slade' was their champion. If he's lifting a finger for working people, it will be the first time in his elected career."[21]

In the middle of these pleasantries, the president of the Sierra Club felt genuinely obliged to visit Gorton's office to thank him for championing legislation that would have required automakers to boost the corporate average fuel economy of their vehicles to 34 miles per gallon by 1995 and 40 mpg by 2001. The auto industry and the Bush administration mounted a full-court press to defeat the bill, arguing that the 20 to 40 percent increases were too costly to achieve. Gorton nevertheless brought the bill

originally sponsored by Nevada Democrat Richard Bryan to within three
votes of passage in the Senate. Had he succeeded, the nation could have
saved five times as much oil as was reputed to be awaiting extraction
from Alaska, environmentalists said—and at what price? Viewed then, as
now, the bill would have been a landmark in the effort to reduce both
carbon-dioxide emissions and America's dependence on foreign oil.
Gorton conceded that environmentally he was "a marvelous paradox."
But "my positions are overwhelmingly consistent. . . .I am frustrated by
groups that demand 100 percent toeing the line."[22]

ON MAY 23, 1991, Judge Dwyer ordered a virtual halt to timber sales and
logging in 17 national forests stretching from the Olympic Peninsula to
Northern California. Dwyer agreed with the Sierra Club and Audubon
Society that the U.S. Forest Service and Fish & Wildlife had engaged in "a
remarkable series of violations" of environmental laws. To push ahead
with the sales "would risk pushing the species beyond a threshold from
which it could not recover." Dwyer ordered the Forest Service to prepare a
plan that would comply with the National Forest Management Act of
1974, which mandated the preservation of "viable populations" of wildlife. The law was the law, Dwyer said, and painful as it might be to those
caught in the crossfire the reality was that "the timber industry no longer
drives the Pacific Northwest's economy. Job losses in the wood-products
industry will continue regardless of whether the northern spotted owl is
protected. The argument that the mightiest economy on Earth cannot afford to preserve old-growth forests for a short time while it reaches an
overdue decision on how to manage them, is not convincing today."[23]

"Judge Dwyer's opinion is a perfect example of anti-human decision
making," Gorton seethed on the floor of the Senate. The ruling was radical and irresponsible, he said. Mourning the recent suicide of a despon-
dent logger, Gorton said judges and other high-level officials "must con-
front the fact that their decisions breed despair and pain . . ." Dwyer's
analysis of the timber industry was flat wrong, Gorton continued. "The
Pacific Northwest is not running out of timber and massive layoffs are
not inevitable. Timber shortages and massive job losses are the inevitable
result of decisions by federal judges and the Fish & Wildlife Service."[24]

Over the next 11 months the Fish & Wildlife Service and the Bureau of
Land Management—both Interior Department agencies—found themselves at loggerheads. The Forest Service's revised plan to protect the owl
was rebuffed by Judge Dwyer. Interior Secretary Manuel Lujan, the God
Squad's chairman, said the Fish & Wildlife owl recovery plan developed

by the Jack Ward Thomas committee would cost the region 32,000 jobs. He unveiled a "balanced" alternative he said would be only half as onerous. Owl biologists dismissed it as "a recipe for extinction" and said the 32,000 job-loss estimate was greatly exaggerated. "I am not going to let anyone rape the earth," Lujan promised. As a creationist, he unapologetically believed, however, "that man is at the top of the pecking order. I think that God gave us dominion over these creatures . . . I just look at an armadillo or a skunk or a squirrel or an owl or a chicken, whatever it is, and I consider the human being on a higher scale. Maybe that's because a chicken doesn't talk." Conceding that his alternative owl recovery plan violated the Endangered Species Act, Lujan said Congress had the power to implement it through a special act. Gorton introduced the legislation but was thwarted at every turn.[25]

Brian Boyle, the Republican commissioner of public lands in Washington State, where timber sales produced millions for public schools, was angry that Lujan and other federal officials had misled the public by downplaying the impact on state and private lands. The new rules meant that on the Olympic Peninsula, for instance, no old-growth could be logged within a 2.2-mile radius of each pair of spotted owls, or at least where one of their nests was found. That added up to 4,000 acres of forest per pair.[26]

AT GROUND ZERO, Jim Carlson felt as if he couldn't win for trying. The years to come brought even more frustration. He had survived the brutal recession of the early 1980s and was doing his best to find life after the spotted owl when the economy tanked all over again in 1992. With Kellie's help, he was making another comeback when 2008 made 1992 seem like a walk in the woods. A natural-born storyteller, Carlson is a connoisseur of irony. "When we first got the news about the reduction in the harvest, they told us the future would be about diversification and value-added products. Even though I was startled at the reduction, I figured, 'Well, we're a small company. We're agile and able to adapt. We'll downsize; invest in remanufacturing operations, buy a dry kiln. We'll do more with less—get more miles per gallon from the reduced supply.' I went for that one hook, line and sinker. So I spent a few million. Invariably the government forwards a solution that requires spending more money to fix the problem. What they didn't tell us was that the harvest reality was going to be approximately zero. I recall standing there after the smoke had cleared asking myself the now obvious question, 'Add jobs and value to what?' Shortly after this revelation I called some of my friends

in Canada and asked, 'Ya got any wood, eh?' Then our government issued an edict: 'Thou shalt not create jobs and prosperity by adding value
to raw lumber imported from the Crown.' And to back it up they slapped
on a tariff—not your little garden variety either. It was a dandy. I should
have quit right then and there. However, my northern European heritage reared its ugly head and prevented such a logical step. The rest is
history."[27]

Kellie Carlson, thinking hard about what she wanted to be when she
grew up, watched what was happening to her dad and her friends' dads,
brothers and uncles. "People were being laid off, losing their jobs. It was
frightening. But Slade cared enough to come to our community and said
he'd do everything in his power to help. The armchair environmentalists
called it cruel demagoguery. I could tell that he really cared. I knew right
at that moment that I wanted to work for that man."

When she graduated from Washington State University in 1994, she
had a "Slade Gorton Works for Me" sticker on her mortar board. A few
weeks later, she became Gorton's western Washington campaign field
director.[28]

GORTON AND THE ENVIRONMENTALISTS were at odds for the rest of the
'90s. They fought about birds and fish, dams and mines. Gorton introduced a 120-page bill to dramatically weaken the Endangered Species Act.
In considering whether a species should be saved, the Secretary of the
Interior would become a biodiversity czar. The secretary would weigh the
overall cost, including the economic impact on a community, and take
into consideration whether the species existed elsewhere. "That might
work under an environmentally savvy leader like Bruce Babbitt," Bill
Clinton's appointee, "but one shudders at the thought of placing the fate
of the American bald eagle in the hands of a reactionary secretary such as
James Watt," one editorial worried. Babbitt and Gorton, in fact, were old
friends from their days as attorneys general.[29]

Under Gorton's plan, the administration in power, be it Democrat or
Republican, would have broad discretion and the last word. It could pull
out all the stops to save a species, even if that spelled disaster for an Aberdeen or an Albany, or it could ignore the biologists and do little or nothing. "Never has a piece of legislation been introduced that has such potential to destroy wildlife," said the president of the Audubon Society.
"Senator Gorton's bill should be rightly called the 'Endangered Species
Extinction Act.'" Poppycock, said Gorton. All his bill did was bring people
into the process. "That's not radical. That's common sense."[30]

Industry groups that opposed the Endangered Species Act helped Gorton draft the legislation. They had contributed more than $50,000 to his 1994 re-election campaign. Ralph Nader's consumer advocacy group asked the Senate Ethics Committee to investigate. Gorton was cleared of any wrongdoing. "No Senate rule prohibits a senator from seeking advice on legislative issues from individuals or organizations outside the Senate," the committee's chief counsel wrote. "Such exchanges are common and acceptable Senate practices." Gorton said he was never reluctant to accept help from experts, noting that environmental groups "do the same thing."[31]

Greenpeace cranked out a thousand posters: "Wanted—Slade Gorton—for threatening the survival of our nation's wildlife and forests." He welcomed their enmity. On the other hand, he still wanted to get re-elected.[32]

George H.W. Bush did, too. But the recession had the country in a funk. Caught between Clinton's Baby Boomer vitality and Ross Perot's cornpone charisma, Bush came across as an amiable relic. "Did you see Bush look at his watch last night during the debate?" Gorton asked an editorial writer at a luncheon. The writer nodded. "He may not have fully realized it," Gorton said, tapping his watch crystal, "but he was saying, 'It's all over.'"

Clinton was promising to convene a "timber summit" to find middle ground for man, birds and beasts. "He's going to win," Gorton said, "and that may be the best possible outcome for timber communities. A centrist Democrat might be able to achieve a compromise."

A few months after taking office, Clinton convened the forest summit in Portland. Vice President Gore and several members of the cabinet listened intently as a parade of witnesses told of the toll. Larry Mason said "a whole way of life" had been destroyed. Hoquiam Mayor Phyllis Shrauger said unemployment on the Harbor was 19.5 percent and climbing.

Late in 1994, with mixed emotions because he believed it was barely legal, Judge Dwyer signed off on Clinton's Northwest Forest Plan and lifted the injunction. "Option 9" was actually the least draconian of the plans presented to the administration, but it still reduced logging in federal forests by three-quarters. Gorton was incensed. Timber communities had trusted the president, he said. They gave him their votes. "They proposed compromises that would impose pain on themselves, and they were patient when every month of further deliberation meant another month of unpaid bills. Amid fear and anxiety, they fought to hold their families together as they waited and waited for a decision. . . . Mr. President, where is the balance in a plan that reduces by nearly 80 percent the productive capacity of these hard-working people in just four years? Is it 'balanced' to exalt the spotted owl at the expense of the human condition?"[33]

NEXT CAME THE MARBLED MURRELET. Gorton said 300 million board feet on the west side of the Cascades was now in bureaucratic gridlock to protect the newest member of what he called "the creature-of-the month club."

Timber industry lobbyists, working with Republicans in the House and Senate, drafted legislation in 1995 that left the environmentalists reeling. "Salvage" riders were appended to an omnibus congressional budget bill. The amendments mandated a two-year program to remove damaged, dead or dying timber. Trees "imminently susceptible to fire or insect attack" and "associated trees" also could be harvested. All such sales, moreover, would be exempt from administrative appeals and environmental regulations. Gorton shrewdly enlisted Senator Hatfield's help for his version, which also insulated from legal challenge all new timber sales authorized by the Clinton plan. Since the administration had been unable to deliver the billion board feet of timber it promised, Gorton said he was pleased to be "helping" with a short-term solution that would also address the "forest health crisis." Apoplectic, environmentalists said the crisis was a hoax and warned that the rider could undo much of what had been accomplished in the past seven years. Loggers surely were warming up their Husqvarnas, they said, because the fine print would allow a full-scale attack on national forests. The salvage rider also directed federal land managers to proceed with all of the timber sales that had been on hold since 1989.[34]

A nationwide environmental SOS produced a deluge of calls and letters to the White House. Clinton duly vetoed the budget bill, denouncing the salvage rider as a blank check that would saddle the taxpayers with the bill "for whatever damage occurs to the environment." Gorton and Hatfield went back to work. Slade couldn't have found a more influential ally. Hatfield headed the Senate Appropriations Committee. Sometimes called "Saint Mark," Oregon's gentlemanly former governor was in Gorton's eyes "the very model of a United States senator" yet also adept at hardball. Hatfield reportedly threatened to attach the salvage rider to every appropriations bill, a move that would leave Clinton with the Hobson's choice of vetoing every one or letting the federal government close up shop. "At the same time, Hatfield promised the president that under the rider, his agencies still would have the latitude to follow environmen-

tal laws and regulations except for those suspending appeals and legal
challenges," Northwest historian Kathie Durbin wrote in *Tree Huggers*,
her chronicle of the old-growth wars. Gore and other members of Clinton's environmental brain trust were adamant that the rider was political
and environmental poison. But the president signed the budget bill, salvage rider largely intact, on July 27, 1995. It went into effect immediately.
The next day, environmental leaders mourned the capitulation with a
"21-chainsaw salute" outside the White House. Looking back, Gore said
surrendering to Gorton was the worst mistake the administration made
during its first term.[35]

Seven months later, Gorton and Hatfield rebuffed an attempt to weaken
the salvage plan. Patty Murray, Brock Adams' successor, was proposing a
compromise that would have suspended sales of old-growth and allowed
salvage sales to be appealed in court. Murray and Clinton warned that a
lot of healthy ancient timber was being harvested under the loophole.
Environmentalists called it "logging without laws." Gorton's rejoinder
was that only 16,000 acres of green timber out of the 24 million protected
by the Clinton forest plan was being expedited for sale. The Senate
chopped Murray's plan, 54-42. The rider expired at the end of 1996. The
best Clinton could do was truncate it by two weeks. From then on, Gorton's efforts to unlock more timber were repeatedly blocked.[36]

Twenty years after it was declared threatened, the spotted owl's numbers were still in decline, despite the dramatic cutbacks. To the bitter
amusement of surviving loggers, the barred owl—a bigger, meaner non-
native interloper—started horning in on its more docile cousin, kicking
the spotties out of their nests or slamming "into their breasts like feath-
ery missiles" before mating with the females.[37]

Mother Nature has always been fickle, Babbitt observed in 2010.
"Though the owl triggered it, what was at stake was the survival of the
old-growth ecosystem." The Clinton plan represented a landmark in conservation planning, the former Interior secretary added, with foresters
examining entire ecosystems rather than just drawing lines on a map.
The Washington Forest Protection Association protested that ignoring
owl conservation efforts on 2.1 million acres of state and private land was
hardly an entire ecosystem approach.[38]

IN THE GLORY DAYS of logging, they'd tried to cut it all. Now Jim Carlson
had nearly lost it all, although his droll sense of humor survived intact.
Kellie had made him a proud grandfather. After several years on Gorton's
staff, she was back home, helping her father regroup and heading the

Chamber of Commerce board, working to attract new industry to Grays Harbor.

In *My Life*, Clinton's thousand-page autobiography, there's not one word about spotted owls or the timber summit. It's as if Air Force One never stopped in Portland or flew over Forks en route to Vancouver, B.C., for a meeting with Boris Yeltsin. Gorton is not the least bit surprised: "Bill Clinton could be intensely engaged and participate intelligently in a conversation on almost any subject and then forget it totally an hour later if it wasn't an element in his own agenda.

"I still find it curious that the one politician in Washington who fought for the people in Grays Harbor—and for eastern Washington to preserve the dams—was an Ivy League lawyer in Seattle who neither hunts nor fishes nor cares much for long walks in the woods. I believe that the Americans most neglected by the establishment are not racial minorities but the working and middle classes in rural and small-city America. . . .The people whose predecessors built America and whose children still fight its wars deserve a voice, and that is what I have tried to provide."

29 | Back at Bat

"Baseball, it is said, is only a game. True. And the Grand Canyon is only a hole in Arizona."—George F. Will

I N HONOR OF HIS SWEAT EQUITY, Gorton has a seat in the owner's box at Safeco Field, home to the Seattle Mariners since 1999 and one of the great baseball venues in America. That's as good as it gets for someone who became a certifiable baseball nut around age 8. If Gorton hadn't stepped up to the plate once again in 1991, the Mariners might be in Tampa Bay as yet another offspring of Seattle's shotgun marriage with Major League Baseball.

The team Gorton put together to save big-league baseball for Seattle a second time included old friends like John Ellis, the CEO of Puget Sound Power & Light, and new high-tech millionaires like Chris Larson, one of the young software wizards at Microsoft. The real savior, however, was nearly 5,000 miles away.

Though they had never met, Hiroshi Yamauchi, the architect of Nintendo's emergence from domestic playing card producer to global power in the burgeoning world of video games, was grateful to Gorton. The senator had prodded U.S. Customs and the FBI to crack down on the counterfeiters who were pirating Donkey Kong, the game that took America by storm. By 1992, Nintendo owned 80 percent of a $6 billion global market. Its American division, overseen by Yamauchi's talented son-in-law, Minoru Arakawa, had 1,400 employees at its headquarters in the Seattle suburb of Redmond, where Microsoft and McCaw Cellular were also in the chips. From his seat on the Senate Commerce Committee Gorton was a tireless protector of their intellectual property rights. His fan club, in other words, included some of the wealthiest people on Earth.[1]

WHEN JEFF SMULYAN BOUGHT the struggling Mariners in 1989, he described himself as cocky. By 1991 he professed to feeling naïve, although many suspected ulterior motives. The bottom line was that he was losing money. Smulyan's entrepreneurial moxie had allowed him to assemble a string of radio stations and buy one of the world's most expensive toys—a baseball team. Unfortunately, a winning season hadn't translated to success at the turnstiles. His creditors were tightening the screws. When *The Seattle Times* reported that a document at Smulyan's local bank indicated he intended to move the M's after the 1992 season, his denial was emphatic: "I will dispute to the death that that is our strategy. (But) I'll tell you this: There are people in that bank who say baseball doesn't work in Seattle. . . . They have concluded this isn't a viable business."[2]

First the Pilots, now the M's. Two strikes probably would be out for Seattle as a baseball town. Gorton introduced legislation that would have required major league teams to share about half their revenues from local broadcasting contracts. National TV revenues were already being pooled. The plan was designed to boost the overall health of Major League Baseball by helping small-market clubs like the Mariners, who expected to end 1991 $10 million in the hole. With radio and TV contracts estimated at $3.5 million that year, the M's take from TV was the lowest in the big leagues while the Yankees were receiving $50 million from the local airwaves alone. Gorton emphasized that his plan was not "a completely even playing field." Clubs in the big media markets would still have far greater resources. He acknowledged, however, that the chances of his bill passing Congress in the near future were "somewhere between slim and none." He was right.[3]

"George Argyros, who sold the Mariners to Smulyan, was always bitching about the Kingdome—rightly," Gorton observes. The concrete coliseum was funded by the taxpayers as one of the Forward Thrust measures Gorton championed as a legislator. It opened in 1976 to mixed reviews. Playing baseball on fake grass under a concrete sky was not a field of dreams. Angled onto what was basically a football venue, the Kingdome's compact ball park was a hitter's delight, a pitcher's nightmare and a fan's frustration. It had lousy sightlines and the ambiance of a mausoleum, especially on days when sunshine was glistening off Puget Sound and the mountains were out.

"Smulyan got a sweetheart deal on his lease, including an escape clause," Gorton says. "In exchange, he had to agree that before he tried to move the team or sell it he would offer it to someone who would keep it here at a price to be set by an appraiser. Smulyan thought that was a good deal because there'd never been anyone here who could make it work. It was obvious that he wanted to move the team to Tampa, one way or another—either by selling it or staying on as owner. We had 120 days to come up with $100 million. No one thought we could do it, and I wasn't so sure myself."

FOUR YEARS EARLIER, after losing his seat in the Senate, Gorton thought his political career was over. If he was home for good, he hated the thought of life without a baseball team. He began trolling for Japanese investors. Washington was emerging as not only the gateway to the Pacific Rim but as a prime location for Japanese high-tech investment. In an increasingly information-based economy, the Japanese genius for cutting-edge technology and marketing propelled Tokyo to one of the world's major financial centers. Affordable, high-quality products like Sony's "Walkman" portable stereo and trouble-free autos generated a yen for investment in real estate at home and abroad. The bubble would burst. While it lasted, however, Japan was on a roll and aggressively acquisitive.

For the hard-working Japanese, the ball park holds an allure that rivals sumo. They're passionate about their baseball—*yakyu*. In 1987, unbeknownst to Gorton and all but the American baseball cognoscenti, Ichiro Suzuki, a 14-year-old with a sophisticated swing, was beginning to attract the attention of scouts for the Orix BlueWave.

Gorton had long admired the Japanese. "Besides loving baseball, they're disciplined and enterprising, now among the richest people in the world. I contacted our ambassador to Japan, Mike Mansfield, and we did a little work on that angle in 1987. But nothing came of it. Then Smulyan stepped in to buy the club. In December of 1991, when he announced the Mariners were for sale, we were once again on the brink of losing our team. I had my secretary call Nintendo and ask for a meeting with Arakawa and Howard Lincoln, who was their number one American." The conversation went like this:

"What's the subject?"

"Baseball."

"Well, we don't have any interest in baseball, but of course if the senator wants to come out and see us we would be honored to meet with him."

They talked for nearly two hours. "For not having any interest in baseball, they certainly had a lot of questions. If Nintendo wasn't interested in making an investment, I hoped Arakawa's father-in-law might give us some leads."

Gorton departed on a trade mission to Russia.

Arakawa dutifully called Yamauchi, who listened intently, then said, "You don't have to look for other companies. I will do it."[4]

Arakawa was stunned. He told his father-in-law it was a bad investment. He didn't care. America had been very, very good to Nintendo and Gorton-*san* had been their friend. Yamauchi told his son-in-law he would finance the investment out of his own pocket.

When Arakawa relayed the latest news from Tokyo, Lincoln was flabbergasted. A baseball fan, he instinctively understood the perils of being the guy who signed the checks. Whether at lunch, Costco or Nordstrom's, there was sure to be at least one lippy fan who felt the bullpen sucked, not to mention snarky sports writers. "It's going to be great for a while," Lincoln told Arakawa, "and Mr. Yamauchi will be perceived as a savior. But mark my words, the day will come when we'll be attacked by the media, and you're going to have people calling you and complaining about the Mariners' performance." Little did Lincoln know just how prescient he was.[5]*

When Gorton returned from the grueling overseas trip, he was tired and cranky. He also had a mild case of pneumonia. But on December 23rd, 1991, he received "the greatest Christmas present I've ever had. It was a call from Minoru Arakawa, who said, 'Mr. Senator, my father-in-law says that we have done very well in America. Seattle and the State of Washington have been very good to us. We're part of the community. Therefore if you need $100 million to buy a baseball team, you have $100 million.' I was instantly restored, but it quickly developed that we were facing a buzzsaw that 'We're not going to have a bunch of goddamn Japs owning a Major League baseball team.' With long memories to our Pilots lawsuit and my recent efforts to force them to share revenues, the team owners hated me, too. Our only chance was to dilute the racism with local partners and outflank the opposition with an effective PR campaign."

JOHN ELLIS, Jim's enterprising younger brother, was one of the first friends Gorton made in 1956 when he returned to Seattle to stay after his Air Force stint and joined the Young Republicans. Approached to help give the plan a leading local face, Ellis was astounded by Yamauchi's offer and supportive. But he said his pockets were nowhere deep enough to help.

Meantime, back in Redmond, there were baseball fans at Microsoft with major amounts of disposable income. When Smulyan announced the team was for sale, Chris Larson, one of Bill Gates' best friends, was disappointed when the boss demurred. A baseball fan since childhood,

---

* In 2010 when Lincoln was CEO of the Mariners, he received a year-end dubious achievement award from a *Seattle Times* columnist for blowing off media criticism of "his consistently embarrassing on-field product by urging team employees via e-mail to remember that 'the dumbest guys in the room are always media guys.'"[6]

Larson was mulling retirement at 32 and daydreaming about owning a piece of the team. When Gorton called, he decided he could spare $25 million or so and immediately began e-mailing other potential investors.

Gorton's next call was to Wayne Perry, a friend and admirer who had ascended to the No. 2 spot at McCaw Cellular. Their paths crossed often in Washington, D.C., where Perry argued the cell-phone industry's case with the FCC and Gorton ran interference on the Commerce Committee. "Wayne is the kind of guy who likes straight talk," Gorton says, "so I just told him, 'You've made a lot of money. It is time to give back.' It helped that he had been a Little League coach—and that John McCaw trusted him implicitly." Gorton, Arakawa and Lincoln then told Ellis he was being drafted. His investment would be his management skill and Seattle bona fides. He'd be the group's glue. "I have never approached anything in my life with less knowledge of how to do it," Ellis recalls. Nonsense, Gorton says. "He was the perfect choice."

For his baseball chops and PR skills, Ellis and Gorton immediately accepted Chuck Armstrong's offer to help. He'd been the team president before Smulyan acquired the M's. With the addition of Boeing CEO Frank Shrontz, the Baseball Club of Seattle was announced to the public on January 23, 1992.[7]

To help offset the team owners' undisguised hostility to Japanese ownership of a piece of the American pastime Hiroshi Yamauchi agreed to reduce his share in the franchise. The political realities were delicately couched by his son-in-law, but Yamauchi already knew the score. Japanese investors were seen as predatory, a new wave of yellow peril. A half century after Pearl Harbor, they'd bought Rockefeller Center, even Gorton's of Gloucester. Now they wanted a piece of the American pastime. Baseball Commissioner Fay Vincent made it instantly clear that Major League Baseball's "strong policy" was to reject investors from outside North America. Gorton found the anti-Japanese sentiment in Major League Baseball shameful. Howard Lincoln, having worked so closely with Arakawa, was profoundly "pissed off" at the disrespect visited on his boss and the chairman.[8]

The Washington State Senate unanimously approved a resolution urging Vincent to "recognize and applaud the international appeal of baseball." Governor Booth Gardner and Seattle Mayor Norm Rice met with the commissioner. "The only foreign ownership I'm concerned about is Tampa Bay," Gardner told him. *New York Times* columnist Dave Anderson wrote, "For those who think of baseball's 26 owners as the only members of a snobbish country club but could never prove it, proof is now available . . . By offering to provide 60 percent of the $100 million purchase price, the Nintendo people weren't trying to buy a baseball treasure, such as the Hall of Fame at Cooperstown or one of Babe Ruth's mustard-stained uniforms. If anything, the Seattle group would be doing baseball a favor. Over its 15 seasons, the Mariners franchise has been all but invisible. Never in a divisional race. Never above .500 until last season. Never willing to bid for any of the expensive free agents." Joining the chorus of hooting at baseball's xenophobia were George Will, *Sports Illustrated*, *Time*, *Newsweek* and the *Washington Post*.9

While the specter of racism was beginning to make them squirm, Gorton played party politics. He called the managing director of the Texas Rangers, an affable young fellow named George W. Bush, and told him his dad would vouch for him as a good guy. Gorton emphasized that he wasn't part of a plot to give foreigners control of the game they both loved. "W" doubtless called the White House, Gorton believes, because the president began making calls of his own.

Ellis had impressed the Major League owners' committee as a "very capable no-nonsense guy." In a move that proved decisive, he was persuaded to dip into his retirement nest egg, ante in $250,000 and become the club's chairman. Yamauchi's investment would be scaled back to a "passive" 49 percent. "During this gut-wrenching, six-month ordeal I frequently thought the Japanese were just going to say forget it," Gorton recalls. "Major League Baseball drove a hard, humiliating bargain. Ellis kept everyone talking, even when tempers flared."10

ON JUNE 11, 1992, the Seattle Mariners were safe at home—at least until the next crisis. The Major League owners voted 25-1 to allow the Baseball Club of Seattle to buy the team from Smulyan. Ellis, who was 63, had been looking forward to partial retirement. "I wake up in the middle of the night and think, 'What's gotten into me?'" The challenge now, he said, was to put the Mariners on a firm financial footing for the first time in their 15-year history.11

"So we have a baseball team," Gorton sums up his second at bat while gazing down at Safeco Field from his law office on the 27th floor of the sleek skyscraper at Fourth and Madison. "But we still have a pretty lousy baseball team. And it's still playing in the Kingdome, which still is not a Major League ball park. Our lease lasted through the 1996 season. I knew we weren't out of the woods, but I didn't think we'd soon be on the brink of losing our team all over again."

30 | New Friends and Old Enemies

TO THE SURPRISE OF MANY, cerebral Slade Gorton and Trent Lott, a former Ole Miss cheerleader who loved to boom "The Old Rugged Cross," bonded quickly. Lott had been in Congress since 1973, ascending to House GOP whip before capturing the Senate seat left open by the retirement in 1988 of the venerable John C. Stennis in increasingly Republican Mississippi. Gorton's status as a former senator put him one rung higher on the seniority ladder when they took office in 1989. They ended up sitting next to one another on the Armed Services and Commerce committees and became fast friends.

They were antsy. Despite Bush's decisive victory over Dukakis, Democrats had retained control of both houses of the 101st Congress. Gorton was not used to being in the minority and Lott's greatest ambition was to lead a majority, although he was nowhere near as single-mindedly crafty as his fellow movement conservative, Georgia Congressman Newt Gingrich.

"A lot of senators don't take the time to read the language in legislation or understand it if they read it," Lott says. "It's strictly a political or a visceral judgment. Slade actually understood the substance. I had to shake my head at the reputation he had in some circles as an uber-partisan because that's not the kind of

Majority Leader Trent Lott, Gorton's good friend. *Library of Congress*

senator he was. He was a fiscal conservative, but his demeanor is very moderate. He is very much his own man—witness the fact that he frustrated Reagan—but he's also a mediator. I told somebody who didn't know him that when Slade first shows up at a meeting people are gonna say, 'Who's the nerd?' and think 'He's not going to be much of a player.' But in the end, he will greatly impact and affect the result."

While Gorton can do a dead-on impression of a straight-from-Central Casting Southern senator, he found Lott, drawl and all, to be as astute as he was charming. "He's an easy guy to like and someone who was going places. As our friendship deepened and he steadily moved up, Trent made me the only non-elected member of leadership because he trusted me and my judgment. I was probably the only one in those meetings not mentally measuring the drapes for a move into the leader's office."

Across the aisle were two upwardly mobile freshmen Gorton came to know and admire: Joe Lieberman of Connecticut—more conservative by far than Lowell Weicker, the Republican he ousted—and former Nebraska governor Bob Kerrey, a free spirit who had seen real combat, receiving the Medal of Honor for his exploits as a Navy SEAL team leader in Vietnam.

Gorton and Mike McGavick, his new chief of staff, hit on an idea for a group they dubbed the S-214 Society. It took its name from an office just off the Senate floor. A group of hand-picked back-benchers, the society met every other week when the Senate was in session. They kicked around ideas; developed strategies; shared their frustrations. Besides the serious stuff, they had fun. S-214 helped Gorton establish his reputation with younger senators who lacked his legislative experience. Connie Mack of Florida was one of the quick learners he admired. It also created a group of friends and supporters that bridged Gorton's admirers from the first term and those who had not known him well.

BROCK ADAMS GREETED GORTON'S RETURN to the Senate with a show of collegiality but their interactions were invariably awkward. Together with Norm Dicks, they found common cause on earthquake preparedness, double-hulled oil tankers and reauthorization of the Magnuson Fisheries Act of 1976, a crucial issue for the stakeholders in the North Pacific fishery.[1]

On the signature issue of their 1986 battle for the Senate, Adams still strongly opposed the Gorton-Morrison proposal to convert an unfinished WPPSS plant to produce tritium. Even though Boeing was a major subcontractor, Adams also opposed a Bush Administration plan, endorsed by Gorton, to build 75 B-2 stealth bombers at a cost of $65 billion. However, they both favored allowing women to fly combat missions and voted for a foreign-aid bill Bush vehemently opposed because it didn't restrict abortion counseling.[2]

When the Navy's Whidbey Island air station was threatened with down-sizing, then closure, Gorton's stance was instructive of his dispassionate approach to problem solving. Although his son-in-law, a combat-ready aviator, was stationed at Oak Harbor, Slade bluntly dismissed the Chamber of Commerce's pitch that the community would be devastated. Every community in the base-closing commission's cross hairs could and would make the same case, Gorton said. The only viable, patriotic argument was that the military's mission would be compromised. With support from Adams and Dicks, Gorton made that case and won. The same fact-based approach later saved the Everett Home Port.

With Dicks leading the way, Adams and Gorton agreed early on that the landmark land-claims settlement with the Puyallup Tribe in the Tacoma area was overdue and just. The tribes saw Gorton's vote as window-dressing, however, and they were miffed when he was named to the Select Committee on Indian Affairs.

In June of 1989, the delegation's power took a quantum leap when Tom Foley of Spokane ascended to Speaker of the House in the wake of an ethics probe instigated against Speaker Jim Wright by Gingrich. In 1991, Gorton was named to Appropriations, making Washington the only state with both senators on the powerful committee.[3]

ALTHOUGH GORTON'S SUPPORT for logging interests infuriated environmentalists, they welcomed his outrage over an historic unnatural disaster. At 12:04 a.m. March 24, 1989, the tanker *Exxon Valdez*—its radar broken and skipper allegedly sleeping off a bender below decks—ran aground on a reef in Alaska's Prince William Sound. The spill fouled 1,300 miles of coastline and 11,000 square miles of ocean. Soon thereafter the tanker *Exxon Philadelphia* lost power and drifted for seven hours off the Olympic Peninsula. In one of the fieriest speeches he ever gave on the Senate floor Gorton denounced Exxon's irresponsibility, calling for heavy monetary penalties, other sanctions, tighter regulations and the CEO's resignation. America needed oil and clean beaches, he said, and the technology to protect both interests was readily available if corporations and regulators did their jobs.[4]

Gorton bucked the Bush White House by teaming up with Nevada Democrat Richard Bryan to push legislation requiring automakers to achieve a 40 mpg fleet average for their vehicles by 2001. It would be the death knell for the midsize American family sedan, Detroit and its allies insisted. "It means smaller cars. It means less safe cars." They'd been saying that since the early 1970s during the Arab oil embargo, Gorton noted. By dragging their heels, the Big Three were losing the battle to their agile overseas competition and wasting millions of barrels of oil. "I refuse to accept the notion that American ingenuity can't produce vehicles that are simultaneously safer, more fuel efficient and less harmful to the environment." Gorton's advocacy of aggressive Corporate Average Fuel Economy standards was repeatedly rebuffed by industry lobbyists and conservatives during his 18 years in the Senate. The CAFE standard for 2012 through 2016 was still only 34.1 mpg.[5]

Gorton also flexed his old consumer-protection muscles, playing a key role in successful legislation to require dual airbags in all cars and light trucks as well as stronger roll-bars and head-injury and side-impact protection. He negotiated a tough toy-safety law and teamed with Al Gore to push legislation to impose competition on the cable TV industry after a dispute that deprived millions of New Yorkers of their inalienable right to view Yankees, Rangers and Knicks games. The senators said the arrogance of cable providers prompted them to think better of their 1984 votes to deregulate the industry. Rather than improving service, they said the industry had gouged consumers with huge rate hikes and increasingly "tiered" offerings. Popular new channels invariably cost more. Regional telephone companies ought to be allowed to offer TV service through their growing fiber-optic networks, the senators said. Gorton, Gore and Adams were in the majority in 1992 when the Senate joined the House in voting to override Bush's veto of legislation subjecting cable franchise holders to FCC and local oversight. It marked Congress's first override of a Bush veto.[6]

GORTON'S PRO-CHOICE VOTES and his break with Bush on fetal-tissue research earned him some grudging kudos from liberals. They were more impressed by his support for the Corporation for Public Broadcasting and the National Endowment for the Arts. He demanded "balanced programming," however, and opposed federal funding of fellowships such as the one that produced the notorious "Piss Christ," a photo of a Jesus figure submerged in the artist's urine. Gorton at first had joined the move to ban public funding of artists whose work is "patently offensive to the average person." The debate over how to define average promptly degenerated into gibberish that had Gorton rolling his eyes. Jesse Helms upped the ante to include anything "indecent" or "denigrating." Gorton, his friend

Warren Rudman and Georgia Democrat Wyche Fowler crafted a substitute focusing on "obscene," which had passed muster with a majority of the Supreme Court. The 65-31 vote was a stinging defeat for Helms, who was furious with Gorton and the other Republican moderates.

A year later, Gorton could be found in opposition to funding works that featured "sexual or excretory activities or organs" in a "patently offensive way," but he never surrendered to the fig-leaf wing of the Republican Party. Between 1995 and 1997, Gingrich's right-wingers in the House repeatedly attempted to zero out the NEA's funding, with Gorton saving the day in the Senate. In 1997, as chairman of the Interior appropriations subcommittee, he even boosted the agency's budget by a modest yet symbolically important $1 million.[7]

Gorton helped sustain Bush's controversial veto of a job discrimination bill, agreeing with the conservative contention that it would force employers to adopt hiring quotas. He also supported Bush's vetoes of "family leave" legislation requiring both public and private employers of 50 or more workers to provide up to 12 weeks of unpaid time off in the event of childbirth or illness in an employee's immediate family.[8]

Gorton was a study in unpredictability. His vote in 1992 helped the Senate achieve an override of Bush's veto of legislation allowing federally funded clinics to provide abortion counseling. The House, however, failed to achieve the necessary two-thirds majority.[9]

During his first term, Gorton frequently described himself as a "passionate moderate." Now he was in orbit with Lott, moving right, yet never in lock-step, always with that libertarian streak. He and Lott found the president eminently likable but a frequent disappointment, especially when he broke his famous "read my lips—no new taxes" pledge. That one cost the party dearly.

GORTON'S VIEWS ON INTERNATIONAL RELATIONS are a blend of Teddy Roosevelt, George C. Marshall and Ronald Reagan. "Passionately pro-liberty" and a student of history, he believes in American Exceptionalism. *Black Lamb and Grey Falcon*, Rebecca West's 1,100-page masterpiece on the Balkans just before World War II, made a huge impression on him when he was a senior at Dartmouth writing a thesis on Yugoslavia. One part travelogue, one part history, all steeped in metaphor, the moral of West's story is the importance of resistance to evil.

Gorton's favorite countries are "small, oppressed democracies—Israel, the Republic of China on Taiwan and Estonia, to name three." In the winter of 1990, the Soviets denied Gorton and McGavick visas to visit Estonia as guests of its Cultural Foundation. Given some leeway to experiment with Western-style government, Estonia was moving too quickly for the Kremlin's comfort, poised to establish its own Congress before Soviet-sanctioned elections. Other members of Congress, including John Miller, a Republican from Seattle, encountered roadblocks when they made plans to visit Lithuania, Ukraine and Latvia to observe elections.[10]

Gorton viewed the Soviet annexation of the Baltic republics as tyranny. He was in close contact with the fair-sized group of Baltic expatriates in Seattle. After his defeat in 1986, his secretary was a Latvian who had come to the Northwest as a teenager. The most active ex-officio ambassador was a man from Estonia who often popped into his path. In fact, he was the last person Gorton met with before returning to the Senate in 1988. "Remember the Baltics, Slade!" he admonished. "I promised I would. Because of him, I was invited to be the keynote speaker at the Congress of Estonia."

Gorton accepted with glee and immediately set to work on a speech enumerating the rights and responsibilities of a democracy—the rule of law and freedom of speech tempered with civility, including "How will you treat your minority—the Russians who will still live among you?"

"One particularly important aspect of equality before the law and equality of opportunity is its relationship to half or more than half of the population of every society: our women," Gorton wrote. "Through most of history and most societies, women have been and still are severely limited in their ability to live up to their full potential. This is profoundly unjust, both to women and to men, and may be the greatest inhibition to the success of human society." At Gorton's urging, a statement addressing the oppression of women in Muslim societies was incorporated into the report of the 9/11 Commission some 15 years later.

"I worked really hard on that speech, but it soon became evident that no way were the Soviets going to let us in." Gorton gave the speech on the floor of the U.S. Senate and airmailed a videotape to Estonia. It was played before some 800 at the inaugural meeting of their Congress. An empty front row seat bore Gorton's name and a bouquet of roses. "It got more publicity, I'm sure, than if I had been able actually to show up. Happily, a few months later, Estonia was free." The grateful new republic awarded him the Order of the Cross of Terra Mariana, 1ˢᵗ Class.

"IN TERMS OF THE ONE ACT that had a profound impact on a significant number of lives," Gorton believes the most significant achievement of his 18 years in Congress was his response to the Chinese government's bloody crackdown on pro-democracy protesters in 1989.

As a menacing column of tanks rumbled into Beijing's Tiananmen Square on June 4, Curtis Hom was glued to the TV in Gorton's Senate office. Famous for his 16-hour days, the young legislative assistant was alone in the office, watching the showdown with anxiety and fascination. He'd been there. Many of the protest leaders were from Peking University, where Hom had spent two years. "The soldiers were dispersing the crowds. Then all of the sudden CNN got chopped off and the studio went crazy. I spent that night, working 'til 3 or 4 a.m., writing a memo to Slade. I told him everyone in Congress was going to be making 'I'm pissed at China' speeches, but he should talk about what needed to be done rather than just say 'I'm outraged.'"

Hom's memo, which impressed Gorton as first-class staff work, outlined a possible overture to Boeing to help evacuate frightened Americans. It explored the opportunity to prod the Bush Administration to play good cop/bad cop to promote human rights and free-enterprise reforms. And, Hom emphasizes, it addressed the question of "what do you do with all the Chinese who are in the United States who are now scared witless about going back. First of all, they have been tainted by America and, second, most them likely had been participating in demonstrations in the United States. So they are quite possibly marked people." There were upwards of 80,000 Chinese nationals in the United States, including 45,000 students. In all, they were among the best and brightest of the most populous nation in the world. The legislation Gorton and Hom drafted offered them the chance to seek permanent residency. It streamlined the often lengthy green card process by waiving some of the visa and interview requirements.[11]

Nancy Pelosi, whose San Francisco-area congressional district is heavily Chinese, picked up on Gorton's idea. Ted Kennedy, who headed the subcommittee on immigration, also championed the plan. Hom was miffed that the Democrats were getting most of the ink but Gorton reminded him that when you're in the minority you can often achieve your goals by greasing the skids with the majority. "Besides being scary smart," Hom says, "Slade is great at strategy. He kept nudging it along, working across the aisle, lobbying Bush."

In 1990, the president signed an executive order staying the deportation of Chinese nationals. Many Chinese students, however, were unable to land the jobs for which they were well qualified because their immigration status was uncertain. The Chinese Student Protection Act finally became law in 1992.

"America is a land of immigrants, but I really like it when immigrants bring special talents to our society," Gorton says. "China's loss was our gain—all those brilliant Ph.D.'s, physicists, physicians, engineers and economists who decided to stay here, 600 of them in Washington State. They were not only a benefit to the United States but their loss was an appropriate punishment of communist China for the way in which it treated its people. The act was a catalyst for the Chinese government to start making reforms. It might not have happened without Curtis Hom, the son of Chinese immigrants—just one of the many remarkable people I was able to recruit to public service."

WHEN SADDAM HUSSEIN'S ARMY invaded Kuwait in the summer of 1990, Gorton and Norm Dicks were among the lawmakers invited to a briefing by the president. Bush said it might mean war if sanctions failed to produce a withdrawal. In that case, Gorton piped up emphatically, "The one most important thing we have to do is win." The room burst into applause. The history of the 20th Century was replete with lessons on the tragic consequences of meeting naked aggression with timidity, Gorton said.

Adams, Seattle Congressman Jim McDermott and Jolene Unsoeld, the Democrat from Olympia who had succeeded Bonker in the state's Third Congressional District, were among the harshest critics of Bush's actions. Unsoeld warned that if the U.S. failed to exhaust all alternatives to war it would be remembered "as a country that threw away the lessons of Vietnam" and became ensnared in a bloody conflict "to make the world safe for cheap American gasoline and Mercedes-driving sheiks." Gorton said Iraq wasn't Vietnam and the issue at hand wasn't oil. Even "more boys will be coming home in body bags" down the road if Iraq wasn't stopped. Kuwait today, Saudi Arabia tomorrow, then Israel, said Gorton. "It means we will face Saddam Hussein again and others who believe that what Saddam Hussein got away with they can get away with as well." Gorton and Dicks, a defense expert, were in agreement that Bush should not act without congressional authorization. "The president derives no authority from the United Nations," Gorton emphasized.[12]

On Jan. 12, 1991, Gorton cast one of the 52 Senate votes in favor of the war powers resolution. As the deadline for Saddam's withdrawal neared, some 15,000 peace marchers took to the streets of Seattle to chant, pray and sing. Some of the more militant converged on the Federal Building. Six were arrested for refusing to leave Gorton's 32nd floor office after his staff fielded their questions for 15 minutes. The senator was occupied elsewhere.

An interdenominational service was held at the Episcopal cathedral,

St. Mark's, but they wouldn't have found Gorton there either. He had boycotted St. Mark's since suffering through a Christmas Eve sermon a decade earlier on the importance of a nuclear weapons freeze. He would have mailed the rector a copy of *Black Lamb and Grey Falcon* if he'd thought there was any chance it would inspire more rational homilies. The book's author, Rebecca West, observed that some people just seemed intent on thrusting the "blunt muzzle" of their stupidity into conclaves of state.[13]

The day after the protests, Bush's generals unleashed the most devastating air assault in history, followed by a ground war that steamrolled Saddam's vaunted Republican Guard in 100 hours. From start to finish, it was five weeks. What the Iraqi dictator had billed as the Mother of All Battles turned out to be the Son of Waterloo.

If the president had ordered the Pentagon to keep on rolling, ousting Hussein right then and there, as many argued we should, would the Mideast have been a safer place by the time the president's son occupied the Oval Office a decade later? "In retrospect, with 20-20 hindsight, yes," says Gorton. "But I can't claim that I held that view at the time because we had reached the limit of the U.N. resolution that gave us our coalition. I exchanged views on the subject with Charles Krauthammer, the Pulitzer Prize-winning columnist. He was right and I was wrong. But Bush was outrageously wrong in not stopping the slaughter of the Shiites in southern Iraq by Saddam immediately after the shooting war was over."

AS SOMEONE who was often at the White House during the administration of the 41st president, endorsed the candidacy of the 43rd early on and later played a key role in investigating the root causes of the 9/11 terror attacks, Gorton's views on the Bushes are intriguing:

"George W. Bush is tougher than his dad. His dad is a very soft personal-

President George H.W. Bush greets Gorton as Vice President Dan Quayle looks on. *Gorton family album*

ity whose overwhelming interest was foreign and defense policy. He presided over winning the Cold War and the first Gulf War and he had nothing left when they were over because he wasn't interested in anything else. He's a wonderful person, but you couldn't get him to take a strong position on something even when Republicans wanted him to do so. George W. Bush inherited a lot from his mother, who is a much more decisive person than his father. That said, the second Bush was probably too indifferent to listening to various voices. He got us into a war without knowing what the goals of the war were, or more precisely what the goals were going to be after the war was over. So he has the 'mission accomplished' banner there on an aircraft carrier to celebrate victory, only to lose thousands of troops over the next several years.

"He came out courageously with the right answer in the last year of his presidency. He would have been a magnificent president if he had called for 'The Surge' in 2003 or 2004 and had done the job then. I said it when his father first told us a war seemed inevitable: If you go to war, you better go to war to win. G.W. Bush thought he could win on the cheap, and he couldn't. It's just as simple as that. Then when he was very unpopular he went in to win—but way too late, with a large number of Americans killed and tens of thousands of Iraqis dead as a result.

"G.W. Bush greatly underestimated the difficulty of creating a democracy. You don't create a Vermont town-meeting democracy in a place like Iraq quickly or on the cheap. His whole presidency after 9/11 was national security, with no longer any priority for domestic policies. He ran an idea up the flag pole to partly privatize Social Security and it died. He never came up with any other big ideas after that. His father's presidency lasted one term because he was indecisive. His own never reached its potential because he didn't learn enough lessons from his father's presidency or follow the instincts he inherited from his mother."

31 | A House Divided

THE RUN-UP TO THE 1992 ELECTIONS found Gorton embroiled in the spotted owl battle, the president with a recession on his hands and Brock Adams' 31-year political career at a sad end. Rumors that there were more Kari Tuppers had dogged Adams since 1987. Perceived as vulnerable within his own party and rebuffed by his old Labor Council allies, Adams already had one announced challenger, the upstart Patty Murray, while Mike Lowry was on the cusp, brandishing a poll he commissioned that documented Adams' vulnerability. Adams put on a brave face. "There's always wannabes. I'm the only winner. I've won eight straight elections."[1]

On Sunday, March 1, 1992, a few weeks after Adams formally announced his bid for re-election and just before the precinct caucuses, *The Seattle Times* front-paged a devastating investigative piece. Eight women claimed the senator had sexually harassed or molested them in incidents that stretched back two decades, sometimes plying them with a mixture of drugs and alcohol. There were even more victims, the newspaper said, but it was relying only on those willing to sign statements that they understood they could be compelled to testify if the senator sued the paper, as his lawyer had threatened. Adams had no comment. But on the afternoon of the day the story appeared he called a press conference at his campaign headquarters. The story "was created out of whole cloth by people that hate me," he said. Nevertheless, it had mortally wounded his bid for a second term and caused great pain to his family. He was withdrawing his candidacy. "This is the saddest day of my life."[2]

Gorton said the new allegations convinced him that Tupper's story was true and that Adams should resign forthwith. Some Democrats recoiled. "What he's trying to do is put his foot on Brock's neck," said Jeff Smith, executive director of the State Democratic Party. "He still holds it against him that Brock beat him. This is a very personal thing." J. Vander Stoep, who had succeeded McGavick as Gorton's chief of staff, said Smith was misinformed. "If you are talking about Republican politics, it's better for the Republicans that Brock Adams stay in office."[3]

Adams stuck it out. It was a sad ending, Gorton says, for someone who had once been "a brilliant and articulate person."

A HOUSE SHARPLY DIVIDED, the Washington State Republican Party convened in Yakima in June with conservative Christian activists in firm control. The congregants immediately adopted a plank that declared "Western cultural values" superior to all others. It called for a constitutional ban on abortion, even in cases of incest and rape, denounced the U.N., the "deviant lifestyle" of homosexuality and public school classes supposedly promoting witchcraft. "This doesn't sound like the party of Abraham Lincoln," said Congressman Morrison, who was running for governor. When King County Prosecutor Norm Maleng, another mainstreamer, told the delegates the protection of children's rights would be his highest priority if he was elected attorney general, some booed; others stood and turned their backs. Booing shook the hall when King County Executive Tim Hill, a pro-choice candidate for Adams' Senate seat, declared, "I support Roe vs. Wade." By plunging into theocracy, Hill said, the party risked relegating itself to "permanent minority status."[4]

Sarah Nortz, Gorton's daughter, was a delegate from Island County. "Give him one vote for guts," she said of Hill. "It was the right thing to do." Hill's strategy, in fact, was to goad the delegates into outrage and boost his bona fides as an electable moderate. He had a camera crew in tow.

Rod Chandler, styling himself as the party's presumptive Senate nominee, steered clear of abortion and the other litmus tests, focusing instead on blasting Murray as a liberal lapdog. Why was he running? "Because I love America!" A week later, however, he put on his progressive cloak and said the platform was "rooted in the Dark Ages."[5]

Chandler and Morrison were profiles in timidity, *The Seattle Times* editorialized. But "first prize for Political Pandering" went to Gorton, "presumably the leader of his party, who delivered a 20-minute keynote address without once mentioning the platform or the divisive, xenophobic principles it embraces. Instead, the senator attacked the 'liberal media' and the Democratic Party platform."[6]

Although the Blethens, who had a controlling interest in *The Times*, had endorsed him in every statewide race he'd run, Gorton concluded there was no longer a dime's worth of difference between Seattle's two daily newspapers. He viewed the *Post-Intelligencer* as habitually hostile. Now *The Times'* "true left-wing political colors" were also on prominent display. Gorton returned fire in a letter to the editor:

I award *The Times* my first prize for a journalistic double standard . . .
and bias against Republicans and conservatives. . . .

On June 18, *The Times* chided Bill Clinton for quarreling with Jesse
Jackson and thus hurting Democratic unity. Who is "the enemy" that is
being ignored when Clinton and Jackson spat? The Republicans, according to *The Times*. After criticizing Clinton for dividing Democrats, on
June 23 they criticized me for not dividing Republicans. That is a double
standard.

The Times took no editorial notice two years ago when I angered GOP
state convention delegates by flatly stating my disagreement with the
platform's anti-abortion plank. . . .

The Times' double standard is also evident in its reaction to the two
parties' platforms. If the GOP platform is written by extremely conservative Republicans, the Democratic platform is an example of left-wing
thinking, endorsing protectionism, a state income tax and single-payer
universal government-mandated health care. . . .

Gone are the days when *The Times* reflected the great wide center
of Washington state political thought.

The new *Times* should state its bias flat out: Conservatives and Republicans are the enemy; *The Times* supports any form of liberalism
espoused by the Democratic state platform.[7]

Lowry opted to run for governor. It was Bonker who challenged Murray for the Democratic senatorial nomination. Continuing her string of
once thought improbable victories, "The Mom in Tennis Shoes" easily
outpolled the former congressman, then trounced Chandler in the general election. The Republican nominee made a fatal error in what came
to be known as "The Year of the Woman." With the fallout still fresh
from the Adams scandal and Anita Hill's charges that she had been
sexually harassed by U.S. Supreme Court nominee Clarence Thomas,
Chandler should have realized that having a female opponent presented
a minefield.* Yet when Murray jabbed him hard during one of their debates, the tall, handsome former TV newsman offered a chauvinistic ren-
dition of the refrain from a popular Roger Miller ditty: *"Dang me, dang
me/They oughta take a rope and hang me/High from the highest tree/Woman
would you weep for me!"*[8]

---

* Gorton finally made up his mind to vote for Thomas' confirmation after meeting with
the 14 women in his Senate office. "They were split among those who believed Thomas'
story, those who believed Hill was harassed and those who, like Gorton, felt both were
telling their own version of the truth." Adams voted against confirmation.[10]

Chandler did the weeping. Murray took 54 percent of the vote, one of four female Democrats elected to the U.S. Senate that year. Her friend from the state Legislature, Maria Cantwell, was elected to Congress, together with Jennifer Dunn, which gave Washington Republicans something to cheer about. With assists from Pat Buchanan, Ross Perot, James Carville and Bush's own haplessness, Democrats not only reclaimed the White House, they maintained their hold on Congress.

While Democrats at home and on the Hill perceived Gorton to be politically dead, he was upbeat. At the urging of Lott and the other members of the Mississippian's emerging kitchen cabinet, he once again challenged Alan Simpson for GOP whip. He lost 25-14, but Simpson's days in leadership were numbered. Lott vowed they'd forge a majority of their own. His optimism—one part Baptist, one part Jaycees—was infectious.[9]

"It was difficult being in the minority with George Bush president," Gorton told a reporter on a rainy day at the dawn of the Clinton Administration. He leaned back in his chair, plopped his old brown wingtips on a coffee table, revealing holes in the soles, and seemed unusually sunny. "Our primary job was upholding his vetoes," Gorton continued. "Bush was without new ideas and Reagan's had played out. That doesn't leave you with much room to create a message. This year has been an intensely liberating experience."[11]

His fund-raising for the '94 re-election campaign was going great guns, he said, and his staff was "terrific"—unquestionably one of the best in Congress. He was traveling home frequently, making thoughtful speeches. Seattle still had a baseball team. He loved his job.

Gorton judged the new president to be an astute policy wonk and the most gifted political animal of his generation. Maybe he could solve the timber crisis. But could he control his party's appetite for higher taxes and profligate spending? He wasn't in Arkansas any more.

On condition of anonymity, a member of Washington State's congressional delegation told a reporter, "If Bill Clinton runs into problems, it will be with conservative Democrats in the House and Republicans in the Senate. Republicans in the House are too stupid and disorganized to make any trouble for the president."[12]

If Newt Gingrich read that line he surely cackled. With a fertile, fomenting mind, he was the conservative equivalent of Che Guevara. Trent Lott had plans of his own. They included Gorton.

32 | Messy and Unpredictable

THE UNITED STATES SENATE was the most frustrating place Trent Lott had ever been. "The process was glacial, messy and unpredictable. All I could do was go along, get along and start making lists of things I would change when I had the opportunity. But I had a hidden strength that, before long, would begin to shatter the status quo." It was a steering committee of "philosophical buddies"—philosophical in the sense that they were more conservative and less patient than the Dole brain trust; buddies because they were loyal to Lott and dedicated to making him majority leader.[1]

Besides Gorton, who always saw opportunities when things were messy and unpredictable, the group included John McCain of Arizona, Dan Coats of Indiana, Don Nickles of Oklahoma and Phil Gramm, the canny Texan. They helped advance Lott to secretary of the Republican Conference. Dole was already weighing a challenge to Clinton in 1996. Lott was thinking big, too. First, however, he told Gorton they needed to get themselves re-elected. By 1994, things definitely were looking up.

"Most new presidents get a honeymoon from Congress, but Clinton got a trench war," Alan Greenspan, the Federal Reserve chairman, observed. Buoyed by his enormous self-confidence, Clinton ignored the flip side of his campaign anthem, "Don't Stop Thinking About Tomorrow," and imagined that 43 percent of the vote actually equaled a mandate. He was stunned by the vociferous Republican resistance to his complex first budget. It reduced spending but added a host of new programs. He and Hillary had over-reached on health care reform and taken on the NRA. While the economy was improving and the deficit declining, reliable polls found Americans anxious. Clinton's approval ratings were tanking; only 28 percent thought Congress was doing a good job. The guy in the last chapter who dismissed Newt Gingrich as stupid and disorganized was now unavailable for comment.[2]

Democrats skedaddled to the middle of the road and agreed with the Republicans' cry to get tough on crime by putting 100,000 more cops on the street and enacting a "three strikes, you're out" law Gorton had championed. Gorton hosted a crime summit of his own and lobbied Attorney General Janet Reno to focus more resources on criminal aliens and drug trafficking, which was epidemic in the Yakima Valley, a narcotics conduit for the entire Northwest. Gorton angered gun owners by backing the Brady Bill, which requires licensed dealers to institute a law-enforcement background check before selling a firearm. He opposed the final version of the crime bill, however, because it banned assault weapons. The left hooted, saying duplicity was Gorton's middle name.[3]

Gorton criticized Clinton for not being tougher on China over human-rights violations but still supported most-favored nation trading status for the world's most populous country. "Trade is too important to be tied to anything but trade," Gorton said, explaining his 180 from the position he'd staked out earlier in his Senate career. "I support the president when he is right, as he was on NAFTA, and I oppose him when he is wrong, as he was on government-run health care."[4]

BY THE SPRING of 1994, King County Councilman Ron Sims and former TV anchorman Mike James were leading a parade of a half-dozen Democrats jockeying for endorsements and money in the race to take on Gorton. The son of a Baptist minister, Sims came of age at the height of the civil rights movement. He was student body president at Central Washington State College his senior year, then became an investigator with the attorney general's Consumer Protection Division during Gorton's tenure. Sims spent four years as an assistant to George Fleming, the state's first black state senator. A linebacker-size man given to hugging friend and foe alike, Sims was a lay minister who worked with street kids and championed affordable housing. At 46, he was 20 years younger than Gorton, whom he accused of practicing the politics of polarization, pitting white fishermen against Indians, loggers against city-dwellers. "Time to say goodbye to Slade!" Sims said, commanding the podium like a pulpit.[5]

James seconded the motion. Handsome and urbane, with a dashing mustache, he had teamed with Lori Matsukawa and Jean Enersen for years to make KING-5 the top newscast west of the Cascades. James said the "divisive politics of Slade Gorton" had propelled him into his first bid for public office.[6]

J. Vander Stoep, a hard-charger in the McGavick mold, stepped down as chief of staff to manage the campaign. Gorton's bid for a third term had a foundation of exceptional constituent relations, a statewide grass-roots organization and a war chest already at $3 million and growing daily toward a $5 million goal. His "Skinny Cat" days were long gone. The agony of his 1986 defeat unforgotten, he wasn't taking any chances. Although midterms are seldom kind to a president's party, Gorton said over-confidence was "poisonous." He was running hard everywhere, even Seattle. All across the state, "real people will stand up and tell what Slade has meant to them," said Tony Williams, Gorton's press secretary. Their theme was "Slade Gorton Works For You."[7]

Although he opposed a ban on semi-automatic assault weapons, Gorton had been relentlessly tough on crime ever since his days as attorney general. He won the first-ever endorsement of the 5,100-member Washington State Council of Police Officers, which didn't even bother to interview Sims or James. The Democrats were flummoxed. "We stick with our friends," said the council's president.[8]

The Democrats ripped Gorton for voting in 1991 to give himself and his 59 colleagues a $23,200 "midnight pay raise." The vote, which aroused public ire, brought senators' pay into parity with members of the House, Gorton countered, adding that the senators also approved a ban on accepting outside speaking fees.[9]

The Gorton campaign mailed an "urgent message" to senior citizens at midsummer. Discounting the lessons Gorton and Lott learned painfully a decade earlier, Clinton had flirted with delaying Social Security COLA increases and pushed through higher taxes on upper-income recipients as part of his 1994 budget. "Now it appears they want even more from our seniors! This is an outrage," the Gorton mailer warned. Ross Anderson, the veteran *Seattle Times* editorial writer and columnist, marveled at the "extra element of hypocrisy to Gorton's missive." Clinton's move, like Gorton's in 1984, was in fact a gutsy decision to put a dent in the deficit, Anderson wrote, and a step toward a solution to the trust fund's lurch toward a demographic crunch when the Baby Boomers hit retirement age. By trying to scare the daylights out of low-income seniors, Gorton was using the same tactics he had decried when he was being bludgeoned by Brock Adams. Anderson concluded the elderly now had a choice: "Would you rather be hugged by Slade or poked in the eye by Slick Willie?"[11]

"As you get closer to an election, things get more tactical and strategic," Gorton admitted. He worked with Democrats, however, to secure $100 million for a Yakima River irrigation project, even though that gave a boost to Jay Inslee's re-election campaign in the 4th Congressional District.[12]

ENVIRONMENTALISTS AND THE TRIBES stepped up their attacks on Gorton when he introduced a bill to force the Clinton Administration and its al-

lies in Congress to pony up nearly $30 million within two years to pur-
chase two dams on the Elwha River on the Olympic Peninsula. Otherwise, a plan to demolish the dams would be scrapped, reopening the
debate over whether they should be relicensed. "The status quo is hurting
everyone," Gorton insisted.[13]

Two years earlier, Gorton had supported an Elwha ecosystem and
fisheries restoration act signed by President Bush. The lower dam was
"older, out-moded and leaky," Gorton conceded. Now the comprehensive study the act mandated had determined that both dams should be
removed. He was shocked by the estimated cost—$200 million, maybe
more. The federal government ought to buy the dams, install fish pas-
sageways and relicense them for another 20 years, he argued. Unquestioned was the fact that the Elwha's wild Chinook salmon were once the
largest on the Olympic Peninsula, sometimes reaching 100 pounds.
The dams, one completed in 1914, the other in 1927, all but rendered the
runs extinct. The anadromous fish no longer had access to more than
180 miles of fresh-water spawning habitat. Hatcheries had been substi-
tuted for fish ladders in direct violation of laws enacted in 1890 by Washington's first legislature.[14]

While the Daishowa America Company paper mill, the second-largest
employer in the Port Angeles area, derived 40 percent of its electrical
power from the dams and appreciated Gorton's support, it was worried
about being thrown back into the regulatory grist mill. So was the Lower
Elwha Klallam Tribe. But Gorton said removing the dams would set a
terrible precedent. "Why is the Pacific Northwest going to reduce the
amount of power available when we're running out of power? . . . My plan
is more likely to preserve jobs and save fish because I do not think the
Congress of the United States, at a time of rapidly declining money, is
going to come up with $200 million to take out these dams and restore
that area."[15]

Gorton was thwarted for the time being. The Sierra Club celebrated by
dropping his Environmental Batting Average to zero. "As a pitcher for the
Senators," his specialty was curveballs, the club said in a mailer designed
like a baseball card.[16]

IN LIGHT OF HIS PREVIOUS POOR SHOWINGS in primaries and despite a
low turnout, Gorton was genuinely overwhelmed by the outcome on September 20, 1994. He had an impressive outright majority—53 percent—
against 14 other candidates. He was the leading vote-getter in all 39 counties, outpolling all the other candidates combined in 32. Sims edged

James for the Democratic nomination. Between them they had only a third of the vote.

Frank Greer, a national political strategist who had worked for Clinton in '92, was now advising Sims. "We can easily run this race with a $1 million budget and win because of Slade's overall record of voting against hard-working families," Greer predicted. If he had seen the returns from owl country, those were strange tea leaves. Still, Sims insisted, "We got to the top of Mount Rainier, and that's gotten us in shape for Mount Denali. We're going to challenge his whole record and show he's out of step with the state."[17]

That Sims happened to be black was irrelevant to Gorton, except in the sense that his opponent's primary victory represented real progress for their state. Sims was the most viable minority candidate for statewide elected office since Gorton's friend Art Fletcher ran for lieutenant governor in 1968 as part of the Evans Action Team. Sims' race, happily, was rarely noted and by all accounts had little to do with the final outcome. His burden to bear in 1994 was being a liberal Democrat from Seattle with $4 million less to spend.

In their debates, Sims painted Slade as a flip-flopping right-winger, while Gorton criticized urban Democrats as "chattering classes" of pseudo do-gooders with little empathy for working stiffs.[18]

Still smarting over a disastrous meeting in 1988 when he bristled at being taken to task over a TV spot used against Lowry, Gorton refused a "pointless" interview with the *Post-Intelligencer's* editorial board. It was an extraordinary snub. Unsurprisingly, the paper endorsed Sims.

The cold war between the senator and the *P-I* began to thaw in the fall of 1995 when Williams and other staffers told Slade it was counterproductive. Joel Connelly, visiting D.C., was spotted by Williams and invited to join him for dinner with Slade. Gorton discovered at least one thing he liked about his perceived nemesis: Connelly had also read *Black Lamb and Grey Falcon*. An hours-long discussion of the Balkans ensued, together with a fragile truce.

It helped when the widely-respected Joann Byrd, a former ombudsman for *The Washington Post*, took over the *P-I's* editorial page in 1997. But Gorton's resentment ran deep. At a Washington News Council roast, he quipped that he and Bruce Babbitt should settle their differences by blowing up the Elwha dams—and the *P-I* building.[19]

The Times endorsed Gorton once again despite chastising him for a late hit—a TV ad that charged Sims "voted 21 times for higher taxes" when what he'd done was vote to place the issues on the ballot.[20]

THE MASTERSTROKE OF GINGRICH'S CAMPAIGN to reclaim Congress was unveiled on the steps of the Capitol six weeks before the midterm elections. The would-be speaker assembled some 300 Republican congressmen and hopefuls to sign a Reaganesque "Contract with America." An unaccountable bloated bureaucracy was usurping personal responsibility and thwarting free enterprise, Gingrich declared. The contract called for a balanced budget amendment, lower taxes, tort reform, term limits, strengthened national security, tougher welfare rules and reduced government spending. Give us a majority, Gingrich declared, and we'll keep the faith by bringing these issues to the floor within the first 100 days. "If we break this contract, throw us out. We mean it."[21]

Gingrich invited Republican senators to join his insurgents on the steps. Lott and Gramm told Dole it was a terrific idea, but the minority leader balked. Dole detested Gingrich. He and the other old bulls saw the Contract as foolish grandstanding. On Election Day, though, they were delighted to be beneficiaries of its coattails. The Republican resurgence made Dole the frontrunner for the 1996 GOP presidential nomination and paved the way for Lott's elevation to whip, with Gorton as one of his deputies.[22]

GORTON WON A THIRD TERM resoundingly, for a change, capturing just shy of 56 percent of the vote. He carried 35 of the state's 39 counties, including, with great satisfaction, Grays Harbor, a Democratic stronghold since the coming of the New Deal. He lost King County by only 22,600 votes out of a half-million cast. The wave of exasperation that cost the Democrats control of Congress swept away five Washington State Democrats, including Maria Cantwell, Mike Kreidler, Jolene Unsoeld and Jay Inslee. But the biggest Republican scalp of all nationwide was Tom Foley's. George Nethercutt, a little-known Spokane lawyer, ousted the speaker of the House.

Republicans now had seven of the state's nine seats in Congress. Norm Dicks and Jim McDermott were the lone survivors. Gingrich wasn't whistling past Dixie when he called Washington State "ground zero of the Republican revolution." As usual, the war in Washington was composed of strategic battles to win independents. Although the state's delegation went from 8-1 Democratic to 7-2 GOP, the total Republican vote for congressional seats exceeded the total Democratic vote by only 15,000 statewide, Stu Elway noted.[23]

For Cantwell, defeat was a great career move. She landed a job as vice president of marketing for a Seattle Internet start-up that became Real-

Networks. Buoyed by the Dotcom bubble, her stock options made her a multimillionaire in nothing flat. As smart as she was lucky, her itch for politics went away only temporarily.

Elway's polling on the weekend before the election found that issues mattered little to voters in the Gorton-Sims race. Gorton's negatives were still high but his positives were way up. While 44 percent of Sims' voters just flat didn't like Gorton, Slade had wide support among all demographic groups statewide, even from a sizable number of Democrats. His integrity, his politics and his experience were cited repeatedly.

Relieved that he'd won an election without worrying about absentees, Gorton was grateful and conciliatory. "We need to remember that this nation of ours is not just Republicans; it's Democrats—even those indifferent people who didn't vote," he told his cheering supporters. "We haven't been given a blank check. We've been given an opportunity. . . . We've got to produce or two years from now we could suffer the same disaster the Democrats did."[24]

He'd never felt better. A month later, he had a heart attack.

33 | Close Calls and Tragedies

AFTER THE 1994 ELECTION, Gorton went East to visit his brothers. He was staying with Nat, a federal judge in Boston, when he set out one morning for his usual run. Halfway through, he began to feel awful. His chest hurt and his legs were heavy. He also had a curious pain near his collar bone. It couldn't be a heart attack, he reasoned. At 66, with his lean runner's body, he was as fit as an active man 30 years his junior and every family doctor's dream patient. He'd never smoked, drank sparingly, handled stress remarkably well and maintained a healthy diet. "It doesn't matter how good something is, he doesn't have a second helping," Sally says, marveling at his self discipline. After his morning routine of stretching, pushups and sit-ups, he ran every day—still does— rain or shine. His cholesterol was low. He slept like a baby.

Something, however, was very wrong. He walked back to Nat's house, thinking the feeling would pass. His sister-in-law, Jodi, thought he looked drawn and extremely serious as he headed straight upstairs. Sally saw how disconcerted he was and had Jodi call Nat's doctor, who listened to 30 seconds' worth of the symptoms and said, "Call 9-11."

Slade was soon at Massachusetts General, undergoing an angioplasty to roto-rooter a clogged artery. He told his brother he felt chagrined because somebody in his condition shouldn't have had a heart attack. When the head of cardiology assured him it was an aberration—a "biological accident"—and predicted no further problems, he was relieved. "How soon can I resume running?"

On January 4, 1995, Gorton was sworn in for his third term. He was out running again by the end of the month.[1]

He exchanged get-well cards with Patty Murray, who was recovering from a hysterectomy. Their relationship was improving after a chilly start. Murray's chief of staff was a hard-nosed New York Democrat averse to any kind of cooperation with a Republican running for re-election. Jealous over Gorton's relationship with Boeing, he even attempted to scuttle a bill Slade's staff had crafted to make it easier for struggling airlines to buy new planes. Murray's office developed a reputation early on for being officious and overly protective of Patty. When her press secretary threatened to resign, Murray consulted Norm Dicks for a reality check, then fired the chief of staff and another flinty aide.[2]

After their hospitalizations, Murray invited Gorton to her office to discuss ways they could work together to advance the state's interests in the new session. Their committee assignments were advantageous, and he was now not only back in the majority but a confidant of Trent Lott. She supported Gorton's vigorous efforts to defend Microsoft against antitrust allegations. They were also united on protecting the Bonneville Power Administration.

While they remained poles apart on most environmental issues, Gorton backed her attempt to derail a bill lifting the ban on the export of Alaskan oil to foreign refineries. When it was clear she lacked the votes to kill it outright, he helped her extract concessions from Alaska Republican Frank Murkowski to protect the environment and jobs at domestic refineries.[3]

Most controversially, both voted for the Defense of Marriage Act— Gorton on the grounds that "for a thousand years marriage has been defined as a joining of one man and one woman," Murray because "I'm willing to fight for gay rights, but I'm not willing to debate over the definition of the word 'marriage.'" Clinton signed the bill and caught the most flak from liberals who accused him of selling out to boost his chances for re-election. A poll found Americans opposed to same-sex marriage 2-to-1.[4]

Most emphatically, they teamed up with John McCain to tighten regulation of the nation's oil and natural gas pipelines. The legislation was spurred by a tragedy that could have been a full-scale disaster.

A 16-inch pipeline delivering gasoline from Cherry Point to facilities at Renton and Seattle ruptured on June 10, 1999. About 240,000 gallons of fuel spilled into a creek less than two miles from downtown Bellingham. Two 10-year-olds playing with a lighter they'd used earlier to set off fireworks unwittingly ignited the fumes, producing a massive fireball. The explosion occurred a block from the middle school where Senator Murray's twin sister taught. Together with a teenager who was fishing nearby, the boys died. They were hapless heroes. If the fuel had ignited closer to town, authorities said the loss of life and damage would have been far greater.[5]

Gorton signed on as a co-sponsor of Murray's Pipeline Safety Act of 2000. The Bellingham explosion was but one of 5,700 pipeline accidents

over the previous 14 years, with 325 dead, 1,500 injured and 6 million gallons of hazardous liquids released. Washington's senators worked with
McCain and John Kerry to fine-tune the bill and lobby for its passage.
Adopted by unanimous consent, it increased fines for safety violations
and provided an additional $13 million for federal oversight. It also man-
dated more training for pipeline operators and instituted protection for
whistle-blowers.[6]

Six years later, Gorton would learn a lot more about refineries in the
wake of an explosion with nearly 200 casualties.

RECALLING THE FALLOUT from the Manion-Dwyer deal 11 years earlier,
many were surprised to see Gorton challenging Murray and the White
House over judicial appointments. By 1997, however, Gorton's fears about
the power of "activist" liberal judges were greater than ever. Ten of the 28
seats on the U.S. 9th Circuit Court of Appeals were vacant or soon to be.
In a classic power play, he challenged a 150-year-old tradition that senators
in the same political party as the president were entitled to propose candidates for the federal bench in their states. Gorton told Murray she ought
to let him choose the next two judges to give "a philosophical balance" to
the federal courts in Washington. He also informed her that henceforth,
unless she sought his advice and gave his views "significant weight" he
would block Senate confirmation of any Clinton judicial nominee for
Washington State. No idle threat was this, with Republicans controlling
the Senate and many Clinton appointees already in limbo.[7]

Murray said she always welcomed his input but beyond that, nothing
doing. She had discussed the matter with Clinton and his White House
counsel. They weren't about to change the rules just because "someone is
upset that his candidate for president did not win." It would be a shame to
see excellent judicial nominees "cut up in partisan battles."

Gorton scoffed. How about all the excellent Republican judicial nominees who'd been cut up in partisan battles? "It shouldn't matter which
party controls the White House. Republicans and Democrats alike should
have a say in nominating federal judges who will serve for life."[8]

Three months down the road, the Mutt and Jeff pair had forged a truce
of sorts, based in part on growing mutual respect but mostly practical
politics. After interviewing three finalists for the U.S. District Court
bench in Seattle, they agreed that King County Superior Court Judge
Robert Lasnik, a highly regarded centrist, should get the job. Then, in
1998, Clinton sealed a deal he'd made with Lott to break a logjam on judicial nominations: Gorton was granted the right to name the next appoin-

tee to the 9th Circuit. He picked Barbara Durham, chief justice of the State Supreme Court. Although Governor Gary Locke and Attorney General Christine Gregoire, both Democrats, endorsed her nomination, liberals lamented the deal as Faustian, saying Durham was a sharply partisan conservative with a "constricted understanding" of individual rights.[9]

The key to Clinton ceding one of the presidency's prime perquisites was a Republican promise to advance the appointment of his friend William E. Fletcher to the 9th Circuit bench, together with two other stalled nominees. Confirmation of the Berkeley law professor had been stonewalled by Republicans for more than three years. Fletcher's mother, the redoubtable former Seattle attorney Betty Fletcher, would move to senior status on the 9th Circuit bench to make way for Durham.[10]

While Gorton and Murray continued to work together on judicial nominees, the Barbara Durham story lacks a happy ending. In the spring of 1999 she withdrew her name, saying her husband's heart problems had grown severe. That fall, she resigned from the State Supreme Court, saying it was time to "take a fresh look at the future." Her colleagues knew the sad truth: With each passing day dementia was dimming her fine mind. The trailblazing Stanford graduate was suffering from early-onset Alzheimer's disease. Durham was dead at the age of 60 within 2½ years.[11]

34 | Refuse to Lose

F OR THE SEATTLE MARINERS in particular and Major League Baseball in general the summer of 1994 was fraught with discontent. Ken Griffey Jr., arguably the most gifted player in baseball, was fed up with losing and wanted to be traded. Jay Buhner, another fan favorite, also went nose-to-nose with Lou Piniella, the club's fiery skipper. Then, during warm-ups on July 19, a pair of 26–pound tiles came tumbling down from the Kingdome's ceiling. If fans had been sitting in the area where they landed someone could have been killed.

Emergency repairs left the team homeless. The up side was that the club bonded on its extended road trip and started winning—only to be sidelined by a players' union strike that canceled the World Series for the first time since 1904. Like millions of other baseball fans, Gorton was disgusted. But when other members of Congress and the White House began talking about intervention he said they should just "butt out." Talk of repealing baseball's antitrust exemption as a way to force an end to the strike could end up prolonging the dispute, Gorton warned.[1]

With its 20–year lease for the Kingdome expiring after the 1996 season, the Baseball Club of Seattle began a campaign for a new, retractable roof stadium. The timing, to put it mildly, was inauspicious. Even baseball's best friends were alienated by the strike. The Legislature authorized a tenth of a percent increase in the sales tax in King County, contingent on approval of the county's voters. Despite being the equivalent of only 10 cents on a $100 purchase, it was going to be a hard sell.

After intense lobbying by the business community, the County Council voted 7–6 to place the proposal on the 1995 Primary Election ballot. The first poll found 70 percent opposed. Some of the Mariners began investigating the housing market in Tampa. Then, as old sports writers used to say, Mo Mentum swapped jerseys. The team caught fire behind the hitting of Griffey, Buhner and Edgar Martinez, with 6–foot-10 Randy Johnson, "The Big Unit," in a zone on the pitcher's mound, firing virtually unhittable left-handed fastballs and wicked sliders.

Then the club dropped a heartbreaker at the polls. On September 19, the stadium plan fell 1,082 votes short out of a half-million cast. The owners said they'd put the team up for sale on Oct. 30 if a suitable fallback plan couldn't be developed. "We cannot further jeopardize our investment by undue delay," team chairman John Ellis said in a letter to Gary Locke, King County's new executive.[2]

The M's were playing like there was no tomorrow.

AT THE BEGINNING OF AUGUST the home team was 13 games behind the California Angels. On October 1 they were tied. Seattle's stunning comeback and California's humiliating collapse were both sealed the next day. Gorton was in a front-row seat at the Kingdome as the Mariners reached the postseason for the first time in their 19–year history by shelling the Angels, 9–1. The team departed for New York that night for a best-of-five series with the Yankees to determine who would play for the American League pennant. The M's returned home four days later, trailing 2–0, with every game do or die. Gorton was in Italy with a congressional delegation, frantically waking himself at 4 a.m. to see if CNN International would at least come up with a score.

In the 11th inning of game five, with Griffey on first and Joey Cora on third, Edgar Martinez ripped a double down the left field line to tie the game. All 57,000 eyes swiveled to Griffey. Arms pumping as he rounded third, he sprinted home, crossing the plate in an emphatic slide as the Kingdome exploded. Junior was instantly at the bottom of a delirious dog pile.

After all that, unfortunately, the Mariners were finally out of juice, losing the American League Championship to a clearly superior Cleveland club in six games. Elvis may have left the Dome but the fans remained on their feet, clapping and cheering until the team returned to the field. The "refuse to lose" Mariners had saved baseball for Seattle. No one put it better than the *Post-Intelligencer's* Art Thiel: It hadn't occurred to the lords of baseball that Seattle, "rather than a bad baseball town, was merely a town of bad baseball."[3]

IN THE MIDST of the M's amazing run, Governor Lowry—no sports fan but an astute bunter—called a special session of the Legislature to pick up the pieces from the bond issue. Just before the deadline, the polarized Legislature—accused by stadium opponents of ignoring the public will, pressured by baseball fans and the worried business community—authorized a tax package providing $320 million for a new ball park. It created a Public Facilities District board to oversee the project.

Fourteen months later, yet another crisis: Ellis called a surprise press conference to announce he and the other owners had reluctantly concluded there was "insufficient political leadership in King County" to complete the new ball park in time for the 1999 season. Besides labor and management issues, the project had become entangled in a controversy over a proposal to demolish the Kingdome and build a new, open-air stadium for the Seahawks. That was a stipulation set by the NFL team's prospective buyer, Microsoft co-founder Paul Allen. The double-dealers, Ellis charged, were four County Council members, Ron Sims, Pete von Reichbauer, Larry Phillips and Cynthia Sullivan. To the "shock and dismay" of M's ownership, they had suggested to the Public Facilities District board that a delay in the construction schedule for the M's stadium would be prudent. "It is clear that they intend for the ball park project to fail," Ellis said. "We've done all we can do." The owners were tired of losing money. More talking was useless. He fought back tears. The team was for sale.[4]

It was Saturday, December 14, 1996. While Ellis was going nuclear, Sims was being endorsed by King County Democrats to succeed Governor-elect Locke as county executive. Certain he had the votes to win the council's appointment, Sims was over the moon. He arrived home to find reporters on his lawn and a lump of coal in his stocking. He realized there was some frustration over the time-line for the ball park, Sims said, but he was flabbergasted by Ellis' announcement.[5]

Gorton believed that Sims and his friend and ally on the council, the politically ambidextrous von Reichbauer, knew exactly what they were up to when they co-authored the not-so-fast letter to the facilities district. Councilman Rob McKenna, a young Republican Gorton was eyeing for bigger things, said the Mariners weren't to blame for the impasse. The letter "was like throwing a stick of dynamite into the fire. . . . It was completely gratuitous," McKenna said.[6]

Some found Ellis' emotional last press conference unconvincing. The owners were playing political hardball "as nasty as it gets," wrote Blaine Newnham, the veteran *Seattle Times* sports columnist. "The Mariners say the politicians have forced them to sell the team. But all the politicians have really done is overrule an electorate that voted against a stadium and come up with $300 million to build one." The owners clearly were in the catbird seat. "Their stadium is funded, drawn up and ready to be built. It seems to me all this noise is just about keeping it that way."[7]

GORTON WAS BLISSFULLY OUT of the loop. He'd said a temporary aloha to politics for a week of sun in Hawaii with his family and a stack of good books. He arrived back home the night of Ellis' announcement. "At SeaTac, every television camera in Seattle was waiting for me: 'Senator Gorton, the Mariners are going to move! What are you going to do about it?' And I go 'Huh?' I quickly learned that John Ellis had had it with the County Council and the PFD, declaring, 'I am never going to speak to another politician for the rest of my life.' Ellis was in a fury and genuinely emotional."

The next day, Gorton met with the members of the County Council, whose phones were ringing off the hook. "They're frantic that they're all going to be recalled: 'Slade, can't you do something? Ellis won't return our calls.'" By Monday Ellis had returned Gorton's call and by Thursday they had put together a "non-negotiable final offer."

In a conversation both recall as terse, Gorton presented Sims with the list of demands. Sims' distress over his untenable dilemma was as palpable as his chagrin at receiving his marching orders from the man he'd failed to dislodge from the U.S. Senate just two years earlier. The angry calls and e-mails had been relentless; his kids were being hassled at school. He was being hammered from all sides—by taxpayers who saw the project as a fat-cat subsidy as well as the baseball faithful and the Chamber of Commerce. He seriously considered not becoming county executive.

The County Council and the Public Facilities District Board ran up the white flag two days before Christmas. Fifteen months later, Gorton and Griffey wielded shovels at the groundbreaking for Safeco Field, which opened on July 15, 1999.

"IT TAKES AT LEAST 25 YEARS to make a city a baseball city," Gorton says. "You have to have had a generation that has grown up watching Major League baseball, then love taking their own kids to the games. The first 25 years are much the hardest. It's very, very difficult to create and sustain interest. But after that you turn into a baseball town. Seattle is still getting there. Someday we're going to have a team to match the best ball field in Major League Baseball."

Getting there is often as serendipitous as the way the Mariners survived their three crises, Gorton says. You beef up the bull pen, make some timely trades, find a great manager, then get hot—and lucky—from August through October.

"Hiroshi Yamauchi, the great hero of all of this, has never seen his

Ken Griffey Jr. and Gorton at the groundbreaking for Safeco Field in 1997. The Kingdome looms in the background. *Seattle Mariners*

team play in person. But they're on TV in Japan where Ichiro is a god. I went to Japan and thanked him. The first thing he said, through his interpreter, was 'Oh Mr. Senator, how is our team doing?'

"Baseball is by far the greatest sport," Gorton says. "Those six months of the year when there is no baseball are just wasted." His daughter Sarah found the perfect Christmas present for a man whose best friend is a dog named Triple Play—a device that provides play-by play updates, batting averages and all the other statistics, as well as trades and news in the off season.

35 | The Council of Trent

TWO AMBITIOUS MEN were at the pinnacle of their political careers in 1996. When Bob Dole resigned from the Senate to run for president, Trent Lott became majority leader, with Gorton as his attorney and ex-officio counsel to the Republican leadership team. While to some they seemed a curious pair, it was a mutual admiration society. Gorton wished he had Lott's charm and charisma. Lott appreciated Gorton's sophisticated sense of humor and legal acumen. He was one smart Yankee. On all matters legal, Gorton was Lott's E.F. Hutton: When Slade talked, people listened.

Lott had another reason for keeping Gorton at his side on what was soon dubbed The Council of Trent: "Our leadership team was all basically from the Deep South. It was also heavily oriented toward conservatives. We needed sort of a contrarian view. After we all came in and slapped each other on the back and said this is what we should do, I needed somebody who'd say, 'Now wait a minute. Have you considered this? Have you considered the impact it would have on the Midwest or the Northwest? Or have you considered the position this puts some of our more moderate members in?' Thanks to Slade, we would frequently stop, think about what we had planned to do and reject it or moderate it in a way that made it more palatable to the largest group of senators. We'd get more done his way.

"We had the majority in the House and Senate, but the Democrats had Clinton, a masterful politician. So we had to find a way to frame our issues in such a way that we could get Clinton to sign them. The record is replete with examples of how we did that on everything from safe drinking water to portability of insurance; balanced budgets, tax cuts—the whole package. Slade was in the middle of all that."[1]

As Lott's confidant, Gorton also knew how much their legislative success owed to the fact that Lott was part of a triad of strange bedfellows. Lott's political adviser for his 1988 Senate campaign was a freewheeling New York consultant named Dick Morris. His main claim to fame in the

South had been managing two of Bill Clinton's gubernatorial campaigns. Right after the Democrats' disastrous 1994 midterms, Clinton confided his frustrations to Morris, who convinced him to open a back-channel dialogue with Lott. Two instinctive Southern politicians who wanted to get things done ought to be able to find common ground, Morris said.

When Lott invited Morris to his home in Pascagoula for a chat before Congress convened, Morris revealed he'd been talking with Clinton. "This could be great," Morris said. "You take over the Senate, I'll take over the White House and we'll pass everything!" Morris was only half joking. He became the intermediary between the president of the United States and the majority leader of the opposing party. The relationship even survived Morris's embarrassing exit from Team Clinton over revelations that he had a paid mistress and some kinky proclivities. The Council of Trent and the White House agreed to the Balanced Budget Act of 1997 and a major welfare reform initiative, with Gorton as a key strategist.[2]

INDIANS AND ENVIRONMENTALISTS were dismayed to find Gorton with more power, especially as chairman of the Interior Appropriations Subcommittee, which oversees the budgets for the Bureau of Indian Affairs and Forest Service. In fact, all of Interior's agencies, including Fish & Wildlife, the National Park Service and the Bureau of Land Management, were now Gorton's turf. His hope was that the 104th Congress would move to amend the Endangered Species Act to allow social and economic concerns as part of the equation. He was prepared to play the budget card "if we don't start moving down a path of meaningful reform."[3]

Gorton was even more adamant after the National Marine Fisheries Service announced its biological opinion on the cost of increasing water flows on the Columbia and Snake Rivers to help save endangered fish. The lost hydropower penciled out to at least $120 million a year. The head of the Bonneville Power Administration expected overall costs to be closer to the $175 million to $180 million estimated under a salmon plan prepared for the Northwest Power Planning Council. "We figure that each saved Chinook would cost its weight in gold," Gorton said. Northwest ratepayers would have to decide whether saving the salmon was worth that much. "When almost everything else is being cut," Congress was unlikely to foot the bill. "There is a cost beyond which you just have to say very regrettably we have to let species or subspecies go extinct."[4]

On the Elwha, the question was nearly moot. Impressed by a compromise forged by a Port Angeles citizens group, Gorton helped secure $30 million in 1997 to buy the lower dam on the Olympic Peninsula river. He agreed to its removal, but urged a 12-year study of the habitat restoration effort before making a decision on the fate of the up-river dam at Glines Canyon.

Over the next 18 months, as dam-breaching advocates gained steam nationwide, Gorton grew increasingly worried. He tried to use his support for the Elwha project as a bargaining chip. Flexing the muscle of his subcommittee chairmanship in what one critic described as his "typical slimy fashion," Gorton threatened to withhold the funds for removal of the Elwha Dam unless the administration agreed to surrender the Federal Energy Regulatory Commission's power to unilaterally remove 250 smaller, nonfederal dams in the Northwest. "The subject is dams," Bruce Babbitt shot back, "but the issue is using them as a straw man to have a wholesale exception to the environmental laws of this country." On the contrary, Gorton said, the issue was whether a federal agency should be able to make wholesale changes to a region's livelihood without a vote of Congress or permission from state or local officials.[5]*

"Determining what is best for salmon is an important question," Gorton said in 1998 as the battle reached a boil, "but it is not the final question." The final question, in his view, was how society valued the various uses of the river—power, irrigation, flood control, transportation and, yes, fish. The challenge was to make the interests as compatible as possible. Everyone might have to settle for less. Maybe in the end, society would conclude the dams were expendable. "I think it is perfectly appropriate to debate the proposition that fish are more important than agriculture and transportation and electricity combined."[6]

Gorton introduced a bill that would have required congressional approval of any plan to dramatically alter any of the hydropower dams on the Columbia-Snake system, even if a federal judge ruled such action was mandated by the Endangered Species Act. When the Seattle City Council endorsed breaching the Snake River dams, he mused bitterly, "How easy it must be for downtown Seattle liberals to cast aside the lives and concerns of people in Eastern Washington's agricultural communities."[7]

---

* The federal government purchased the Elwha River dams in 2000. Removal was scheduled to begin by 2012. Gorton maintains that the cost of dam breaching in the Northwest is now even more prohibitive: "The removal of so many kilowatts of hydropower will necessarily be replaced by the same number from the most polluting marginal producer. The argument that we can just conserve is false because no amount of conservation will ever replace the final marginal production that will always be coal."

Murray, up for re-election, tiptoed. However, she said she knew at least two things for sure: Holding the Elwha dams hostage was the worst sort of political power play and "we are going down a long line toward not saving any fish. We have to make some decisions that turn that around. We cannot bury our head in the sand on this one."[8]

ON BOTH COMMERCE AND APPROPRIATIONS, Gorton was at odds once again with his old adversary, Senator Ted Stevens, who fought like a grizzly to maintain Alaska's dominance in the North Pacific fishery against some of the Seattle-based factory trawlers. Gorton was also pushing for individual quotas in the pollock fishery. One of many heated hearings was held in Seattle in 1995. On hand was Jeanne Bumpus, a young lawyer Gorton and Tony Williams had just hired to serve as Slade's legislative counsel on the committee. "If she had known the issue was going to be so messy, I'm guessing she might have turned us down," Williams says.

Bumpus, now with the Federal Trade Commission, admits she left the hearing a bit dazed. As if differences with Stevens were not challenge enough, there were tremendous conflicts among the Washington State interests. When she got to Capitol Hill, she grasped the enormous power Stevens wielded as Appropriations Committee chairman. "One time I'd been up for days on end. I came back to the office and burst into tears when I got back to my cubicle. Slade put his arm around me and listened to me sniffle. It was very sweet."

Stevens seized on the fact that a lot of the Seattle-based processing fleet was foreign-owned. In fact, some of the vessels were foreign built, he thundered. "So there was a large amount of jingoism," Bumpus says. But in fairness to Stevens, he was intent upon defending his constituents—including smaller, Alaska-based catcher boats and tribal interests—as resourcefully as Gorton. "One of Slade's key principles was that the little guys weren't going to get run over, which was no small goal since the Seattle interests were hugely divided in the beginning." One hearing erupted in fisticuffs.

For a while it looked as if Stevens would prevail. In 1998, however, Gorton worked with the Alaskan to broker a deal that balanced the interests of the myriad players, large and small, including the Seattle-based fishing fleet and factory trawlers. "Ted still held all the high cards," Gorton says, "but the ace of trumps was my friendship with Trent," who was now the majority leader. Lott informed Stevens that his amendment was going nowhere until he reached a compromise with Gorton. "After all that," Slade says, "the paradox is that a good 90 percent of the industry was delighted at the result." Paul MacGregor, who represented the At-sea Processors Association, calls Gorton "the white knight who rode in and slayed the dragon and then went off to do other work."9

GORTON'S OTHER WORK INCLUDED EDUCATION. He decided in 1997 that the $11 billion directed at helping needy students would be far better spent if it was handed over to the states and local school districts. Give it to the people who know where the money's really needed, he said. Let them experiment and innovate. He pointed to a program aimed at lowering grade-school class sizes by hiring 100,000 new teachers. Some schools already had small classes, Gorton said, but federal rules prevented their principals from spending the money on other programs. "I'm talking about restoring authority over this money to the people who have dedicated their lives to education."10

Sometimes these brainstorms of his went from inception to the legislative hopper overnight. And if they died aborning—as this one did, with Clinton threatening a veto—he would regroup and attempt to recruit more allies. After brainstorming with teachers, principals and school board members from around the state at education summits, he produced "a more moderate but no less revolutionary proposal to provide federal money with fewer federal strings." Gorton's "Straight A's Act" of 1999 would have given the states authority to pool the budgets of a number of federal programs designed to assist underprivileged kids. There was a stick and a carrot: Schools that accepted the no-strings-attached federal money would have to produce better test scores. Otherwise, they'd be forced back into the old programs. But if their students' grades or test scores improved, there'd be a 5 percent bonus.11

The state association of grade-school principals endorsed the plan, as did a dozen school superintendents. Senator Murray, a former school board member, was diametrically opposed. She gave it "straight F's," asserting that "his bill shows a complete misunderstanding of what the federal role is and why it's important. . . . He is saying that we'll take away the red tape, which is very appealing and certainly sounds good to everyone. But I guarantee you this flexibility, as nice as it sounds, will mean that over time, money will transfer from low-income students to higher-income students."12

Gorton made adjustments, inserting a provision to ensure that money from Title I, the nearly $8 billion-a-year "War on Poverty" program to improve the academic achievement of disadvantaged children, still would be distributed mostly to poor districts. Vociferous critics, including teachers' unions, had the president on their side.[13]

No adjustments could placate the nation's Indian tribes after Gorton antagonized them once again.

36 | 'Dump Slade 2000'

E ARLY ON THEY HAD DUBBED HIM "the new General Custer," vow-
ing that sooner or later he'd meet his Little Bighorn. When the slot
machines started jingling they had many more arrows in their
quiver.

From the banks of the Columbia to Narragansett Bay, where Gorton's
famished forefathers were befriended by the natives in the 1600s, the
tribes were once independent nations. "They say they are sovereigns, but
the courts call them *quasi*-sovereigns," Gorton said in 1997, italics his.
"They're nations within a nation." Ultimate authority still rested with the
Great White Father, the senator said, and Congress still helped distribute
the beads. Gorton's subcommittee chairmanship gave him wide latitude
over appropriations for the Bureau of Indian Affairs.[1]

The tribes' long-festering grudge against Gorton became flat-out war
when he cut their federal assistance by 28 percent in 1995 as part of the
Republican deficit-reduction plan. He also took up the complaints of non-
Indians living on reservations, saying it was fundamentally unfair for "a
closed, ethnic group" to have immunity from lawsuits. Inholders on the
Lummi reservation near Bellingham told Gorton their wells were virtually dry because the tribe was hogging the ground water aquifer. Pointing
to a treaty signed in 1855, the Lummis maintained they had senior status
in the water rights dispute. Nevertheless, they said they were attempting
to reach an equitable settlement. Gorton threatened to slash half of the
tribe's federal assistance if it persisted in restricting water use by non-
Indians, who comprised nearly half of the reservation's population.[2]

Conrad Burns, Gorton's Republican colleague from Montana, joined
the fray that year when the Crow Tribe, in a delicious turn of events, levied
a 4 percent B&O tax on businesses catering to tourists visiting the Custer
battlefield. "Taxation without representation!" cried the non-Indian businesses, refusing to pay. Some 40 percent of the reservation was owned by
non-Indians. Much of Indian Country in both states was a checkerboard
of Indian and non-Indian ownerships.[3]

Gorton and the tribes even fought over "Kennewick Man," an ancient skeleton discovered in 1996 along the banks of the Columbia. Five tribes claimed him as an ancestor and demanded the remains for reburial under the Native American Graves Protection and Repatriation Act. It was patently obvious, Gorton said, that the remains were of archaeological importance. If anthropologists in England unearthed a 9,000-year-old skeleton in his ancestral village, he said he would be eager to have it studied. Ron Allen of the Jamestown S'Klallam Tribe, a longtime Gorton adversary, was president of the National Congress of American Indians. He said Gorton clearly had little respect for Indian religious traditions. "Once a body goes into the ground it's supposed to stay there."4

When the Makahs set off an international controversy by declaring their intention to harvest a whale for the first time in 70 years, Gorton joined the save-the-whale environmentalists as they squared off with cultural liberals. Literally caught in the cross-fire was one 32-foot female gray whale. As the tribe exulted in the revival of an ancient practice, some characterized Gorton and other opponents as blubbering "eco-racists." They had the right to kill the whale, the senator said, but the responsibility to be more sensitive. "This gruesome event, documented on live television, has rightly offended the great majority of Americans."5

WHILE THEY LOATHED HIS STANDS, they respected his power and his talented staff, which always returned calls. By the 1990s, Indian leaders had become sophisticated political operatives. Ron Allen was—of all things— a Republican. Joe DeLaCruz was the champion frequent flier of Indian Country, one part warrior, one part lobbyist, going from office to office in D.C. with a sack of the finest Quinault smoked salmon. Billy Frank Jr., the wily sage of the Nisquallys, knew how to close a deal. Though he cussed like a sailor and drove a hard bargain, he was always respectful of public officials, even when they were his adversaries. Frank said the senator was frequently sadly misguided but that didn't make him a racist.

In 1996, when a flood wiped out the Wa He Lut Indian School at Frank's Landing east of Olympia, Billy and Tom Keefe, the superintendent, called Slade. He quickly secured $1.8 million for a new school. "Unless Slade Gorton had taken an interest, there would have been no money for this school," said Keefe, a former Magnuson aide who well understood how much power a committee chairman wielded. He told reporters that for Gorton, "sovereignty is just another legal argument, and the part about limiting financial aid is his conservative desire to get the tribes to wean themselves from federal dependence. It's very consistent with his

approach to a whole range of issues that have nothing to do with Indians."
Keefe had married a Nez Perce, which gave him some reservation cred.
Gorton also secured money for a new school for the Lummi Tribe, but the
vast majority of the minority still despised him.[6]

Across the street from the Capitol that same September day, the National Congress of American Indians was in emergency session. They
were there, 230-strong, to fight two riders Gorton had appended to a
spending bill containing a host of provisions the Clinton Administration
wanted passed. Some $700 million was earmarked to protect parks and
ancient redwoods. Gorton was threatening to slash nearly half of the
tribes' federal funding—$767 million—unless they agreed to waive sov-
ereign immunity from civil lawsuits. He was out to "overturn almost two
centuries of jurisprudence," Secretary Babbitt said. Gorton shot back, "I
find nothing in any Indian treaty that says they must be continuously
supported by the federal taxpayers."[7]*

The other rider—a "chairman's mark" in the parlance of prerogatives—
called for a need-based formula to distribute subsidies. Wealthier tribes,
especially those with lucrative casinos, would see their payments sharply
reduced, Gorton acknowledged, but "the poorest of the poor in Indian
Country" would benefit.[8]

The Indians snorted at the notion of Custer as a born-again Robin
Hood. "The only reason we are all here is Senator Gorton," said Henry
Cagey, chairman of the Lummi Nation and newly-elected leader of the
Northwest's Affiliated Tribes. "He will take any chance he can get to at-
tack our sovereignty. If anything, he has become more hard-line and anti-
Indian and devious in his attacks on us, and he's been fighting us for as
long as anyone can remember. . . .We see him as an individual that will
wipe out future generations."[9]

Ben Nighthorse Campbell, the only Native American in the Senate,
criticized Gorton for adding his proposals to the Interior appropriations
bill without a hearing and promised they would be passed only "over my
dead body." The Colorado Republican was chairman of the Indian Affairs
Committee, so it was a big body. Senator McCain told tribal leaders they
could count on help from him and Senator Domenici. Gorton was a good
man, McCain said. "This is not some personal vendetta of his. He has a
philosophical, intellectual difference with me and many others here

---

* Babbitt and Gorton enjoyed their sparring and mutual respect, based on a 30-year relationship. "He's very liberal and a very good friend, somebody I really liked, even when we
were profoundly disagreeing on issues," Gorton says.

about the nature of Indian treaties and what the federal government's responsibilities to the tribes should be. I think the treaties are very clear. They are solemn agreements in which we got their land and we agreed to treat them as nations as well as help provide for their health and education."[10]

Gorton called a news conference of his own. With their special understanding of what it means to be cheated and oppressed, Gorton said Indians ought to recognize that having separate standards for due process and other civil rights was un-American. He was joined by the father of a youth fatally injured three years earlier in Toppenish when his car was broadsided by a squad car driven by a tribal police officer. Because the Yakama Tribe had sovereign immunity, the family was unable to sue for damages in a state or federal court. "Now is that fair?" Gorton asked on the floor of the Senate the next day. "If you are injured by a New York City policeman, you can sue New York City. But if you are injured by a Yakama tribal policeman, you cannot sue the tribe." New York City and most other governments had long ago waived sovereign immunity in public-safety cases as a way of balancing the power of government with the rights of individual citizens, Gorton said. "I just don't see how that is a racist view. I think cries of racism are an escape from having to argue the merits. . . . I have always supported Indian tribes when it comes to their health and educational opportunities. What this is about is whether rights also carry with them responsibilities, such as supporting yourself and coexisting fairly with the rest of society."[11]

Gorton took pains to distance himself from the rabid wing of the anti-sovereignty movement, which was calling for an end to tribal governments. He believed in self-governance, he emphasized, noting that Republicans could legitimately claim it as their own initiative, Indians having found an unexpected champion in President Nixon. What he was advocating was a cross between welfare reform and means-testing: "Do we have a permanent, 100 percent obligation to fund all of the activities of these governments, or, as we give them increasing self-determination, do they have some responsibility to pay for their own government services? . . . It's a taxpayer issue. We're spending three-quarters of a billion dollars subsidizing these governments."[12]

He took his riders out of the saddle after Campbell, McCain and Domenici agreed to allow congressional hearings on tribal sovereign immunity during the next session. The General Accounting Office was instructed to re-evaluate its tribal-aid formulas. It was a truce of sorts, but short-lived.[13]

IN THE SPRING OF 1998, officials from Washington and several other states arrived on the Hill to tell the committee they were losing hundreds of millions annually because some tribes were selling cigarettes to non-Indians at reservation smoke shops without collecting sales tax. In the space of two months a new revenue swat team in Washington State had confiscated nearly 300,000 packs of contraband cigarettes being trucked to three reservations. Some were intent on defying a U.S. Supreme Court decision Gorton had won as attorney general 18 years earlier when he asserted that the tribes had no constitutional right "to be, in effect, parasites on the state system."[14]

Tribal leaders said it was Gorton once again at work with a broad broom. DeLaCruz argued that only a few tribes maintained the high court had no jurisdiction over them. Most were following the law. If Gorton had his way and states were allowed to sue them it would spell even bleaker times for impoverished reservations. Tax disputes could be solved in negotiations between state and tribal governments. "The problem is not us, but that the state has never acted in good faith toward the tribes. It dates back to him," the Quinault leader said, pointing at Gorton. "It's his legacy in the state that we've continued fighting and that has made it hard to move forward."[15]

Gorton unveiled his "American Indian Equal Justice Act." Its key provision was the end to legal immunity for tribal governments, a protection derived from a series of Supreme Court rulings dating from 1830. Individuals of any ethnicity, as well as states and other governments, would have the right to file suit against tribes in state or federal courts. "The U.S. Supreme Court is an Indian court just as it is a court for all the rest of us," Gorton said.[16]

"These hearings really are about whether the aboriginal Americans are members of this nation, or members of a multitude of nations within the U.S.," said Senator Campbell. "My own view is that they can be both."[17]

"Would the State of Washington feel comfortable waiving its legal immunity and going into a tribal court?" Henry Cagey asked. "I don't think so. But he wants us to take our chances in a state court." Gorton pounced, asserting that the Lummi leader was glossing over an importance difference: Indians are American citizens, assured a fair hearing in American courts. But non-Indians are not citizens of any Indian nation and therefore not assured a fair hearing in a tribal court. "It's a gross injustice," Gorton said, and even if his measure failed "at least I can see to it that this has been argued."[18]

At a hearing in the Seattle suburb of Tukwila a month later, the crowd of 500 overflowed a large hotel ballroom. "Some were forced to stand impatiently behind red velvet ropes. . . . Hushed but fierce debates took place on subjects from tribal autonomy to the Constitution, to who are better stewards of local natural resources. Property-rights proponents in T-shirts and caps stood next to lawyers in suits, who sat talking with citizens who had steeped themselves in treaty rights and constitutional law." Gorton supporters began to recite the Pledge of Allegiance. When they were drowned out by tribal drummers and chanting, they shouted, "WITH LIBERTY AND JUSTICE FOR ALL!"[19]

"This bill fails to recognize that tribes have already taken steps to ensure fairness and due process to all who live on (reservations) or have contact with tribes," one tribal leader testified. Private-property owners groaned and shook their heads. Several held signs that read "End Treaty Abuse." Some said they hoped Gorton's proposal would also spawn action on non-Indians' hunting, shellfish and water rights—precisely what the tribes feared. An attorney for the Lummi Nation said Gorton's plan was like using a "bulldozer . . . to remove a dandelion weed from the front lawn." Poor tribes could be wiped out by one large court settlement, others argued. Tribal courts could be paralyzed by lawsuits. Gorton's measure was unnecessary, they said, because there was a growing trend for tribes to waive their immunity on a case-by-case basis, "particularly when nontribal businesses might be reluctant to do business with a tribe unless the immunity was dropped."[20]

"The difference between Indians and most minority groups," Senator Campbell observed, "is that minorities came here from somewhere else and upward mobility is their driving force. That is secondary to Native Americans. Their driving force has always been don't lose any more than we have already lost."[21]

With all due respect to the chairman, Gorton replied, that was beside the point. They were there to weigh these issues:

> Is it necessary for a governmental body to be free from litigation in order to carry out its governmental functions? If so, then the United States is no longer a sovereign nation because it can be sued on a wide range of issues. . . . Sovereign immunity and sovereignty are two separate issues. . . . It should also be noted that the doctrine of sovereign immunity is not protected directly or indirectly by any Indian treaty. The American Indian Equal Justice Act is an attempt to find a solution to the problems which constantly exacerbate the day-to-day relations among governments, individual citizens and America's 554 Indian tribes. I seek an answer to this question: How does the doctrine of sovereign immunity fit into the 20th

Century world of Endangered Species Act listings, private property rights, Supreme Court rulings on tribal tax evasion and Indian Civil rights?

Due to the sensitive nature of this issue, most of my colleagues prefer to take a pass and not deal with this issue. I disagree by saying the individual rights of all citizens are too important to ignore as we re-evaluate the relationship among the states, the federal government, Indian tribes and individuals. As part of the United States of America, individual citizens and Indian tribes are all subject to the Constitution. We should strive for equal application of its laws. The U.S. Supreme Court has described Indian Tribes as "domestic dependent sovereigns."

The critics of my proposal have misled the public by saying the intent of my bill attempts to do away with Indian tribes altogether. Nothing could be further from the truth. I have and will continue to recognize Indian tribes as sovereign nations. This is not the issue. The issue at hand is accountability on the part of Indian tribes and a restoration of constitutional rights for both Indians and non-Indians. The enactment of my proposal would mean that individual citizens will be able to take their grievances with Indian tribes to neutral courts.[22]

AFTER THE HEARINGS, no further action was taken on Gorton's bill. The Indians, however, got busy. With the casino tribes leading the way, they set a $4 million fundraising goal for the 2000 elections and launched a voter registration drive. They wanted at least $1 million in "soft money" for TV ads to target Gorton. "There's no limit to the amount of money you can contribute to bring him down," Allen told the National Congress of American Indians, reminding tribal leaders that "no one can know" who donated to the First Americans Education Project. Gorton shrugged but also girded. "I am firmly of the belief that we cannot constitutionally limit the amount of money groups can raise for campaigns, and what's sauce for the goose is sauce for the gander. They have a constitutional right to do that." He promptly mailed an urgent fund-raising letter of his own, saying "Indian tribes flush with gambling dollars" were willing to spend "whatever it takes" to defeat him.[23]

"We certainly were out to beat him," Ron Allen told Gorton's biographer in 2011. "We're still recovering from the way he hammered us with that budget cut in 1995. To be fair and balanced, he also did good things for us—on infrastructure, education and the environment, especially fisheries restoration. 'You have a legal right to co-manage,' he always said. . . . But when it came to sovereignty issues we collided time and again. No one person has caused a stronger unification of tribes across America than Slade Gorton."[24]

Joe DeLaCruz missed the big showdown he'd been itching for since 1971. He died of a heart attack at 62 in the spring of 2000 while waiting for a flight to an Indian health care meeting in Oklahoma. By then, though, thousands of those "Dump Slade 2000" buttons were being distributed.[25]

37 | High Crimes or Misdemeanors?

WHEN BOB DYLAN OBSERVED that "even the president of the United States sometimes must have to stand naked" he hadn't imagined Bill Clinton with a cigar and an intern.

The Clinton-Gingrich brinksmanship over Medicare, Medicaid, education and the environment caused two shutdowns of non-essential federal services between mid-November of 1995 and the new year. A million federal employees were furloughed, with the overall cost estimated at $800 million. Clinton was already winning the public relations war when Gingrich bragged to reporters that he forced the shutdown because the president had made him and Dole sit in the back of Air Force One on a flight to Israel for Prime Minister Yitzhak Rabin's funeral. "What had been a noble battle for fiscal sanity began to look like the tirade of a spoiled child," wrote Tom DeLay, the majority whip in the House. The budget standoff also kept Dole from the campaign trail and boosted Clinton's approval ratings.[1]

In the middle of the government shutdown, the short-staffed White House took on "the giddy atmosphere of a slumber party." Monica Lewinsky, a 22-year-old unpaid intern, was filling in at the office of Clinton's chief of staff. She was curvy and flirty. The president noticed.[2]

Clinton's flings were legendary. Lewinsky was far from the first woman to note that he exuded sexual energy. "Power," Henry Kissinger observed in his political prime, "is the ultimate aphrodisiac." A former Arkansas state employee named Paula Jones was suing Clinton for sexual harassment in a case that dated to his days as governor. Kenneth Starr, the independent counsel appointed to investigate the Clintons' involvement in Whitewater, a failed Arkansas real estate development, broadened his probe to embrace Jones' allegations and discovered Monica.

The news broke in January of 1998. The *Drudge Report* lit the fuse on the Web, then Starr craftily leaked the story to *The Washington Post*, with a spin that had the president suborning perjury. Lewinsky had confided her affair to a fair-weather friend and allegedly said the president had urged her to lie if she was asked to testify in the Paula Jones case. A week later, with Hillary at his side, Clinton called a press conference. Punctuating each sentence with a jabbing index finger, he indignantly declared: "I want to say one thing to the American people. I want you to listen to me. I'm going to say this again: I did not have sexual relations with that woman, Miss Lewinsky. I never told anybody to lie, not a single time. *Never.* These allegations are false."

To paraphrase Clinton's second-most famous sound bite, it depends on what fellatio is. Sexual relations or not, he would later admit, it was wrong. And he did it "for the worst possible reason—just because I could."

The single-minded salaciousness of the Starr Report and the wide-ranging impeachment inquiry authorized by the House produced a backlash in the 1998 midterm elections. Defying all precedent, the embattled president's party rallied. Democrats picked up five seats in the House, where the GOP's majority was already thin, and lost none in the Senate. Hillary Clinton had been "a one-woman campaign machine," and Black voters turned out en masse. Polls indicated a solid majority of Americans opposed impeachment. Within a month, Clinton's job approval rating reached its apex: 73 percent.[3]

Dogged by his own moral lapses and polarizing image, Gingrich was already in trouble. The latest disappointment at the polls stoked the discontent that had been growing in the Republican ranks for two years. The dissidents included Gorton's friend, Congressman Steve Largent of Oklahoma, the Seattle Seahawks' Hall of Fame pass-receiver. Largent likened the election to hitting an iceberg and said the "question is whether we retain the crew of the *Titanic* or we look for some new leadership." Gingrich resigned as speaker three days after the election and also quickly resolved to leave Congress, despite having won an 11th term.[4]

ON DEC. 19, 1998, after 13½ hours of bruising debate, the House impeached a president for the first time in 130 years, approving two of the four charges presented for debate. Gorton believed the strongest was abuse of power, but that article was rejected. The House concluded that Clinton lied to the grand jury about both his relationship with Lewinsky and the Arkansas sexual harassment case. Further, he had obstructed justice by concealing evidence and encouraging Lewinsky and others to commit perjury.

Now it fell to the United States Senate to conduct a trial to determine if the president should be removed from office. With sadness and anxiety, Lott watched the impeachment process unfold on TV from his 1854 home overlooking the Gulf of Mexico. He remembers thinking a bomb was being pitched onto his lap. Lott believed Clinton was guilty as charged and ought to do the honorable thing, like Nixon, and resign. As majority leader, however, it was up to him to prove the system still worked. He and Gorton knew one thing for certain: Absent some devastating new evidence, there was no way, no how, the Republicans could muster a two-thirds majority, 67 votes, to convict Clinton.[5]

Gorton called from Seattle. Early on he'd told Lott impeachment was barreling their way "like a freight train," and most of the senators were in serious denial. Equally worrisome, few of their fellow Republicans seemed to grasp the realpolitik: how they handled impeachment could spell success or failure at the polls in 2000.[6]

Gorton reported that his friend Joe Lieberman had suggested they team up on a plan to ensure the trial would be dignified, bipartisan and as a brief as possible. Have at it, said Lott.

En route to Hawaii for a holiday with his family, Gorton phoned Lieberman. Between the middle of the Pacific and a car heading down a rural road in Connecticut, the two senators began to craft what became the Lieberman-Gorton Plan. It called for a "rapid and reasonable" trial based on the House proceedings. That meant they could avoid calling witnesses. The Starr Report was "almost pornographic," Gorton said, and they wanted none of that. Congress had a full plate and shouldn't waste its time on a pointless, divisive, long-drawn-out trial.[7]

On opening day, the two former attorneys general proposed, the House prosecutors would present their evidence. Day two would feature rebuttals from the Clinton defense team. The third day would be devoted to questioning of both sides. On the fourth and fifth days, the Senate would debate Clinton's guilt, then take what amounted to a test vote. If the votes were there to convict the president on either charge—a highly unlikely event—only then would a full-blown trial ensue, with House prosecutors allowed to call witnesses. If two-thirds majorities were lacking, as surely would be the case, the Senate would have the option of ending the trial and considering censure as an alternative to impeachment. Censure would require only a simple majority.[8]

Lott liked it. So did Tom Daschle, the minority leader. Lott was worried, though, about blowback from his right flank. When the press got wind of the idea and erroneously labeled it the "Lott-Lieberman Proposal," it was party time. The arch-conservatives said their majority leader, who had already raised their eyebrows by collaborating with Clinton, was now wimping out. Why should they let the president off the hook and short-circuit justice? Henry Hyde, the House's chief impeachment prosecutor, was outraged.[9]

Lott regretfully backed away from Lieberman-Gorton. But as the ground rules were being hashed out on January 8, 1999, discouragement gave way to candor. "It was one of the few occasions during my 18 years when all the senators were on the floor together," Gorton recalls. "It was like being transported back to the Senate of the 19th Century."

West Virginia's courtly Robert Byrd warned that they were "teetering on the brink" of the black pit that had swallowed the House. Lieberman said 67 votes was out of reach—face it. Calling witnesses would only prolong the trial. Gorton said the Senate's reputation would be sullied by sordid details. It was time for compromise. Others agreed. Finally, Phil Gramm rose to say there was real merit to the key thrust of Lieberman-Gorton: Brevity is the soul of wit. For starters, the tough Texan said, give the House prosecutors and Clinton's lawyers 24 hours apiece to make their cases and deal with other stuff as it arises. Ted Kennedy said they could deal with the witness business later, too.[10]

"Let's vote!" Lott declared. Lieberman, Lott, Gorton, Gramm and Kennedy decamped to the majority leader's office to draft the final deal, which was approved 100-0. Gorton's intellect, coupled with his attention to detail and grasp of nuance, sometimes annoyed his colleagues. Now he basked in their praise. "We have enjoyed cussing and discussing him and his proposals for the last week," said Don Nickles, the assistant majority leader. "He has shown great courage and leadership, and he has worked with all of us . . . Republicans and Democrats, to try to forge a bipartisan resolution to this challenge. And I compliment him for his legislative skills in doing so." It was Gorton's 71st birthday.[11]

THERE WAS A TEMPORARY SETBACK. When Monica Lewinsky arrived back in town in late January, she set off "agitated scrums of reporters and gawkers that foretold the commotion that would ensue if she was to testify in the Senate. Partisan tempers had flared, reminding senators that their hold on dignity was tenuous." The Republican Conference balked when Gorton and Lieberman once again made their case to forgo witnesses. In the end, the Senate voted to allow House prosecutors to question Lewinsky in a closed-door deposition and the trial was largely devoid of partisan venom. "Working with Senator Lieberman on this issue was one of the most rewarding experiences of my life," Gorton told reporters. Their first conversations had been practically "telepathic."[12]

On February 12, 1999, the Senate acquitted the president on both counts. The perjury allegation was defeated 55 to 45, with Gorton among the 10 Republicans who voted "not guilty." The obstruction of justice charge failed on a 50-50 tie. Gorton and 49 other Republicans voted to convict Clinton; 45 Democrats and five Republicans were opposed. Lieberman, a religious man deeply disappointed by Clinton's "immoral and disgraceful behavior," nevertheless voted "not guilty" on both counts, as did Patty Murray.[13]

Gorton's rationale for voting as he did was this: "The first count was lying about sex, and there's no question that he did. But an impeachment trial is different than any other trial, and the punishment was so disproportionate to the crime that I couldn't bring myself to say he should be thrown out of office for that offense. The second count was lying under oath to a grand jury—obstruction of justice. And that seemed to me to be a much more serious offense. My split vote created all kinds of problems for me with my Republican constituency—Clinton haters who were outraged that I voted 'not guilty' on even one count. They didn't pay any attention to the second vote. And of course I got no credit from any Democrat for being reasonable by voting 'guilty' on only one of the charges. So from a political standpoint it was a *terrible* choice, although I don't think my votes had any impact on my race for re-election in 2000."

In the heat of the impeachment battle, the Washington State wing of the ultraconservative American Heritage Party announced it would probably field a candidate against Gorton. "I don't think he understands the critical nature of our Constitution and his duty toward it," said the state chairman.[14]

A Libertarian would prove more problematic.

"When the history of this is finally written, I think Gorton will turn out to be one of the heroes . . .," said Stephen Hess, a veteran political analyst at the Brookings Institution. Joni Balter, a *Seattle Times* columnist and seasoned Gorton-watcher, pronounced his performance "somewhere between cunningly brilliant and all over the map."[15]

SOME COMIC RELIEF in the midst of the impeachment crisis was provided by Senator McCain, who was often at odds with Gorton and Lott. Gorton thought the Arizonan too mercurial to be president. Accompanied by Tony Williams, J. Vander Stoep and Veda Jellen, his state director, Gorton went to Austin in December of 1998 to meet with Bush and Karl Rove, the governor's calculating, moonfaced strategist. "It was a *great* talk; two or three hours. We talked about everything. I *really* liked the guy," Gorton says. "I thought he was smarter than his old man—that he took after his mother. I *loved* his old man but I was frustrated by him as my president. We signed up on the spot for G.W. for president."

When they told Bush that a Democrat couldn't fashion an electoral vote victory without Washington and Oregon but a Republican could, Bush leaned back in his chair and twanged, "Ah like to keep the other guy pinned back!"

Deed done, Gorton wondered how he'd break the news to McCain. "He had been running for months but he had never said a word to me about it. I assumed that since I was a fellow Republican United States senator, he would make an appointment and come to my office to lay out his case."

They were in the third day of the Clinton impeachment trial, one of the few times in his 18 years when every senator was in his seat. Gorton always sat in the back row because he liked to see what was happening. McCain was in the row ahead. Someone was droning away down in front. McCain stretched crankily, walked over to the aisle, turned and walked behind Gorton. Dick Lugar was on one side, Connie Mack on the other. "Hey Slade," McCain said, "I've got to talk to you about supporting me for president." Gorton was so startled that he just blurted out, "Sorry John, I've signed up with G.W." McCain's eyes blackened. "Well, fuck you!" he declared and walked briskly away. Lugar and Mack almost fell off their chairs they were laughing so hard: "Good job, Slade!" said one. "That's the way to do it, Slade!" the other chimed in.

"Those were the only two words we ever exchanged over his 2000 presidential race," says Gorton.

38 | A Dubious Honor

AFTER IMPEACHMENT WAS PUT TO BED, the 2000 elections were only 18 months away. Who would challenge Gorton in his eighth and likely last statewide race? Gary Locke was strongly inclined to seek a second term as governor. The Democrats' consensus next best bet was Chris Gregoire, fresh from her star turn leading the team that extracted a $206 billion public-health settlement from the tobacco companies. Many speculated, however, that the attorney general might be reluctant to challenge Gorton, who was something of a mentor. He had taken note of her fastidious gumption when she clerked at the AG's Office while attending law school at Gonzaga University.[1]

"Periodically, he would arrive at the airport in Spokane. A law clerk was assigned to drive him to wherever he was going," Gregoire recalls. "The talk around the office was that when you picked him up you got a crisp 'Good morning' and then up goes the newspaper. There's no conversation. On the way back he's reading something else. Then he bids you adieu. And that was that."

Gregoire was determined to engage the boss in a meaningful conversation. The worst that could happen, she figured, was an icy, "I'm not going to talk to you." So when Gorton buckled his seat belt and reached for the *Spokesman-Review* she immediately brought up a recent Supreme Court case. "Down comes the paper and off we go! He loved a debate. He's a lawyer's lawyer. If you have something to say, it's easy to engage him."

Having worked for the Department of Social & Health Services, where controversy was a constant, Gregoire had resolved she was "never going back" to a state job. As graduation approached in 1977, she was polishing her resume. Gorton called. "You've got a great future," he said. "How about coming to work in the AG's office?" Gregoire was flattered and impressed. "When you're a law clerk, graduating from law school and the attorney general himself calls, you do not say no."

Twenty-three years later, family considerations—a husband, two teenage daughters and an elderly mother—more than mixed emotions con-

vinced her to say no to a bid for the U.S. Senate. "Politics is politics,"
Gregoire said, adding that Gorton had made that "real clear when he went
out of his way" to support her Republican opponent in 1992. The possibility of a cabinet post in a Gore administration was also enticing.[2]

Ron Sims was reluctant to risk his job as King County executive, arguably the second-most important office in the state, for a bruising rematch
with Gorton. State Supreme Court Justice Phil Talmadge, a brainy former
state senator, was thinking it over. Many found him as astringent as
Gorton.

While Gorton seemed vulnerable over his run-ins with Indians, environmentalists, senior citizens, unions, right-wingers and Clinton defenders, it seemed for months that he might luck out.

Deborah Senn, the state's two-term insurance commissioner, was running hard. She was a divisive figure, however, even in her own party.
With her spiky hairdo and piercing eyes, Senn projected the butt-kicking
bravado of Chicago's South Side, where she grew up. She dismissed most
of her enemies as anti-Semites.[3]

Jim McDermott, Seattle's unabashedly liberal congressman, was also
mentioned as a potential challenger. But he was demonstrably unelectable
statewide. Those two would be "like bugs on the senior senator's wind-
shield," Joni Balter wrote.[4]

Some said former congresswoman Maria Cantwell, still smarting over
her re-election loss in 1994, might be the party's last best hope. Would
she really risk a major lump of the millions she'd made at RealNetworks
for a shot at a seat in the Senate in what was certain to be an exhausting,
contentious campaign—first against the pugnacious Senn, then against
Gorton if she won the primary?

She would. Extremely bright, determined and often perceived as
aloof, Cantwell, 41, shared another trait with Gorton: She loved being in
Congress.

"YOU'RE CRAZY!" RON DOTZAUER, an old friend, told Cantwell when she
showed up at his consulting firm in Seattle and told him she was going to
run for the Senate.

"No I'm not," she said with a confident smirk.

"Yes you are. Look, if you really want to do good things and get back
into public policy take some of your money and set up a foundation."

"No. This is important to me. I think it's the right thing to do, and it's
the right time to do it."

"Good luck. I'm going to Mexico!"

"No, no. You don't understand: You're going to run my campaign."

"No, no, no. You don't understand. I'm not going to run your campaign. I'm too old to be running campaigns. That's not my deal any more. I'm leaving for Mexico."

Two weeks later when Dotzauer returned from vacation, Cantwell was waiting. "You don't understand," she said. "I'm going to do this, and you're going to do this. We're going to do this." Then she pulled out the last stop. Their fathers had died of cancer. "You know, my dad would want this and your dad would want this." He sighed. "What the hell? OK. I'll do it."

"I guess I wanted to see if I still had it in me to run a race."

One of the most successful political operatives in Washington State history, Dotzauer won his spurs managing Scoop Jackson's 1982 re-election campaign. In 1984 he was the architect of the "Booth Who?" campaign that propelled the relatively unknown Booth Gardner from Pierce County executive to governor. Afterward, he formed a public affairs firm, with Cantwell as his first employee, and soon attracted a stable of clients.[5]

SENN HAD BEEN ON THE STUMP for 10 months when Cantwell made it official on January 19, 2000. "It's something she's got to do," said Cathy Allen, a Democratic political consultant. She compared Cantwell to a bungee jumper with a phobia for heights: "She can't live with that last loss. This is her confronting and overcoming her greatest fears."[6]

Cantwell had never run statewide. Senn had. The insurance commissioner also boasted a number of union endorsements. It had taken Senn nearly a year, however, to raise $800,000. Cantwell had ready access to five times that. Besides Dotzauer, her brain trust included former House speaker Joe King and Christian Sinderman, an experienced political operative. King and Cantwell had worked together closely during her six years as a state legislator, focusing on health-care, economic development and growth management.[7]

A woman had never defeated an incumbent elected U.S. senator. One of the women dedicated to making sure Gorton was not the first was the indefatigable Veda Jellen, his state director. A huge personality, Jellen had emerged from the PTA and Campfire Girls to become one of the most influential women in the Washington State Republican Party. She was a past master of grass-roots organizing, phone banks and direct-mail. Gorton was in awe of her moxie. "You ignored her advice at your peril."[8]

Given Slade's perennially high negatives, they took nothing for granted.

Jellen worked with Tony Williams, Gorton's chief of staff, to develop a strategy that Tony would oversee down the stretch while she worked with the Bush people and other Republican candidates. Goal No. 1 was to offset Cantwell's money advantage by keeping the National Republican Senatorial Committee and well-heeled GOP donors fully engaged and writing checks. Nor could they be content to watch Senn and Cantwell duke it out, à la Lowry and Bonker 12 years earlier. They knew they wouldn't get 50 percent of the primary vote; they just couldn't afford to be second. If Cantwell was the winner, which they fully expected, given Senn's proclivity to go shrill and Maria's money, they had to style her as a classic tax-and-spend liberal disguised as a high-tech centrist. Their ads would also emphasize Slade's constituent-relations credentials, reprising the "Slade Gorton Works for Me" theme. They had Bush's state manager in their fold early on, and resolved to prop up the Texas governor in every way possible. "We knew 'W' wouldn't win Washington but we didn't want him to lose big," Williams says. They needed to energize the Republican base. It was likely to be another nail biter. They scheduled fundraisers all around the state, with guest stars as diverse as Charlton Heston and Bill Gates. Guns and software. The race would shatter the state's campaign spending records.

IT WAS HALF PAST 9 on the night of May 12, 1999. Danny Westneat, *The Seattle Times'* man in Washington, was watching a master at work. Gorton was down on both knees in a room deep in the basement of the U.S. Capitol. "He wasn't praying," Westneat wrote. "Pen in hand and surrounded by staff and lobbyists from the mining industry, the Republican senator was furiously scratching out the words to give Eastern Washington a gold mine."[9]

In 12 hours of wheeling and dealing by House and Senate conferees, the emergency appropriations bill President Clinton needed to underwrite the NATO air war in the Balkans and assist Kosovo refugees had acquired a remarkable array of expensive appendages and special pleadings. There were subsidies for reindeer ranchers and sewers for Salt Lake City. A senator from Alabama was out to prevent the White House from listing sturgeon as an endangered species. Senator Byrd, who could play piggyback better than anyone, added a rider to help a West Virginia steel mill hurt by imports; Domenici was going to bat for small oil and gas companies; $566 million was earmarked to help Midwest farmers hurt by low commodities prices. The tinkering totaled $9 billion. Lacking a line-item veto, Clinton would have to take it or leave it.[10]

Gorton finished drafting the gold mine measure less than an hour before it was approved, still in his handwriting, by the conference committee. "Indignant as hell," he persuaded his fellow lawmakers that the project had been unfairly blocked by the Clinton Administration. Battle Mountain Gold Co. of Houston had invested $80 million over seven years to secure dozens of state and federal permits and win legal battles with environmentalists and the tribes, Gorton said. Now the Interior Department was citing a little-known provision of an 1872 mining law limiting the amount of federal land that could be used for mining waste. It wouldn't stop in Okanogan County, Gorton warned. Babbitt was trying to shut down mines and confiscate vast stretches of land across the West "by fiat as a dictator."[11]

Opponents said the company's plan to blast 97 million tons of rock off the back side of Buckhorn Mountain would be a body-blow to the landscape. They also noted that the site of the proposed Crown Jewel mine—a name tailor-made for irony—was largely on federal land. Their main fear was that the cyanide-water mixture used to leach gold from powdered rock would pollute waterways. Nevertheless, the state Department of Ecology had signed off on the project, which offered the promise of 150 jobs in one of the state's poorest counties. "An honorable government doesn't treat its citizens the way they treated Crown Jewel," Gorton said. "Bureaucrats in the bowels of the Interior Department don't make the laws of the United States."[12]

Norm Dicks backed Gorton, saying the company had been treated unfairly, but Murray said it was flat wrong to rewrite mining laws "in the middle of the night."[13]

ENVIRONMENTALISTS AND THE TRIBES christened Gorton "Cyanide Slade," the "Midnight Rider," galloping once more with industry lobbyists. First the forests, then the dams; now an open-pit gold mine. Even if you liked the idea, "watching this law's birth would be like watching your own surgery for hemorrhoids. It might be good for you in the end, but you'd just as soon avert your eyes," one columnist wrote. Dotzauer's collection of clippings was growing.[14]

Gorton observed testily that no one ever complained when he worked with lobbyists for consumer-advocate groups. Environmentalists and the tribes routinely sent their lobbyists to help senators write bills. "It happens all the time." And why would he turn down advice from great lawyers and experts in specialized fields? "I don't want to write something that doesn't meet the purpose it's designed for." As for riders, "The administration asks us to put riders on bills; environmentalists ask us to put riders on bills." There'd been riders since the first Congress in 1789.[15]

The $15 billion spending bill—gold mine and reindeers intact—passed Congress. Clinton signed it, wagging his finger about all the ornaments. The final twist was that Gorton had voted no, which outraged the gold mine opponents all the more. If you could do your "dirty work" in the dead of night, then vote against it in the light of day and still see it pass, something was terribly wrong, they said. Gorton said it was more important "to stand on principle" and vote against the "folly" of the NATO airstrikes than support the spending bill just because it included his rider. Clinton hadn't convinced him that military intervention in the Balkans was necessary or working.[16]

ON EARTH DAY 2000 the Sierra Club kicked off an $8 million campaign to elect a more environmentally friendly Congress by targeting Gorton. The club's Cascade Chapter hoped to reach a million viewers with TV ads—some of them set to air during Mariners games—slamming Gorton for "sneaking in special deals for polluters, even letting lobbyists write our laws." Poised to name Gorton to its Dirty Dozen, the League of Conservation Voters was readying a $700,000 blitz of its own.[17]

A few weeks later, Cantwell chartered a plane to haul Seattle reporters and a film crew to Buckhorn Mountain. Standing on a bluff overlooking the fir-covered hills, she denounced Gorton for his "insensitivity" to the environment and open government. Mining company officials had trailed her party to the site, angry that she didn't tell them she was coming. "See these kids?" said the company's environmental superintendent, showing Cantwell's staff photos of his children. "You are putting us out of work."[18]

Gorton said it was strange indeed that a politician who was promising to listen to the people hadn't bothered to ask the locals how they felt about the mine. "It does show that the rest of the state outside Seattle can expect the same kind of treatment from (Cantwell), and I expect the other one (Senn) as well," Gorton told reporters. "She will tell them they are to take down their dams. She will tell them how they're going to live. She shows no interest in listening to what people's concerns are."[19]

The other one couldn't afford a plane but she agreed with Cantwell that Gorton's "backroom maneuver" was an affront to democracy. Both Democrats said they opposed breaching the dams.

Secretary Babbitt, meantime, was touring the Hanford Reach, one of the last wild stretches of the king Columbia River, its flow swollen by the spring runoff. The former Arizona governor found the vista "staggering." The area had been appropriated by the federal government in 1943 as a security buffer for its A-bomb project. Patty Murray desperately wanted it designated a national monument. Her attempts at achieving a compromise between the counties and conservationists had all failed. Gorton was siding with irrigators and property rights advocates, fighting a vociferous battle to stave off federal control. Resorting once again to a rider, he said the administration's plan was indifferent to the real-world needs of farmers.[20]

Babbitt promised to make "every provision I reasonably can" to give locals a say in managing the monument. Gorton scoffed. But no rider could stop them now. Idaho Congresswoman Helen Chenoweth-Hage shared his chagrin, fuming, "This president is engaging in the biggest land grab since the invasion of Poland." Using the Antiquities Act of 1906 with a vigor that might have "dee-lighted!" Teddy Roosevelt, one of Gorton's heroes, Clinton had designated nearly 4 million acres of land in the West as national monuments. On June 9, 2000, he added 200,000 more, sending Al Gore to make the announcement in a state that might prove crucial to his veep's hopes for the presidency. Gorton predicted the photo-op would make page one of *The New York Times*.[21]

While the greens were pillorying him, Gorton glowered that they showed their true colors by ignoring his "40-year track record" of environmental activism, including billboard-control legislation, King County's landmark Forward Thrust initiatives and higher vehicle fuel-economy standards. From his seat as chairman of the Interior appropriations subcommittee, he had secured $10 million for the Mountains to Sound Greenway project and was the major architect of a land-exchange along Interstate 90. Now he was looking for at least $8 million to help a conservation partnership protect 16,000 acres of privately held timber land in the Cascades. Long Live the Kings, a group dedicated to salmon and steelhead restoration, said Gorton had appropriated tens of millions for salmon recovery. Congressman Brian Baird, a Democrat from Vancouver, criticized the Sierra Club's TV ads for not crediting Gorton for his work to preserve land in the Columbia River Gorge.[22]

In June a senior Sierra Club official felt obliged to stand next to Gorton at a news conference as the senator announced his plan to push higher emissions standards for sport-utility vehicles. Bill Arthur, the club's Northwest regional director, was unimpressed. "His record is pathetic. Every six years he puts on the green lipstick and tries to get a date with the public." The tribes' attack ads featured environmental themes, leading off with a charge that Gorton had "bargained away our state's natural beauty to polluters."[23]

DOTZAUER ADMIRED the "Washington's next great senator" theme Paul Newman had executed flawlessly for Gorton against Magnuson 20 years earlier. At 72, Slade was now only three years younger than Maggie had been in 1980. He was so vigorous, however, and as sharp as ever that there was no way to portray him as a geezer—although TV lights irritated his sensitive eyes and caused him to blink like a signal light on a battleship. Dotzauer said Gorton wasn't so much old as he was old-school politics, writing riders in the dead of night. Still, youth must be served. Slade came in with tail fins and Sputnik. Maria would take him out with laptops and BlackBerries. They'd be aggressive but cool. What Washington State needed, Cantwell said, was fewer angry words. Gorton represented the "politics of division." When the Cantwell campaign bus departed on a 20-day road trip, she quoted JFK: "It's time for a new generation of leadership, for there is a new world to be won."[24]

In May, Cantwell edged ahead of Senn and was gaining on Gorton. By August, she was well clear of Senn and in a dead heat with Gorton, with 20 percent undecided. Americans for Job Security, a Virginia-based trade group funded by the insurance and forest products industries, was spending $548,000 on airtime to attack Cantwell as a creature "from the other Washington."[25]

A week before the primary, Senn and Cantwell had a sizzling debate. Senn said she was tired of being characterized as a pit bull, then barked that RealNetworks had been caught spying on its customers. Cantwell eyed her with icy disdain. "We already have a senator who pits the people of this state against each other," she said. " . . .Why would we want to elect another?"[26]

Nomination in the bag, Dotzauer was rooting for the Libertarian candidate, Jeff Jared. "I was praying for that guy to get enough votes to qualify for the general election ballot. He was critical to our success. *Critical.*" Cantwell's campaign manager figured most of those Libertarian votes would otherwise go to Gorton come November.

Tony Williams was also wary of Jared, but his immediate concern was Slade finishing first in the primary. "We were playing for perception. If Slade came in second, our fundraising in D.C. would have dried up. Cantwell didn't have to spend money to raise money like we did, or expend a lot of time and energy dialing for dollars. She just got out her checkbook or met with her banker. She spent $5 million just to make sure she'd win the nomination."[27]

Brock Adams sent Cantwell $500, telling reporters, "I just want to see Gorton defeated."[28]

Gorton and Maria Cantwell square off in a televised debate on Oct. 10, 2000.
Both candidates said the debate may have come too late in the race for some
voters. *Jimi Lott/The Seattle Times*

Gorton finished first in the primary, with nearly 44 percent of the
votes cast. Cantwell was the runner-up with 37 percent, crushing Senn by
300,000 votes. The Libertarian's 1.3 percent advanced him to November.
Cantwell had momentum, and Gorton had a problem. "With the general
election seven weeks away we only had enough money in our budget to do
five weeks of TV," Williams recalls. "We figured that since Maria had
been on TV all summer, she wouldn't let up. But if we stayed dark for the
first two weeks of the general we'd be toast. So we gambled."

They launched their TV ads immediately, hoping they could raise the
money they'd need for the last two weeks. Then they caught two breaks:
Surmising that Williams was winging it, Dotzauer held fire. When the
National Republican Senatorial Committee jumped in with a $1.5 million
anti-Cantwell blitz of its own, Dotzauer made a course correction. But
Maria had been pounded for 10 days on her votes for higher taxes. "If we
had won," Williams says, "I would be telling you that the key to victory
was those two weeks."

AT MID-OCTOBER, ELWAY'S POLL had Gorton up 3 percent. Given the margin of sampling error, the race was too close to call, although Slade was
ahead everywhere except greater Seattle. Surprisingly, Cantwell led only

46 percent to 44 percent among women, and respondents who followed politics on the Internet favored Gorton by 4 percent. They set out to push her negatives even higher. Crucially, with Washington a battleground state for the presidency and Congress, Gorton had raised enough money to stay on TV down the stretch, even though they'd be outspent $10 million to $7 million.[29]

Their third debate, a week from Election Day, was the most contentious and clearly Cantwell's best showing. She had been hitting him hard on the gold mine rider with a TV ad featuring a picturesque view of Buckhorn Mountain, birds chirping serenely in the background. Then a black cloud covered the screen. The next image was a child drinking from a faucet.[30]

Gorton said the ad implied the mine would poison kids. "It's totally false. The people overwhelmingly want the mine. They don't think their children will be poisoned. . . .Maria Cantwell thinks she knows better." It wasn't the first time she had played fast and loose, he charged. Seeking re-election to Congress in 1994, she ran an ad suggesting that her Republican opponent backed oil drilling in Puget Sound, which was untrue. Gorton complained that she had accepted money from political-action committees in the past, but now that she was rich she was making a holier-than-thou show of swearing off PAC money. "The hypocrisy of Maria Cantwell is breathtaking."[31]

Cantwell defended the ad, asserting that the company had been cited for mining violations in the past. Gorton's rider was a perfect example of special-interest politics that represented "the worst of our political system."[32]

The moderator asked Gorton if the company had asked him for the rider. "Of course they did, as they have every right to do." He accused Cantwell of "stiffing" the people of Okanogan County and said Election Day would be a referendum on the mine.[33]

"Let me make one point clear," Cantwell said, jaw set. "I will listen to people over special interests." Dotzauer grinned.[34]

While one of Cantwell's recurring themes was that she had the savvy to bridge the digital divide and bring the New Economy to rural areas, O. Casey Corr, a *Seattle Times* editorial columnist, found Gorton's grasp of the issues "far more impressive." He wrote:

> Given her five years as an executive with RealNetworks, Cantwell should be able to talk circles around Gorton. He's the suit. She's the geek. But if you ask about telecommunications policy, anti-trust issues affecting the software industry, mergers affecting online content, and rural-economic development, she's short on specifics. . . . Take Microsoft. That company is hugely important to this region and by far is the most powerful player

in the computer industry. Where do they stand on the government's proposal to break up the company?

Although her employer called the break-up proposal "thoughtful and
reasonable," Cantwell has given conflicting statements on the litigation.
In one interview, she said she agreed with the government's prosecution
of the case, but not the proposed breakup. In a later interview, she said
she did not support the filing of the lawsuit.

Gorton's position has been clear. From the start, he opposed the lawsuit as reckless and unnecessary. Adopting Microsoft's language, he complained that the litigation threatens industry innovation. . . .

Cantwell and Gorton both want to see an eventual end to a federal
moratorium on Internet taxes. But Gorton has been a leader on that point
for years. When Gov. Gary Locke appeared before a group of officials
from Oregon, Washington and British Columbia last year, he repeatedly
cited a policy letter by Gorton and other senators on the topic.

"Me too" is all Cantwell can say.[35]

The Times, nevertheless, endorsed Cantwell, saying her "expansive
view of the future, and Washington's role in it, makes her more compelling. As Gorton said 20 years ago, it's time to start rebuilding Washington's team in the U.S. Senate." In his eight bids for statewide office, it was
the first time Seattle's largely home-owned daily had deserted Gorton.[36]

WHEN THEY CALLED IT A NIGHT on November 7, 2000—one of the most
tumultuous election days in American history—King County had pushed
Cantwell to a 4,800-vote lead. But there were nearly a million votes yet to
be counted. Cantwell's headquarters was an emotional roller coaster.
They were sobbing over Gore's apparent defeat but jubilant over Maria's
lead. "No more Slade!" they chanted. Accustomed to nail-biters, Gorton
told his supporters, "You may have to hang around for a while longer,
perhaps for even a week or two." Dotzauer had warned Cantwell and her
family that it might take "a few days."[37]

It took 24.

About the time Gore was retracting his concession call to Bush, Gorton was pulling ahead by 3,000, with an estimated 500,000 absentees
still to be tabulated. Control of the U.S. Senate hinged on the outcome.
Lott called Gorton to offer encouragement. "Patience is a virtue in this
business that you must cultivate, or you're in deep trouble," Gorton said.
Cantwell seemed cool. Dotzauer shook his head and summed up the tension with one word: "Crazy."[38]

Gorton's lead grew to 12,000 after a week of counting and wavered between 5,000 and 8,000 until the afternoon of Nov. 21 when the last ballots were tallied, including 3,000 more than expected in King County. Cantwell had won by about 1,900 votes—0.08 percent. State law required a recount.

While Florida roiled, Washington State's photo-finish was drama free—save for the outcome on December 1. Cantwell, who was born the year Gorton first won elective office, sent him into retirement by 2,229 votes out of nearly 2.5 million cast. He had carried 34 of the state's 39 counties. Their votes weren't quite enough to offset her 153,000 margin in King.

Slade told Sally to keep the engine running. This wouldn't take long.

"It's a dubious honor to come in second in what must have been the closest major election in our state's history," Gorton told reporters as his staff looked on in stunned resignation. "And the stress on my outstanding staff, my family and myself of an election night that has lasted for more than three weeks cannot be overstated."[39]

And that was that.

"It will take time to brush away the recent election—the view that he is a throwback and has divided the state," said Dan Evans. "He hasn't divided the state. But what he has done, in recent years, is to try to represent that there is more to this state than Seattle."[40]

WHILE ANGRY DEMOCRATS denounced Green Party candidate Ralph Nader as a spoiler in the amazingly close presidential race, Washington State Republicans pointed to the 64,734 votes won by the Libertarian in their Senate contest. "In a race that close there are a gazillion small reasons that end up costing you victory, but without Jeff Jared, Slade would have won," says Tony Williams, who took the loss even harder than Gorton. Slade is like a second father to him; McGavick and Vander Stoep like brothers.

The Libertarian; the gold mine ads perfectly timed to mobilize Democrats; those 9,000 new Indian voters; *The Times'* endorsement of Cantwell. It all hurt.

Bitter that Gorton had helped Bush win a crucial victory in Washington's presidential primary, McCain boasted later that his unwillingness to campaign for Slade also contributed to his defeat. (Observing that "in politics, one important characteristic is selective amnesia," Gorton says he didn't ask for McCain's help.)

Gorton believes the last straw was the disclosure four days before the election that Bush had been arrested for drunken driving in 1976. Karl

Rove agreed. The revelation "knocked us off message at a critical time," flipped a lot of voters to Gore and caused many social conservatives to sit on their hands, Bush's strategist wrote in his autobiography.[41]

There was one more twist: Washington State Republicans were infuriated to learn a week after the recount that $1.1 million in contributions was still in the bank. When Rove met with Don Benton, the newly elected state GOP chairman, before the National Convention, his first question was, "Are you holding up your end?" Benton said yes. "Holding up" now took on a whole different meaning.[42]

The party's coffers were so flush that Benton had decided to buy a new headquarters for $360,000. When the executive board blew a gasket over the unspent contributions, he emphasized that most of the money came from restricted national party funds, and much of it arrived too late to buy TV time or hire consultants to design last-minute mailings. Sam Reed, the party's candidate for secretary of state, said he asked Benton for help in those final days and was told the cupboard was bare. "I'm upset, disappointed and feel like I was out there giving my all," said Reed, who was $22,000 in debt after winning a squeaker. "To not have my party give me money when they had it was very disappointing."[43]

Benton countered that campaign representatives for Gorton and Jennifer Dunn shared check-signing responsibility for the national committee money. He said he had no idea so much money was sitting in the account. One board member shot back, "Maybe we should name this building the 'Maria Cantwell Building' because it will have been constructed on the political grave of Slade Gorton." Benton protested that he was being scapegoated and refused to comply with a call for his resignation. Come January, he was defeated for re-election by Chris Vance, a King County councilman.[44]

A DECADE AFTER THE LOSS, Gorton gave a lecture at Seattle University on the findings of the 9/11 Commission. Afterward, he says a woman came up to him and confided she had been stewing over something ever since the 2000 campaign. She claimed the Cantwell campaign had stiffed her on the rent for one of its offices. "I knew if I went to the press she might lose. I wasn't particularly for her, but I finally decided I just couldn't do that. So I've come to you to apologize for being partly responsible for your loss."

When he stopped laughing, Gorton said, "Don't worry about it. You greatly improved my life!"

39 | An Outbreak of Candor

O N DECEMBER 7, GORTON'S COLLEAGUES, led by Senator Murray, rose on the Senate floor to offer farewells. Murray's was particularly eloquent and gracious:

"As my colleagues know, there is also no greater adversary in the United States Senate than Slade Gorton. When Senator Gorton took on an issue everyone knew they had better prepare for an energetic and spirited fight. . . . Ask the Clinton Administration and the Justice Department what it is like to differ with Slade Gorton. He was a champion for Microsoft in its ongoing legal battles with the Department of Justice. . . .Ask the Bush Administration what it was like to do battle with Slade Gorton when he fought his own party to save the National Endowment for the Arts. Slade Gorton also fought for the U.S. Senate. When the Congress was struggling through a very partisan impeachment process, it was Slade Gorton who, along with our colleague Senator Lieberman, stepped forward with a plan for the Senate. . . .Senator Gorton, on behalf of the people of Washington State, thank you for your many years of dedicated service—one proud part of a dedicated and accomplished career in public service."[1]

"The thing that stands out most about Slade," said Phil Gramm, "is that he is wise . . . exactly the kind of person the founders had in mind when they wrote the Senate into the Constitution." Judd Gregg of New Hampshire compared Gorton to Daniel Webster. Jay Rockefeller of West Virginia called him "a master craftsman" grasping all the nuances of complex legislation. Domenici, who had served with Gorton for 18 years, said that "wherever he touches things, either by committee work or by being called in by our majority leader to discuss issues, he leaves an imprint." Gordon Smith of Oregon said he was "the champion of many things, but I think he was the greatest champion for rural people. . . . He stood by farmers. He stood by fishermen. He stood by those who logged. . . .He fought for them to have a place."[2]

The accolades caught Gorton by surprise. He was working in his office, listening to the proceedings on the floor, when Murray began her tribute. He listened with growing gratitude, although he confessed that the experience "bore some resemblance to attending one's own wake." The following day, he told his colleagues:

"Friendships become both broad and deep during the course of a career here in the Senate. When one comes to the end of such a career, it is those personal relationships, in my view, that are the most deep and most profound and that have the greatest effect on one as an individual. To listen to expressions from people who are not accustomed to speaking emotionally or personally is an extremely moving experience." He was especially pleased that Murray and others had praised the caliber of his staff. "I think I can say unequivocally that I am and have been a creature of my staff over the period of my entire 18 years in this body. My proudest achievement is that so many young people—almost all from my own state—have worked on my staff, either here or in the State of Washington. The great majority of them, of course, have already gone on to other careers—most of them in the state—a return that I find particularly gratifying."[3]

Peggy Noonan, Reagan's talented speechwriter who had gone on to a career as an award-winning author and columnist, took note of the farewells in *The Wall Street Journal*:

Candor broke out on Capitol Hill yesterday, and a few hearts got worn on a few blue pinstriped sleeves. Members of the U.S. Senate stood on the floor of their chamber and spoke, usually without text or notes and often at some length, about a man they admired. . . . It was personal and passionate and bipartisan. . . . The speeches were so emotional, so much like eulogies, that the senators had to keep reminding themselves out loud not to use the past tense. But they couldn't help it, any more than they can help feeling that when you're a senator and you lose your seat you're dead. But also because, as each made clear, they couldn't stand the thought of losing all the experience, talent, shrewdness and seriousness that Mr. Gorton had brought to the chamber. . . .

In all of the praise you could hear the sound of an institution defining itself, showing through what it said what it values and honors. I think it was saying this: In the clamor of big egos bumping into daily events that is Congress, we do notice who gets things done, who really works. Who really thinks, who contributes, who has a long-term historical view, who is a patriot, who doesn't care who gets credit, who will quietly counsel and help you with your problem and not capitalize on it or use it against you . . .

People who write for newspapers don't really get to be very positive about people in politics very often. It's sort of a sign of being a sissy. You get the best laughs, and you're quoted most often, by putting someone down in a witty or interesting way. To do the opposite—to laud someone in politics—is like wearing a sign that says This Guy Fooled Me. But it's good to write about those you admire, and to explain why. . . . So now, inspired by the Senate, I'm going to do some more of it about Slade. . . .

He has been famous in his 18 years in the Senate for several things, one being that he often called influential columnists, friends, and political operatives to lobby them in support of important pieces of literature. He is a voracious and possibly compulsive reader of novels and history. . . .

I want to say he is unusual for a political figure but actually he is unusual, period: a genuine intellectual who lives in the world of ideas and yet a person who is simply delighted to be alive. Everything he does is so much fun. This sounds corny, and sometimes is, but every stranger he meets is interesting and says the smartest things. Every hockey game yields up fascinating glimpses into his athletic young niece's character. His constituents, especially the recent immigrants, are simply the most brilliant and hardworking people in the world. And his wife just said the most amazingly on-target thing about Al Gore, would you like to hear it?

He has zest. I have simply never known anyone who enjoys life as much as he does. . . . Among political figures, rarely have shrewdness and idealism been so intertwined. His career has been marked by the pursuit of progress within a framework of politics as the art of the possible, as they used to say. He has a conservative's insights and a moderate's instincts. . . .

The bad news is all that capacity for work and wisdom has been removed from the Senate, where it did a lot of good. The good news is that a new administration is about to begin, with many leadership appointments yet to be made. Trent Lott's loss could be President-elect Bush's gain. The new administration will need respected nominees who will get a fair hearing in the evenly split Senate. "Slade was not just a member of the club, Slade was an admired member," Mr. Lott told me. "I think he would be overwhelmingly favorably received for any position. Solicitor general—he's got the demeanor, the experience. He could be an attorney general, a Supreme Court justice."

Maybe that's what they were saying Thursday morning and afternoon in the Senate.[4]

If that's what they were saying, Bush and his transition team weren't listening.

40 | Commissioner Gorton

S LADE GORTON IS A PLUPERFECT EXAMPLE of how wrong F. Scott Fitzgerald was when he famously observed, "There are no second acts in American lives." His name was floated for attorney general, secretary of the Interior or secretary of Energy in the Bush cabinet. Next to AG, the job he wanted was solicitor general. Arguing government cases before the Supreme Court was right up his alley. The solicitor general also plays a key role in selecting federal judges. "Palpably ill at ease with self-promotion," Gorton met with Vice President Cheney and talked with John Ashcroft, the attorney-general designate. The job went to Bush's campaign attorney, Ted Olson, who had been in the trenches in Florida.[1]

Ashcroft's appointment as AG—widely seen as a sop to the GOP's right wing—was particularly galling to Gorton. "Among Senate Republicans, Ashcroft was considered an intellectual lightweight," especially compared to Gorton, a top-rank lawyer who had argued 14 cases before the U.S. Supreme Court.[2]

Forty-nine Senate Republicans urged Bush to nominate Gorton to the Ninth Circuit Court of Appeals or the appellate court in the District of Columbia. The lone holdout was McCain, who declined to sign the letter because tribal sovereignty cases in the West would be on the Ninth Circuit's docket. He said he might change his mind if the nomination were to the D.C. court. The tribes had a conniption fit over the notion of Gorton on the federal bench.[3]

Despite his early endorsement of Bush, Gorton's candidacy for a seat on the Ninth Circuit apparently was never seriously considered by Alberto Gonzales, Bush's counsel. He had three strikes against him for any plum job: His intellectual feistiness; his friendship with Trent Lott, also viewed by the White House as too independent, and his age. At 73, Gorton was a remarkable specimen of physical and intellectual vitality, but the administration wanted to install young conservatives. Some said Bush and Karl Rove were sore because Gore carried Washington State.

That clearly carried no weight. Several cabinet appointees who faced contentious confirmation hearings were from states Bush lost.[4]

"I was very lucky they didn't give me one of those cabinet jobs," Gorton says. "Any one of them would have been over after four years because Bush replaced most of his cabinet in his second term. It would have been prestigious but very, very frustrating and it would have cost me some of the most interesting opportunities I ever had."

GORTON JOINED a leading Seattle law firm, Preston, Gates & Ellis (now K&L Gates), where his talents as lawyer, legislator and lobbyist would produce many billable hours, not just add luster to the letterhead. Preston, Gates also maintained an office in D.C., where Gorton would work a few days a month. On the side, he hooked up with ex-aides Tony Williams, J. Vander Stoep and Nina Nguyen, who had founded a bicoastal consulting firm, Washington² Advocates. Seattle City Light and the state's Public Utility Districts were first in line for Gorton's "strategic and tactical advice" to defend their access to low-cost federal power.[5]

He was re-engaged in civic life practically before the movers left, joining Jim Ellis on a committee reviewing Sound Transit's troubled light-rail project. The Forward Thrust program championed by Ellis and Gorton included rapid transit. When the bond issue to finance light rail failed at the polls, it cost the region billions in federal matching money. Now, some 30 years down the road, the project was three years behind schedule and $1 billion over budget, despite the federal money Gorton had secured for it as a senator. Project planners faced an array of obstacles, including topography, tunneling, new safety rules and neighborhood concerns about intrusiveness and eminent domain. It would be worth all the trouble, Gorton said, recalling a trip on the system Atlanta built with the federal money that could have been Seattle's. "It was a wonderful ride. My strong feeling is that for this community to abandon light rail would be suicide . . . To run this city with buses only seems to me the height of foolishness."[6]

Soon he was popping up everywhere, headlining fundraisers, writing guest editorials, campaigning for progressive projects. He joined the opposition to initiative guru Tim Eyman's statewide ballot measure to limit property taxes, saying it was no time to be cutting back on support for law enforcement. (Eyman won big.)

In a piece for the P-I's editorial page, Gorton and his favorite Democrat, Governor Gary Locke, backed a plan to require out-of-state online retailers to collect sales taxes. Besides eroding state revenues, "remote sales also pose a fundamental fairness issue," they wrote. "Why should merchants on Main Street be required to collect sales taxes while online merchants are not?" Then they hit the road to promote a referendum on the 2002 ballot to boost the gas tax by 9 cents to fund highway projects, mass transit and ferries. "This is roads, not government," Gorton emphasized. "The future of the state in terms of its economic vitality, safety of its highways and the lifestyle we live depends on our willingness to make the investments we've ignored over the years." (Sixty-two percent were unwilling. But the 2003 Legislature adopted the "nickel" package, upping the gas tax by 5 cents to finance congestion-relief projects.)[7]

WITH HIS ANALYTICAL MIND and half century in politics, Gorton was on the A-list for commissions, boards and think tanks. Howard Baker recruited him for an important project sponsored by the University of Virginia's Miller Center of Public Affairs: a commission to study what lessons could be learned from the fiasco in Florida, where the White House was hanging on chads for weeks before Bush won the Supreme Court and graduated from the Electoral College. Gerald Ford and Jimmy Carter were the honorary co-chairmen; Gorton and Kathleen Sullivan, dean of the Stanford Law School, vice chairmen. Other members included Daniel Patrick Moynihan, Leon Panetta, Bill Richardson, former attorney general Griffin Bell, Slade's friend Rudy Boschwitz and John Seigenthaler, the noted newspaperman.

The commission's director was Philip Zelikow, who managed the Miller Center. An academic who was also a lawyer, historian and former National Security Council aide, Zelikow "was known to be indefatigable, able to go without sleep for days, surviving on whatever was available from the nearest vending machine." A debate champion in college, he was also known for not suffering fools gladly. If that sounds like someone Gorton would like a lot, you've been paying attention. He was "wowed by Zelikow's intelligence, his writing skills, and his all-important ability to meet a deadline." Zelikow, in turn, found Gorton a kindred intellectual soul who was also dispassionate.[8]

Major bones of contention in Florida were late-arriving military ballots and the provisional ballots issued to voters who showed up at the wrong polling place or whose status seemed otherwise questionable. Washington State also used provisional ballots as a safety net to ensure no voter was disenfranchised. Gorton told the commission that provisional ballots from college students helped cost him his seat in the Senate. "But I am for it, and I think we ought to recommend it to the whole country." It got everyone's attention, Zelikow says. "It was public spiritedness of a rare kind."[9]

The commission did recommend it to the whole country. It also endorsed making voting easier for members of the military and other citizens living overseas, as well as the restoration of voting rights to felons who had served their sentences. Election Day should be designated a national holiday, the commission said, a "civic day" of participatory democracy. It urged Congress to appropriate matching funds to help states upgrade their registration systems and voting equipment. It asked the media to hold off reporting results until polls were closed across the country. The commission endorsed the adoption of computerized registration lists and uniform standards for vote counting and recounting. One of the report's underlying themes, however, was that state-by-state election reform was preferable to a larger federal role.[10]*

The commission's report was laced with Zelikow. His reputation for abrasiveness had preceded him, but Gorton was impressed by his persuasive diplomacy. "He did a marvelous job of deferring to everyone but leading the commission in the direction that he wanted."[11]

After Lott appointed him to the 9/11 Commission, the first thing Gorton did was call Tom Kean and Lee Hamilton, its chairman and vice-chairman. "Your executive director has to be Philip Zelikow," Gorton said. "He is absolutely the smartest guy around."

---

* Bush signed the Help America Vote Act in the fall of 2002. It created the U.S. Election Assistance Commission and authorized $3 billion in grants to the states. Funds were earmarked to buy out antiquated punch-card and lever voting machines. Statewide voter registration databases were mandated, together with provisional ballots nationwide.

41 | Confrontation and Consensus

A HMED RESSAM, A 32-YEAR-OLD ALGERIAN MUSLIM, was at the wheel of the last car off the ferry from Victoria, B.C. It was 5:45 p.m. on December 14, 1999. "Where are you going?" said Diana Dean, one of the U.S. Customs inspectors at Port Angeles on the Washington side of the Strait of Juan de Fuca. Ressam was sweaty-faced and jittery. When she asked him more questions, he started rummaging in the console. "The minute the hands disappear," Dean says, "you get nervous."[1]

She told him to get out of the car, a dark green Chrysler from a rental agency. Hidden in the spare-tire well inspectors found 10 plastic bags filled with white powder. Ressam fled into the drizzly dark, bouncing off startled pedestrians and cars before he was finally tackled and cuffed. On further inspection, the trunk also yielded several black plastic boxes containing watches wired to circuit boards, as well as bottles and jars filled with chemicals. The powder wasn't drugs, as they had surmised. It was urea fertilizer and sulfates. Ressam was an al-Qaida foot soldier, headed to California. His goal was to bomb a busy passenger concourse at Los Angeles International Airport at the dawn of the new millennium. But nobody realized that for nearly a year. Seattle's mayor canceled the New Year's Eve gala at Seattle Center, fearing the Space Needle was a terrorist target.[2]

The scheme—foiled by chance and Diana Dean's inquiring mind—prompted heightened security and an outbreak of intelligence sharing. The FBI, CIA, Justice Department and national security operatives at the White House were actually talking to one another and passing along terrorist information to police departments and airport managers. The FBI's new attitude was particularly remarkable because at other trying times it had shared practically nothing. The fear that the dawn of the 21st Century would cause the mother of all computer crashes—the "Y2K"

bug—contributed to the epidemic of comity. Soon, however, they retreated to their fiefdoms and reverted to form. Counterterrorism went
back to being a secret preserve. "But the experience showed that the government was capable of mobilizing itself for an alert against terrorism,"
the 9/11 Commission would conclude. "Everyone knew not only of an abstract threat but of at least one terrorist who had been arrested *in the
United States*. Terrorism had a face—that of Ahmed Ressam—and Americans from Vermont to Southern California went on the watch for his
like."[3]

Convicted in the spring of 2001, Ressam faced a life sentence unless
he cooperated. He told how he was recruited and trained and revealed
there were al-Qaida sleeper cells in the U.S. and Canada. He knew more,
however, than he was asked about.

President Bush's briefing book at his Texas ranch on August 6, 2001,
included a report headlined "Bin Ladin Determined to Strike in U.S."
Thirty-six days later nearly 3,000 people died in hideous tangles of
twisted steel and crushed walls. Clinton and Bush administration officials would argue over who had taken the terrorist threat more seriously
and whether either administration did enough to try and prevent what
happened when all hell broke loose on Sept. 11, 2001.[4]

Helping uncover the truth would be the most important assignment of
Gorton's life.

GORTON AND JAMIE GORELICK, a former deputy attorney general in the
Clinton Administration, came to the 9/11 Commission with misconcep-
tions about one another. She expected him to be "reliably conservative"
and he figured she would be "a really partisan Democrat." Two astute legal tacticians quickly realized how much they had in common. "Jamie's
goal was the same as mine: The commission was vital to America's safety,
and we both wanted to get it right." An honors graduate of Radcliffe and
Harvard Law School, the only woman on the commission was collegial
but definitely not compliant. Gorton was impressed when she held her
own against the strong-willed Zelikow. Long before their work was done,
Zelikow concluded that Gorelick was helping Gorton set the bipartisan
bar for conscientious intensity. They would wield major influence on the
commission's final report.

Invariably working with Gorelick, Gorton was the commission's consensus builder. In the middle of a particularly difficult meeting he would
jot down language that ended up serving as the commission's compromise position. "Time and again, he was able to bridge disagreements and

divisions," according to Tom Kean and Lee Hamilton, the chairman and vice chairman.[5]

Of the friendships forged by the commission, none were closer than Gorton and Gorelick. Bob Kerrey was already an old friend from the Senate—someone Slade respected enormously. Gorton relished the moments—frequent—when Kerrey was deliciously blunt. Told that the Federal Aviation Administration's point man for a teleconference on September 11 had zero experience with hijacking situations, Kerrey demanded, "What the hell is going on that you would do such a thing?"[6]

Lee Hamilton, a personable Indiana Democrat who had spent 34 years in Congress, immediately recognized Gorton as a key player. Kean, a former two-term New Jersey governor, also got along well with the Democrats on the commission. "Tom Kean is one of the world's nicest people," Gorton says. "Nobody ever wanted to disappoint him."

Early on, the commission set out to examine the performance of the FAA and the North American Aerospace Defense Command. What security measures were in place at airports? What happened after air traffic controllers lost cockpit contact with the four hijacked jetliners on 9/11? How quickly did NORAD scramble fighters? The commission's request for disclosure of tapes and transcripts met with foot-dragging at the FAA, which Gorton already believed deserved "the shameful distinction of being the most culpable for the attacks." A frequent flyer for 25 years, Gorton recoiled in horror as the commissioners inspected a folding blade—nearly four inches of razor-sharp forged steel—that FAA regulations allowed passengers to carry aboard a plane. He also found it unbelievable that before 9/11 the agency's security chief was unaware that the State Department had a terrorist watch list. As a former Air Force colonel, Gorton was also infuriated with NORAD, which had engaged in butt-covering PR, even outright lies, over its indecisive response to the hijackings. "[T]hey are responsible for a lot of the conspiracy theories that we have to deal with to this day," he said of the generals.[7]

The FAA's intransigence convinced several commissioners they ought to subpoena every agency of the Executive Branch. Gorton counseled they should save their hand grenades. They decided to subpoena the FAA and issue a stern warning that everyone else could expect the same absent "full compliance" with the commission's requests for documents.[8]

After months of haggling to gain access to the Presidential Daily Briefs prepared by the CIA—a trove spanning the Clinton and Bush administrations—the commission had another tense meeting in the fall of 2003. The White House was unwilling to let the entire commission review the memos. The news didn't go down well, but they finally settled on a review team: Kean and Hamilton, with Gorelick and Zelikow doing the heavy lifting. "By that time most of the other Republicans also had full confidence that Jamie would do things right," Gorton recalls, emphasizing that consensus was crucial to the credibility of the commission. "We never had a vote that was partisan—that was tied 5 to 5. In fact, you could count on one hand the number of times we voted at all. We worked out the difficult questions."9

It's easy to see why Gorton and Gorelick were so simpatico. She even talks like him, reeling off measured compound sentences: "Slade would look at a problem that divided the commission and look for ways we could find common ground. Fortunately for me, the person to whom he turned, because I am similar in approach, was me. Working through issues like that, seeing how another person's mind works, watching his dedication to taking the facts wherever they might go, was a remarkable experience for me and forged an unbreakable bond between the two of us." That bond—and Gorton's disdain for duplicity—led to one of the commission's most dramatic moments.

ATTORNEY GENERAL JOHN ASHCROFT was convinced the commission was plotting to portray him as lackadaisical about al-Qaida. His staff scrambled for evidence that the Justice Department had done due diligence prior to the terrorist attacks. Plopping down a sheaf of classified internal memos from Gorelick's tenure at the department, they told Ashcroft he could make a case that America's guard was down because of her.

"Had I known a terrorist attack on the United States was imminent in 2001, I would have unloaded our full arsenal of weaponry against it, despite the inevitable criticism," Ashcroft assured the commission on April 13, 2004. "The simple fact of September 11th is this: We did not know an attack was coming because for nearly a decade our government had blinded itself to its enemies. Our agents were isolated by government-imposed walls, handcuffed by government-imposed restrictions, and starved for basic information technology. The old national intelligence system in place on September 11th was destined to fail."10

Ashcroft charged that a 1995 memo had imposed evidence rules in terrorism cases that amounted to the "single greatest structural cause for September 11th." It constructed "a wall that segregated or separated criminal investigators and intelligence agents" and kept them from sharing evidence. "Government erected this wall; government buttressed this wall and—before September 11—government was blinded by this wall.

Somebody did make these rules. Somebody built this wall. . . . Full disclosure compels me to inform you that the author of this memorandum is a member of this commission."[11]

In truth, Gorelick's 1995 memo did little more than reiterate the Justice Department's longstanding policy on terrorism cases. "The first bricks of the so-called wall were put into place in the 1980s as a result of court orders intended to protect civil liberties," wrote Philip Shenon, the *New York Times* reporter who covered the commission. The "wall" was largely a legacy of the Watergate-era enemies list paranoia, a response to the danger of giving the FBI and CIA carte blanche to spy on American citizens. After Gorelick left the Justice Department, "the memo was widely misinterpreted by the FBI to bar almost all evidence sharing—but she was not its creator."[12]

Kerrey realized it was a setup when his BlackBerry began vibrating. As Ashcroft was somberly detailing how the Democrats had blood on their hands, e-mails were pouring in. "You traitor, you should be ashamed of yourself for having somebody like Gorelick on the 9/11 commission," one said. Ashcroft had greased the skids.[13]

They all knew the wall was made of straw. Zelikow and the staff had parsed the issue for the commission. Gorton was shocked, however, that the Attorney General of the United States would stoop so low. Though they were never close friends in the Senate, "I had a high regard for Ashcroft's character. But this attack was unprincipled. I was astounded and infuriated. Jamie was frantic and clawing through her papers, trying to get ready to respond." Gorelick turned anxiously to commission staffers, asking them to dig out more documents. Slade was sitting next to her. He leaned over, tapped her arm and whispered, "Let me do this."[14]

The verbal dexterity that so many Democrats have denounced as arrogance was now unleashed on a conservative Republican, with Gorton saying in essence, "Mr. Ashcroft, why didn't *you* tear down this wall?" He displayed a memo from Ashcroft's top deputy. Dated August 6, 2001—one month before the terrorist attacks—it informed Ashcroft that "the 1995 procedures" remained in effect. "If that wall was so disabling," Gorton asked, "why was it not destroyed" during the eight months before 9/11 that Ashcroft was running the Justice Department?[15]

Ashcroft bobbed and weaved, saying the memo was "a step in the direction of lowering the wall . . ." When Gorton observed that the steps seemed insignificant, Ashcroft replied, "I missed your question, commissioner."[16]

Despite his fumbling performance, Ashcroft was hailed by Republican lawmakers and *The Wall Street Journal's* editorial page, as well as Rush

Limbaugh and other conservative firebrands. They all demanded Gorelick's resignation. There were death threats against her and members of her family. The other commissioners, Republicans and Democrats alike, were outraged and unified. "Jamie Gorelick ended up with nine big brothers," Gorton says. "John Ashcroft did us a huge favor in trying to break us up."[17]

Gorton, in demand as a pithy guest, denounced Ashcroft on several nightly news shows. He had been telling Andy Card, Bush's chief of staff, that the White House was its own worst enemy. "When push came to shove we'd go to the big newspapers and they would excoriate the president for not cooperating with us. Then he'd give us what we wanted. But Bush got a reputation for stonewalling. The problem was all Alberto Gonzales." Bush's ham-handed counsel had seriously compromised the president's reputation. "We kept asking to talk with the president about 9/11. First it was 'No.' Finally, 'OK, yes. The chairman and the vice-chairman can come and talk to him for 15 minutes.' We applied more pressure and the White House finally grudgingly agreed that we could all come."

The 9/11 Commission: Back row, from left, Richard Ben-Veniste, John F. Lehman, Timothy J. Roemer, James R. Thompson, Bob Kerrey, Gorton; front row, from left: Fred Fielding, Lee Hamilton, Tom Kean, Jamie Gorelick. *9/11 Commission, AE/WPPi.com*

IT HAD BEEN TWO WEEKS since Ashcroft confronted the commission with Gorelick's alleged complicity in undermining the war on terror. On the day before the commission was set to interview the president and vice president, Ashcroft posted more memos on the Justice Department's Web site, including some that hadn't been shared with the commission. That was too much for even the preternaturally patient Kean. The chairman told Card he was mad as hell.

When the commission arrived at the White House, Bush met privately with Kean and Hamilton. Straightaway he apologized for Ashcroft's attacks on Gorelick, especially the new batch of memos. When the other eight members joined them in the Oval Office, Bush repeated his apology. "Jamie, this shouldn't have happened," the president told her earnestly. Bush and his brain trust had finally wised up. They had opposed creating the 9/11 Commission, fearing it might portray him as a bungler. That was now water over the dam. Creating a hostile commission was the last thing they needed in the middle of a re-election campaign.[18]

Bush could be terrific one-on-one. He came across as genuinely apologetic, eager to help. "I spent more time in the Oval Office on that one errand than I did in my entire 18 years in the United States Senate," Gorton says. "Bush answered every question. In fact, two commissioners had to leave for other appointments because the meeting went so long. What I found most amusing was that the tigers on the commission turned into pussy cats when they were sitting in the Oval Office."

It was a bravura performance, with political expediency for an encore. Bush had never been close to Ashcroft, so, as they say in Texas, he took him to the woodshed. From then on Ashcroft's days were numbered.

Gorton viewed Ashcroft's departure with mixed emotions. The attorney general had been a hero to some for refusing to reauthorize a warrantless domestic spying program that the Justice Department had determined was illegal. (Gonzales and Card brought the papers to Ashcroft's hospital room while he lay ill in the winter of 2004. Ashcroft's deputy got there first, sirens blaring on his police escort.)[19]

After Ashcroft was "unceremoniously canned at the end of the first Bush Administration," Gorton says, Bush appointed "a much worse attorney general as a result—Alberto Gonzales. I could have done that job with my eyes closed better than either of those people did."

WHEN DONALD RUMSFELD, Bush's alternately charming and imperious secretary of defense, appeared before the commission on March 23, 2004, he knew full well that Gorton and Kerrey were particularly immune to what a former chairman of the Joint Chiefs of Staff characterized as the brilliant bureaucratic BS he shoveled out to "stay afloat" when he was challenged or proven wrong.[20]

Clearly well prepared, Rumsfeld began by earnestly praising the commission's diligence. He also empathized with the difficulty of its mission. It was his as well, he said. "You've been asked to try to connect the dots after the fact, to examine events leading up to September 11th and to consider what lessons, if any, might be taken from that experience that could prevent future dangers. It isn't an easy assignment. . . . Our task is to connect the dots not after the fact but before the fact, to try to stop attacks before they happen. That must be done without the benefit of hindsight, hearings, briefings or testimony. Another attack on our people will be attempted. We can't know where, or when, or by what technique. That reality drives those of us in government to ask the tough questions: When and how might that attack be attempted and what will we need to have done, today and every day before the attack, to prepare for it and to, if possible, to prevent it?"

Having heard Gorton remark to William Cohen, Clinton's second-term secretary of defense, that he found "actionable intelligence" to be "a very troubling two-word phrase," Rumsfeld said, "I knew of no intelligence during the six-plus months leading up to September 11th that indicated terrorists would hijack commercial airliners, use them as missiles to fly into the Pentagon or the World Trade Center towers."

Kerrey and Gorton were poised to probe.

"Mr. Secretary," said Kerrey, "you're well-known as somebody who thinks about all kinds of terrible possibilities that might happen that nobody else is thinking about. I mean, that's what you do so well when you're going into a difficult situation. I mean, it seems to me that a declaration of war, either by President Clinton or by President Bush, prior to 9/11 would have mobilized the government in a way that at least would have reduced substantially the possibility that 9/11 would have happened. Do you agree or not?"

"Possibly. Let me put it that way. The problem with it—it sounds good the way you said it. I try to put myself in other people's shoes. And try to put yourself in the shoes of a new administration that had just arrived. And time had passed. We were in the process of bringing people on board. And the president said he wanted a new policy for counter-terrorism. . . ."

Gorton picked up where Kerrey left off, noting that in 1998 Osama bin Laden had declared an Islamic holy war—jihad—against the Jews and their allies in the West. American embassies in Kenya and Tanzania were bombed that summer. Next came the millennium plot, inadvertently foiled at Port Angeles. The deadly attack in the fall of 2000 on the *USS Cole*, a Navy destroyer deployed to Yemen, was a full-fledged al-Qaida operation that galvanized bin Laden's recruitment efforts. With multiple wakeup calls, why didn't the Bush Administration have a more aggressive counterterrorism strategy?

Gorton and Bob Kerrey listen to testimony from National Security Adviser Condoleezza Rice at a 9/11 Commission hearing on April 8, 2004, in Washington, D.C. *AP Photo/Charles Dharapak*

" . . . You say nothing was done. A great deal was done," Rumsfeld insisted. "The Cole Commission did a good job. They made a whole series of recommendations and the Department of Defense implemented those recommendations. In my view, that is not nothing. . . . And the other thing that was happening is that the policy was being developed to deal with al-Qaida and the country that was harboring them. . . ."

Gorton said the commission's understanding was that the policy had three parts. "First, there would be one more diplomatic attempt with the Taliban to see if they would give up Osama bin Laden. Second, we would begin to arm the Northern Alliance and various tribes in Afghanistan to stir up trouble there and hope that perhaps they could capture Osama bin Laden. And third, if those didn't work, there would be a military response that would be substantial, much more than . . . lobbing cruise missiles into the desert. But as we understand it, this was seen as a three-year program, if we had to go to the third stage. My question is, Given World Trade Center one, given the embassy bombings, given the millennium plot, given the *Cole*, given the declaration of war by Osama bin Laden, what made you think that we had the luxury of that much time—even seven months, much less three years, before we could cure this particular problem?"

"Well, let me answer two ways," Rumsfeld said. "Number one, I didn't come up with the three years. I tend to scrupulously avoid predicting that I am smart enough to know how long something's going to take because I know I don't know. Where that number came from, I don't know. In fact, dealing with the terrorism threat is going to take a lot longer than three years. . . . And the other concern we had was that we had precious little information about the groups in Afghanistan. . . .And the part you left out was that we decided—*I decided*, the president decided, everyone decided—quite early that we had to put U.S. forces in that country. And that was not a part of that plan. That was something that came along after September 11th."

"Well, Mr. Secretary, that's a good answer. But it isn't an answer to the question that I asked you," Gorton said. "The question that I asked you was: What made you think even when you took over and got these first briefings, given the history of al-Qaida and its successful attacks on Americans that we had the luxury of even seven months before we could make any kind of response, much less three years?"

"And my answer was on point," Rumsfeld bristled. "I said I didn't come up with three years, and I can't defend that number. I don't know where that came from. With respect to seven months, I've answered. My testimony today lays out what was done during that period. Do you have—you phrase it, do you have the luxury of seven months? In reflecting on what happened on September 11th, the question is, obviously, the Good Lord willing, things would have happened prior to that that could have stopped it. But something to have stopped that would have had to happen months and months and months beforehand, not five minutes or not one month or two months or three months. And the counter argument, it seems to me, is do you have the luxury of doing what was done before and simply just heaving some cruise missiles into the thing and not doing it right? I don't know. We thought not. It's a judgment."[21]

The commission concluded that Rumsfeld's prepared statement offered some major truths. "Even if bin Laden had been captured or killed in the weeks before September 11th," Rumsfeld submitted, "no one I know believes that it would necessarily have prevented September 11th. Killing bin Laden would not have removed al-Qaida's sanctuary in Afghanistan. Moreover, the sleeper cells that flew the aircraft into the World Trade Towers and the Pentagon were already in the United States months before the attack. Indeed, if actionable intelligence had appeared—which it did not—9/11 would likely still have happened. And ironically, much of the world would likely have called the September 11th attack an al-Qaida retaliation for the U.S. provocation of capturing or killing bin Laden."

Was there actionable intelligence much earlier? Maybe. Maybe not. But Gorton would disgustedly conclude that the Bush White House thought it had "all the time in the world" to deal with al-Qaida, as if Osama bin Laden and his wily operatives were just "a bunch of people off in a cave." While "hindsight is always 20-20," Gorton said, you didn't need glasses to see "they screwed up." Nothing Gorton was doing or saying endeared him to the White House. As if he cared.[22]

RICHARD A. CLARKE, the counter-terrorism czar for the first Bush and Clinton, was retained by George W. Bush but with diminished authority and access. He placed much of the blame for that on Zelikow, who had been a key member of Bush's transition team. Clarke departed in 2003 to write a scathing memoir. Opening fire on CBS' *60 Minutes*, he asserted that the Bush administration turned a deaf ear to the terrorist threat, then launched a half-baked war with Iraq just to show the colors. That Zelikow, a friend of Condoleezza Rice, ended up as staff director of the 9/11 Commission only underscored Clarke's belief that its report would be a whitewash of the Bush administration's ineptitude. Clarke's testimony before the 9/11 Commission, one day after Rumsfeld's appearance, was high drama.

"I welcome these hearings because of the opportunity they provide to the American people to better understand why the tragedy of 9/11 happened and what we must do to prevent a reoccurrence," Clarke began. "I also welcome the hearings because it is finally a forum where I can apologize to the loved ones of the victims of 9/11. To them who are here in the room; to those who are watching on television, your government failed you. Those entrusted with protecting you failed you. And I failed you. We tried hard, but that doesn't matter because we failed. And for that failure, I would ask, once all the facts are out, for your understanding and for your forgiveness. With that, Mr. Chairman, I'll be glad to take your questions."[23]

At first there was stunned silence, Shenon writes. Some of the 9/11 family members were still returning from lunch, but as the words sank in some in the audience gasped; others sobbed. No one of any importance had ever apologized to them. Clarke's critics called it political theater.[24]

When it was his turn, Gorton politely but unapologetically cut to the chase. If your recommendations had been implemented, he asked Clarke, "is there the remotest chance that it would have prevented 9/11?

"No."

Gorton followed up: "It just would have allowed our response, after 9/11, to be perhaps a little bit faster?"

"Well, the response would have begun before 9/11," said Clarke.

"Yes, but there was no recommendation, on your part or anyone else's part, that we declare war and attempt to invade Afghanistan prior to 9/11?"

"That's right."[25]

Gorton had deftly "punctured the political balloon," Zelikow said. He refocused the hearing on trying to determine what could have been done—*what could be done*—to combat a disciplined, fanatical enemy that views America as the "head of the snake," the font of all evil. "I was glad I had Slade in my foxhole," Zelikow said. "He was statesmanlike, but he was savvy, too."[26]

RELISHING 12-HOUR DAYS, Gorton was always well-prepared for the hearings and intensely interested in the staff's research. In the space of 17 months, the commission sorted through two million documents, interviewed more than a thousand people in 10 countries and heard 160 witnesses during 19 days of hearings.

"He's analytical rather than polemical," Zelikow observes. "The way he handled the questioning of Clarke was so deft. It didn't involve any ad hominem attacks. He was setting a standard that we're going to really take this seriously in a factual way and not just get caught up in political name-calling."

Gorton's real influence, however, was behind the scenes, according to Kean, Hamilton, Gorelick and Zelikow, who sums it up like this: "Basically, in a lot of small ways, Slade elevated the quality of the internal work of the commission. . . .The commission was in some ways foreseen to be a likely failure. It was created under highly political circumstances, and the commissioners—five Republicans and five Democrats—were selected in a highly political process. You had a powerful chair and vice chair and a powerful staff, but it would have broken apart if you'd had a really fractious, polarized tone among the commissioners. The situation was so intense that there were constant dangers of that. Slade was a critical person in mitigating and heading off that danger. These are the qualities that end up deciding whether or not political institutions succeed. The essence of political institutions—the reason they are called political institutions—is they are places where power is shared. And whenever power is shared there is friction. . . . So, the challenge to make a political institution work is to find norms and ways of doing business that manage that natural and even healthy friction in productive ways. That's where the qualities of someone like Slade Gorton turn out to make the difference between success and failure. Slade raised the level of everyone's game."

The difference between success and failure in this case is a life-or-death issue. Yet dealing with the challenge of an enemy who embraces martyrdom and rationalizes mass murder "as righteous defense of an embattled faith" is a terrible dilemma for a free society with a short attention span. It demands to be safe but bristles at full-body scanners and wants its boys back home.[27]

42 | The Nature of the Enemy

Pogo, THE COMIC STRIP POSSUM, famously observed, "We have met the enemy and he is us." The commission concluded that 9/11, like Pearl Harbor, stemmed in large part from bureaucratic inertia, compounded by politics. When Bill Clinton gave his successor a final briefing on national security issues just before leaving office, he recalls saying, "One of the great regrets of my presidency is that I didn't get him (bin Laden) for you, because I tried to."

After the attack on the *USS Cole*, ambiguous reports about al-Qaida's culpability caused indecision among the Pentagon, the State Department, the FBI and CIA. Should the U.S. give an ultimatum to the Taliban to cough up bin Laden or else? And what about collateral damage that might further inflame the Islamic world? Absent actionable intelligence—that phrase punctuates everything—the lame-duck president was worried about being accused of launching "wag the dog" air strikes in Afghanistan to try and help elect his vice president.[1]

The protracted battle for the White House complicated the transition to a new administration and created a dangerous period of vulnerability, Gorton and Gorelick wrote later. "As always, the crowd coming in was dismissive of the concerns of the crowd going out." With nominations to some key posts delayed, Bush took too long to set priorities for his national-security team. By then the attack on the *Cole* was yesterday's news. They decided to regroup and push ahead with a new plan. It was a rational political decision, Gorton says, "but that guy in the cave in Afghanistan is thinking, 'What a bunch of paper tigers! We kill 17 sailors and almost sink one of their ships and they don't even shoot a rocket over here.'"[2]

Gorton believes the decision to not follow up forcefully on the attack on the *Cole* led directly to 9/11, a view shared by Bob Kerrey and John Lehman, the former Navy secretary who served on the commission. "Al-Qaida didn't think we'd react to 9/11," Gorton says. "They must have thought we'd just find somebody and put him on trial in New York City after six or seven years. Can't you hear Bin Laden and his lieutenants saying,

'What a wonderful world we live in! We can do whatever we want to do to the Great Satan!'"

GEORGE TENET, THE DIRECTOR of Central Intelligence during Clinton's second term and most of Bush's first, told the commission "the system was blinking red" in the Intelligence Community in July of 2001. Yet some at the Pentagon and White House surmised that the threats might be merely al-Qaida deception. There were in fact few specifics. Some 9/11 family members pointed to the August 6 Presidential Daily Brief warning that bin Laden was determined to strike in the U.S. There's the smoking gun, they said. The brief went on, however, to assure the president that the FBI was conducting 70 "full field" investigations throughout the nation. Bush recollected that Rice told him there was no actionable intelligence of a domestic threat.[3]

The September 11 attacks fell into a void between the foreign and domestic intelligence agencies of an unwieldy government, the 9/11 Commission concluded. No one was looking for a foreign threat to domestic targets from al-Qaida foot soldiers who had infiltrated into the United States. But here they were, busy learning how to fly Boeing 767s and practicing how to butcher anyone who tried to intervene. "The terrorists exploited deep institutional failings within our government." Gorton vividly recalls a CIA supervisor telling the commissioners that no one was looking at the bigger picture. "No analytic work foresaw the lightning that could connect the thundercloud to the ground."[4]

Besides a failure to communicate, Gorton says 9/11 was caused by a dearth of something that's second nature to Bill Gates and Steve Jobs: Imagination. The blame really had no one face or handful of faces. It was a systemic "failure of imagination," as Kean and Hamilton put it. The lesson was as old as December 7, 1941, when "in the face of a clear warning, alert measures bowed to routine," one contemporary historian wrote.[5]

What if al-Qaida decided to launch latter-day kamikaze attacks, with suicide pilots at the controls of huge jetliners instead of single-engine Mitsubishi Zeros? The FBI had inklings in July of 2001 that terrorists were interested in U.S. flight schools. That August, FBI and INS agents arrested an al-Qaida operative in Minnesota. Zacarias Moussaoui had Boeing 747 flight manuals and a flight simulator program for his laptop. Intense publicity surrounding his arrest might have disrupted plans for the attack, according to Zelikow and Gorton. But no one connected the dots. Institutionalizing the exercise of imagination requires breaking down fiefdoms and creating creative teams able to think like the enemy. Not only does intelligence win wars, it can prevent wars. Information must be collated and shared, telltale indicators developed and monitored. What the counterintelligence community really needs, Gorton says, is a few Tom Clancys.[6]

Gorton barely suppressed a shudder when the commission learned that Khalid Sheikh Mohammad, the mastermind of 9/11, had even more ambitious plans. The 76-story Bank of America Tower in downtown Seattle, where some 5,000 worked, was one of the original targets, together with a skyscraper in L.A., nuclear plants, the White House or the Capitol. Mohammad suggested simultaneously hijacking 10 planes. Bin Laden authorized the scaled-down mission.[7]

A LIFELONG STUDENT OF HISTORY, Gorton had strong feelings about defining "the nature of the enemy." Kerrey was of the same mind. Gorton drafted an overview and worked with Kerrey to polish it. For the chapter outlining a global strategy to combat terrorism, the commission voted unanimously to substitute their version for the language drafted by the staff. Kerrey and Gorton wrote:

> Because the Muslim world has fallen behind the West politically, economically and militarily for the past three centuries, and because few tolerant or secular Muslim democracies provide alternative models for the future, Bin Ladin's message finds receptive ears. It has attracted active support from thousands of disaffected young Muslims and resonates powerfully with a far larger number who do not actively support his methods. The resentment of America and the West is deep, even among leaders of relatively successful Muslim states.
>
> Tolerance, the rule of law, political and economic openness, the extension of greater opportunities to women—these cures must come from within Muslim societies themselves. The United States must support such developments. But this process is likely to be measured in decades, not years. . . .
>
> Islam is not the enemy. It is not synonymous with terror. Nor does Islam teach terror. America and its friends oppose a perversion of Islam, not the great world faith itself.[8]

To Gorton's great annoyance, Barack Obama—like Bush and Clinton before him—"keeps telling Muslims what true Islam believes in. Utter nonsense! We are not going to tell Muslims what Islam requires of them. They are going to have to do that themselves. This war is going to be over when the terrorists have created more problems for their co-religionists than they do for us. We can contribute to that struggle, but it has to be won internally, and the Muslim world's decline will never be reversed or even arrested as long as so much of Islam discriminates against the 50 percent of its population that is female. Education is a huge part of the war against terrorism."

OF ALL THE RECOMMENDATIONS made by the 9/11 Commission, none was more imperative than the admonition to make structural changes in intelligence gathering and sharing. To paraphrase the Peter Principle, in a huge government hierarchy every agency tends to protect its turf at the risk of incompetence.

The commission concluded that the job of Director of Central Intelligence should be scrapped. Downgraded was another way to put it. (George Tenet announced his resignation before the final report was released.) The commission believed it was impractical and counterproductive for the CIA chief to do double duty. He should be strictly an agency manager, reporting to a new supreme spymaster. The cabinet-level Director of National Intelligence would also oversee America's other intelligence-gathering agencies, including the FBI's National Security Branch, Homeland Security's threat analysts, the National Security Agency and the Defense Intelligence Agency.

The commission also called for a new National Counterterrorism Center to integrate information on terrorist threats. It was crucial for the new director to have real power, including budget and personnel authority. Otherwise, the outcome would be just another layer of bureaucracy. The turf wars would continue.

IT HAD BEEN A LONG HOT SUMMER. Literally and figuratively. With both national conventions imminent, the political atmosphere was supercharged as the commission's final report was released on July 22, 2004. Massachusetts Senator John Kerry, Bush's challenger, had been warning that the White House would try to spin the report to blame Democrats for the nation's intelligence snafus. The White House returned fire with its own flurry of e-mails to reporters and editorial writers.[9]

Flanked by Rumsfeld, Ashcroft and other administration notables, Bush gave the 9/11 report the full Rose Garden photo-op treatment. By executive order, he created the counterterrorism center, but balked at cabinet-level status for the new Director of National Intelligence. The director would have "significant input" but not the final say. Bush was also reluctant to hand over to the new office full operational control of the $40 billion annual intelligence budget. Rumsfeld had the president's ear on that score, Gorton says, and soon was telling Congress it was prudent to go slow.[10]

Democrats pounced. Kerry gave the report his "unequivocal endorsement," declaring, "If there is something that will make America safer, it should be done now, not tomorrow." *The Wall Street Journal* called it a "rush to czardom," suggesting the members of the commission make themselves scarce until after the election.[11]

With a runaway best-seller to help make its case, the commission had no such inclination. The 9/11 Commission Report—567 pages—sold more than a million copies in its first month on the market. Reviewers raved. "Distilling an enormous amount of information in plain language, with unerring pitch," said *Publishers Weekly*, "this multi-author document produces an absolutely compelling narrative. . . . Given what hangs in the balance, it is not a stretch to compare it to The Federalist Papers . . ." *Time* magazine called the report "one of the most riveting, disturbing and revealing accounts of crime, espionage and the inner workings of government ever written."[12]

"It's a remarkable achievement for any committee to produce readable writing," Gorton says proudly, let alone one with nearly 100 authors. They worked in drafts, consulted historians and literature professors; read passages aloud to make sure the narrative had pace; took pains to avoid dumbing down the details. The credit for the literary quality of the narrative largely belongs to Zelikow and Harvard Professor Ernest May, Gorton says, "but the entire commission went through it paragraph by paragraph three times or more to make sure we agreed with everything it said.

"Perhaps the most surprising and gratifying reaction was the dramatic shift in the attitude of 9/11 family member groups. They were critical from the beginning, first at the makeup of the commission, including my appointment to it. Their hostility and anxiety continued when several of the commissioners asked partisan questions in open hearings. They thought that we would whitewash Bush. They were astounded at the unanimous result and the thrust of our report. They became our fiercest defenders and our most effective advocates."

KEAN AND HAMILTON TESTIFIED at two-dozen congressional hearings while Gorton and the other commissioners fanned out to lobby lawmakers, appear on news shows and make speeches.

The sister of a firefighter who died on 9/11 was one of many family members who spoke out about the opponents. "There is a clear attempt afoot to marginalize the findings and recommendations of the commission," she wrote in a guest editorial. "I was horrified to hear one former FBI agent call the commission 'a traveling circus' in a television interview. . . . It is completely irresponsible to demean this essential and important work. . . .Congress must force federal agencies to make changes."[13]

John Warner, the Virginia Republican who headed the Senate Armed Services Committee, was a staunch defender of the Pentagon's intelligence prerogatives. He worried that the commission was out to reduce the secretary of defense to a "payroll clerk." Lieberman, McCain and Senator Susan Collins of Maine warned that terrorism was a real and present danger. Al-Qaida doubtless was busy planning its next attack and enjoying the woolgathering. It was time to get the lead out. "Nothing else we do is more important," Lieberman said.[14]

By the third anniversary of 9/11, Bush was offering concessions; ready to give the Director of National Intelligence "full budgetary authority" over most of the Intelligence Community yet still hedging his bets on whether the new spymaster should control all military intelligence-gathering.[15]

BUSH DEFEATED KERRY on the strength of Ohio's 20 electoral votes. Republicans solidified control of Congress, and the 9/11 Commission was confident it had the popular vote. Still, it took another month of jawboning—especially among reluctant Republicans in the House—to pass the Intelligence Reform and Terrorism Prevention Act. It cleared the House on December 7; the Senate a day later, and was quickly signed into law by Bush. Gorton and the other nine commissioners looked on. It was a day of somber satisfaction and optimism, Gorton recalls. A year later, however, as its final act, the commission issued a report card rating the response to its recommendations: Five F's, 12 D's, nine C's, 11 B's, two "incompletes" and one A minus (for "significant strides" against terrorist financing, although the State Department and Treasury were still engaged in "unhelpful turf battles"). Uncle Sam couldn't even make it to junior college with a grade-point average of 1.76. The F's included airline passenger prescreening. Bag and cargo screening got a D.[16]

In particular, little progress had been made on information sharing. The good news was that the harsh report card opened a lot of eyes in Congress—part of the commission's strategy. Gorton was hopeful that the new Counterterrorism Center would be the intelligence conduit America needs to help protect itself from such cunning and resourceful enemies. His 18 years in the Senate had impressed upon him the need for independent oversight of security issues. That was the message he brought to the Senate Republican Caucus, where his counsel was always welcomed whenever he was in town.

Now, however, he was needed on a new commission.

43 | Petroleum and Beyond

BRITISH PETROLEUM LAUNCHED a $200 million public-relations campaign in 2000 to style itself as "Beyond Petroleum." It emphasized, however, that its safety motto was still "No accidents. No harm to people and no damage to the environment."[1]

At BP's refinery in Texas City, Texas, a sobering safety study was released in January of 2005. While profits were soaring after rounds of cost-cutting, the plant's 2,000 workers had an "exceptional degree of fear" that a catastrophe could occur at any moment. Corporate culture prevented critical safety information from reaching the top levels of BP management. "Telling the managers what they want to hear, **that** gets rewarded," a worried worker told the auditors. "For example, one person who had cut costs, done a lot of Band-Aids with maintenance and had a quit-your-bellyaching attitude was rewarded in the last reorganization. . . . His replacement found that not a single pump was fit for service. . . ."[2]

On March 23, 2005, workers accidentally filled a tower with 138 feet of flammable liquid when $6\frac{1}{2}$ feet was the threshold of safety. "The window on the tower that the workers might have used to spot their mistake was so dirty that they couldn't see how much fluid was inside, and the gauge that was supposed to measure the height of the liquid wasn't designed to measure more than 10 feet. Some safety devices that should have sounded an alarm failed—others were ignored."[3]

A cloud of gas spewed from a containment drum next to the overfilled tower. It "sank to the ground in a clear fog, bending the air in wavy lines like the ones that settle on the horizon on a hot day. When the gas found a spark in an idling truck 25 feet away, it triggered an explosion so powerful that it shattered windows of nearby homes." Fifteen people died and more than 180 were injured.[4]

At the mandate of the U.S. Chemical Safety Board, BP funded an independent safety review. Former secretary of state James A. Baker III agreed to head the 11-member panel, promising it would "let the chips fall where they may."[5]

That Gorton knew Baker wouldn't have it any other way was the key reason he signed up immediately when the Houston attorney called. Other panelists included Skip Bowman, a retired admiral who had commanded the Navy's fleet of nuclear-powered vessels without an accident; Irv Rosenthal, a chemical industry safety expert; Paul Tebo, a widely respected retired DuPont executive, and Glenn Erwin, an up-from-the ranks petrochemical worker who headed his union's safety program.

BP had paid a $21 million fine to settle 300 federal safety violations and agreed to set aside $700 million for victims' compensation. The Baker panel's mission was not to investigate the Texas City blast. Rather, it would spend a year evaluating BP's corporate safety culture, visiting all five of the company's U.S. refineries, including Cherry Point near Bellingham.

Unwilling to come to Houston for an interview, British Petroleum's CEO, John Browne—that would be Lord Browne of Madingley to you—flew the commissioners and an equal number of their support staff to London first class and put them up in a posh hotel. "He spent a lot of money on us," Gorton says, "but it was probably one-ten-thousandth of one percent of BP's daily profits."

The interview began with a 30-minute monologue that reeked of arrogance. He was a small man, Gorton says, and he seemed to have a refined chip on his shoulder. If Browne actually wanted nothing less than the unvarnished truth you couldn't tell it from the way he responded to Erwin's questions. A plain-spoken guy with an accent Gorton describes as "from the deepest, hilliest part of the Ozarks," Erwin fixed Browne with a steely gaze. "I heard what you did," he said. "I'd like you to tell me *what you felt* when you learned that 15 people had been killed at one of your refineries." Browne proceeded to repeat practically everything he'd said in his opening statement, with not one word about how he felt. Erwin and Gorton exchanged incredulous glances. Sitting right behind them was David Sterling, a lawyer from Baker's firm. "A perfect Michael Dukakis answer," Sterling leaned forward to whisper. Gorton nearly burst out laughing. "That quip was perfection. Lord Browne left that meeting thinking he'd snowed us. We stood there and said, 'What an asshole!'"

THE BAKER PANEL and its staff interviewed more than 700 people, including refinery managers, front-line workers and union shop stewards. Published in 2007, its report focused on what the Department of Labor calls process safety, as opposed to personal safety. Avoiding slips, falls and forklift mishaps is different from preventing leaks, spills, metal fatigue, equipment malfunctions and overfilling a pressurized tower. Process safety is systemic. It focuses on design and engineering, thorough regular inspections, diligent maintenance, effective alarms and continuous training. Texas City was a process safety accident, the report said. Under no illusion that the problems were limited to BP, the panel urged the entire industry to take its recommendations to heart.[6]

BP's deadly error had been interpreting a significant improvement in personal safety rates as proof of vigilance. High turnover of plant managers made things worse, Gorton says. So did the emphasis on the bottom line. The neglect, tragically, was not benign. "BP has not demonstrated that it has effectively held executive management and line managers and supervisors, both at the corporate level and at the refinery level, accountable for process safety performance at its five U.S. refineries," the Baker report concluded. Browne promised to implement the panel's recommendations, saying, "BP gets it, and I get it, too." Gorton said that was encouraging, but he had his doubts.[7]

Tony Hayward soon succeeded Lord Browne in the wake of a classic British sex-and-perjury scandal that supplied the last straw. Given that distraction and the transition at the top, did BP take seriously the panel's admonition that process safety leadership—especially integrated auditing of risks—was Job 1 for its entire executive management team, including its board of directors?

On April 20, 2010, a spectacular blowout at BP's Deepwater Horizon drilling platform in the Gulf of Mexico killed 11 workers. Before the underwater wellhead was finally capped on July 15, it had gushed 206 million gallons of crude. Cleanup costs and compensation at this writing top $40 billion. Some predict the eventual bill will be triple that. Long-term ecological impacts are unknown. The culpability of BP and its partners, Transocean and Halliburton, became a blur of finger-pointing. A contractor testified that he warned BP that it risked gas leaks in the well if it cut back on stabilizers for the pipe into the wellhead. "We're talking the culture of BP," Gorton said. "If this was going to happen to an oil company, it would happen to BP."[8]

A seven-member commission appointed by President Obama issued a report that emphasized the importance of process safety "from the highest levels on down" as opposed to a "culture of complacency." It implicated the entire oil and gas exploration and production industry, and called for "systemic reforms."[9]

It was the Baker Report in a new dust jacket. Two blue-ribbon panels in the space of four years, and the only thing that had changed was the

toll. "To change hearts and minds and the attitudes individuals have toward their jobs is a difficult and a human task, and it's never complete,"
Gorton says.

GORTON WAS ALSO BUSY recruiting young Republican candidates. He
liked everything about Rob McKenna. They'd first met 22 years earlier
when McKenna was a student at the University of Washington. In 2004,
when Attorney General Chris Gregoire decided to run for governor, Gorton was on the phone to McKenna within an hour of her announcement.
He tracked him down in Canada where the 41-year-old King County
councilman was vacationing with his family.

"Slade was very persuasive that attorney general was the best job you
could have in the realm of public service," McKenna says. "He's a particularly good mentor and role model because he's so intellectually vibrant—
so mentally acute. I think he proves that you ought to stay active, first of
all for your mental sharpness, but it applies to your physical health as
well. It's use it, or lose it."

McKenna comes across as a blend of Gorton and Evans. Tall and slender, with a narrow, bespectacled face, he's a young Slade without the
sharp elbows. Like Evans, McKenna is an Eagle Scout with an air of even-
tempered confidence. He was student body president his senior year at
the UW, graduating with a Phi Beta Kappa key. Law school was followed
by a job with a leading law firm, then politics.

To Gorton's delight, McKenna was elected attorney general, handily
outpolling Deborah Senn. To his disappointment, former state senator
Dino Rossi lost to Gregoire by 133 votes out of a record 2.8 million cast in
a race that rivaled Bush-Gore for contentiousness. Still smarting from his
narrow loss to Cantwell, Gorton was in the thick of it, calling for an independent investigation of King County's ham-handed elections division. It
was "breathtaking," Gorton said, that 93 valid absentee ballots primarily
from Republican-leaning precincts weren't counted. How many more
were out there? While he staunchly defended the use of provisional ballots, King County had tallied whole batches before verification. The public deserved to know whether it was outright fraud or just "colossal incompetence." In any case, "I think it's appropriate to come to the conclusion
that King County has the worst election administration in any county in
the United States of America."[10]

County Executive Ron Sims, Gorton's old adversary, said his call for an
investigation was "pure partisanship." Jenny Durkan, the lead attorney
for the State Democratic Party, pronounced it "hypocritical beyond be-

lief," asserting that Republicans didn't make a fuss over errors in other counties that might have helped Rossi.[11]

MIKE MCGAVICK'S BID for the U.S. Senate in 2006 began with high hopes. As CEO of Safeco, Seattle's home-grown insurance industry giant, Gorton's former chief of staff had engineered a hugely successful restructuring. Along the way, however, 1,200 jobs were jettisoned. McGavick departed with rewards worth $28.4 million.[12]

Maria Cantwell was perceived early on as vulnerable. McGavick had demonstrated he was an astute campaign manager. But could he run his own? Gorton wasn't worried about that. His antennae told him it was a bad year for Republicans. Polls found 60 percent disapproved of the war in Iraq, which had turned up no signs of the ballyhooed weapons of mass destruction. Further, the administration's handling of Hurricane Katrina disaster relief was a huge snafu, and the GOP-controlled Congress had been wracked by scandals.[13]

McGavick didn't ask Gorton whether he should run. "He told me he was thinking about it, and he told me when he decided he definitely was doing it. I supported him wholeheartedly, of course, but I believed it was an impossible task."

Gorton campaigned energetically, hopping aboard McGavick's RV for stops from Port Angeles to Pullman. He introduced his prize protégé at rallies and joined him for editorial board interviews. McGavick's themes were civility and real-world administrative moxie. He made a preemptive confession to a DUI arrest in 1993 and apologized for the marijuana-baiting ad he'd run against Mike Lowry in Slade's 1988 campaign. Some called it "refreshing candor," others "manipulative."[14]

The campaign's eponymous, exclamatory signage—MIKE!—was appropriated for a news release claiming there was "Mike!Mentum." In reality, McGavick was getting little traction against the cool, competent Cantwell. She had won admiring reviews for standing up to Ted Stevens over drilling in the Arctic National Wildlife Refuge and oil tanker traffic on Puget Sound. McGavick chided her for voting to authorize the use of force in Iraq in 2002—her most vulnerable spot—and distanced himself from Bush, saying the president ought to fire Donald Rumsfeld and do something decisive. "Partition the country if we have to and get our troops home in victory."[15]

Down 16 points, McGavick asked Gorton to fly to Spokane with him for his last big rally. "I am very critical of people's speaking ability," Gorton admits, "but I could not have corrected a comma in what Mike said that day. He stood up there knowing there wasn't the remotest chance he could win. He balanced his message, thanking his supporters with humor and grace. It was absolute total perfection as a dead loser—one of the handful of most impressive performances I've ever seen. Mike McGavick would have been a great United States Senator."

Maria Cantwell, smiling her Maggie Gyllenhaal smile, won a second term with nearly 57 percent of the vote. Democrats regained control of both houses of Congress for the first time in a dozen years as Republicans absorbed what Bush pronounced "a whuppin'."

"The one grace that comes with an event like this," McGavick said with his boyish smile, is that "you don't sit around and say, 'If I had just done this one thing differently.'"[16]

JOEL CONNELLY GAVE GORTON a nice salute that year when Greater Seattle's greens and the U.S. Forest Service invited the former senator to help dedicate a new campground and celebrate the resuscitation of the valley bisected by the Middle Fork of the Snoqualmie River. Before leaving office, Gorton had secured $2 million for the campground, as well as money to transform a pigpen back to paradise. The area had been littered with garbage, derelict autos, old refrigerators and the toxic detritus from meth labs. "Not bad for a guy on the 'dirty dozen' list whom the Sierra Club spent $300,000 in 'voter education' money to defeat," Connelly wrote. To contrast Gorton's dubious achievements rap sheet, he proceeded to itemize all the genuinely good things Slade had done over the years—from recruiting female attorneys to defending John Goldmark and Jamie Gorelick; from the Mountains to Sound Greenway to saving the Mariners.[17]

When a friend observed that it was such a nice piece, Gorton barked, "Now he writes it!"

44 | Not So Super

ORTON SAVED BASEBALL FOR SEATTLE but couldn't come up with a buzzer-beater for basketball. By the end of a bruising game, in fact, he was charged with a technical foul that complicated the city's case and called into question his ethics.

Three decades after their stirring championship season of 1979, the SuperSonics were less than super. The arena where Lenny Wilkens, Dennis Johnson, Jack Sikma, Shawn Kemp and Gary Payton once packed them in was now the smallest in the National Basketball Association. Despite a $100 million remodel in 1995, it also lacked the requisite luxury boxes, plasma screens and sushi bars. It was soon clear, as many feared from the outset, that when Clay Bennett's Oklahoma-based group purchased the team from Howard Schultz in 2006 it had one goal in mind: Moving it to Oklahoma City. Absent a new arena, Seattle was a money pit, Bennett said, asserting that the team stood to lose $60 million if it was forced to stay until its KeyArena lease expired in 2010.

See you in court, said Mayor Greg Nickels. A lease is a lease. The city retained K&L Gates, Gorton's law firm, and filed suit in U.S. District Court. Hoping to duplicate his success with the Mariners, Gorton was already working his Rolodex to find a local buyer. McGavick, a basketball fan now between jobs, volunteered to help.[1]

Microsoft CEO Steve Ballmer soon emerged as the leader of a local investment group that committed half of the $300 million it would take to renovate KeyArena, as well as the money to purchase an NBA franchise. Bennett insisted the Sonics weren't for sale. The city said it would contribute $75 million, and lobbied the Legislature to authorize the remainder by extending the King County car-rental and restaurant taxes paying for the Mariners' Safeco Field.[2]

At the beginning of 2008, Bennett offered the city $26.5 million to drop its lawsuit. The mayor stood his ground, but it was liquefying. Ballmer withdrew his group's offer after the Legislature balked. With the NBA's Board of Governors poised to approve the move, Seattle had lost its leverage to keep the team or land a replacement. Gorton criticized the governor and legislative leaders for "a failure of both imagination and courage."3

The board voted 28-2 to send the Sonics to Oklahoma City. NBA Commissioner David Stern, livid that the city persisted in taking its case to trial, accused Gorton of waging a "scorched-earth" campaign. If Gorton and the mayor persisted in attempting "to exact whatever pound of flesh is possible here," Stern warned, they might jeopardize Seattle's chances of landing a replacement team anytime soon.4

Gorton replied evenly that the city would be pleased to negotiate an exit settlement with Bennett if Seattle was guaranteed a replacement team. "My goal from the very beginning has been to have a team," Gorton said. "Revenge, I'm not interested in, as such. The city has a financial stake in all this. The mayor and I are in complete accord that what we want is a team. . . . Whatever David Stern said about me, my principle unhappiness is not directed at David Stern. At this point, we have not given him a plan with an arena adequate for the NBA in the 21st century. If we do and he doesn't respond, my attitude will be different. But at this point, we haven't given him that chance."5

WHEN THE CASE WENT TO TRIAL in U.S. District Court in Seattle, dueling tales of duplicity unfolded. Unsealed e-mails, memos and PowerPoints yielded juicy quotes. Sonics attorney Brad Keller, for starters, charged that the city had "unclean hands." Gorton, McGavick, Ballmer and former Sonics CEO Wally Walker were part of a strategy to bleed Bennett's group into submission, Keller said. Walker, like Gorton, was a contracted consultant to the city when the group met at his home in the fall of 2007. They reviewed a presentation developed by McGavick. "The Sonics Challenge: Why a Poisoned Well Affords a Unique Opportunity" was duly entered into evidence. The section labeled "making them sell" described a "pincer movement" to boost the Oklahomans' costs "in an unpleasant environment while increasing the league's belief that an alternative solution gains it a good new owner and keeps it in a desirable market." The role of Gorton and the others would be to "increase pain" of trying to leave.6

Paul Lawrence, one of Gorton's K&L Gates colleagues, told the court the pain was self-inflicted. Bennett and the other Oklahoma investors were "all sophisticated businessmen who know what it means to sign and assume a contract." That the Sonics had been losing money at KeyArena they knew full well. They assumed that risk when they bought the franchise and assumed its obligations. The city was merely holding the team to a valid lease.7

The poisoned well wasn't "as nefarious as the title seemed," Art Thiel noted in the *Post-Intelligencer*, since it "referred to how much Bennett had fouled things, not that Ballmer was dumping Drano in Oklahoma City's water supply."[8]

There was plenty of hemlock to go around. Among the documents reviewed in court was a Gorton e-mail summing up an underwhelming meeting he'd had with Gregoire, Sims and House Speaker Frank Chopp: "Not one of them has a stake in the Sonics' loss or retention at the present time. None of them can be effectively blamed for a loss which, to the extent that if blame can be laid at anyone's feet, belongs to (former owner) Howard Schultz. Nor does any one of them see much personal glory in a win on our terms except for the mayor, who will deserve credit for any success. He owns KeyArena and the (Seattle) Center and sees the viability largely dependent on the presence of the Sonics."[9]

"Say what you will about Gorton," Thiel wrote, "he nailed that assessment. In the run-up to the litigation, many in the community were furious with political leadership for not stepping up with a comparatively small contribution."[10]

Keller's closing arguments focused on portraying Bennett as the victim of a full court press that had morphed into conspiracy. "[T]he end does not and never will justify the means," Keller said. A new piece of evidence was an e-mail from Gorton to Ballmer, McGavick and Walker describing a meeting he and Deputy Mayor Tim Ceis had in New York with an NBA official and two of Bennett's attorneys. Gorton, who was representing the city, had signed a confidentiality agreement. "What is he doing turning around the next day and violating the city's promise?" asked Judge Marsha Pechman. Lawrence called the e-mail a "major misstep" but denied Gorton had sent it on behalf of the city.[11]

Under cross-examination, Mayor Nickels proved to be a contradictory witness, conceding afterward that if Keller's job "was to make me look feeble . . . I would say he did a pretty good job."

Thiel, Jerry Brewer, a sports columnist for *The Seattle Times*, and practically every other pundit in town agreed that no one had clean hands, including the vainglorious NBA. Both, however, singled out Gorton. His e-mail had allowed the Oklahomans to drag Seattle into "that dark, nearly irresistible place of prevarication, dissembling and obfuscation where powerful men see their reputations implode," Thiel wrote.[12]

Brewer concluded that Gorton had "entangled the city in a vile conflict of interest." All things considered, however, "there are no victims in this trial. There are only villains ... plaintiffs, defendants, everyone—wearing sullied suits, looking like rivals after a schoolyard brawl."[13]

Gorton was furious to have his integrity impugned but constrained from comment at the time. Here is his side of the story:

"At the time at which the mayor asked me and K&L Gates to represent the city I was already involved with Mike McGavick and Wally Walker in trying to find a purchaser to keep the team here. The only potential buyer was Steve Ballmer, whom both Wally and Mike knew well. It took very little persuasion to get Steve to offer the city $150 million to pay half of the cost of remaking KeyArena into a satisfactory venue for the NBA. In her usual lackluster fashion, Gregoire supported the idea of authorizing the city to extend the Safeco Field taxes but Speaker Chopp killed it. If it had not been for Frank Chopp, the Sonics would still be here.

"The NBA was right in its position that the present KeyArena is vastly inadequate. However, it would have had to agree that the remodel would make it OK, and the Oklahomans didn't want to sell. They wanted to move. We could only retain the Sonics by persuading the league to reject their application and that required an unequivocal commitment to the changes and to a new purchaser—Ballmer. Of course we played hardball, the only game a sports league would understand. Once the Legislature failed to act, the league was certain to approve the move to Oklahoma City. The city was left with only a lawsuit to keep the team here for two more awful years or to get as large a settlement as possible.

"The meeting I had with the NBA in New York was set up by Wally Walker, whom the NBA knew and liked. He and McGavick and Ballmer were the team to save the Sonics that preceded my representation of the city, so of course they were told about its results, and properly so. But during the course of the trial, when Keller made his charges, Lawrence failed to defend me or to allow me to do so myself—during or after the trial, probably because the settlement negotiations were at a crucial point. Whatever, I was furious and seriously considered leaving the firm. I'm still unhappy today."

THE CITY AND THE OKLAHOMANS settled out of court for $45 million in the summer of 2008, just before Pechman was set to release her ruling. Seattle kept the Sonics' name. Oklahoma City gained a young team rechristened the Thunder. Seattle stood to receive another $30 million on two conditions. The first was the linchpin: The Legislature in 2009 had to approve funding to renovate KeyArena or build a new venue. If that happened and the city failed to land a new NBA team by 2013, the Oklahomans had to write the second check. Stern said the NBA "would be happy to return" to Seattle at a future time.

The Legislature balked once again. In his bid for a third term, Nickels was defeated in the 2009 primary—the loss of the Sonics adding to the voters' general dissatisfaction with City Hall.

"The settlement was highly favorable," Gorton maintains, "yet still denounced by the sporting press and others. They wanted what we couldn't get—a permanent team. So it ended up hurting Greg Nickels, the only politician who really had the courage to do something positive."

At this writing, Seattle has no replacement team. Even more gallingly to Sonics fans, Kevin Durant, the club's blue-chip 2007 draft pick, emerged as a superstar. The Thunder made the playoffs in its first season. By 2011 it was a genuine contender.[14]

45 | The Extraordinary Octogenarian

A SHADOW FELL across his cream of broccoli soup. It was lunch hour one busy Tuesday in the spring of 2011 at Wagner's Bakery & Cafe, an Olympia institution just below the Capitol. He looked up to see a pleasant-faced woman smiling down at him.

"Are you who I think you are?"

"That depends on who you think I am."

"I think you're Slade Gorton!"

"You're right!"

"Well, I always liked to vote for you. *We miss you.*"

"Thank you!" he said, beaming. Turning back to his companions, he joked, "If all the people who tell me that had actually voted I'd still be in the Senate."

At 83, Slade Gorton was remarkably content. Among the multiple irons in his fire was the Redistricting Commission, charged with rearranging the state's political geography to create new legislative and congressional districts. Another new mission was bringing China to heel on intellectual

The 2011 Washington State Redistricting Commission: from left, Tom Huff, Dean Foster, Chairwoman Lura J. Powell, Tim Ceis and Gorton. *Genevieve O'Sullivan/Washington State Redistricting Commission*

Slade at Safeco Field in 2010. *Dan Schlatter/Puget Sound Business Journal*

property protection through a congressional initiative he dreamed up and testified on.

Besides undiminished energy, he has more disposable income. His lawyering and lobbying for K&L Gates' clients is more lucrative by far than the Senate. He's delighted to be able to help with college tuition for his grandchildren and glad he's had more time to watch them grow up and take them out to the ball game. Safeco Field is just a few blocks from his office.

The past three years have been laced with boards and commissions. He was a member of the National War Powers Commission and co-chairman of a panel reviewing federal transportation policy for the Bipartisan Policy Center. Formed in 2007 by former Senate majority leaders Howard Baker, Bob Dole, Tom Daschle and George Mitchell, the center incubates ideas to meet major challenges. To modernize surface transportation in America, Gorton's group concluded that federal funds need to be allocated through a performance-based system that ties spending to national goals, including economic growth, connectivity, safety, security and environmental protection.[1]

Gorton also joined the advisory board of the William D. Ruckelshaus Center, a regional think tank to promote collaborative problem solving. The center is named in honor of his longtime friend, a widely respected former administrator of the Environmental Protection Agency. It works with faculty and students at Washington State University and the Evans School of Public Affairs at the University of Washington. In 2008 the center set out to assist the Legislature by mediating talks between environmentalists and farmers over land-use regulations. Gorton is an enthusiastic participant, stimulated by the chance to tackle diverse problems and the caliber of the board. Besides Ruckelshaus, it includes Dan Evans, Bill Gates Sr., Billy Frank Jr. of the Northwest Indian Fisheries Commission, former secretary of state Ralph Munro and ex-House speaker Joe King. "The methodology of the Ruckelshaus Center is, I am convinced, the wave of the future," Gorton says.[2]

THE 2008 PRESIDENTIAL CAMPAIGN featured a measured reconciliation of Gorton and McCain. Besides refusing to endorse Gorton's candidacy for the federal bench, the Arizonan had been a sworn enemy of Trent Lott. The grudge stemmed from McCain's conviction that Lott had helped spread scurrilous rumors about him to boost Bush during their bitter fight for the GOP nomination in 2000. Two years later, however, McCain rose to Lott's defense when Bush joined the push to oust him as majority leader over a racially-charged remark Lott ad-libbed at Strom Thurmond's

100th birthday party. "I know how you are feeling," McCain told Lott. "You have been treated unfairly." The shared grievance forged a new alliance. McCain, like Gorton, profited greatly from being in Lott's orbit, diminished though it was for the time being. "Previously a marginal player better known for heckling the Senate"—and flipping off colleagues who annoyed him—than wielding major influence, McCain tempered his maverick image with new political sophistication.[3]

A delegate to the GOP National Convention for only the second time in his life, Gorton signed on as honorary state chairman of McCain's campaign. Though annoyed by this development, most of the state's tribal leaders understood that Indians accounted for only 150,000 of Washington's six million voters. "So it's just pure math," said Ron Allen of the Jamestown S'Klallams, Gorton's old adversary. McCain's alliance with Gorton didn't diminish their faith in his commitment to Indian country, Allen said.[4] Despite McCain's strong record on Indian affairs, a hundred tribal leaders nationwide defected to Obama.

If McCain had a fighting chance for the Indian vote in the Evergreen State, Boeing workers likely were less pliable. They would not soon forget his vociferous opposition to the Pentagon's plan to lease air-refueling tankers from their employer. It was "one of the great rip-offs in the history of the United States of America," McCain fumed. Gorton doubted the dustup would have much impact. "I think I can say with some confidence he isn't going to be prejudiced against Boeing in any fairly competitive procurement."[5]

Washington stayed resoundingly blue. Obama and Biden won nearly 58 percent of the vote. Rossi lost again to Gregoire, this time decisively. Gorton's former assistant attorney general racked up almost 64 percent of the vote in King County, home to one out of every three voters. McKenna's re-election as attorney general was one of the few bright spots for Republicans. Absent a candidate—Gorton hopes it's McKenna—who can capture something beyond 40 percent in King, he concedes that Republican chances of reclaiming the governor's office or a seat in the U.S. Senate are slim. Gorton's old boa constrictor strategy of strangling King by carrying most everything around it increasingly has become a garter snake. Patty Murray made Rossi a three-time loser in 2010, winning a fourth term in the Senate with 63 percent of the King County vote. Cantwell took 66 percent against McGavick four years earlier.[6]

Gorton and J. Vander Stoep took hope from the success of Jaime Herrera Beutler, who was elected to Congress from Southwest Washington in 2010. Gorton hosted a D.C. fundraiser for the telegenic young Hispanic state representative. Vander Stoep was a campaign adviser. Herrera, 32, was the only Republican on the West Coast to capture a seat that had been held by a Democrat.[7]

IN 2009, GORTON JOINED THE BOARD of the Markle Foundation, a national group that brainstorms solutions to health and national security issues, particularly through information technology. He also joined the Partnership for a Secure America. The brain child of Lee Hamilton and Warren Rudman, it focuses on foreign policy and national security. Together with Hamilton, Rudman, Howard Baker, Tom Kean, Robert Mc-Namara, Sam Nunn, Ted Sorensen, Gary Hart and two dozen other prominent Republicans and Democrats, Gorton endorsed a statement that urged the Obama Administration to work diligently to improve America's ties with Russia. The former Cold War adversaries now have many urgent shared interests, the leaders said, notably nuclear non-proliferation and the war on terror. Addressing critical issues in concert rather than competition is vital to both countries, Gorton says. "It also aids the cause of democratic reforms in Russia."[8]

Unrepentant mugwumps 50 years after they mobilized the progressive wing of the Washington State Republican Party, Gorton and Evans declared their opposition in 2009 to Tim Eyman's latest creation, Initiative 1033. Although the party had endorsed the plan to limit city, county and state tax-revenue increases to the rate of inflation and population growth, the two old campaigners denounced the initiative as "ill conceived and unreasonable." It would make "already tough times worse in our state and our communities" by crimping education, law enforcement and job-creation projects. Their cross-generational message also emphasized the potential impact on home care for senior citizens. Initiative 1033 was soundly rejected.[9]

HARD ON THE HEELS of the massacre at Fort Hood, the narrowly thwarted bombing of a jetliner on final approach to a Detroit airport on Christmas Day 2009 was fresh evidence to Gorton that there was still too much "sand in the gears of the bureaucracy." The 9/11 Commission Report emphasized that information-sharing in the intelligence community was critical to keeping the homeland safe. Congress moved earnestly to adopt its recommendations, Gorton said, yet deadly inertia clearly remained, together with potentially lethal political correctness.[10]

The father of the 23-year-old Nigerian jihadist who nearly brought down the plane was so concerned about his growing radicalization that he spoke with CIA officers at a U.S. embassy five weeks before the close call. But the engineering student's name was not added to the FBI's Terrorist Screening Database or the "no fly" list. Nor was his U.S. visa revoked. Gorton noted that his wife, in her upper 70s with an artificial hip, is screened carefully every time they go through airport security "and yet people like this," the would-be bomber, "were given just the most superficial examination and waved on through." It remained for passengers on Northwest Airlines Flight 253 to subdue him as he attempted to light an explosive device attached to his underwear.[11]

"Intelligence wasn't shared," Gorton told reporters. "It's a crashing disappointment that this happened. I hope this is a significant wake-up call. . . . This isn't completely the fault of the Obama Administration. The problem predates the 9/11 attacks, as the commission made abundantly clear. But the president has the definitive bully pulpit to emphasize that we're in a very real, ongoing war against determined extremists . . . and make it a priority of his administration."[12]

Two years later, Obama showed the colors in a big way. Together with millions of his countrymen, Gorton listened with satisfaction as the president announced that Osama bin Laden had been killed by an elite Navy SEAL team in a helicopter raid on a compound in Pakistan. "It's eight or nine years past due," Gorton said, "but the president deserves high marks for persistence and willingness to act on intelligence no better than Bill Clinton had more than a dozen years ago and took a pass on." It was a symbolic victory as well, he added, and that's not to be undervalued, "but the reality is that we are maybe two decades into a war the end of which no person living now will see. The struggle will go on until Islam decides massively that jihad is more harm to itself than it is to the West, a realization that is only beginning to permeate through to a few."

As for our ostensible allies, that bin Laden could hide so successfully for so long in Pakistan was "a massive illustration of the dilemma we face in a country only a step or two removed from the status of a failed state—and one with nukes. The basic problem is that Islam is perfectly consistent with absolutism and terrorism and from the time of the prophet himself has no philosophical distinction between church and state." In short, Gorton said, anyone tempted to unfurl a "Mission Accomplished" banner is a delusional fool. More al-Qaida foot soldiers with jihad in their hearts and explosives in their pants doubtless were figuring out new ways to elude scanners.

IN HIS SPARE TIME, Gorton became a columnist, joining *The Washington Post*'s lineup of "On Leadership" contributors. The editors pose questions about how leadership—or the lack of it—is affecting the most pressing issues of the day. A diverse group of contributors offer answers. Gorton's 200-word pieces appear two or three times a month on the *Post's* Web page, often generating hot debate in the comments string.

Given his personality and the breadth of his reading since childhood— all 12 volumes of Toynbee twice, Shakespeare and a smorgasbord of fiction from Mark Twain to Tom Clancy—he writes like he talks. "Better to be silent and thought insensitive than to speak out and prove it," Gorton concluded one column, borrowing from the Bible, Confucius, Lincoln and Ben Franklin.[13]

He saw no reason to be silent on a subject of insensitivity when Harry Reid, the already embattled Senate majority leader, faced more trouble in 2010. *Game Change*, the newly published best-seller about the 2008 race for the presidency, featured Reid's observation that Obama had a good chance to become the first black president because he was "light-skinned" and had "no Negro dialect, unless he wanted to have one." Reid issued an abject apology, which Obama accepted. The GOP national chairman, an African American, was unmollified. He called for Reid's resignation.[14]

Recalling Lott's gaffe in saying that if Thurmond had been elected president on the segregationist Dixiecrat ticket in 1948, "we wouldn't have had all these problems over all these years . . .," Gorton wrote:

> The nation cannot be deprived of the opportunity for a frank and open discussion of issues relating to race, no matter how controversial. That's a policy that obviously must apply to members of Congress as well as to the press and public.
>
> Neither the comment of Senator Lott, which cost him his post as Senate Majority Leader, nor that of Senator Reid, which threatens his, however, dealt with contemporary political issues.
>
> Senator Lott's was a throwaway to a 100-year-old retiring senator that, ill-advised as it was, was not true, nor did it represent Senator Lott's actual views. It should not have cost him his position.
>
> Senator Reid's comment, as inelegant and inadvisable as it was, was probably a correct description of election reality at the time. It is now almost two years in the past, and it should not affect Senator Reid's post.[15]

In 1989, Gorton and Norm Dicks had followed through on an idea hatched by Scoop Jackson. They helped Rich Ellings and Kenneth Pyle found The National Bureau of Asian Research in Seattle. Pyle was the director of the Jackson School of International Studies at the University of Washington. Ellings, a former Gorton aide, in 2010 established an integrated offshoot:

The Slade Gorton International Policy Center. Housed in NBR's new high-tech building adjacent to the university campus, the center plans to offer fellowships and internships and sponsor seminars on global economics, emerging technology and national security. Gorton is the mentor in residence. Creigh H. Agnew, another former Gorton aide, is its president.

Ellings is leading a campaign to raise $13 million in public and private money to ensure the center's long-term success. Gorton has already moved his 14 framed quills from his Supreme Court appearances.[16] The Gorton Center is supported by a host of Slade's old friends and former staff, including Dan Evans, Bill Ruckelshaus, Jim and John Ellis, Trent Lott, Pete Domenici, Rudy Boschwitz, Tom Daschle, Mike McGavick, J. Vander Stoep, Mariana Parks and Chris Koch.[17]

AN INITIATIVE PROPOSING AN INCOME TAX on the rich—defined as individuals earning more than $200,000 and couples twice that—found Gorton and Bill Gates Sr., two old friends, in opposite corners. Although Gorton also qualifies as genuinely rich, his net worth pales in comparison to Gates', the co-chairman of the philanthropic foundation endowed

Bill Gates Sr. and Gorton leave the stage following their debate of Initiative 1098 at the University of Washington Tacoma. I-1098 would have established an income tax on the state's highest earners. *Janet Jensen/The News Tribune*

by his son and daughter-in-law. A teddy bear of a man with a sweet smile, Gates Sr. argued earnestly that the wealthy in Washington State aren't paying their fair share. The state's commitment to education in terms of investment per $1,000 of income is declining precipitously, he said. Health care programs were also suffering under the state's regressive tax system. The recession was making everything that much worse. The poorest 20 percent of Washingtonians pay 17 percent of their income to support state services while the richest get richer, Gates said, contributing only 2.6 percent. "They have been riding free on the payment of other people for year after year."

Gates felt so passionately about the proposal that he perched over a dunk tank for a memorable TV spot. "Some say Initiative 1098 is about soaking the rich, but it's really about doing something for the next generation," he testified. Just then, a kid with a good arm gave him a chilly bath. The 84-year-old popped up good-naturedly, blinked the water from his eyes and declared, "Vote yes on 1098. It's good for Washington!"

A few weeks before the election, Gates and Gorton were the big draw when some 300 people packed a meeting room at the University of Washington's Tacoma campus. A crew from CBS' *60 Minutes* was on hand for the debate. Gorton played the populist, warning that no taxpayer's wallet is safe when a Democratically-controlled Legislature is in town. If I-1098 won approval, the tax-and-spend lawmakers would view it as "a bonanza the likes of which they have never seen, and they will go wild." Sooner or later—bet on sooner—the income tax would be extended to everyone. Moreover, it would be a disincentive to economic growth, Gorton argued, asserting that an income tax handicaps Oregon, which has lost business and industry to Washington as a result. Any way you cut it, he said, an income tax would add up to even less money for education.[18]

Gates saw it though a different prism. He agreed that Oregon was a cautionary tale for Washington. Each state, however, was relying on a two-legged stool to generate revenue. Budget cuts and a lack of vision had left Oregon's schools and universities in even worse shape than Washington's, Gates said. Economic development was being stifled. Unemployment was nearly 1½ percent higher there. Oregon's once vaunted quality of life was steadily eroding.

Connelly was on one side of the dais, Gorton's biographer on the other. Between them they had covered his career since 1966. Both smiled as they jotted down his rejoinder to Gates. It was vintage Gorton, never at a loss for a rapier comeback.

"As soon as this campaign is over," Gorton said with a wicked grin, "we'll have to send Bill down to Oregon to campaign for a sales tax." The audience laughed, and Gates had to chuckle, too. Initiative 1098 went down in a landslide.[19]

AS 2011 DAWNED, the Republican caucus in the state Senate appointed Gorton to the bipartisan Redistricting Commission created by constitutional amendment in 1983. House Democrats chose Dean Foster, Bob Greive's aide when the wily majority leader

Dean Foster and Gorton, who sparred over redistricting in the 1960s, reminisce after a hearing conducted by the 2011 Washington State Redistricting Commission. Foster represents the House Democratic Caucus, Gorton the Senate Republican Caucus on the five-member commission. *John C. Hughes/The Legacy Project*

and Gorton fought their landmark battles over apportionment a half century earlier.

Sitting side by side on the five-member panel, Gorton and Foster helped hash out a timeline to achieve consensus on a plan to present to the Legislature by Jan. 1, 2012. "There are two good and valid reasons for beating the Dec. 31 deadline," Gorton observed. "We need to be sure everyone is heard and we need to give aspiring candidates more time to start working on campaigns. . . .We can't cheat each other on a partisan basis. That's the genius of this commission. There are only four votes. Let's see if we can do it as early as possible." In the audience, multiple representatives of several members of congress nodded approvingly—doubtless some aspirants as well. The 2010 Census had granted Washington a tenth seat in Congress.

During a break, Gorton's biographer mused that Greive's bow-tied ghost would be hovering nervously when they started crunching numbers, this time with computers instead of adding machines and Shell Oil roadmaps. "He's here somewhere," Foster joked. Gorton grinned and nodded.

That afternoon one of his former Senate aides called to say she had the perfect title for this book: "Slade Gorton: The first 80 years."

Acknowledgements

WHAT A POORER PLACE the world would be without librarians and archivists. How would historians determine whether it snowed on a winter's day along Cape Cod in 1637? Or locate a 30-year-old political commercial and find a Betamax player to view it? One floor below me at the Washington State Library, which Secretary of State Sam Reed saved from closure, is a repository of priceless books, manuscripts and microfilm—and the people who ensure it's all accessible. The State Archives is another trove for historians, history buffs and genealogists, as well as lawmakers and their staffs. You can pore over documents and touch artifacts or access 100 million documents on line for free. Washington State's archives are in the forefront of the digital revolution. I am also indebted to the staffs of the Washington State Law Library, the Tacoma Public Library and the historic Hoquiam Timberland Library, my second home for the past 45 years.

Invaluable to telling Slade Gorton's life story were six books you ought to read: Art Thiel's *Out of Left Field, How the Mariners Made Baseball Fly in Seattle;* Philip Shenon's *The Commission, What We Didn't Know About 9/11;* William L. Dwyer's *The Goldmark Case, An American Libel Trial;* Senator Trent Lott's memoir, *Herding Cats,* and Mary Ellen McCaffree's autobiographical *Politics of the Possible,* written with Anne McNamee Corbett. In *On the Harbor, From Black Friday to Nirvana,* Doug Barker, my former longtime colleague in journalism, offers the best account of what it was like to be at ground zero in timber country during the spotted owl war.

In my biography of Booth Gardner, I mentioned the famous observation by Phil Graham, the late publisher of *The Washington Post,* that journalism is a "first rough draft of history." While Gorton, like Gardner, often groused about the media's "negativism," his career was insightfully chronicled by some of the most talented newspaper people the state has ever seen, notably David Ammons, Ross Anderson, Joni Balter, Knute Berger, Les Blumenthal, Rebecca Boren, David Brewster, Peter Callaghan, Joel Connelly, O. Casey Corr, William Dietrich, John Dodge, Adele Ferguson, John Hendren, Henry Gay, David Horsey, Dean

Katz, Richard W. Larsen, Mike Layton, Neil Modie, Bob Partlow, David Postman, Eric Pryne, Shelby Scates, Art Thiel, Doug Underwood, Emmett Watson and Danny Westneat. I worry that a whole new generation of readers now expects quality information for free. That said, thank God for P-I.com, seattletimes.com, Crosscut.com, HistoryLink, TVW, C-Span and search engines like ProQuest and NewsBank, which gave me access to some 8,000 articles about Gorton in hundreds of newspapers and other periodicals.

Hundreds of others made this work possible, including Creigh Agnew, Gerry L. Alexander, Dick Allen, Ron Allen, Rick Anderson, Phil Austin, Mike Bay, Chris Bayley, Steve Bell, Stephanie Benna, Katie Blinn, Dave Boardman, Rudy Boschwitz, Sharon Boswell, Don Brazier, Casey Bruner, Angelo Bruscas, Jeanne Bumpus, Ritajean Butterworth, Jim Carlson, Wendy Coddington, Monte Dahlstrom, Kellie Carlson Daniels, Pete Domenici, Robert J. Doran, Ron Dotzauer, Mark Doumit, Rich Ellings, Jim Ellis, Stuart Elway, Lori Enholm, George Erb, Dan Evans, Steve Excell, Dean Foster, Grahame J. Gadman, Dawn Kendrick Gibb, Tommi Halvorsen Gatlin, Jamie Gorelick, Mike Gorton, Nat Gorton, Chris Gregoire, Jody Gripp, Rebecca Hale, John Hamer, Shane Hamlin, Jerry Handfield, Nick Handy, Dave Hastings, Ben Helle, Curtis Hom, Patsy Hughes, Becky Gorton Jack, Peter Jackson, Bob Johnson, James M. Johnson, Keith Kessler, Anne Kilgannon, Chris Koch, Bud Krogh, Greg Lamm, Sean Lanksbury, Crystal Lentz, Trent Lott, Ed Mackie, Richard Mattsen, Howard McCurdy, Mike McGavick, Rob McKenna, Carl Molesworth, Sid Morrison, Ralph Munro, Patty Murray, Paul Newman, Sarah Gorton Nortz, Mariana Parks, JoAnn Poysky, Frank Pritchard, Sam Reed, Chris Rush, Mary Schaff, Dan Schlatter, George W. Scott, Kim Smeenk, Gary T.

Bobblehead by David Horsey.

Smith, Payton Smith, Sid Snyder, John Spellman, Linda Thompson, Mary Thornton, LeRoy Tipton, Robert Utter, Ian Stenseng, J. Vander Stoep, Tony Williams, Hans Zeiger, Philip Zelikow and Al Ziontz.

Trova Heffernan and Lori Larson, my teammates at the Legacy Project, have been amazing, together with Carleen Jackson and Laurie Mott of the Heritage Center. Special thanks to Sally Gorton, a former reporter whose vocabulary doesn't include "no comment." Doubtless I have forgotten to acknowledge someone. It always happens. My apologies and sincere thanks.

While the Slade Gorton International Policy Center, its host, The National Bureau of Asian Research, the Gorton Legacy Group and other donors helped fund the printed edition of this book, it is in no way an "official" biography. No one outside the Office of the Secretary of State asked for or received any editorial oversight.

One last word about Thomas Slade Gorton III: He was an open book, warts and all, and never once attempted to steer or interfere. No biographer could ask for more. By any objective assessment, Washington State is lucky a young man opted out of the fish business and decided to go West.

John C. Hughes, 2011

Donors

DONATIONS TO THE WASHINGTON State Heritage Center Trust by the following organizations made the publication of this book possible.

The National Bureau of Asian Research

NBR IS A NONPROFIT, nonpartisan research institution dedicated to informing and strengthening policy in the Asia-Pacific. It conducts advanced independent research on strategic, political, economic, globalization, health, and energy issues affecting U.S. relations with Asia. To attract and train the next generation of Asia specialists, it also provides internship and fellowship opportunities to graduate and undergraduate students. NBR was established in 1989 with a major grant from the Henry M. Jackson Foundation.

Slade Gorton International Policy Center

THE CENTER HONORS Senator Gorton's living legacy of service to state and nation by sponsoring world-class policy research and inspiring the next generation of leaders. It was founded in 2010 by a group that includes former Gorton staffers, Senate colleagues, friends, and family. The Center is a core program of The National Bureau of Asian Research, focusing on three areas: policy research, fellowship and internship programs, and the Gorton History Program.

The Gorton Legacy Group

THE GLG WAS FOUNDED in 2001 by women who have worked with Gorton during his six decades of public service—from the Legislature to the Attorney General's Office to the U.S. Senate and a host of other public service endeavors. Long before women were regarded or treated as equals in the workplace, Slade opened the doors of opportunity. Over the years he has recruited hundreds of women for key positions. Women and men who worked for Slade received equal pay, equal respect and the same obligation to meet the high standards he always sets. The result is three generations of women who owe much—professionally and personally—to their mentor. The GLG's mission is to perpetuate this legacy. Soon after its inception, the GLG altered its bylaws to include former male staffers. They were equally resolute in wanting to honor their mentor.

Source Notes

ABBREVIATIONS: Seattle Post-Intelligencer, P-I; Seattle Times, Times; Tacoma News Tribune, TNT; Olympian, Oly; The Seattle Weekly, Weekly; New York Times, NYT; Associated Press, AP; United Press International, UPI.

INTRODUCTION: SLIPPERY SLADE?

Interviews with Kellie Carlson Daniels, Sally Gorton, Dan Evans, Joel Connelly, Jamie Gorelick, Rudy Boschwitz and Booth Gardner; Gorton voting record analysis from NationalJournal.com, congressional vote analysis; www.govtrack. us, *Gorton voting record*; "This half of the 20th century . . ." quote from Geov Parrish, *Slate Gorton's Indian Wars*, Eat the State!, 3-17-98

CHAPTER ONE: THE GORTONS AND SLADES

Editor's note: Grahame Gadman's research on Samuell Gorton is the most exhaustive and nuanced.

1. Gadman, *A Strenuous Beneficent Force: The Case for Revision of the Career of Samuell Gorton, Rhode Island Radical*; Gorton, Adelos, *The Life and Times of Samuel Gorton*

2. Ibid.

3. Ibid.

4. McLoughlin, *Rhode Island, a Bicentennial History*

5. Gadman, *A Strenuous Beneficent Force*

6. Ibid.; Gorton, Thomas, *Samuel Gorton of Rhode Island & his Descendants*; McLoughlin, *Rhode Island, a Bicentennial History*

7. Gadman, *A Strenuous Beneficent Force*

8. Ibid.; Gorton, Thomas, *Samuel Gorton of Rhode Island & his Descendants*; McLoughlin, *Rhode Island, a Bicentennial History*

9. Gorton, Thomas, *Samuel Gorton of Rhode Island & his Descendants*

10. Ibid.

11. The Woonsocket Call, 7–18–81, p. 22; *History of Essex County, Massachusetts, Volume 2*, p. 1379

12. Seafood.Com, *Mass Moments*, 4-4-05; Kurlansky, *Cod: A Biography of the Fish that Changed the World*; Gorton's of Gloucester, *How it All Began*

13. Kurlansky, *Cod*, p. 137

CHAPTER TWO: DUMB AND DUMPED

Interviews with Mike Gorton, Nathaniel Gorton and Frank Pritchard

   1. Time, 7–21–52, *National Affairs: Keep it Clean; On the Harbor*, p. 139

CHAPTER THREE: THE CHANGE AGENTS

Interviews with Dan Evans, Joel Pritchard, Frank Pritchard, Jim Ellis and Sally Gorton; *Joel M. Pritchard*, An Oral History; *Don Eldridge*, An Oral History; *Tom Copeland*, An Oral History; Tedlow, Richard, *Intellect on Television: The Quiz Show Scandals of the 1950s*, American Quarterly, Vol. 28, No. 4

   1. *Joel M. Pritchard, An Oral History*, p. 34

   2. Ibid., p. 9

   3. Ibid., pp. 6–13

   4. Scates, *Warren G. Magnuson*, p. 171

   5. Watson, *Digressions of a Native Son*, p. 192

   6. *Don Eldridge, An Oral History*, p. 107, 273

   7. *Tom Copeland, An Oral History*, p. 272

   8. *Eldridge*, p. 273

CHAPTER FOUR: THE FRESHMAN

Interviews with Dan Evans, Sally Gorton and Ritajean Butterworth

   1. Alan Thompson, TVW, 12–10–10

   2. Clark, *The Dry Years*, pp. 258–260; Times, 9–19–04, p. B-5, *Tommy raincoat*

   3. *Richard O. White, Washington State Code Reviser, An Oral History*, p. 9

   4. Dwyer, *The Goldmark Case*, p. 16

   5. Ibid, pp. 16–17

   6. Ibid., p. 15

   7. Ibid., p. 47; Time, 1–31–64

   8. Dwyer, *The Goldmark Case*, p. 52

   9. Ibid., p. 104

   10. Ibid., p. 104–105

   11. *Albert F. Canwell*, An Oral History, p. 332–333

   12. Dwyer, *The Goldmark Case*, p. 284

CHAPTER FIVE: A POWER STRUGGLE

   1. P-I, 7–3–84, p. C-2

   2. Brazier, *History of the Washington Legislature, 1854–1963*, p. 160–161; Billington, *People, Politics & Public Power*, pp. 175–181

   3. Ibid.

   4. Chasan, *Speaker of the House*, p. 114; *Eldridge, An Oral History*, p. 280; *Margaret Hurley, An Oral History*, p. 100

   5. *Washington State House Journal*, 1961 Session

   6. Smith, *Rosellini*, p. 200–201; Brazier, *History of the Washington Legislature, 1854–1963*, p. 160–161

7. Chasan, *Speaker of the House*, p. 116
8. Ibid., p. 124
9. *Hurley, An Oral History*

CHAPTER SIX: THE COALITION

Interviews with Dan Evans, Sid Snyder, Don Brazier, Adele Ferguson, Howard McCurdy and Dean Foster; Eldridge, Hurley and Copeland oral histories.
1. Oly, 1–15–63, p. A-1
2. The Bremerton Sun, 1–7–63, p. A-1
3. McCaffree and Corbett, *Politics of the Possible*, pp. 28–51
4. Copeland, p. 237
5. Ibid. 238
6. Evans to Hughes
7. McCaffree and Corbett, *Politics of the Possible*, p. 69
8. Brazier, *History of the Washington Legislature*, p. 163
9. *Elmer Huntley, An Oral History*, pp. 35–37
10. The Bremerton Sun, 1–15–63, p. A-1
11. House Journal, 1963
12. Ibid.
13. Ibid., pp. 11–12
14. The Bremerton Sun, 1–15–63, p. A-1
15. Democratic Caucus Report, 38th Session, 1963
16. *R.R. "Bob" Greive, An Oral History*, p. 130–136
17. Copeland, p. 256–257
18. Eldridge, p. 351
19. McCurdy, *Redistricting Wars*, p. 6
20. Greive, p. 144, 162
21. Foster to Hughes
22. McCurdy, p. 51

CHAPTER SEVEN: TAKING ON GIANTS

Interviews with Dan Evans, Nancy Evans, Frank Pritchard, Don Brazier, Howard McCurdy and Dean Foster
1. *Joel M. Pritchard, An Oral History*
2. *Dolliver, An Oral History*, p. 24; McCaffree and Corbett, *Politics of the Possible*, p. 143
3. *Pritchard, An Oral History*
4. Brazier, *History of the Washington Legislature*, 1965–1982, p. 1

CHAPTER EIGHT: WEIRD AND WONDERFUL SHAPES

1. *House Journal*, 1995 Session
2. McCurdy, *A Majority of the People*, p. 72
3. *Copeland, An Oral History*, p. 308

4. Evans Inaugural Address, Washington State Library
5. *Hallauer, An Oral History*, p. 182
6. McCurdy, *Redistricting Wars*, p. 15
7. McCurdy, *A Majority of the People*, p. 92
8. *House Journal*, 1995 Session
9. Ibid.
10. Ibid.
11. Ibid., pp. 476–478
12. Scott, *A Majority of One*, p. 182
13. Ibid., pp. 185–186

CHAPTER NINE: MAJORITY RULES

Interviews with Jim Ellis, Don Brazier and Dan Evans
1. *Eldridge, An Oral History*, p. 394
2. *Copeland, An Oral History*, p. 471
3. Brazier, *History of the Washington Legislature*, 1965–1982, pp. 1–5

CHAPTER 10: GENERAL GORTON

Interviews with Don Brazier, Dan Evans, Sam Reed, Chris Bayley, Robert Doran, Ed Mackie and Dick Mattsen
1. McCaffree and Corbett, *Politics of the Possible*, p. 509
2. Seattle Argus, 1–19–68, p. 1
3. TNT, 9–11–68, p. B-14
4. 1968 Washington State Voters Pamphlet, p. KC-32
5. TNT, 9–11–68, p. B-14
6. Ibid.
7. Puget Soundings, Junior League of Seattle, October 1968, p. 13
8. *The Action Team*, advertising supplement to The Seattle Times, 11–3–68
9. Gorton campaign brochure, Washington History File, State Library
10. Seattle magazine, Politics 68, pp. 84–85, December 1968
11. Ibid.
12. McCaffree and Corbett, *Politics of the Possible*, p. 516
13. Seattle magazine, *Politics 68*, December 1968, p. 85
14. Times, 11–5–68, p. A-1
15. Oly, 1–1–69, p. A-1
16. Bayley and Reed interviews
17. Doran interview
18. Ibid.
19. Mackie interview
20. Mattsen interview
21. Oly, 1–1–69, p. 7; Times, 2–5–69, p. 18, 4–30–69, *Gambling Opinion 'Soft' on Bingo, Pinball Games Even Without Payoff Illegal*
22. *Copeland, An Oral History*, p. 616–617

23. P-I, 10–2–72, p. A-10

24. Times, 5–12–71, p. A-11; P-I, 5–12–81, p. 2

25. Ibid.

26. *Copeland, An Oral History*, p. 699, 709

27. Times, 6–3–70, p. E-1

28. Oly, 2–3–70, p. 12; Times, 3–28–72, p. A-4

29. P-I, 4–30–72, p. C-2

30. Ibid.

31. Oly, 2–3–70, p. A-12

32. Oly, 4–2–72, p. A-1

33. Brazier, *History of the Washington Legislature*, 1965–1982, p. 17

34. Times, 9–3–71, p. A-13

35. Ibid.

36. Ibid.

37. Ibid.

CHAPTER II: UNHAPPY DAYS

1. Times, 7–25–72, p. B-8; P-I, 7–26–72, p. A-13

2. P-I, 11–5–72, p. A-12; 11–8–72, p. A-5; HistoryLink.org Essay 3105, *Madrona Memories*; Times, 5–19–96; 11–12–07

3. Smith, *Rosellini*, pp. 218–226

4. Measuring Worth calculator, using average of CPI, GDP and other benchmarks; Oly, 8–14–72, p. 7

5. Ibid., 8–14–72, p. 7

6. Ibid., 9–20–72, p. 6

7. Gorton, Utter and Bayley to Hughes, 2010

8. P-I, 10–6–72, p. A-1; 10–9–72, pp. A-12 to A-13; Ibid., 10–19–72, p. A-1; Ibid., 10–10–72, p. A-5

9. Oly, 10–26–72, p. A-1; P-I, 9–22–72, p. A-1; Oly, 10–27–72, p. A-1

10. P-I, 10–14–72, p. A-1; 10–15–72, p. A-1; 10–24–72, p. A-1

11. Ibid., 7–26–03; Times, 10–28–72, p. A-1; Oly, 10–29–72, p. A-6; Times, 10–31–72, p. A-1; P-I, 7–26–03

12. Corr, *KING*, p. 199, and Times, 10–31–72, p. A-1; Times, 10–31–72, p. A-1

13. Corr, *KING*, pp. 206–208; Times, 10–28–72, p. A-1; Slade & Sally Gorton to Hughes, 2010

14. Times, 10–29–72, pp. A-1 & A-10; P-I, 10–29–72, p. A-10; Times, 10–31–72, p. A-8; 10–30–72; Oly, 10–31–72, p. 6; P-I, 11–1–72, p. A-4

15. P-I, 11–1–72, p. A-4

16. Times, 10–29–72, p. A-25; 10–30–72

17. Ibid., 10–29–72, p. A-1; 10–29–72, p. A-24; P-I, 10–29–72, p. A-1; Times, 10–30–72, p. A-18

18. Ibid.

19. Ibid., 10–30–72

20. P-I, 10–29–72, p. A-10; Ibid., 7–26–03; Ibid., 1–22–05
21. Corr, *KING*, p. 207; Times, 10–28–72, p. A-1
22. P-I, 10–30–72, p. A-1 & A-5
23. Times, 10–29–72, p. A-25
24. Official election returns, Election Division, Sec. of State; P-I, 10–29–72, p. A-10
25. Evans and Ferguson interviews, 2010
26. Smith, *Rosellini*, p. 7
27. Smith to Hughes
28. P-I, 1–22–05; Dolliver oral history, p. 54
29. McGavick and Vander Stoep to Hughes, 2010
30. Times, 10–30–72, p. A-9; Ellensburg Daily Record, 6–20–73
31. Krogh to Hughes, 2010
32. Times, 8–30–73, p. C-4; Oly, 8–30–73, p. 11; P-I , 8–30–73, p. A-1
33. Rule, *Stranger Beside Me*

CHAPTER 12: RIDING WITH HISTORY

1. Mercer Island Reporter, 9–29–2009
2. P-I, 9–3–71, p. A-14; Oly, 9–6–71, A-10
3. Slade & Sally Gorton to Hughes, 2010
4. Times, 8–19–73
5. Sarah Gorton Nortz to Hughes, 2010
6. Oly, 3–1–73, p. A-6
7. P-I, 7–22–73, p. A-1
8. TNT, 6–9–74, magazine section; Times, 8–19–73
9. Becky Gorton Jack to Hughes, 2010
10. Sarah Gorton Nortz to Hughes, 2010
11. P-I, 7–13–73, p. A-3; Becky Gorton Jack to Hughes, 2010
12. P-I, *Northwest* magazine, 10–14–73
13. Watergate timeline, *Watergate.info*

CHAPTER 13: GORTON AGONISTES

1. Becky Gorton Jack to Hughes, 2010
2. Washington Post, 11–18–73, p. A-1
3. Ibid., 12–7–73, p. A-1
4. P-I, 3–21–74, p. A-1
5. Ibid., 3–21–74, p. A-4; Times, 3–21–74, p. C-1; P-I, 3–22–74, p. A-2
6. Ibid.
7. Ibid.
8. Ibid.
9. P-I, 3–21–74, p. A-1
10. P-I, 3–22–74, p. A-9
11. Ibid.

12. Ibid., 3–26–74, p. A-3; Times, 3–26–74, p. B-2

13. Times, 3–21–74, p. C-1

14. TNT, 3–24–74, p. A-7

15. Ibid., 3–21–74, p A-1

16. Ibid., 3–26–74, p. A-3

17. TNT, 3–25–74, p. A-3

18. Nixon Resignation Speech, 8–8–74, Library of Congress

CHAPTER 14: THE JOLT FROM BOLDT

1. *Land of the Quinault*, pp. 205–206; Brown, *Mountain in the Clouds*, pp. 36–42

2. Ziontz, *A Lawyer in Indian Country*, pp. 51–53; AP, Columbian, 10–8–2005; *Answers.com*, Adams biography; Indian Country Today, 1–11–06

3. Ziontz, pp. 84–85; *Uncommon Controversy*, pp. 18–21

4. Ibid., pp. 94–95; pp. 108–109; Ulrich, *Empty Nets*, p. 121

5. Ibid.

6. Kershner, *Maxey*, pp. 168–177

7. Ziontz, p. 95

8. Ibid., p. 109

9. Ibid., p. 106

10. P-I, 2–15–74, p. A-5

11. Ziontz, p. XII, forward by Charles Wilkinson; NYT, 9–6–92

12. TNT, 2–12–74, p. A-1; Times, 2–12–74, p. A-1; P-I, 2–13–74, p. A-1; Times, 2–14–74

13. Schwantes, p. 373; NYT, 9–6–92; P-I, 1–25–95

14. Ziontz, p. 125

15. P-I, 11–20–04; Johnson interview, 7–30–10; Ulrich, *Empty Nets*, p. 150

16. Ziontz speech and Q&A, 4–13–10, Northwest Historians Guild, Seattle Public Library Northeast Branch

17. *U.S. v. Washington*, 520 F.2d 676

18. Ziontz, pp. 125–127

19. Congressional Record—Senate, December 7, 2000, p. 26430; Washington State Bar Association newsletter, 2010

20. *Puget Sound Gillnetters Ass'n v. US Dist. Court*, 573 F. 2d 1123—Court of Appeals, 9th Circuit 1978; *State of Washington v. Washington State Commercial Passenger Fishing Vessel Association*, 443 U.S. 658 (1979); Ziontz, p. 128.

21. *Tribes, Casinos and Hardball Politics*, Gaming Law Review, W. Dale Mason, Volume 5, Number 4, August 2001

22. TNT, 9–29–96

23. Gorton Oral History

24. Ziontz speech and Q&A, 4–13–2010

25. *Tonasket v. Washington*, 411 U.S. 451, 1973

26. *Antoine v. Washington*, 420 U.S. 194, 1975

27. *Colville v. Washington*, 447 U.S. 134, 1980; Ziontz, page 139

28. *Oliphant v. Suquamish Indian Tribe*, 435 U.S. 191, 1978; Ziontz, p. 171

29. P-1, 2–12–2004; U.S. District Court, Western District of Washington, Seattle, CV 9213RSM; Times, 1–24–2008

30. TNT, 5–9–76, p. A-1

31. Ibid., 5–10–76, p. A-1

32. Ibid., 5–11–76, p. A-2

33. Ed Mackie to Hughes, 2010

34. Ziontz, p. 97; Johnson interview, 7–30–2010

35. *DeFunis v. Odegaard*, 416 U.S. 312, 1974; Times, 2–26–74

36. P-I, 2–15–74, p. A-5; Gorton to Hughes, 2010

37. Times, 2–26–74

38. *Hunt v. Washington State Apple Advertising Commission*, 432 US. 333, 1977

CHAPTER 15: DESIGNATED HITTERS

1. Carlin, *Brain Droppings*

2. P-I, 7–6–2001; Bouton, *Ball Four*, p. 107, p. 164

3. HistoryLink.org Essay 2164, *Kingdome*

4. Thiel, *Out of Left Field*, p. 70; Seattle Pilots History interviews, Jerry McNaul, http://seattlepilots.com/

5. Thiel, *Out of Left Field* pp. 12–13

6. McNaul interview, 2010

7. Thiel, *Out of Left Field*, p. 13; McNaul and Dwyer; http://seattlepilots.com/

8. Seattle Pilots History interviews, Bill Dwyer, http://seattlepilots.com/dwyer_int.html

CHAPTER 16: BICENTENNIAL FOLLIES

1. Kaufman, *Henry M. Jackson*, p. 225, pp. 301–303.

2. Ibid, p. 309, p. 320, p. 336–337; Evans interview 2010; P-I, 11–16–75, p. B-2

3. Oly, 11–3–76, p. A-1

4. Times, 9–19–76, p. A-23; P-I, 9–29–76, p. G-2; Argus, 4–8–77, p. 1; P-I, 11–4–76, p. A-16

5. "No Smoking" sign in Washington State Archives; HistoryLink Essay 8535, 2008; Mardesich oral history, pp. 118–120

6. P-I, 5–12–76, p. A-1; Oly, 11–3–76, p. A-8; P-I, 11–3–76, p. A-1; Clark, *The Dry Years*, pp. 263–266; Times, 9–24–71; Ibid., 9–30–71; P-I, 6–2–73; Times, 6–5–76; Washington Supreme Court, 93 Wash.2d 603, 611 P.2d 758; Eldridge oral history

7. Ibid.

8. Oly, 8–20–76, p. B-5; Carter, *White House Diary*, p. 5, 123

9. Guzzo, *Is It True What They Say about Dixy*, pp. 184–186; Scates, *Warren G. Magnuson*, p. 307

10. Washington Secretary of State Legacy Project Timeline, www.sos.wa.gov/ legacyproject/timeline; Times, 10–5–86, p. B-6

11. Weekly, 2–2–77, p. 11;

12. Brazier, *History of the Washington Legislature, 1965–82*, p. 32; Argus, 4–8–77, p. 1

13. Weekly, 2–2–77, p. 11

14. Scates, *Warren G. Magnuson*, p. 305

15. HistoryLink.org Essay 5620; Times, 10–31–77, p. A-7; *Ray v. Atlantic Richfield Co., 435 U.S. 151* (1978); Scates, *Warren G. Magnuson*, p. 305; tanker traffic comparisons from Kathy Fletcher, executive director, People for Puget Sound, 2010

16. Oly, 12–13–2009; Whidbey News Times, 5–16–10; Times, 1–16–08; Munro interview, 2010

17. Scates, *Warren G. Magnuson*, pp. 294–295

18. P-I, 11–28–78, p. A-6

CHAPTER 17: A GOLD WATCH FOR MAGGIE

1. U.S. Forest Service report on the Mount St. Helens National Volcanic Monument and U.S. Geological Survey Fact Sheet 036–00; Scates, *Warren G. Magnuson*, p. 298, 324

2. Scates, *Warren G. Magnuson*, p. 317, pp. 309–314; P-I, *Northwest* magazine, 2–8–81, p. 6

3. Jimmy Carter "crisis of confidence" speech, 7–15–79, Carter Presidential Library; White, *America in Search of Itself*, p. 258, pp, 266–269

4. Watson column in Times, 12–20–92; Corr, *KING*, pp. 201–202; P-I, 6–10–80, A-14

5. Newman interview, 2010; P-I, 7–19–80, p. A-5; P-I, 10–26–80, p. A-23

6. P-I, 5–7–80, p. A-8

7. Newman interview, 2010

8. Times Centennial feature, 9–29–96; Scates, *Magnuson*, p. 127

9. Lois and Pitts, *The Art of Advertising*

10. Times, 10–26–80, p. B-2

11. Scates, *Magnuson*, pp. 268–269, p. 310; Kaufman, *Jackson*, p. 405; P-I, 8–26–80, p A-2, p. A-23

12. Times, 10–26–80, p. B-2; P-I, 10–26–80, p. A-23

13. Times, 11–2–80, p. A-1; P-I, 11–5–80, p. A-3, A-5

14. Gorton campaign ad comparing endorsements, Washington State Archives

15. Scates, *Magnuson*, p. 318–319; AP, 11–4–80; P-I, 11–4–80, p. A-1; White, *America in Search of Itself*, p. 387, p. 409

16. P-I, 11–5–80, pp. A-3, A-5; Spokane Daily Chronicle, 11–5–80, p. 1

17. Ibid.

18. Ibid.

19. Times, 11–9–86, p. A-18

CHAPTER 18: THE GIANT KILLERS

1. P-I, 7–12–85, p. A-1
2. NYT, 6–14–81, p. A-5
3. Ibid., 10–22–82, p. A-14; P-I, 10–22–86, p. A-12
4. Interview transcripts for "Slade Gorton: Ladies Man?", *Washington Law & Politics* magazine, June 1998
5. Agnew interview with Hamer and Parks, 1998; Koch and Vander Stoep Legacy Project interviews, 2010
6. Ibid.
7. McPherson, *Best of My Ability,* pp. 285–286, p. 442
8. NYT, 1–25–81, p. A-5
9. *Sen. Pete Domenici: nuclear Renaissance man,* msnbc.com, 1–24–07; Domenici to Hughes, 10–20–10; P-I, 10–22–86, p. A-12
10. Ulrich, *Empty Nets,* pp. 161–163; Oregon Historical Society CN 020037; Times, 8–14–82, p. A-20
11. NYT, 6–14–81, p. A-5
12. Ibid.
13. Ibid.
14. Hayward, *Age of Reagan,* pp. 155–156; Boston Globe, 5–26–81, p. A-1; Oly, 10–10–81, p. A-1
15. Ibid.

CHAPTER 19: DEFICIT HAWKS

1. White & Wildavsky, *Deficit and the Public Interest,* p. 118
2. Boston Globe, 2–20–81, p. 1; Ibid., 3–19–81, p. 1; NYT, 11–13–81, p. A-21
3. Ibid.
4. Boston Globe, 2–20–81, p. 1; Ibid., 3–19–81, p. 1
5. National Journal Magazine, 3–28–81; P-I, 3–3–06, *Indian clinic's budget number being called again*
6. P-I, 10–29–81, p. A-1; Kaufman, *Jackson,* p. 146, 416; P-I, 10–29–81, p. A-4
7. AP, Boston Globe, 10–9–81, p. 1; *Thicker Than Oil,* p. 160; Safire, NYT, 10–8–81, p. A-27
8. Ibid.
9. Boston Globe, 10–14–81, p. 1; NYT, 10–29–81, p. A-1
10. Kaufman, *Jackson,* p. 419; Jackson, Amendment 1448, Congressional Record, 5–13–82; Durbin, *Tree Huggers,* pp. 55–56; *"What's Good for Boeing,"* Forbes, 6–21–82, pp. 36–37; Boston Globe, 7–22–82, p. 1; Gorton interview with Zeiger, 4–13–10; Jackson press release 5–2–83
11. AP, 2–1–05, Wyoming trib.com; The Columbian, 5–16–10, p. A-1
12. AP in Boston Globe, 2–25–1982, p. 1; Washington v. Seattle School Dist. No. 1, 458 U.S. 457 (1982); Weekly, 10–19–88, p. 2
13. NYT, 4–2–82, p. A-18; AP in Fort Lauderdale Sun Sentinel, 3–26–86, p. A-1
14. Ibid., 5–15–82, p. 2

15. NYT, 9–25–82, p. 1

16. Marguerite Del Giudice, Boston Globe, 12–29–1981, p.1; Copyright 1981, The Boston Globe. Reprinted with permission

CHAPTER 20: SHIP SHAPE

1. Charles Fager, op-ed, NYT, 3–23–81, p. A-17; Ibid., 5–21–82, p. D-7; Ibid, 7–27–82, p. A-22; Ibid., 2–16–83, p. D-4.

2. NYT, 7–14–82; Zeiger interview with Gorton, 4–13–10; NYT, 2–16–83, p. D-4; Philadelphia Inquirer, 8–28–83, p. A-3; Legacy interview with Chris Koch, 10–7–10

3. Carter, *White House Diary*, p. 123, 200, 282

4. Kaufman, *Jackson*, pp. 14–15, pp. 25–26

5. Hans Zeiger, *Scoop and Slade: Partners in the Senate*, unpublished Independent Study paper, 2010

6. Ibid.; Legacy Project interviews with Sally Gorton and Peter Jackson, 2010

7. Kaufman, *Jackson*, pp. 420–423; Gorton interview with Zeiger, 4–13–10

8. Dotzauer to Kaufman and Hughes; Kaufman, *Jackson*, pp. 428–43.

9. Ibid; Butterworth interview with Hamer and Parks, 1998; Gorton to Hughes; Hayward, *The Age of Reagan*, p. 8.

10. Tate, HistoryLink.org Essay 7167, 2004; Hughes, *Nancy Evans*, pp. 52–54, 245–247

11. Ibid.; Dan Evans and Ralph Munro interviews, 2009

12. P-I, 11–9–83, p. A-1, A-4; HistoryLink Essay 8600

13. Kaufman, *Jackson*, p. 162, p. 165; Evans, *Bipartisanship protects Washington's wilderness*, Times, 9–8–2003; Wall Street Journal, 5–15–84, p. 1

14. Whitesell, *Defending Wild Washington*, pp. 180–181; Times, *The gift of Wilderness*, 7–2–09; Durbin, *Tree Huggers*, p. 62

15. Kaufman, *Jackson*, p. 424; Time magazine, 10–17–83, *Dimming Watt*; Creigh Agnew to Hughes, 10–26–10; NYT, 5–27–84

16. Ibid.

CHAPTER 21: THE YEAR OF LIVING DANGEROUSLY

1. NYT, 1–7–94, p. 1; Hayward, *Age of Reagan*, p. 36, p. 140; Max Friedersdorf oral history, Miller Center of Public Affairs, University of Virginia

2. White & Wildavsky, *The Deficit*, p. 309

3. Ibid., p. 38; Stockman, *Triumph of Politics*, pp. 369–70; *Reagan on the Defense*, Newsweek, 4–18–83, pp. 22–24

4. NYT, 3–16–83, p. A-1; Washington Post, 8–21–83, pp. A-1, A-6; Hayward, *Age of Reagan*, pp. 275–276

5. Ibid.

6. Ibid.

7. *Reagan on the Defense*, Newsweek, 4–18–83, pp. 22–24; Domenici to Hughes, 10–20–10

8. White & Wildavsky, *The Deficit*, pp. 369–371; NYT, 6–3–83, p. A-18; Ibid., 10–8–83, p. 1; *A ticking time bomb*, Times, 1–22–84

9. White & Wildavsky, *The Deficit*, pp. 396–397

10. Times, 5–9–84, p. A-24; 5–10–84, p. G-2

11. Ibid., 3–9–84, *Gorton offers plan*

12. Ibid., 3–21–84, p. A-13

13. Times/P-I, 12–16–84, p. A-13; Hayward, *Age of Reagan*, p. 338

14. Times, 11–4–84, p. A-2

15. Hayward, *Age of Reagan*, p. 341, 375, 387–388

16. Times, 1–19–84, p. A-16

17. John Dumbrell, *The Carter Presidency*, p. 6, 34

18. Hayward, *Age of Reagan*, p. 341, 375, 387–388

19. Times, 11–29–84, p. A-16

20. NYT, 11–29–84, p. A-1; Ibid., *A long climb gets tougher*, 5–13–95

CHAPTER 22: DÉJÀ VU ALL OVER AGAIN

1. L.A. Times, 5–10–85, *Wilson Wheeled in to Cast Key Vote*

2. White & Wildavsky, *The Deficit*, p. 435; P-I, 7–12–85, p. A-1

3. Ibid.

4. NYT, 8–4–85, p. A-4

5. Ibid.

6. Boschwitz to Hughes, 10–26–10

7. Times, 10–18–85, p. D-12; P-I, 4–10–2006, *Alaska's Sen. Stevens stomps . . .*

8. NYT, 8–4–85, p. A-4; White & Wildavsky, *The Deficit*, p. 438

9. White & Wildavsky, *The Deficit*, pp. 425, 431–432, 442

10. Ibid.

11. National Journal, 1–4–86, pp. 15–21; U.S. News & World Report, 2–3–86, pp. 20–21

12. White & Wildavsky, *The Deficit*, p. 432

13. White & Wildavsky, *The Deficit*, p. 484

14. Ibid., pp. 490, 498; Newsday, 10–22–86, p. 15

CHAPTER 23: GORTON V. ZAPPA

1. Senate Commerce Committee hearing transcript, 9–19–85; qotd.org; Lowe, *The Words and Music of Frank Zappa*, pp. 194–195

2. Senate Commerce Committee hearing transcript, 9–19–85

3. Ibid.; Lowe, *The Words and Music of Frank Zappa*, pp. 194–195

4. Senate Commerce Committee hearing transcript, 9–19–85

5. Ibid.

6. Ibid.

7. UPI, 12–6–93, *Frank Zappa dies*

8. Ibid.

9. Hamer and Parks interview of McGettigan for *Slade Gorton: Ladies Man,* Washington Law & Politics magazine, June 1998

10. Prerau, *Seize the Daylight,* pp. 206–209

11. Ibid.

12. Times, 1–10-86, p. B-2; 3–20-86, p. D-2; 9–11–04, p. A-11; Houston Chronicle, 9–18–86, p. 7; Newsday, 10–22–86, p. 15

13. HistoryLink.org Essay 5739 ; P-I, 9–11–94, *Former senator dies*

14. Ibid.

15. Ibid.

16. Counterpoint, 2–24–86, Henry Seidel, *Will the real Brock Adams please stand up and expose the real Slade Gorton?*

17. P-I, 3–21–86, p. A-3; Times, 5–5–86, *"People mutter, 'Where's Brock?'"*

CHAPTER 24: LET'S MAKE A DEAL

1. NYT, 7–6–86, p. A-10; Times, 2–13–2002, p. A-1, A-11.; NYT, 12–3–87, p. A-36; Times, 7–13–86, p. A-14

2. Ibid.; NYT, 7–25–86, p. A-31; P-I, 6–28–86, p. A-3; Ibid., 7–2–86, p. A-12

3. Evans to Hughes, 10–19–10; Manion to Hughes, 10–20–10; NYT, 7–25–86. P. A-31

4. Ibid.

5. NYT, 7–6–86, p. A-10; Newsday, 10–22–86, p. 15; Elway Research Inc. polling data 1986

6. Times, 7–7–86, p. B-1

7. Newsday, 10–22–86, p. 15

8. AP and NYT, 12–20–83, p. A-29

9. Wall Street Journal, 11–13–86, p. 1

10. UPI, NYT, 10–10–86, P. A-19

11. Wall Street Journal, 11–25–86, p. 1

CHAPTER 25: TRICK OR TREAT

1. Newman to Hughes, 8–11–10

2. John Carlson, Weekly, 1–2–88, p. 32; Newman to Hughes, 11–7–10; Excell to Hughes, 11–1–10

3. P-I, 11–16–86, p. F-4

4. Times, 7–6–86, p. B-1; P-I, 8–30–86, p. 1; 10–26–86, p. A-1; P-I, 10–22–86, p. A-12; Boston Globe, 11–1–86, p. 4; AP, Oly, 10–30–86, p. A-2; NYT, 10–22–86, p. A-28

5. Ibid.

6. Oly, 6–15–86, p. A-2

7. Times, 9–18–86, *Both sides stumped*; P-I, 10–22–86, p. 1

8. P-I, 5–5–97, p. A-3

9. Newsday, 10–22–86, p. 15; NYT, 10–22–86, p. A-28; P-I, 11–3–88, p. A-6

10. NYT, 10–22–86, A-28

11. P-I, 11–1–86, p. A-4

12. Newman to Hughes, 8–11–10; Excell to Hughes, 11–1–10

13. P-I, 10–22–86, p. A-14; Connelly, Seattle P-I.com, 6–30–10, *Nuclear waste in Senate race*

14. Connelly to Hughes, 11–10–10

15. Richard Larsen, Times, 5–8–88, *Gardner's petty, peevish campaign kickoff*; Times, 11–2–86, p. D-1; AP in Oly, 10–20–86, p. A-1; P-I, 10–29–86, p. 1; Boston Globe, 10–23–86, p. 8; P-I, 10–28–86, p. A-16; Times/P-I, 10–26–86, p. A-1

16. Oly, 11–3–86, p. A-1; NYT, 10–22–86, p. A-28; Times, 11–9–86, p. B-1

17. Times, 10–30–86, p. B-1; AP in Oly, 10–30–86, p. A-2

18. Boston Globe, 11–1–86, p. 4; NYT, 10–22–86, p. A-28

19. Excell to Hughes, 11–1–10, 11–8–10; Newman to Hughes, 11–8–10

20. Times, 10–25–86, p. A-11; AP, Oly, 10–29–86. P. 1; Ibid., 10–31–86, *Senate campaign heavy hitters head for Spokane*

21. Spokane Spokesman-Review, 10–31–86, p. 1; Ibid., 11–1–86, p. 1; Boston Globe, 11–1–86, p. 4; Times, 11–1–86, p. A-20; Hayward, *Age of Reagan*, pp. 260, 513; O'Neill with Novak, *Man of the House*, p. 370

22. Spokesman-Review, 10–31–86, p. 1

23. Connelly to Hughes, 11–10–10

24. Spokesman-Review, 10–31–86, p. 1

25. Transcript of Reagan speech at the Spokane Coliseum, 10–31–86, Reagan Presidential Papers; Spokesman-Review, 11–1–86, p. A-1

26. Ibid.

27. Times, 11–2–86, p. D-1; P-I, 11–3–86, p. A-1; Ibid., 11–4–86, p. A-9. Boston Globe, 11–2–86, p. 28; Spokesman-Review/ Chronicle, 11–1–86, p. A-6

28. Oly, 11–3–86, p. A-1

29. Elway Research Inc. polling data

30. P-I, 11–4–86, p. A-8

31. Ibid.

32. Ibid.

33. Times, 11–5–86, p. B-1

34. Oly, 11–5–86, p. A-1

35. Times, 11–5–86, pp. A-1, B-6

36. Times, 11–5–86, p. B-1; P-I, 11–6–86, p. A-1

37. Ibid.

CHAPTER 26: POST-MORTEMS

1. P-I, 11–20–86, p. D-1; Times, 11–20–86, p. F-1

2. Newman to Hughes, 11–7–10

3. Times, 11–9–86, p. B-1

4. Oly, 9–21–86, p. A-1; Times, 11–5–86, p. A-1; Ibid., 11–9–86, MacLeod, *Avoiding perils of polling voters*; Ibid., *Hanford seen as Gorton's Iran*, p. B-1

5. Oly, 11–12–86, p. B-1; Times, 11–2–86, p. A-22
6. Boston Globe, 11–7–86, p. 20

CHAPTER 27: THE COMEBACK

1. P-I, 11–25–86, p. A-5
2. *The Reagan Diaries*, p. 501
3. San Francisco Chronicle, 12–13–86, p. 7; San Diego Tribune, 2–5–88, p. A-20; New York Times, 3–26–88, *Reagan nominee for judgeship urged to withdraw*
4. P-I, 11–25–86, p. A-5
5. P-I, 3–11–87, p. A-1
6. David Ammons, *The Daily World*, Aberdeen, 6–29–91, p. A-4
7. NYT, 6–9–87, p. A-18
8. NYT, 6–9–87, p. A-18, 12–3–1987, p. A-36; National Journal, 11–12–83; Times 2–13–02, p. A-1
9. Washington Post, 11–6–87, p. A-32
10. NYT, 10–21–87, p. A-21; 12–1–87, p. A-22
11. NYT, 4–17–88, Daniel J. Evans, *Why I'm quitting the Senate*
12. Times, 10–21–87, p. A-1
13. P-I, 10–21–97, p. A-1; Times, 10–21–87, p. A-1; Washington Post, 10–27–87, p. A-3
14. Ibid.
15. P-I, 11–3–88, p. A-6
16. Times, 9–12–88, p. B-1
17. Quoted in Siefert, *Extending the borders of Russian History*, p. 450
18. P-I, 11–3–88, p. A-6
19. P-I, 1–9–88, p. A-4
20. P-I, 1–9–88, p. A-1; USA Today, 11–9–8
21. Charles H. Sheldon, *The Washington High Bench*, p. 166; P-I, 4–20–88, p. A-1; Seattle Times, 3–4–88, p. A-1
22. Times, 4–19–88, p. B-1; P-I, 4–20–88, p. A-1; Seattle Times, 9–12–88, p. B-1
23. Ibid.; Julian P. Kanter Political Commercial Archive, University of Oklahoma
24. Partlow to Hughes, 11–13–10; Connelly to Hughes, 11–29–10
25. NYT, 9–22–88, p. A-31; Frank Chesley, HistoryLink Essay 8600, 2008
26. Times, 10–30–88, p. A-16; McGavick to Hughes, 12–1–10
27. Bremerton Sun, 8–26–88; P-I, 8–18–88; Bellingham Herald, 9–3–88; Times, 5–19–2003, *A future in politics?;* Weekly, 9–28–88, p. 23
28. NYT, 9–22–88, p. A-31; Weekly, 9–28–88, p. 23
29. Boston Globe, 10–2–88, p. 9; NYT, 11–3–88, p. B15
30. P-I, 9–30–88, Kari Tupper interview; Times/P-I, 10–2–88, p. A-4; Weekly, 10–5–88, p. 2
31. Times/P-I, 10–2–88, p. A-1; Washington Post, 10–25–88, P. A-7

32. Times, 10–28–88, p. C-4

33. P-I, 10–5–88, p. A-1; Times, 10–16–88, p. A-1; 10–30–88, Richard W. Larsen, *A plea for decency*

34. Times, 10–16–88, p. B-1

35. Times, 10–16–88, p. B-1; P-I, 10–5–88, p. A-1; 10–8–88, p. B-1

36. P-I, 10–8–88, p. B-1; 10–11–88, p. A-5; 11–3–88, p. A-6

37. UW Daily, 11–21–79, p. 11

38. P-I, 10–12–88, B-1; Times, 9–7–06, *McGavick's apology*

39. Times, 10–14–88, p. E-1; 10–13–88, p. D-4; 10–17–88, p. B-1; Weekly, 11–2–88, p. 32

40. Ibid.

41. Ibid.

42. NYT, 11–3–88, p. B-15; Times, 9–7–06, *McGavick's apology strategy*

43. Ibid.

44. Times, 7–28–06, *Father was taproot*; David Postman, *Times* blog, 8–24–06; McGavick to Hughes, 12–1–10

45. P-I, 11–3–88, p. A-1

46. Weekly, 11–2–88, p. 32

47. P-I, 11–2–88, p. B-1

48. Julian P. Kanter Political Commercial Archive, University of Oklahoma

49. Times, 11–6–88, p. D-2; Chesley, HistoryLink Essay 8600, 2008

50. P-I, 10–20–88, p. B-1; Times, 9–7–06, *McGavick's apology*; Julian P. Kanter Political Commercial Archive, University of Oklahoma; Evans to Hughes, 11–18–10

51. Evans to Hughes, 11–10–10 and 2–8–11; McGavick to Hughes, 12–1–10; Gary T. Smith to Hughes, 2–1–11

52. Evans to Hughes, 11–10–10 and 2–8–11; McGavick to Hughes, 12–1–10; Gary T. Smith to Hughes, 2–1–11

53. P-I, 11–9–81, p. A-1; Weekly, 11–16–88, p. 23

54. Times, 11–9–88, p. A-1; Ibid., 9–7–06, *McGavick's apology*

CHAPTER 28: WHO GIVES A HOOT?

1. Werner Mayr, *The Cinderella Tree*, pp. 1–3, 35–39

2. Ibid.; Doug Barker, The Spotted Owl, *On the Harbor*, pp. 170–174

3. Ibid.

4. Ibid.

5. Ibid.

6. Tipton to Hughes, 12–9–10

7. Doug Barker, The Spotted Owl, *On the Harbor*, pp. 174–175; Hughes interviews

8. Time, 6–25–90, *Owl vs. Man: Who Gives A Hoot?*

9. Doug Barker, The Spotted Owl, *On the Harbor*, p. 170; Durbin, *Tree Huggers*, p. 93

10. Transcript of Hamer and Parks interviews for *"Slade Gorton: Ladies' Man?"*

11. Times, 6–30–90, *Standing tall for timber*

12. Ibid.

13. Times, 6–15–90, *Timber-dependent families come to Seattle*

14. Times, 6–16–89, p. A-7

15. Ibid; Durbin, *Tree Huggers*, pp. 117–118

16. Times, 1–5–90, *Warning: Expect Timber Cutbacks*; Durbin, *Tree Huggers*, pp. 106–109

17. Barker, *On the Harbor*, p. 175

18. NYT, 4–27–89, p. A-18; Times, 6–28–90, *Gorton sowing false hopes*

19. Ibid.

20. Ibid.

21. Oregonian, 9–27–90, p. C-10; Times, 9–30–90, *Gorton's positions confound labeling*

22. Ibid.

23. Times, 5–24–91, p. A-1

24. Times, 6–27–91, *Gorton calls Dwyer "anti-human"*; David Wilma, HistoryLink.org Essay 5321, 2003

25. Time, 5–25–92, *Manuel Lujan: The Stealth Secretary*; Durbin, *Tree Huggers*, pp. 135–139

26. Times 8–28–90, *Washington halting a lot of logging*

27. Jim Carlson and Kellie Carlson Daniels interviews, 12–9–10

28. Ibid.

29. Times, 5–21–95, *Gorton's ESA*

30. Times, 5–9–95, *Gorton puts Endangered Species Act on Notice*

31. Ibid., 6–14–95, *Gorton cleared*

32. Times, 5–10–95, *Greenpeace wanted posters*

33. Ibid. , p. 188; Gorton, *Congressional Record*, 6–30–93

34. Durbin, *Tree Huggers*, pp.254–258; Whitesell, *Defending Wild Washington*, pp. 190–192

35. Ibid.

36. Ibid.; Times, 3–14–96, *U.S. Senate rejects logging-repeal efforts*; P-I, 12–14–96, p. P-1

37. Eureka, Calif., Times-Standard, 6–15–2005, *Clash of Cousins*; Smithsonian magazine, January 2009, *The Spotted Owl's New Nemesis*

38. Barker, *On the Harbor*, p. 174; Dietrich, *The Final Forest*, p. 237; Times, 9–11–10, *20 years after protections*; WFPA Annual Report 2010

CHAPTER 29: BACK AT BAT

1. Thiel, *Out of Left Field*, pp. 5–52; Times, 2–13–92, *What would baseball say . . .?*

2. Thiel, p. 47; P-I, 6–12–92, p. A-1

3. Times, 9–19–91, *Strikeout legislation?*
4. Thiel, pp. 50–51
5. Ibid.
6. Times, 12–26–10, p. A-3
7. Thiel, pp. 60–61.
8. Ibid., p. 72
9. NYT, *Sports of the Times,* 1–29–92; Times, 2–13–92, *What would baseball say . . .?*
10. P-I, 6–16–92, p. 1
11. P-I, 6–12–92, p. 1; 6–13–92, p.1; 6–16–92, p. 1

CHAPTER 30: NEW FRIENDS AND OLD ENEMIES

1. Anchorage Daily News, 106–89, p. B-1; Times, 1–20–90, *Meeting on quakes;* 4–1–90, *Double-hulls provision;* P-I, 11–30–90, p. C-1
2. Times, 1–22–90, *How will Northwest states fare?;* 8–3–90, *B-2 critics;* 7–27–91, *Abortion issue may spur veto;* 8–4–91, *How your lawmaker voted*
3. Ibid., 1–9–91, *Gorton joins key panel*
4. Times, 5–4–89, p. A-14; Houston Post, 5–4–89, p. C-1
5. USA Today, 3–9–90, p. 4; Globe & Mail, Toronto, 9–25–90, p. B-4
6. Newsday, 5–18–89, p. 42; UPI, Richmond Times-Dispatch, 5–18–89, p. 23; Times, 1–31–92, *Cable regulations win Senate approval;* 10–11–92, *How your lawmaker voted;* 5–30–94, *Gorton to look for credit*
7. Washington Post, 6–16–89, p. B-1; San Francisco Chronicle, 9–30–89, p. 1; Richmond Times-Dispatch, 10–18–90, p. 2; Times, 10–26–90, 9–29–91, 6–7–92, 9–27–92, *How lawmakers voted;* Seattle Weekly, 1–21–98, *Clean Slade*
8. Ibid.; 136 Cong. Rec. 33406
9. Times, 10–11–92, How your lawmaker voted
10. Times, 3–7–90, *Gorton denied visa*
11. The Sun, Baltimore, 7–1–93, p. A-12; P-I, 10–22–92, p. A-2
12. Times, 8–29–90, p. A-5; P-I, 11–2–90, p. A-2, 12–4–90, p. A-5; Times, 1–4–91, *Lawmakers differ over gulf timing;* 1–11–91, *Foley calls coming vote an 'Issue of conscience'*
13. Times, 1–15–91, *Thousands take to streets;* West, *Black Lamb and Grey Falcon;* also in The Atlantic Monthly, January 1941

CHAPTER 31: A HOUSE DIVIDED

1. Ibid., 12–12–91, *Adams is plowing on*
2. Ibid., 3–1–92, p. A-1, 3–2–92, p. A-1; HistoryLink.org Essay 5739
3. Times, 3–31–92, *Gorton says he believes Adams allegations,* 4–1–92, *Gorton says Adams should quit*
4. P-I, 6–18–92, p. A-1, 6–19–92, p. A-1, 6–20–92, p. B-1; Times, 6–20–92, p. A-1, 6–23–92, p. B-1
5. Ibid.

6. Times, 6–23–92, p. A-8
7. Ibid., 6–28–92, p. A-15, *Letters to the editor*
8. NYT, 10–19–82, *In Northwest, Free-for-All Elections*
9. Times, 11–13–92, *Where will Gorton take his party?*
10. Ibid., 4–13–93, *Slade Gorton—Portrait of a political enigma*
11. Ibid.
12. Times, 10–16–91, *Gorton, Adams stuck to their guns throughout*

CHAPTER 32: MESSY AND UNPREDICTABLE

1. Lott, *Herding Cats*, pp. 117–119
2. Greenspan, *The Age of Turbulence*, p. 148
3. Times, 3–6–94, *Can Gorton win another term?*; 11–16–93, *Gorton plans crime summit*; 11–3–94, p. A-14
4. Ibid.
5. Ibid., 5–8–94, *If Slade is no slam dunk . . .*
6. Ibid.
7. Ibid., 5–30–94, *Gorton to look for credit*; 9–21–94, *Sims clinches primary*
8. Ibid., 6–7–94, *Gorton wins police support*
9. AP, 6–16–94, *Gorton got over $16,000*; Times, 10–2–94, *Political Notebook*
10. Times, 7–15–94, *Gorton learned his lesson*; Clinton, *My Life*, p. 488, 496, 621
11. Times, 7–15–94, *Gorton learned his lesson*; Clinton, *My Life*, p. 488, 496, 621
12. Times, 10–23–94, *Gorton vs. Sims*
13. Ibid., 8–16–94, *Gorton voted for law he's fighting*; Brown, *Mountain in the Clouds*, Chapter Four; *Defending Wild Washington*, pp. 296–298
14. Ibid.
15. Ibid.
16. Gorton file, Washington State Archives, Olympia
17. Times, 9–21–94, *Sims clinches primary*
18. Ibid., 10–23–94, *If you want nasty . . .*, 11–9–04, p. B-1
19. Weekly, 5–11–98, *'P-I' intelligence*; 12–1–99, *Slade slays 'em*
20. Times, 11–3–94, p. B-10
21. Clinton, *My Life*, p. 621; Lott, *Herding Cats*, pp. 126–127
22. Lott, p. 127
23. Washington Secretary of State Web site, *Resources*, 1994 elections; New York Times, 7–12–10, *Times Topics*; Washington Post, *Who runs GOV Web site*; The Elway Poll, May 2000
24. Times, 11–9–94, p. A-1, B-1

CHAPTER 33: CLOSE CALLS AND TRAGEDIES

1. Times, 12–7–94, *Gorton vows quick return*, 12–12–94, *Gorton will be home for holiday*
2. Ibid., 5–4–93, *Inside Politics*; 2–6–95; *Murray, Gorton trying to get along*

3. Times, 10–2–10, *Suburban mom to D.C. power broker*

4. Times, 9–8–96, *Senate takes up Defense of Marriage Act*; 2–3–97, *Vote puts lawmakers in a bind*

5. Bellingham Herald, 6–7–09, *Timeline of Bellingham pipeline explosion*; HistoryLink.org Essay 5468; Times, 3–13–00, *Father calls for pipeline scrutiny*

6. Ibid.; Times, 9–8–00, *Senate supports pipeline scrutiny*

7. Ibid., 4–24–97, *Gorton seeks role in naming federal judges*

8. Ibid.

9. Ibid., 5–5–1998, *Deal To Break Senate Logjam*; Weekly, 10–14–98, *Appeals Court Barbie*; P-I, 1–27–99, p. A-2

10. Ibid.; NYT, 5–28–99, *A nomination is withdrawn*

11. Times, 9–16–99, *Durham resigning*; 12–31–02, *Ex-chief justice blazed trail*

CHAPTER 34: REFUSE TO LOSE

1. Vancouver Columbian, 2–2–95, p.1

2. Times, 9–28–95, *M's set Oct. 30 deadline*

3. Thiel, *Out of Left Field*, p. 138

4. Times/P-I, 12–15–96, p. A-1

5. Ibid., 12–15–96, p. B-1

6. Ibid.; Thiel, *Out of Left Field*, pp. 156–158;

7. Times/P-I, 12–15–96, p. C-1

CHAPTER 35: THE COUNCIL OF TRENT

1. Lott to Hughes, oral history interview, 2010

2. Lott, *Herding Cats*, p. 102–104, 120, 129–144; Washington Post, 2–3–99, p. C-1

3. Times, 1–11–95, *Gorton to head Interior panel*

4. Times, 1–20–95, *Gorton: Salmon might have to go*

5. Times, 4–9–98, *Free the Elwha*; 10–25–98, *Dam-removal politics*

6. Times, 4–12–98, *Salmon issues split NW delegation*

7. P-I, 9–8–00, p. A-1

8. Times, 4–12–98, *Salmon issues split NW delegation*

9. Bumpus and Williams to Hughes, 1–18–11; Puget Sound Business Journal, 4–30/5–6, 2010, *Citizen Slade*

10. Times, 8–30–99, *Gorton bill shows his new interest in education*

11. Ibid.

12. Ibid.

13. Ibid.

CHAPTER 36: 'DUMP SLADE 2000'

1. Weekly, 10–8–97, Nina Shapiro, *Slade's Indian War*

2. Times, 8–17–95, *NW tribes, Gorton are again clashing*; *Endangered Peoples of North America*, p. 104, 107–109

3. Native Americas, Fall 2000 issue, *The New Terminators*, Bruce E. Johansen
4. Times, 7–18–97, *Gorton, Tribes at odds over remains*
5. TNT, 5–19–99, *Pride, sorrow emerge from kill*
6. Times, 9–4–97, *Nations Tribes gather*
7. Ibid.; Weekly, 7–15–98, *Gorton rides again*
8. Ibid.
9. Times, 9–4–97, *Nations Tribes gather*; NYT, 8–27–97, *Senate measures would deal blow to Indian rights*; Weekly, 10–8–97, Nina Shapiro, *Slade's Indian War*
10. NYT, 8–27–97, *Senate measures would deal blow to Indian rights*
11. Ibid.
12. Weekly, 10–8–97, Nina Shapiro, *Slade's Indian War*
13. Ibid.
14. Times, 3–12–98, *Gorton calls for right to sue tribes*
15. Ibid.
16. Ibid.
17. Ibid.
18. Ibid.
19. Times, 4–8–98, *Tribal-Immunity Issues Debated*
20. Ibid.
21. Ibid.
22. Gorton testimony on sovereign immunity, Tukwila, WA, 4–7–98, Gorton file, Washington State Archives
23. L.A. Times, 4–30–00, *Tribes top target in 2000: Sen. Slade Gorton*
24. Allen to Hughes, 2–7–2011
25. Seattle Times, 4–18–2000, *Quinault Indian leader dies*

CHAPTER 37: HIGH CRIMES OR MISDEMEANORS?

1. DeLay, *No Retreat, No Surrender*, p. 112
2. Gartner, *In Search of Bill Clinton*, p. 308
3. Boston Globe, 10–31–1998, *Energized first lady . . .*; Gallup Poll, 12–19/20–1998
4. Washington Post, 11–7–98, p. A-1
5. Gormley, *The Death of American Virtue*, p. 614; Lott, *Herding Cats*, p. 176
6. Lott, *Herding Cats*, p. 179
7. Times, 1–4–99, *Gorton proposes short Clinton trial*; 1–5–99, *Dealmaker Gorton*
8. Ibid.; Lott, *Herding Cats*, pp. 180–182; Washington Post, 1–5–99, p. A-5
9. Gormley, *The Death of American Virtue*, p. 617; Lott, *Herding Cats*, pp. 180–183
10. Lott, *Herding Cats*, pp. 193–196; Times, 1–9–99, *Senate turned to Gorton*; P-I, 1–9–1999, p. A-4
11. Ibid.

12. NYT, 1–26–99, *The president's trial;* Tri-City Herald, 8–8–2000, *Lieberman, Gorton have friendly history;* Washington Post, 1–5–99, p. A-5

13. Lott, *Herding Cats,* p. 179

14. P-I, 1–9–99, p. A-4; Yakima Herald-Republic, 1–10–99, p. C-5

15. Times, 1–24–99, *Gorton's role;* 2–14–99, *Stench of impeachment*

CHAPTER 38: A DUBIOUS HONOR

1. Times, 2–13–99, *Gregoire wooed . . .*

2. Ibid.

3. Times, 2–14–99, *Stench of impeachment makes Gorton vulnerable*

4. Ibid.

5. Dotzauer to Hughes, 2011

6. Times, 1–19–00, *Cantwell announces run;* P-I, 5–5–00, p. B-2

7. Times, 1–19–00, *Cantwell announces run*

8. Times, 2–25–03, *Veda Jellen was a force in GOP*

9. Times, 5–13–99, *Gorton known as the master, Gorton revives E. Wash. gold mine;* P-I, 5–13–99, p. A-3; 5–14–99, p. A-1

10. Ibid.; P-I, 5–14–99, *Spending package provides for Balkans;* Times, 5–19–99, *House passes bill to fund war*

11. Times, 5–13–99, *Gorton known as the master of slipping new laws into bills;* Times, 7–5–93, *Gold—and discord—in those Okanogan Hills;* P-I, 5–14–99, p. A-1

12. Ibid.

13. Ibid.; P-I, 5–13–99, p. A-3

14. Columbian, 5–30–99, p. B-6

15. P-I, 5–14–99, p. A-1

16. Times, 5–19–99, *Gorton to oppose bill*

17. Times, 4–26–00, *Sierra Club TV ad;* 5–18–00, *Cantwell takes on Gorton;* P-I, 5–18–00, p. A-1; 5–20–00, p. B-1

18. Ibid.

19. Ibid.

20. Whitesell, *Defending Wild Washington,* pp. 324–328; Seattle Weekly, 6–7–2000, *Reaching for it*

21. P-I, 5–17–00, p. A-1; 6–16–00, p. A-3; 6–9–00, p. A-1

22. P-I, 5–18–00, p. A-1; 10–2–00, p. A-3; Times, 6–12–00, *Gorton, Sierra Club in rare agreement;* 10–10–00, *Gorton's complicated environmental record;* 8–15–00, *Tribal ads criticize Gorton;* 10–18–00, *Taking a peek inside the political lockbox*

23. Ibid.

24. P-I, 5–5–00, p. B-2

25. The Elway Poll, May and October 2000; P-I, 8–31–00, p. B-1

26. P-I, 9–11–00, p. B-1

27. Times, 9–22–00, *Adams donates to fight Gorton*

28. Ibid.
29. The Elway Poll, October 2000; P-I, 9–30–00, p. B-1
30. Times, 11–3–00, *Cantwell, Gorton trade barbs on mine*
31. Ibid.
32. Ibid.
33. Ibid.
34. Ibid.
35. Times, 10–4–00, *The high-tech candidate for senator is . . .*
36. Ibid., 10–29–00, *Maria Cantwell for U.S. Senate*
37. P-I, 11–8–00, p. A-1; Times, 11–8–00, p. A-1
38. AP in Yakima Herald-Republic, 11–9–00, p. A-1; P-I, 11–8–00, p. A-1
39. Times, 12–2–00, *Cantwell: I will be a senator for all Washington*
40. Times, 12–3–00, *Gorton leaves pragmatic legacy*
41. NYT, 7–21–08, *After 2000 run, McCain learned to work levers of power*;
Rove, *Courage and Consequence*, pp. 192–193
42. P-I, 8–1–00, p. A-10
43. Times, 12–6–00, *Angry state Republicans*
44. Ibid.

CHAPTER 39: AN OUTBREAK OF CANDOR

1. Congressional Record—Senate, 12–7–00, pp. 26427–26437
2. Ibid.
3. Congressional Record, 12–8–00, *Senate Relationships*
4. Wall Street Journal, 12–8–00, *A good man gets his due*

CHAPTER 40: COMMISSIONER GORTON

1. P-I, 1–29–01, p. A-3
2. Shenon, *The Commission*, p. 26
3. Times, 2–16–01, *Gorton backed for appeals-court bench*; Spokesman-Review,
2–22–01, p. B-1
4. Shenon, *The Commission*, p. 26; TNT, 1–7–01, p. B-7
5. P-I, 5–4–01, p. A-2
6. Tate, HistoryLink.org Essay 7833, *James Ellis*, 2006; P-I, 3–10–01, p. B-1;
Times, 3–30–01, *Group studying light-rail viability*
7. P-I, 10–20–01, p. B-1; 12–9–01, p. E-7; Columbian, 5–19–02, p. C-2;
7–13–02, p. C-1; P-I, 11–1–02, p. B-4
8. Shenon, *The Commission*, pp. 58–62
9. Puget Sound Business Journal, 4–30/5–6–2010, *Citizen Slade*
10. Election Law @ Moritz, Daniel P. Tokaji, *The Help America Vote Act:
An Overview*; 107th U.S. Congress, Help America Vote Act of 2002 (Pub.L.
107–252)
11. Shenon, *The Commission*, p. 58

CHAPTER 41: CONFRONTATION AND CONSENSUS

1. PBS, #2004, *Trail of a Terrorist Program*; Times, 11–25–01, *An otherwise ordinary day*; Times, 4–12–04, *Clarke book has errors;* The 9/11 Commission
2. Ibid; PBS, Frontline, *Ahmed Ressam's Millennium Plot*
3. Times, 7–23–04, *Ahmed Ressam held valuable clue . . .; 9/11 Commission Report, p. 359*
4. Ibid.
5. Kean and Hamilton, *Without Precedent*, p. 32
6. Ibid., p. 266
7. Shenon, *The Commission*, pp. 114–115, 208
8. Ibid.; Kean and Hamilton, *Without Precedent*, pp. 83–84
9. Ibid., pp. 97–99
10. 9/11 Commission transcript, 4–12–04
11. Ibid.
12. Shenon, *The Commission*, p. 329
13. Ibid.
14. Ibid., pp. 328–333; Gorton and Gorelick to Hughes, 2010
15. Kean and Hamilton, *Without Precedent*, pp. 193–196
16. Ibid, p. 196
17. Shenon, *The Commission*, p. 401
18. Kean and Hamilton, *Without Precedent*, p. 207; Shenon, *The Commission*, p. 338, pp. 341–343
19. Washington Post, 5–16–07, *Gonzales hospital episode detailed*
20. Hugh Shelton, *Without Hesitation: The Odyssey of an American Warrior*, p. 413
21. Transcript of 9/11 Commission hearing, 3–23–04
22. Shenon, *The Commssion*, p. 233
23. Ibid., p. 282; Kean and Hamilton, *Without Precedent*, p. 166
24. Shenon, *The Commission*, p. 282; Kean and Hamilton, *Without Precedent*, p. 166
25. Shenon, *The Commission*, pp. 282–284; Washington Post, 3–24–04, Transcript of 9/11 Commission hearing, 3–24–04
26. 9/11 Commission Report, p. 362; Puget Sound Business Journal, 4–30/5–6, 2010, *Citizen Slade*
27. 9/11 Commission Report, p. 51

CHAPTER 42: THE NATURE OF THE ENEMY

1. 9/11 Commission Report, pp. 192–199; Shenon, *The Commission*, p. 315
2. NYT, 7–16–08, p. A-19
3. Ibid, p. 259–262
4. Ibid, p. 263–265, 277
5. Ibid., p. 406; Gordon Prange, *At Dawn We Slept: The Untold Story of Pearl Harbor*, quoted in the 9/11 Commission Report, p. 344

6. 9/11 Commission Report, p. 347

7. P-I, 6–17–04, *Seattle was an early 9/11 target*; KOMOnews.com, 6–16–04, *Seattle among original targets*

8. Ibid., pp. 362–363

9. Kean and Hamilton, *Without Precedent*, p. 297

10. NYT, 8–3–04, p. A-1; Newsday, 8–3–04, p. A-3; Wall Street Journal, 8–5–04, p. A-6

11. Ibid.

12. Publishers Weekly, 8–16–04; Chicago Tribune, 8–18–04, p. A-1

13. Kathleen Lynch, Buffalo News, 9–5–04, p. H-2

14. Christian Science Monitor, 9–9–04, p. 2; Connecticut Post, 9–8–04, *Nothing else we do is more important*

15. Chicago Tribune, 9–9–04, p. 1

16. Kean and Hamilton, *Without Precedent*, pp. 341–345

CHAPTER 43: PETROLEUM AND BEYOND

1. Rick Outzen, Rick's Blog, 6–30–10, *Baker Panel Report*

2. Pro Publica, 7–2–10, *Blast at BP Texas Refinery in '05 Foreshadowed Gulf Disaster*

3. Ibid.

4. Ibid.

5. BP news release, 10–24–05, *Baker to chair independent safety review panel*

6. *The Report of the BP U.S. Refineries Independent Safety Review Panel*

7. Ibid; KLTV.com, 1–18–07, *Panel blames BP in Texas City blast*

8. P-I, 5–21–10, *Strange Bedfellows*

9. Harvard Business Review, 1–17–11, *How the BP Commission Dropped the Ball*; National Legal & Policy Center, 2–21–11, *BP Oil Spill Commission Chief Counsel Blames BP*

10. Times, 5–7–05, *Slade Gorton calls for criminal probe*

11. Ibid.

12. P-I, 11–3–06, p. B-1; Encyclopedia of Business, Second Edition; National Journal, 7–29–06, *The Cook Election Preview*

13. AP in Columbian, 11–2–06, p. A-1

14. Washington Post, 8–29–06, *McGavick confesses*

15. AP in Columbian, 11–2–06, p. A-1; Times, 11–10–06, p. A-1, *Campaign mental floss*; P-I, 4–10–06, *Stevens stomps into town*

16. Knight Ridder Tribune Business News, 11–9–06, p. 1

17. P-I, 5–17–06, *What will they say about Gorton now?*

CHAPTER 44: NOT SO SUPER

1. TNT, 4–8–08, *Arena plan to keep Sonics in Seattle dies*

2. Ibid.

3. Ibid.

4. McClatchy-Tribune Business News, 4–19–08, *NBA owners approve Sonics' move*

5. P-I, 4–22–08, p. D-1

6. Journal Record, Oklahoma City, 6–23–08, *Okla.-owned Sonics plan reveals 'poisoned well' plan*; Deseret News, 7–17–08, p. D-4

7. AP in Deseret News, 1–17–08, p. D-4

8. P-I, 6–21–08, p. D-1

9. Ibid.

10. Ibid.

11. McClatchy-Tribune Business News, 6–27–08, *Sonics' closing arguments*

12. P-I, 7–27–08, p. C-1; 10–30–08, p. E-1; Times, 6–21–08, *Sonics case exposes city's dirty hands, too*

13. Ibid.

14. P-I, 7–3–08, *Sonics are Oklahoma City-bound*

CHAPTER 45: THE EXTRAORDINARY OCTOGENARIAN

1. U.S. Newswire, 8–27–09, *Former Senator Slade Gorton advocates for federal transportation policy reform*

2. Tri-City Herald, 12–10–08, p. A-1

3. NYT, 7–21–08, *McCain learned to work levers of power*

4. Indian Country Today, 9–26–08, *Strategies diverge at the Indian border*

5. The Herald, Everett, 2–5–08, *Boeing has a tense past with McCain*

6. P-I.com, 11–5–10, *King County continues to stymie Washington Republicans*

7. P-I.com, 9–29–10, *Herrera goes to Washington, D.C.*

8. AP, 2–25–09, *Former top officials back renewed U.S.-Russian ties*

9. Times, 10–28–09, *Mainstream Republicans oppose Eyman's initiative*; Washington Post, 11–9–09, p. A-17

10. KOMO Radio interview, 12–31–09

11. Washington Post, 12–27–09, *Uninvestigated terrorism warning*; The Sunday Times, London, 1–2–10, *One boy's journey to jihad*

12. KOMO Radio interview, 12–31–09

13. Washington Post, 8–4–09, *Self-created problems*

14. NYT, 1–10–10, *GOP chairman urges Reid to step down*

15. Washington Post, 1–14–10, *No exceptions for Congress*

16. Puget Sound Business Journal, 4–30–10, *Slade Gorton's political legacy*; Gorton Center Campaign brochure, The National Bureau of Asian Research, Washington State Archives

17. Ibid.

18. P-I.com, 10–11–10, *Gates Sr., Gorton spar over income tax*; Oly, 10–12–10, p. A-3

19. Ibid.

Bibliography

American Friends Service Committee, *Uncommon Controversy, Fishing Rights of the Muckleshoot, Puyallup and Nisqually Indians*, University of Washington Press, Seattle, 1970

Beckwith, Ryan Teague, *Where the Sun Almost Always Shines*, from *On the Harbor*, The Daily World, Gorham Printing, Rochester, WA, 2001

Billington, Ken, *People, Politics & Public Power*, Washington Public Utility Districts' Association, Seattle, 1988

Bone, Hugh A., *The 1964 Election in Washington*, Western Political Quarterly, June 1965

Bouton, Jim, *Ball Four, The Final Pitch*, Bulldog Publishing, North Egremont, MA, 2000

Boswell, Sharon, *Elmer Huntley, An Oral History*, Washington State Oral History Program, Office of the Secretary of State, State Printer, Olympia, 1996

Boswell, Sharon, *R.R. "Bob" Greive, An Oral History*, Washington State Oral History Program, Office of the Secretary of State, State Printer, Olympia, 2001

Boswell, Sharon, *August P. Mardesich, An Oral History*, Washington State Oral History Program, Office of the Secretary of State, State Printer, Olympia, 200

Boswell, Sharon, and McConaghy, Lorraine, *100 Years of a Newspaper and its Region*, The Seattle Times Centennial Project, 1996

BP U.S. Refineries Independent Safety Review Panel Report, January 2007, Washington State Library, Tumwater

Brands, H.W., *American Dreams, The United States Since 1945*, The Penguin Press, New York, 2010

Brazier, Don, *History of the Washington Legislature, 1854–1963*, Washington State Senate, Olympia, 2000

Brazier, Don, *History of the Washington Legislature, 1965–1982*, Washington State Senate, Olympia, 2007

Bronson, Rachel, *Thicker Than Oil: America's uneasy partnership with Saudi Arabia*, Oxford University Press, New York, 2006

Brown, Bruce, *Mountain in the Clouds, A Search for the Wild Salmon*, Simon & Schuster, New York, 1982

Capoeman, Pauline K. (editor), *Land of the Quinault*, Quinault Indian Nation, Taholah, WA, 1990

Carlin, George, *Brain Droppings, Hyperion*, New York, 1997

Carter, Jimmy, *White House Diary*, Farrar, Straus and Giroux, New York, 2010

Chasan, Daniel Jack, *Speaker of the House, The Political Career and Times of John L. O'Brien*, University of Washington Press, Seattle, 1990

Clark, Norman H., and McKeehan, Susan, *James M. Dolliver, An Oral History*, Washington State Oral History Program, Office of the Secretary of State, State Printer, Olympia, 1999

Clark, Norman H., *The Dry Years, Prohibition & Social Change in Washington, Revised Edition*, University of Washington Press, Seattle, 1988

Clinton, Bill, *My Life*, Alfred A. Knopf, New York, 2004

Cosell, Howard, with Bonventre, Peter, *I Never Played the Game*, William Morrow & Co., New York, 1985

Dietrich, William, *The Final Forest, The Battle for the Last Great Trees of the Pacific Northwest*, Simon & Schuster, New York, 1992

Dietrich, William, *Northwest Passage, The Great Columbia River*, Simon & Schuster, New York, 1995

Dumbrell, John, *The Carter Presidency: A Re-evaluation*, Manchester University Press, Manchester, U.K., 1995

Duncan, Don, *Washington: The First One Hundred Years, 1889–1989*, The Seattle Times Company, 1989

Durbin, Kathie, *Tree Huggers, Victory, Defeat & Renewal in the Northwest Ancient Forest Campaign*, The Mountaineers, Seattle, 1996

Dwyer, William L., *The Goldmark Case, An American Libel Trial*, University of Washington Press, Seattle, 1984

Farrell, John Aloysius, *Tip O'Neill and the Democratic Century*, Little, Brown & Company, Boston, 2001

Frederick, Timothy, *Albert F. Canwell, An Oral History*, Washington State Oral History Program, Office of the Secretary of State, State Printer, Olympia, 1997

Gadman, G.J., *A Strenuous Beneficent Force: The Case for Revision of the Career of Samuell Gorton, Rhode Island Radical*, master's degree thesis, Manchester Metropolitan University, Manchester, England, 2004

Gartner, John D., *In Search of Bill Clinton*, St. Martin's Press, New York, 2008

Genealogical Publishing Co. Inc., *Genealogies of Rhode Island Families Vol. I*, Baltimore, 1983

Gormley, Ken, *The Death of American Virtue, Clinton vs. Starr*, Crown Publishers, New York, 2010

Gorton, Adelos, *The Life and Times of Samuel Gorton*, George S. Ferguson Co., Philadelphia, 1907

Gorton, Thomas, *Samuel Gorton of Rhode Island & his Descendants*, Gateway Press Inc., Baltimore, 1982

Greaves, Tom (editor), *Endangered Peoples of North America*, Greenwood Press, Westport, CT, 2002

Greenspan, Alan, *The Age of Turbulence*, Penguin, New York, 2007

Guzzo, Louis R., *Is It True What They Say About Dixy*, The Writing Works Inc., Mercer Island, WA, 1980

Harden, Blaine, *A River Lost, The Life and Death of the Columbia*, W.W. Norton & Co., New York, 1996

Hayward, Steven F., *The Age of Reagan, The Conservative Counterrevolution*, 1980–1989, Crown Forum, New York, 2009

Heffernan, Trova, *The Aura of Jennifer Dunn*, Legacy Project biography for the Office of the Secretary of State, Olympia, 2009

Heilemann, John, and Halperin, Mark, *Game Change*, HarperCollins Publishers, New York, 2010

Hurd, Duane Hamilton, *History of Essex County, Massachusetts, Volume II*, J.W. Lewis & Co., Philadelphia, 1888.

Hughes, John C., and Beckwith, Ryan Teague, *On the Harbor, From Black Friday to Nirvana*, Gorham Printing, Rochester, WA., 2001

Hughes, John C., *Booth Who?*, The Legacy Project, Office of the Secretary of State, Gorham Printing, Centralia, WA, 2010

Hughes, John C., *The Inimitable Adele Ferguson, A Biography and Oral History*, The Legacy Project, Office of the Secretary of State, Gorham Printing, Centralia, Wash., 2011

Hughes, John C., *Nancy Evans, First-rate First Lady, A Biography and Oral History*, The Legacy Project, Office of the Secretary of State, Gorham Printing, Centralia, WA, 2010

Jacobson, Sid, and Colon, Ernie, *The 9/11 Report, A Graphic Adaption*, Hill and Wang, New York, 2006

Kaufman, Robert G., *Henry M. Jackson, A Life in Politics*, University of Washington Press, Seattle, 2000

Kean, Thomas H., and Hamilton, Lee H., with Rhodes, Benjamin, *Without Precedent, The Inside Story of the 9/11 Commission*, Alfred A. Knopf, New York, 2006

Kerr, Thomas J., *Wilbur G. Hallauer, An Oral History*, Washington State Oral History Program, Office of the Secretary of State, State Printer, Olympia, 2001

Kershner, Jim, *Carl Maxey, A Fighting Life*, University of Washington Press, Seattle, 2008

Kilgannon, Anne, *Joel M. Pritchard, An Oral History*, Washington State Oral History Program, Office of the Secretary of State, State Printer, Olympia, 2000

Kilgannon, Anne, *Dan Evans, Further Thoughts, an oral history within Joel M. Pritchard, An Oral History*, Washington State Oral History Program, Office of the Secretary of State, State Printer, Olympia, 2000

Kilgannon, Anne, *Thomas L. Copeland, An Oral History*, Washington State Oral History Program, Office of the Secretary of State, State Printer, Olympia, 2007

Kilgannon, Anne, *Don Eldridge, An Oral History*, Washington State Oral History Program, Office of the Secretary of State, State Printer, Olympia, 2005

Kilgannon, Anne, *Donald H. Brazier, An Oral History*, Washington State Oral History Program, Office of the Secretary of State, State Printer, Olympia, 2005

Kilgannon, Anne, *Richard O. White, Washington State Code Reviser, An Oral History*, Washington State Oral History Program, Office of the Secretary of State, State Printer, Olympia, 2004

Krogh, Egil "Bud", with Krogh, Matthew, *Integrity: Good People, Bad Choices and Life Lessons from the White House*, BBS Public Affairs, New York, 2007

Kurlansky, Mark, *Cod: A Biography of the Fish that Changed the World*, Walker & Company, New York, 1997

Larsen, Randall J., *Our Own Worst Enemy*, Grand Central Publishing, New York, 2007

Lien, Carsten, *Olympic Battleground, The Power Politics of Timber Preservation*, Second Edition, The Mountaineers Books, Seattle, 2000

Lois, George, and Pitts, Bill, *The Art of Advertising, George Lois on Mass Communication*, Harry N. Abrams Inc., New York, 1977

Lott, Trent, *Herding Cats, A Life in Politics*, ReganBooks/HarperCollins, New York, 2005

Mayr, Werner, *The Cinderella Tree, The Story of Mayr Bros. Logging*, Keokee Publishing Co., Sandpoint, Idaho, 1992

McCaffree, Mary Ellen, and Corbett, Anne McNamee, *Politics of the Possible*, McCaffree's life in Washington State politics, Gorham Printing, Centralia, WA, 2010

McCurdy, Howard E. Jr., *A Majority of the People: A Case Study on the Redistricting of Washington State, The Inter-University Case Program Inc.*, Syracuse, N.Y., 1967

McLoughlin, William Gerald, *Rhode Island, a Bicentennial History*, W.W. Norton & Company, New York, 1978

McPherson, James M. (general editor), *To the Best of My Ability, The American Presidents*, DK Publishing, New York, 2001

Mercier, Laurie, *Margaret Hurley, An Oral History*, Washington State Oral History Program, Office of the Secretary of State, State Printer, Olympia, 1995

Mitchell, Greg, *Tricky Dick and the Pink Lady*, Random House, New York, 1998

Newell, Gordon, *Rogues, Buffoons and Statesmen, Superior Publishing Co.*, Seattle, 1975. (Dysart page 504)

9/11 Commission Report, Authorized Edition, W.W. Norton & Company, New York, 2005

O'Neill, Tip, with Novak, William, *Man of the House*, Random House, New York, 1987

Prerau, David, *Seize the Daylight, The Curious and Contentious Story of Daylight Saving Time*, Thunder's Mouth Press, New York, 2005

Reagan, Ronald, *The Reagan Diaries*, Harper Collins, New York, N.Y., 2007

Rove, Karl, *Courage and Consequences*, Threshold Editions, New York, N.Y., 2010

Ruby, Robert H., and Brown, John A., *The Chinook Indians*, University of Oklahoma Press, Norman, 1976

Rule, Ann, *The Stranger Beside Me*, W.W. Norton & Co., New York, 1980

Sale, Roger, *Seattle Past to Present*, University of Washington Press, Seattle, 1976

Scates, Shelby, *Warren G. Magnuson and the Shaping of Twentieth-Century America*, University of Washington Press, Seattle, 1997

Schlesinger, Arthur M. Jr., *Journals, 1952–2000*, The Penguin Press, New York, 2007

Schwantes, Carlos A., *The Pacific Northwest, An Interpretive History*, Revised and Enlarged Edition, University of Nebraska Press, Lincoln, 1996

Sheldon, Charles H., *The Washington High Bench*, WSU Press, Pullman, 1992

Shenon, Philip, *The Commission, What We Didn't Know About 9/11*, Twelve, Hachette Book Group, New York, 2008

Smith, Payton, *Rosellini, Immigrants' Son & Progressive Governor*, University of Washington Press, Seattle, 1997

Stratton, David H., editor, *Washington Comes of Age: The State in the National Experience*, Washington State University Press, Pullman, 1992.

Thiel, Art, *Out of Left Field, How the Mariners Made Baseball Fly in Seattle*, Sasquatch Books, Seattle, 2003

Thomas, Helen, *Front Row at the White House*, Scribner, New York, 1999

Ulrich, Roberta, *Empty Nets, Indian Dams and the Columbia River*, Second Edition, Oregon State University Press, Corvallis, 2007

Watson, Emmett, *Digressions of a Native Son*, The Pacific Institute, Seattle, 1982

Weeden, William B., *Early Rhode Island, A Social History of the People, 1636–1790*, The Grafton Press, N.Y., 1910

West, Rebecca, *Black Lamb and Grey Falcon, A Journey through Yugoslavia*, The Viking Press, New York, 1941

White, Joseph, & Wildavsky, Aaron, *The Deficit and the Public Interest*, University of California Press, Berkeley, 1991

White, Theodore H., *America in Search of Itself, The Making of the President 1956–1980*, Harper & Row, New York, 1982

Whitesell, Edward A. (editor), *Defending Wild Washington, A Citizen's Action Guide*, The Mountaineers Books, Seattle, 2004

Zeiger, Hans, *Scoop and Slade: Partners in the Senate*, unpublished master's degree thesis

Ziontz, Alvin J., *A Lawyer in Indian Country*, University of Washington Press, Seattle, 2009

HISTORYLINK.ORG ESSAYS:

MacIntosh, Heather, *Kingdome: The Controversial Birth of a Seattle Icon*, HistoryLink.org Essay 2164, 2000

McRoberts, Patrick, *Forward Thrust*, HistoryLink.org Essay 2168, 1999, revised 2002 and 2007

Oldham, Kit, *Mardesich Not Guilty of Extortion and Tax Evasion*, HistoryLink.org Essay 8535, 2008

Tate, Cassandra, *James Reed Ellis*, HistoryLink.org Essay 7833, Seattle, 2006

Tate, Cassandra, *R.R. "Bob" Greive*, HistoryLink.org Essay 5717, 2004

Tate, Cassandra, *Dan and Nancy Evans*, HistoryLink.org Essay 7167, 2004

Wilma, David, *King County Grand Jury Indicts Public Officials in Police Payoff Scandal*, HistoryLink.org Essay 3289, 2001

OTHER ELECTRONIC SOURCES:

Web site on "The Coalition": http://www.sos.wa.gov/legacyproject/timeline_event.aspx?e=40

Index

About the author

JOHN C. HUGHES joined the Office of the Secretary of State as chief oral historian in 2008 after a 42-year career in journalism, retiring as editor and publisher of *The Daily World* at Aberdeen. He first met Slade Gorton as a young reporter covering the Legislature in 1966. Hughes is a trustee of the Washington State Historical Society and the author of five other books: *On the Harbor, From Black Friday to Nirvana,* with Ryan Teague Beckwith; *Booth Who?,* a biography of Booth Gardner; *Nancy Evans, First-rate First Lady; Lillian Walker, Washington State Civil Rights Pioneer,* and *The Inimitable Adele Ferguson.*